The Philosophy of Literature

**Foundations of the Philosophy of the Arts**

*Series Editor: Philip Alperson, Temple University*

The Foundations of the Philosophy of the Arts series is designed to provide a comprehensive but flexible series of concise texts addressing both fundamental general questions about art as well as questions about the several arts (literature, film, music, painting, etc.) and the various kinds and dimensions of artistic practice.

A consistent approach across the series provides a crisp, contemporary introduction to the main topics in each area of the arts, written in a clear and accessible style that provides a responsible, comprehensive, and informative account of the relevant issues, reflecting classic and recent work in the field. Books in the series are written by a truly distinguished roster of philosophers with international renown.

1. The Philosophy of Art    *Stephen Davies*
2. The Philosophy of Motion Pictures    *Noël Carroll*
3. The Philosophy of Literature    *Peter Lamarque*

**Forthcoming:**
The Philosophy of Music    *Philip Alperson*
Black is Beautiful: A Philosophy of Black Aesthetics    *Paul Taylor*

# The Philosophy
# of Literature

## Peter Lamarque

**Blackwell**
Publishing

BLACKWELL PUBLISHING
350 Main Street, Malden, MA 02148-5020, USA
9600 Garsington Road, Oxford OX4 2DQ, UK
550 Swanston Street, Carlton, Victoria 3053, Australia

First published 2009 by Blackwell Publishing Ltd

1   2009

*Library of Congress Cataloging-in-Publication Data*

Lamarque, Peter.
   The philosophy of literature / Peter Lamarque.
      p. cm. — (Foundations of philosophy of the arts)
   Includes bibliographical references and index.
      ISBN 978-1-4051-2197-2 (hardcover : alk. paper)—ISBN 978-1-4051-2198-9 (pbk.: alk. paper)
   1. Literature—philosophy. I. Title.

PN49.L33 2009
801—dc22                                          2007046034

A catalogue record for this title is available from the British Library.

Set in 11.5/13pt Perpetua
by SPi Publisher Services, Pondicherry, India
Printed and bound in Singapore
by C.O.S. Printers Pte Ltd

For further information on
Blackwell Publishing, visit our website at
www.blackwellpublishing.com

# Contents

*In memory of my mother*
*Patricia Lamarque*
*(1916–2006)*

# Preface

What exactly is it to view literature as *art*? It is widely acknowledged that at least some poems, novels, and plays are genuinely works of art, but it is far from clear exactly what that means. Why does it exclude sentimental rhymes on birthday cards or risqué limericks or genre novels like murder mysteries or sci fi? Is this merely a bald judgment of taste or is it also a category judgment? Are there objective grounds for making these distinctions? What counts as "literature" in the first place? And once something has been recognized as literature in the relevant sense, what implications does that hold for how it is read, what is sought from it, what kinds of benefits it bestows, and what place it holds among other things humans value?

What follows is a philosophical exploration of these and similar questions. Why "philosophical"? Is this inquiry different from that of literary critics themselves? In fact it is not different in kind; literary critics can be, and often are, philosophical. But it can still seem an unusual perspective. The philosopher looks at fundamental principles, conceptual connections, unnoticed consequences of lines of thought, significance and insignificance, boundaries where these are possible and desirable. In theory-constructing mode, he or she might then hope to develop an overarching theory of the phenomena that helps unify, explain, and clarify diffuse elements. The philosophical investigation of literature is a probing into practices and procedures but it does not offer a history of those practices or a sociological analysis of them. It looks at the underlying conventions and assumptions that give the practices what distinctive identity they have and seeks to find a coherent perspective that makes sense of them. However, the investigation is of little use if it is too abstract, if it loses touch with the very works – either the works of art themselves or the works of criticism that comment on them – it purports to encompass. Throughout this inquiry these works will be to the fore. Any principles identified or concepts clarified or theories constructed will find their justification only among the familiar practices of readers and appreciators of literature.

The book is aimed not just at philosophers but at those – critics or "common readers" alike – with an interest in literature and a taste for pursuing questions beyond unreflective commonplaces. The method is largely "analytical" and tends to tackle philosophical problems head-on rather than through the history of the problems. But it seeks no confrontation with other methodologies. Styles of philosophizing are largely a matter of temperament and training. In the end what is important is the illumination that is afforded. It is hoped that those who are puzzled by certain aspects of literary creation and literary appreciation will gain some clarity, even some insight, from the treatment on offer.

In Chapter 1 the nature of the inquiry is set out, its methods and its aspirations. What does "philosophy of literature" entail? How does it relate to literary or critical theory? What is involved in thinking of literature as "art"? Can literature be accommodated within aesthetics or does that presuppose a hopelessly outdated conception of *belles lettres* or "fine writing"? Is there any room for talk of aesthetic experience or aesthetic qualities or aesthetic pleasure in relation to literature? In fact a warning is sounded early on against reductionist views of literature, views, for example, that take one literary mode as paradigmatic (the poem, the novel) or see the pleasures of literature in purely sensuous terms or give priority to "natural" or untutored responses.

In Chapter 2, detailed and critical examination is offered of attempts to define literature. Just what is distinctive about literary art? Is there some essence of the literary, its use of language perhaps or its "imitation" of the world or its powers of expression? If there is nothing intrinsic to literary works – properties common to all such works – that signals their literariness, might there be "institutional" factors that set them apart? This idea is carefully explored and different kinds of institutional analyses evaluated. The idea of the "mode of existence" of the literary work is also pursued. Could literary works be merely strings of sentences?

Chapter 3 examines the idea of the author. In twentieth-century literary criticism the author took quite a beating with the rejection of biography-based criticism, the promotion of "impersonality," the emphasis on "autonomy," all the way to the "death of the author." What reasons might there be for demoting the author in this way? Is it not paradoxical that works ostensibly created by authors should be thought to have a life of their own apart from their authors? Arguments about the role of intention in criticism, whether there is an "intentional fallacy," are also put under the spotlight.

Chapter 4 is pivotal in that it looks at fundamental principles of reading that seemingly must underlie any conception of literature as art. Far from being prescriptive, though, the chapter simply seeks to identify deep and common interests that readers have when approaching literary works of art *as* art. Attention is given to "interpretation," what it aims to do, what grounding it has, and what relation it bears to the "appreciation" of literature.

In Chapter 5 the many facets of fictionality are explored: for example, whether there is a clear line between fiction and non-fiction, what it is to tell a story or make up a character, how we can talk meaningfully about fictional events. What kind of reality, if any, do fictional characters have? What is a fictional world and how do we build up a picture of it? How similar are fictional characters to real people? How can readers get emotionally attached to characters knowing that they are merely "made up"?

Chapter 6 is about truth in relation to literature. Is truth an aspiration of literature: in poetry, perhaps, even works of fiction? What might it mean to say that a work of fiction expresses some profound truth about human life? Is propositional truth remote from literature? Are literary truths *sui generis*? Can we learn from fiction both facts and ways of viewing the world? Can the great works of literature give us a better understanding of ourselves and human life? Caution is advised here. It is not always clear how to sustain some of the grander claims of the "truth" theorists.

Finally, Chapter 7 directly examines other putative values of literature. What is the mark of a great work of literature? Can such judgments be made objectively? What is meant by a literary "canon"? Do works becomes canonical through their intrinsic literary merits or are there political factors at work? How does literary value relate to interpretation? Does ethics have anything to do with literary value? Could an unethical work be valuable from a literary point of view?

These, then, are just some of the questions that come up in the philosophy of literature. This book seeks to probe such questions in detail, not just characterizing the principal arguments on different sides – though it does attempt that – but also contributing to the debates and evaluating the arguments. The book is not entirely neutral in its stance but develops a line of thought that binds the issues together into an overall perspective which it is hoped the reader will find persuasive and congenial. But in the end, seeing what the problems are and thinking them through can be as important as settling on some final conclusions. The literary realm is one in which we all partake to some degree; reflecting on just what place literature does have in our lives can enhance our appreciation of it and make us all the more aware of the genius that underlies its greatest productions.

The ideas presented in this book continue and develop earlier explorations of mine on fiction and the aesthetics of literature, notably in two books: Peter Lamarque and Stein Haugom Olsen, *Truth, Fiction, and Literature: A Philosophical Perspective* (Oxford: Clarendon Press, 1994) and Peter Lamarque, *Fictional Points of View* (Ithaca, NY: Cornell University Press, 1996).

I have also drawn on other previously published articles of mine, to a greater or lesser degree:

"The Death of the Author: An Analytical Autopsy," *The British Journal of Aesthetics*, vol. 30, no. 4 (1990), pp. 319–331; "Appreciation and Literary Interpretation," in Michael Krausz, ed., *Is There a Single Right Interpretation?* (University Park, PA: Penn State Press, 2002), pp. 285–306; "Fiction," in Jerrold Levinson, ed., *Oxford Handbook of Aesthetics* (Oxford: Oxford University Press, 2003), pp. 377–391; "How to Create a Fictional Character," in Berys Gaut and Paisley Livingston, eds., *The Creation of Art* (Cambridge: Cambridge University Press, 2003), pp. 33–52; "Cognitive Values in the Arts: Marking the Boundaries," in Matthew Kieran, ed., *Contemporary Debates in Aesthetics and the Philosophy of Art* (Oxford: Blackwell, 2006), pp. 127–139; "The Intentional Fallacy," in Patricia Waugh, ed., *Oxford Guide to Literary Theory and Criticism* (Oxford: Oxford University Press, 2006), pp. 177–188; "On the Distance Between Literary Narratives and Real-Life Narratives," in Dan Hutto, ed., *Narrative and Understanding Persons*, Royal Institute of Philosophy Supplement (Cambridge: Cambridge University Press, 2007), pp. 117–132; and "Aesthetics and Literature: A Problematic Relation?" *Philosophical Studies* vol. 135, no. 1 (2007), pp. 27–40. I am grateful to Oxford University Press, Penn State Press, Blackwell, and Springer for permissions to reprint excerpts from this material.

# Acknowledgments

My biggest intellectual debt is to my friend and co-author Stein Haugom Olsen, now of the University of Bergen in Norway, who is the pioneer of analytical literary aesthetics and to whom I owe so much of my thinking on the subject. Just how great his influence is on this book will be evident to anyone who knows Olsen's work. Other friends and fellow toilers in these pastures include Malcolm Budd, Noël Carroll, Greg Currie, David Davies, Stephen Davies, Susan Feagin, Berys Gaut, Eileen John, Matthew Kieran, Peter Kivy, Michael Krausz, Jerry Levinson, Paisley Livingston, Joe Margolis, Alex Neill, Jenefer Robinson, Mark Rowe, Bob Stecker, Amie Thomasson, and Ken Walton, with whom I have had enjoyable and beneficial discussions on these topics over many years. Needless to say, we haven't always agreed. I should thank as well the students in two Philosophy of Literature classes at the University of York, in 2005 and 2007, who went through this material with me, prompting further thoughts and questions. My thanks to Phil Alperson, the editor of the series, for inviting me to contribute to it, to Jeff Dean at Blackwell, who is not only a commissioning editor but a respected contributor to philosophy of literature in his own right, and to an anonymous referee who made many pertinent and perceptive suggestions, all of which I have followed. Much gratitude also to David Williams for his meticulous copy-editing and friendly advice on several literary matters. Finally, fond thanks to the family, Mary, Toby, and Hugh for their remarkable tolerance of these enduring obsessions.

# Chapter One

# Art

This is a book about literature written by a philosopher from a philosophical point of view. What interest might a philosopher have in literature, writing *as* a philosopher? What is distinctive about a philosophical point of view on the subject? The task of this chapter is to give special attention to the nature and bounds of the inquiry.

## First Steps

There is a vast body of writing *about literature*, from analyses of individual works, descriptions, interpretations, evaluations, recommendations, to general reflections on what the term "literature" means and whether there is such a thing as literature in the first place. Such writing is described in different ways, including "literary criticism," "literary history," "literary biography," "critical theory," "literary theory," "poetics," "metacriticism." Literary critics themselves have engaged a seemingly limitless number of "approaches" to literature, from the psychological, historical, sociological, or political to the linguistic, stylistic, or rhetorical. This outpouring, if nothing else, attests to the extraordinary amount of interest that the literary realm evokes.

"Philosophy of literature" reflects one kind of interest although this designation is relatively new and largely unfamiliar. In fact the inquiry designated by the phrase "philosophy of literature" is not itself new and dates back to the ancient Greeks. Aristotle's *Poetics*, one of the most influential works in the canon of literary criticism, is an exemplary instance of philosophy of literature in the modern sense. It is not just written by a philosopher but exhibits a quintessential philosophical methodology: a careful delineation of the subject matter – the nature of poetry in general, its modes, aims, and objects – then a detailed analysis of one literary genre, tragedy, outlining its constituent parts (plot, character, action, thought, diction) and the key concepts for describing its aims and effects, concluding finally with remarks about and comparisons with another genre of poetry, the epic.

Surprisingly, however, in spite of this model set by Aristotle, there has been little systematic interest in literature by philosophers. Even Plato's treatment of poetry, although immensely important, is hardly systematic and more often than not occurs in discussions where other, non-literary, issues are to the fore, like the education of the guardians or the good of the state. Many philosophers make passing reference to literature, either to particular works or (following Plato) to the moral effects of the literary or (like Hume, Hegel, Nietzsche, and Schopenhauer) to genres such as tragedy, but detailed philosophical explorations of the very practice of writing, reading, appreciating, and valuing works of literature are rare. The history of "theoretical" writings about literature is not primarily a history of philosophical writing. More common, at least up to the beginning of the twentieth century, are reflections by poets or critics: for example, offering advice to poets in the manner of Horace's *Ars Poetica* or, as with Sidney and Shelley, defending poetry against Puritans and moralists, or through prefaces and critical essays (Fielding, Wordsworth, Matthew Arnold) proposing new ways of showing the importance of literature in human life.

In philosophy of literature the first task – already a philosophical task – is to position this newly designated inquiry among other inquiries about literature. Is it a species of criticism or theory? Is it another "approach" to literature alongside those mentioned? Is it a study of individual works? In fact it is not really any of those things. Above all, it is, as is obvious, a *philosophical* inquiry, a branch of philosophy, with all that that entails. As Aristotle showed, this is a foundational inquiry into the very nature of the literary, classifying the subject matter, delineating aspects, analysing concepts, exploring norms and values, locating the whole practice of writing and reading literary works in its proper place among related but distinct practices. More on this will emerge in due course.

It is not hard to find *some* connections between philosophy and literature, yet not all such connections can count as philosophy *of* literature. A good place to start in explaining the aims and scope of our inquiry is to compare it with some other philosophical interests.

## Philosophy *in* Literature

To begin with, philosophy *of* literature is not the same as philosophy *in* literature, although it has indirect connections with that conception. This is not a book that will be mining individual novels and plays for their philosophical insights.

The presentation or exploration of broadly philosophical themes in poetry, drama, or the novel is widespread and well acknowledged. Underlying

Tolstoy's *War and Peace* is a philosophy of history and of human destiny; there is existentialism in the novels of Sartre and Camus; mysticism versus rationalism in Blake's poetry; pantheism in Wordsworth's *The Prelude*; atheism painstakingly debated in Dostoievsky; divine providence and free will in Milton's *Paradise Lost*; egoism in George Eliot and George Meredith, and so forth.

Philosophical themes in literature can figure in reflections on literature in at least three different ways.

First, they can be characterized in direct critical readings, as in this brief observation by a literary critic about *War and Peace*:

> since Tolstoy's approach is always *sub specie aeternitatis*, he has created human beings working out their destiny in accordance with the eternal implacable laws of humanity. … It is a pantheist philosophy, and Tolstoy is obsessed by the thought of man's greatest efforts and best hopes being defeated by death.[1]

This is a summary comment making a claim about central themes in the novel. The identification and characterization of these themes are not part of a philosophical exercise but an attempt to make sense of the novel and its aims. The content identified might be philosophical but the skills in eliciting this content are more literary critical than philosophical. It is enough for the critic to notice the themes and connect them to incidents in the novel. The validity of the critic's interpretation rests not on the philosophical validity of the ideas themselves but on the support offered from the details of the work. At this level, then, the level at which a literary critic identifies themes, there is a clear distinction between philosophy *in* literature and philosophy *of* literature.

At a second level, though, philosophical skills and philosophical interests are directly engaged. Philosophers look to the literary exploration of philosophical ideas to help clarify, deepen, or expound a philosophical topic. Philosophers interested in Sartre's views on the "absurdity of existence" or the relation between objects and consciousness would do well to read his first novel *Nausea*. That novel is a philosophical novel in the sense that it uses a fictional (and literary) context to provide an imaginative realization of a conception of consciousness that Sartre presents in his non-fictive philosophical writings.

Another example might be the purported contributions to moral philosophy in the novels of Henry James, as claimed by the philosopher Martha Nussbaum:

> there are candidates for moral truth which the plainness of traditional moral philosophy lacks the power to express, and which *The Golden Bowl* expresses

---

[1] Rosemary Edmonds, "Introduction," in L. N. Tolstoy, *War and Peace*, vol. 1, trans. and with an introduction by Rosemary Edmonds (Harmondsworth: Penguin, 1969), pp. x–xi.

wonderfully. Insofar as the goal of moral philosophy is to give us understanding of the human good through a scrutiny of alternative conceptions of the good, this text and others like it would then appear to be important parts of this philosophy.[2]

For Nussbaum, it is not just that James's novels have philosophical themes but rather they are supplementary works of philosophy themselves. Although Nussbaum makes a strong case for this kind of reading of James, it is not uncontroversial, either as Jamesian interpretation or as a general view of literature as philosophy.[3] Arguably this is more an *appropriation* of literary works into philosophy than an illumination of the works as literature. The issues are taken up further in Chapters 6 and 7.

There is a third level, however, at which philosophy *in* literature intersects with philosophy *of* literature. That is the level at which the very possibility of using fictional works to expound, develop, or challenge philosophical ideas is addressed. How could a work of fiction, a product of the imagination, be a vehicle for conveying serious theses? How can fiction support truth? Is it part of the very essence of literature that it "instruct" as well as give pleasure? These are the kind of issues that go to the heart of philosophy of literature for they explore not just the purpose of literature but the question of how it relates to other kinds of discourse and what special values it possesses.

## The Philosophy of _____

Many branches of philosophy are characterized by filling in the blank in "philosophy of _____" with the name of another area of inquiry: for example, science, history, law, psychology, religion, mathematics, linguistics, or logic. Sometimes, though, the blank is filled with a concept such as mind, knowledge, action, language, morality, freedom, or art. Perhaps the difference is not always great: e.g., between philosophy of psychology and philosophy of mind. Yet there is a difference even in that example. Where a discipline or area of inquiry is highlighted then the philosophical investigation looks at

[2] Martha C. Nussbaum, "Flawed Crystals: James's *The Golden Bowl* and Literature as Moral Philosophy," in *Love's Knowledge: Essays on Philosophy and Literature* (Oxford: Oxford University Press, 1990), p. 142.

[3] For a discussion of Nussbaum's reading of James, see Richard Posner, "Against Ethical Criticism," *Philosophy and Literature*, vol. 21, no. 1 (1997), pp. 1–27; and Peter Lamarque and Stein Haugom Olsen, *Truth, Fiction, and Literature: A Philosophical Perspective* (Oxford: Clarendon Press, 1994), pp. 386–394.

foundational issues in the inquiry itself, its methods, aims, presuppositions, modes of argument or evidence or reasoning, the status of its central claims, and its basic concepts. It also inquires into how this area relates to adjacent areas. But where a concept is more directly invoked – mind, action, language – then the analysis begins there, with the concept itself and theoretical reflections about it. A philosophical study of the nature of mind is not quite the same as an inquiry into the foundations of psychology.

The position of philosophy of literature is complicated. First of all, crucially for how we are to proceed, it is to be understood as a sub-branch of the philosophy of art, standing on a par with philosophy of music, of dance, of film, of the visual arts. This is not to say that there might not be other conceptions of the philosophy of literature which do not take literature to fall under the general category of art. There are, as we shall see, branches of literary theory which make no such assumption, indeed would challenge it (although literary theorists rarely lay claim to the expression "philosophy of literature"). However, the field is not so well established that there is clearly a right or wrong way to define it, and it seems inevitable within philosophy of art that we should have some way of bracketing the literary arts in the way that philosophy of music, of dance, etc., gives specific focus to the other arts. If need be, we can simply stipulate that for the purposes of this inquiry philosophy of literature will be a sub-branch of philosophy of art, with the implication that literature so considered is an art form. What this *means* is a key issue in our investigation. Although this is a stipulation about a kind of inquiry it is hardly an arbitrary one, for the literary arts (*ars poetica*) have been recognized as such since the ancient Greeks.

### *Philosophy of literature and philosophy of literary criticism*

Philosophy of literature seems to fall somewhere between those inquiries that investigate other disciplines (philosophy of science, philosophy of history) and those exploring fundamental concepts (philosophy of mind, philosophy of action). In philosophy of literature it is not just the concept of literature that is under investigation but rather the wider practice – involving complex interactions between readers and authors – within which literature acquires its identity and value. Yet it would be misleading, without further explanation, to redescribe this focus as the "philosophy of literary criticism."

A simple tripartite division is sometimes proposed to explain the status of "philosophy of _____" inquiries where subject disciplines are involved. Take, say, the philosophy of physics. At the base level, according to this proposal, are physical events in the natural world; at the "first-order level" are the statements, hypotheses, reasonings, experiments of physics itself; at a "second-order level" the philosopher of physics investigates the methods, presuppositions, etc., at the first-order level. The distinction is helpful in a rough and ready way in distinguishing the roles of the physicist and the philosopher. The latter is not a scientist and need not undertake experiments or test physical hypotheses.

However, the distinction looks far less clearcut when probed further. For example, the separation of data and theory, between the ground level and the first-order level, is by no means straightforward. What counts as data "in nature" might depend essentially on the theoretical framework within which it is classified. It should not be assumed that there is a simple "given," nature "carved at the joints," waiting to be investigated. Nor is the first-order/ second-order distinction entirely secure, resting, in some instances, on a dubious dichotomy between conceptual statements (by the philosopher) and descriptive statements (by the scientist), and also on an assumption that reasoning about methodology is not a valid part of physics itself.

In philosophy of art or aesthetics a parallel tripartism is sometimes proposed, where the base level is works of art and the activities of artists, the first-order level the pronouncements of art critics, and the second-order level reflections on the first-order level by philosophers.[4] This translates in obvious ways to philosophy of literature, with the poet, the critic, and the philosopher assigned their distinct roles. Although there are strong reasons, as we shall see, for being wary of this simple division of labour, there is also something appealing about it that should not be lost. It highlights, for example, distinct kinds of expertise. The ability to write a poem is different from the ability to write about poetry, and skill at the former by no means converts into skill in the latter. Poets are not necessarily good critics, nor of course critics good poets. But more fundamentally the modes of "discourse" are entirely different. Novelists or poets on the one hand and critics on the other are all users of language, but their aims and the norms for judging what they write are obviously different. Attempts to blur the kinds of achievement at these levels, by promoting the critic's writing to an "art form," fail to acknowledge deep differences in the aims and expectations involved. Somewhat similar remarks can be made about the first-order and second-order levels. Philosophers do not necessarily make good critics, where criticism is seen as a mode of commentary on and assessment of works of literature, nor critics necessarily good philosophers.

---

[4]   This picture of the role of aesthetics is clearly laid out in Monroe C. Beardsley's *Aesthetics: Problems in the Philosophy of Criticism*, 2nd ed. (Indianapolis, IN: Hackett, 1981), pp. 3–7: e.g., "As a field of knowledge, aesthetics consists of those principles that are required for clarifying and confirming critical statements. Aesthetics can be thought of, then, as the philosophy of criticism, or *metacriticism*" (pp. 3–4).

Whatever its initial appeal, though, the tripartite conception of philosophy of literature should be rejected. Difficulties begin at the base level. Literary works are not "natural kinds," they have no existence apart from the nexus of activities and judgments within which they are identified and evaluated. To put it somewhat more tendentiously, the works are not just the objects of critical discourse but in some sense also the products of it. Literary works acquire their identity as literature partly through the kinds of interest they invite from literary critics. There is an internal or logical connection between the works and the discourse dedicated to them, so merely to put these on different levels, as if they were logically distinct, is not satisfactory.

There are problems too with the first-order and second-order levels, between the criticism and the philosophy. The philosopher of literature, conceived as an investigator of the logic and aims of literary criticism, is not in a comparable position to, say, the philosopher of physics because the field of inquiry, "criticism," is too diverse to present a methodologically coherent and unified subject. The view of philosophy of literature as "metacriticism" seems doomed to fail in either of its two primary manifestations: as a descriptive or as a normative exercise. Viewed descriptively, metacriticism sets out to identify the underlying principles of criticism by observing current practice and abstracting from it. But confronted with the array of critical "approaches," the best such an exercise could deliver would be a set of principles relative to each "approach": principles of psychoanalytic or feminist or desconstructionist or historical materialist readings. This could not form the basis of an interesting philosophy of literature.

The alternative, normative metacriticism, seeks not merely to abstract from the array of critical practices but to formulate principles that *ought* to be in place even in cases where they are not. Normative metacriticism is most likely to arise when one particular critical methodology is in the ascendancy, as was the case in the 1950s and 1960s with New Criticism.[5] At that period it seemed natural for philosophers or metacritics, like Monroe C. Beardsley and others, to formulate principles, such as the Intentional Fallacy, the Affective Fallacy, the Heresy of Paraphrase, etc., which underpinned New Criticism, and present them as universal principles of criticism. In fact subsequently, with the declining influence of New Criticism, the validity of such principles has itself become the focus of debates within philosophy of literature. In effect these debates amount to challenges to the authority of New Criticism.

---

[5]   For a discussion of normative metacriticism, see Stein Haugom Olsen, "Literary Theory and Literary Aesthetics," in *The End of Literary Theory* (Cambridge: Cambridge University Press, 1987), pp. 199–201.

But if philosophy of literature is not philosophy of criticism, or meta-criticism, what is it? Clearly the answer will be revealed in the questions, debates, and discussions undertaken in this book. In summary, the inquiry is not concerned narrowly with the "concept" of literature, conceived as a merely definitional matter, but rather with what might be called the phenomenon of literature, the phenomenon, common to most if not all cultures, of elevating certain kinds of linguistic activities – notably story-telling or poetry-making or drama – to an art form issuing in products that are revered and of cultural significance. What kinds of qualities are required for linguistic works to acquire this status? What fundamental assumptions are in place for those who attend to such works as literature and as art?

Again, though, we need to focus this inquiry, for as described it might seem impossibly wide-ranging. The philosopher's interest is not the same as the sociologist's or the ethnographer's. It is a perfectly valid and important exercise to examine the actual shaping of a literary tradition in some given society – the specific values, genres, styles, or interests that underlie that tradition. These might differ significantly from culture to culture. Not every culture has sonnets or tragedies or romantic novels. We will see in the next chapter that there are two radically different conceptions of "institution" to explain the ethnographer's and the philosopher's focus of inquiry. The literary institutions that the ethnographer investigates are particular to each culture, resting on local social and cultural facts, while the "institution" of literature investigated by the philosopher concerns far more fundamental structures, those that, in Kantian terminology, "make possible" any relevant interactions between participants in a practice. The philosopher of literature is not a historian of culture, nor a sociologist.

Nor in any other sense will the focus of this inquiry be historical. It will neither examine the history of any given literary tradition nor will it examine, in any detail, the history of previous philosophical attempts to inquire into literature. The principal method will be "analytical," broadly conceived. It will seek to analyze the logical foundations of the "practice" of literature, rather as the philosopher of law examines neither particular legal systems nor the history of law but the grounds on which any such system depends, such as the putative justifications for punishment, the relation of law and morality, or the obligations of citizens to obey the law.

## Literary Theory

Perhaps surprisingly, philosophy of literature has little direct connection with "Literary Theory" as that is normally understood. Literary Theory, as a heterogeneous collection of "isms," flourished in literary studies roughly between the late 1960s and the late 1990s. A standard list of such theories would include: structuralism, feminism, Marxism, reader-response theory, psychoanalysis, deconstruction, post-structuralism, postmodernism, new historicism, and post-colonialism, with the principal luminaries including Mikhail Bakhtin, Walter Benjamin, Roland Barthes, Louis Althusser, Jacques Derrida, Paul de Man, Jacques Lacan, Julia Kristeva, Luce Irigaray, and Michel Foucault.[6] It is widely assumed, even among its strongest supporters, that the heyday of Theory (as it became known) is past. Terry Eagleton begins his book, aptly titled *After Theory* (2003), by stating unequivocally "The Golden Age of cultural theory is long past."[7]

Generalizations in this area are fraught with danger but it doesn't seem too cavalier to claim that a feature of Theory, as a whole, was that it rejected the notion of literature as art and also rejected the relevance of aesthetics and analytic philosophy in any investigation of the literary realm. As these are at the center of the present inquiry it is not surprising that the connections are weak.

A recent commentator has noted another but related feature of Theory:

> What theorists of all these persuasions have in common, whatever their individual differences, is a decisive turning away from literature as literature and an eagerness to transmogrify it into a cultural artefact (or "signifying practice") to be used in waging an always antiestablishment ideological political struggle.[8]

It is a curious consequence of this stance that Literary Theory became increasingly remote from literature as such. Admittedly this was not entirely unintended as Theory self-consciously adopted both an anti-essentialist and a reductive view of literature. The very concept of literature was thought to reside in a discredited "liberal humanist" ideology and in its place was substituted the more neutral and supposedly value-free notion of "text" or undifferentiated *writing* (*écriture*). We shall be looking in more detail at this move as we proceed. What it means, though, is that Theory is equally applicable to any kind of text and has no special interest in demarcating a sub-class as "literary," far less trying to discern its fundamental aspects. Literary Theorists were happy to apply their methods to any texts, not just non-literary genres such as popular fiction but also newspapers, comics, films, even philosophy.

The critic and theorist J. Hillis Miller sees Theory not just as an attempt to kill off literature but as a symptom of its decline:

> Literary theory arose in its contemporary form just at the time literature's social role was weakening. If literature's power and role could be taken for granted as still in full force, it would not be necessary to theorize about it. ... The efflorescence of literary theory signals the death of literature.[9]

---

[6]   The list is taken from Valentine Cunningham, "Theory, What Theory?" in D. Patai and W. Corral, eds., *Theory's Empire* (New York: Columbia University Press, 2005).

[7]   Terry Eagleton, *After Theory* (London: Allen Lane, 2003), p. 1.

[8]   Introduction, Patai and Corral, eds., *Theory's Empire*, p. 8.

[9]   J. Hillis Miller, *On Literature* (London and New York: Routledge, 2002), p. 35.

In the event, though, it is Literary Theory that has shown its mortality rather than literature. Arguably, the decline of Theory marks the revitalization of literature. A serious philosophy of literature will show that literature as an enduring social phenomenon is far more robust than this pessimistic prognosis suggests.

In the early days of Theory there was an undeniable sense of excitement at new possibilities: "New perspectives and ways of thinking opened up on issues such as human subjectivity, power, responsibility, gender, class, race, sexuality, mind, the construction of history, disciplinary boundaries, truth-effects, and the nature of the linguistic sign."[10] But as each theory settled down into its own methodology and styles of reading, a degree of staleness became inevitable; if you believe that all texts exhibit *aporias* (contradictions) or repression or class conflict or sexism, the chances are you will find this in any given text. "If, for example, semantic indeterminacy of a certain sort (e.g., the varieties yielded by 'structures of supplementarity') is one of the 'always already' or transcendental conditions of language, it comes as no surprise to learn that more of the same can be spotted in 'the text of Baudelaire' or anywhere else."[11]

However, it is no part of the purpose of this book to confront Literary Theory; indeed, described in neutral terms, many of the concerns of Theorists are also concerns of the philosopher of literature: about authorship, or meaning, or the limits of interpretation, or fictionality. In fact judging from a recent student-focused anthology on *Literary Theory and Criticism* (2006), there is evidence of a tamer post-theory theory emerging among literary critics which virtually coincides with the interests of the philosopher of literature. It addresses, for example,

> questions about authority and authenticity: how do we know whose voice we are hearing when we read a poem? And what is the role of the critic in mediating or explicating the text? If we cannot access authorial intention, whose voice are we listening to? Are we actually in any more privileged epistemological relation to our own activity of interpretation? Do readers construe texts or construct them? Is the activity of criticism one of discovery or performance?
>
> As soon as we begin to ask such questions, we are, in effect, 'doing theory'; but is hard to conceive of a critical practice which could proceed in blithe ignorance or wilful suppression of such problems.[12]

[10]  Introduction, Patricia Waugh, ed., *Oxford Guide to Literary Theory and Criticism* (Oxford: Oxford University Press, 2006), pp. 3–4.

[11]  Paisley Livingston, "Literary Aesthetics and the Aims of Criticism," in Patai and Corral, eds., *Theory's Empire*, p. 659.

[12]  Introduction, Waugh, ed., *Oxford Guide to Literary Theory and Criticism*, p. 10.

It is very much problems of this kind that exercise the philosopher of literature, not least because they do relate directly to critical practice and to the special features of reading literature as literature. Theory, in its older manifestations, often seemed remote from such questions because the focus was seldom on literature as such (the concept was rejected) and the framework for discussion was defined by, and concentrated on, theories from quite distinct intellectual areas, such as psychology, politics, linguistics, or metaphysics. Furthermore, many of the specific theses or presuppositions from those areas that gave shape to Theory have been subjected to devastating criticisms from philosophers: radical meaning-skepticism, radical kinds of anti-realism and constructivism, radical relativisms about everything from truth to morality, radical attacks on objectivity, rationality, authority, liberal politics, the autonomy of the self, and the author.[13] Of course just to state that these theories have been criticized is not enough in itself to undermine them, only a careful assessment of the arguments could do that, but it does suggest that Literary Theory might not be the most reliable starting point for a philosophical inquiry about literature. Where similar topics come up – as in the questions in that last quotation – it is best to see where the philosophical inquiry leads without constant reference to Theory which is either anti-philosophical or at times philosophically suspect.

Another danger with nearly all species of Critical Theory is also endemic in reflections on the nature of literature, one we will encounter in different guises: the danger of reductionism. When literary works are approached with a general all-embracing theory in hand, such as Marxism, psychoanalysis, feminism, linguistics, or radical politics it is all too easy to reduce the works to mere instances of a wider class of phenomena which themselves possess no distinct literary qualities. Reduction here is a semi-technical term, often used in philosophy, although not always with a clear meaning. Reductive or "eliminative" materialism, for example, is the view that only material things are ultimately real, implying there is no distinct realm of mental phenomena and all reference to such can be eliminated in favor of descriptions of matter and its properties.[14] Reduction in the literary realm can take different

[13] Many of theses criticisms have been collected in Patai and Corral, eds., *Theory's Empire*; see also David Novitz, *Knowledge, Fiction and Imagination* (Philadelphia, PA: Temple University Press, 1987); Raymond Tallis, *In Defence of Realism* (London: Hodder Arnold, 1988); J. R. Searle, "Reiterating the Differences: A Reply to Derrida," *Glyph*, 1 (1977), pp. 198–208.

[14] E.g., P. S. Churchland, *Neurophilosophy: Toward a Unified Science of the Mind/Brain* (Cambridge, MA: MIT Press, 1986).

forms, but one way or the other it denies the "autonomy" of literature. It either explains ("explains away") the phenomena of literature – the writing, reading, and evaluating of works – in terms of causal processes (social, ideological, or psychological) or it treats the works themselves as manifestations of essentially non-literary phenomena like the "play of signifiers" or undifferentiated "writing." We shall look in more detail at particular cases in later chapters. It would be wrong to maintain that all the principal branches of Theory are reductive; it is often the case that theories that began in crudely reductive forms – notably psychoanalysis and Marxism – developed much more sophisticated variants. In general, care has to be taken with the charge of reduction that it does not beg the question about what literary qualities are.

## Literature as Art

The focus of our inquiry, as noted, is on literature as an art form. Our central question is what this means and what its implications are. This focus is rarely found within Theory, and where literature as art does get mentioned it is usually in dismissive terms. Yet literature – primarily in the modes of poetry and drama – has been designated an art form for over two millennia. Aristotle described it as "an art which imitates by language alone," although he notes that there is no "common name" covering both verse and prose forms: "we have no common name for a mime of Sophron or Xenarchus and a Socratic Conversation; and we should still be without one even if the imitation in the two instances were in trimeters or elegaics or some other kind of verse."[15] Admittedly, Aristotle and the ancient Greeks did not have a conception of art directly comparable to our own. Aristotle's term *techne* is usually translated as "art" but more literally means skill or craft. Nevertheless, by according poetry a special status among uses of language and indeed by offering a systematic study of one poetic form, tragedy, Aristotle established a clear tradition for elevating poetic art as a proper object of study in its own right.

The Roman poet Horace entitled his famous treatise on poetry (c. 18 BC), itself written in verse form, *Ars Poetica*. He drew an explicit comparison between the art of poetry and the art of painting, "*ut pictura poesis*" (as in painting so in poetry), a comparison that became a subject of ongoing debate, not least in the eighteenth century when Gotthold Lessing, in

---

[15] Aristotle, *Poetics*, in *The Complete Works of Aristotle: The Revised Oxford Translation*, ed. Jonathan Barnes, vol. 2 (Princeton, NJ: Princeton University Press, 1984), p. 2,316.

*Laocoön* (1766), proposed a fundamental definition of the relations between the two art forms. Horace saw poetry not just as beautiful language but as an instrument for learning, thereby addressing Plato's charge that poetry does more harm than good. Horace writes: "It is not enough for poems to be 'beautiful'; they must also yield delight and guide the listener's spirit wherever they wish" (line 99). Also: "Poets wish to either benefit or delight us, or, at one and the same time, to speak words that are both pleasing and useful for our lives" (lines 333–334) [*Aut prodesse uolunt aut delectare poetae | aut simul et iucunda et idonea dicere uitae*].

A more modern attempt to bring poetry in line with the other arts appeared in a landmark work in art theory *Les beaux arts réduits à un même principe* (1746) [Fine arts reduced to a single principle] by Abbé Charles Batteux. This work was the first to offer a definitive grouping of arts under the heading "fine arts." Batteux listed those fine arts whose aim is pleasure as music, poetry, painting, sculpture, and dance. In another category, he added arts that combine pleasure and usefulness, namely eloquence and architecture, while theater is deemed a combination of all the arts. The "single principle" is "the imitation of beautiful nature," invoking again the ancient Greek conception of *mimesis*. For our purposes it is worthy of note that when the modern notion of fine art took shape one of the principal literary arts, poetry, found its place alongside more easily recognizable art forms such as music, painting, and sculpture. This served to consolidate the artistic standing of poetry already anticipated in Aristotle and Horace.

For G. W. F. Hegel (in lectures on aesthetics delivered in the 1820s), poetry was recognized not only as one among other arts but as the highest art of all, moving beyond the sensuous media of music and painting into a purer form of realization:

> As regards the *third* and most spiritual mode of representation of the roman-tic art-type, we must look for it in *poetry*. Its characteristic peculiarity lies in the power with which it subjects to the mind and to its ideas the sensuous element from which music and painting in their degree began to liberate art. For sound, the only external matter which poetry retains, is in it no longer the feeling of the sonorous itself, but is a *sign*, which by itself is void of import. ... Yet this sensuous element, which in music was still immediately one with inward feeling, is in poetry separated from the content of con-sciousness. In poetry the mind determines this content for its own sake, and apart from all else, into the shape of ideas, and though it employs sound to express them, yet treats it solely as a symbol without value or import. ... [T]he proper medium of poetical representation is the poetical imagination and intellectual portrayal itself. And as this element is common to all types of

art, it follows that poetry runs through them all and develops itself independently in each. Poetry is the universal art of the mind which has become free
in its own nature, and which is not tied to its final realization in external sensuous matter, but expatiates exclusively in the inner space and inner time of
the ideas and feelings. Yet just in this its highest phase art ends by transcending
itself, inasmuch as it abandons the medium of a harmonious embodiment of
mind in sensuous form, and passes from the poetry of imagination into the
prose of thought.[16]

It is easy enough to establish as a historical fact the longstanding recognition
of poetry as one of the arts, indeed as a "fine art." Of course nothing
presented in this brief survey goes any way toward explaining what
exactly the implications are in thinking of poetry as an art form. Indeed,
surprisingly, although the New Critics gave primacy to poetry in illustrating their critical principles, when modern philosophers of literature
examine the literary arts they give little attention to poetry as such. There
is not a "philosophy of poetry," and the issues that philosophers raise about
literature in general – meaning, interpretation, cognition, morality –
apply as much to prose narrative as to poetry narrowly conceived. In the
chapters that follow, where the implications of recognizing literature as
art are explored, poetry will figure in roughly equal measure with other
literary forms.

When we speak of literature nowadays we do not restrict ourselves to
poetry in the narrow sense. Literature in prose – the novel or short story or
prose drama – is arguably seen as an even more important or central literary form. The idea of imaginative literature as it developed in the nineteenth
century encompassed both prose fiction and writing in verse. It is a moot
point, one that should not simply be taken for granted, whether there is a
viable and clearly defined conception of literature that covers both poetry,
as traditionally conceived, and the novel. However, it will be one of the
arguments of this book that there is such a conception and that therefore a
philosophy of literature does possess an overall coherence and need not fragment into a philosophy of poetry, a philosophy of the novel, a philosophy of
drama, etc.

Does prose fiction qualify as an art? Novels, characteristically, are not
obviously "artistic" in the way that poetry is. When the novel first developed
in the eighteenth century, novelists looked less to poetry for their model so
much as other styles of prose writing, such as histories, letters, journals,

---

[16]   G. W. F. Hegel, *Introductory Lectures on Aesthetics*, trans. Bernard Bosanquet, ed. with an
introduction and commentary by Michael Inwood (Harmondsworth: Penguin Books, 1993),
pp. 95–96.

biographies. To acquire the kind of verisimilitude they sought they gave their works titles like *The Fortunes and Misfortunes of the Famous Moll Flanders*, *The Life and Opinions of Tristram Shandy*, *Clarissa: The History of a Young Lady*, *The Life and Strange and Surprising Adventures of Robinson Crusoe*. The authors sought to give the impression of telling the truth, not just good stories but stories that looked as if they were from journals or biographies. If anything they wanted to hide the artistic intent, perhaps to heighten verisimilitude or to distance their writing from fable or fantasy. Rather than relying, as had earlier writers, on mythology or legend or standard plots and stock characters, it was a feature of this new literary form that it used new and invented plots (hence the name *novel*) and particularized characters. Unlike poetic forms, such as the sonnet, the ode, the epic, or tragic drama, there were no fixed conventions for the novel. The critic Ian Watt explains this in terms of the early aims of the novelists:

> When we judge a work in another genre [e.g., sonnet or ode], a recognition of its literary models is often important and sometimes essential; our evaluation depends to a large extent on our analysis of the author's skill in handling the appropriate formal conventions. On the other hand, it is surely very damaging for a novel to be in any sense an imitation of another literary work: and the reason for this seems to be that since the novelist's primary task is to convey the impression of fidelity to human experience, attention to any pre-established formal conventions can only endanger his success. What is often felt as the formlessness of the novel, as compared, say, with tragedy, or the ode, probably follows from this: the poverty of the novel's formal conventions would seem to be the price it must pay for its realism.[17]

But if the "artistry" of the novel rests less than that of poetry on the manipulations of formal conventions it does not follow that the novel exhibits no artistry at all. As the genre developed, now-familiar criteria emerged for judging better or worse novels: to do with plot, character, structure, good writing, thematic interest, verisimilitude, originality. Such criteria, which are not too distant from those proposed by Aristotle for tragedy, are artistic criteria in the sense that they concern the artifice of the whole and the pleasures to be derived from it. In an early review (1847) of Charlotte Brontë's *Jane Eyre*, a reviewer remarks:

> Almost all we require in a novelist she has: perception of character, and power of delineating it; picturesqueness; passion, and knowledge of life. The story is not only of singular interest, naturally evolved, unflagging to the last, but it

---

[17]  Ian Watt, *The Rise of the Novel* (Harmondsworth: Penguin, 1966), pp. 13–14.

fastens itself upon your attention, and will not leave you. The book closed, the enchantment continues.[18]

As the novel grew and diversified, it developed into an art form as readily recognizable as poetry, even if, like poetry, manifesting strikingly different modes. When Henry James published an essay describing "The Art of Fiction" (1884)[19] there was no sense that the term "art" was unduly extended; and a hundred years later, at the height of Theory, when the idea of literature as art seemed at its most precarious, the title of Milan Kundera's book *The Art of the Novel* (1988) was not thought to be unduly provocative or controversial. As with poetry, merely popular genres, which did not aspire to be works of art so much as ephemeral entertainments, developed side by side with self-consciously "artistic" modes.

What should be emphasized is that appreciating literature as art is not simply one among other critical "approaches." It is more fundamental. Admittedly there are critics who do not give priority to reading literature as art – this might be true of deconstructionists, new historicists, or psychoanalytical critics. But proponents of such views might be reluctant to describe their readings as attending to the *literary* qualities of a work, or to the work *as literature*. In that sense their attention is not primarily to the work's *artistic* aspects. Again it remains to be seen what this entails. But there is a conceptual connection between literature and art such that it would be paradoxical to speak of appreciating a work *as literature* but not *as art*. In contrast, there is nothing paradoxical in speaking of appreciating a work as literature but not in deconstructionist, new historicist, or psychoanalytic terms. Such categories, whatever independent merits they might have, do not seem essential to explaining the literary viewpoint.

## Aesthetics and Literature

To think of literature as art is, minimally, to think of works as artifacts or designs of some kind, exhibiting "artistry," comparable in certain respects with other arts, and capable of affording distinct kinds of pleasure. An initial question is whether the relevant kind of pleasure and the relevant

---

[18]  George Henry Lewes, Review of Charlotte Brontë, *Jane Eyre*, *Fraser's Magazine*, December, 1847. Extract reprinted in Charlotte Brontë, *Jane Eyre*, edited by Richard J. Dunn (New York: Norton, 1971), p. 447.

[19]  Henry James, "The Art of Fiction," in *Longman's Magazine*, 4 (September 1884), reprinted in *Partial Portraits* (London: Macmillan, 1888).

literary qualities are essentially explicable in *aesthetic* terms. Must we look specifically to aesthetics to give substance to philosophy of literature? The matter is complicated because it is at least not obvious that aesthetic appraisal – perhaps in terms of aesthetic experience or aesthetic qualities or aesthetic values – is indispensable in understanding what is distinctive about the literary arts. Yet notions like the pleasures of literature and the designs of literary artifacts seem indisputably aesthetic. In the end, as will be argued, we cannot escape reference to the aesthetic even though there are important properties of literary works, e.g., fictionality, only indirectly connected to aesthetic properties.

For some, the artistic and the aesthetic are conceptually related. P. F. Strawson asserts that "the concepts 'work of art' and 'aesthetic assessment' are logically coupled and move together, in the sense that it would be self-contradictory to speak of judging something *as a work of art*, but not from the aesthetic point of view."[20] Marcia Eaton has proposed a definition of art that links it essentially with aesthetic perception or reflection:

> This necessary component of the aesthetic [perception or reflection] must also be a necessary component of the artistic if artworks are to be distinguished from other things that are skilfully and intentionally produced. Thus I define "art" as follows:
>
>> X is a work of art if and only if X is an artefact and X is treated in such a way that someone who is fluent in a culture is led to direct attention (perception and/or reflection) to aesthetic properties of X.[21]

Yet conceptions of art have been proposed that distance the artistic and the aesthetic. Most famously, perhaps, Arthur Danto has made the striking claim that it is not how an object *looks* or how it is *perceived* that determines whether it is a work of art but rather its embeddedness in an "artworld."[22] Two objects, Danto suggests, could be indistinguishable to the eye but only one is a work of art. His well-known example is Andy Warhol's facsimile reproductions of Brillo Boxes; Warhol's Brillo Boxes are art but the ordinary Brillo Boxes,

[20] P. F. Strawson, "Aesthetic Appraisal and Works of Art," in Peter Lamarque and Stein Haugom Olsen, eds., *Aesthetics and the Philosophy of Art: The Analytic Tradition: An Anthology* (Oxford: Blackwell, 2003), p. 237. Originally published in P. F. Strawson, *Freedom and Resentment* (London: Methuen, 1974), pp. 178–188.

[21] Marcia Muelder Eaton, "Art and the Aesthetic," in Peter Kivy, ed., *Blackwell Guide to Aesthetics* (Oxford: Blackwell, 2003), p. 74.

[22] Arthur C. Danto, *The Transfiguration of the Commonplace* (Cambridge, MA: Harvard University Press, 1981).

to which they appear identical, are not.[23] Conceptual art in general is often thought to be a challenge to any essential connection between art and aesthetic qualities.[24]

There is no need in this context to examine or assess rival definitions of art. It is enough to note that the relation between art and the aesthetic is contested. Whatever is said on that front, however, there is a fairly broad consensus that a useful distinction can be drawn between purely aesthetic qualities and artistic or art historical properties. To describe a work as elegant or finely balanced or unified or beautiful is to characterize its aesthetic nature, but to describe it as a sonnet or alluding to Marvell or symbolizing hope is to offer an art-related or more broadly literary characterization. The former seem to rely on something analogous to perception, while the latter call on classification or interpretation.

It is sometimes thought helpful to distinguish a narrow from a more inclusive sense of "aesthetic qualities." Berys Gaut has done so:

> In the narrow sense of the term, aesthetic value properties are those that ground a certain kind of sensory or contemplative pleasure or displeasure. In this sense, beauty, elegance, gracefulness, and their contraries are aesthetic value properties. However, the sense adopted here is broader: I mean by "aesthetic value" the value of an object *qua* work of art, that is, its artistic value.[25]

It is not just values but the qualities themselves that concern us, qualities that a work has *qua* work of art. If being a sonnet is such a quality then, in this broad sense, it becomes an aesthetic quality. Perhaps the terminology is not very important. It seems clear that being a sonnet is *relevant* to an aesthetic appreciation of a work.

Nevertheless, there are connotations of "aesthetic" that many critics find troubling in relation to literature. In particular they are the connotations of a specific kind of *experience*, a specific kind of *quality*, and a specific kind of *pleasure*.

### Aesthetic experience

The idea that art yields a distinctive kind of experience and is valued as such is a commonplace in aesthetics. But the nature of that experience,

[23] Arthur C. Danto, "The Artworld," in Lamarque and Olsen, *Aesthetics and the Philosophy of Art*.

[24] See Peter Lamarque, "On Perceiving Conceptual Art," in Peter Goldie and Elisabeth Schellekens, eds., *Philosophy and Conceptual Art* (Oxford: Oxford University Press, 2007).

[25] Berys Gaut, "The Ethical Criticism of Art," in Lamarque and Olsen, *Aesthetics and the Philosophy of Art*, pp. 283–284. Originally published in Jerrold Levinson, ed., *Aesthetics and Ethics* (Cambridge: Cambridge University Press, 1998), pp. 182–203.

particularly when characterized as "aesthetic experience," is subject to perennial controversy.[26] One idea is that aesthetic experience rests on a kind of disinterested contemplation of an object, a state of mind involving "psychical distance."[27] There might be certain applications of this idea to literary appreciation, where forms of detachments are appropriate, but on the whole, conditions of disinterestness and distance do not seem to capture the essence of what is valued in literature, especially where serious reflection on subject and theme is demanded. Weaker notions of aesthetic experience might be more relevant. Noël Carroll, for example, defines aesthetic experience merely as "the detection and discrimination of aesthetic properties, on the one hand, and design appreciation, on the other."[28] On the reasonable assumption that literary works exhibit design and are characterizable in aesthetic terms they would become amenable to aesthetic experience under this conception.

Paisley Livingston builds in a value component to aesthetic experience: "a direct, active contemplative attention to the qualities of some item, where this contemplation is an intrinsically valued experience." He adds that it "embraces thought and imagination as well as perception and sensation."[29] This last clause is particularly germane because the idea of experience defined narrowly in perceptual terms seems barely pertinent to literature. While a text needs to be perceived (by sight or by touch) to be read, no intrinsic quality of this perceptual experience is integral to literary value. As Hegel notes, poetry moves beyond the sensuous medium. Of course this is not to deny factors like the layout of a poem on the page or the mellifluous sounds of a work read aloud, both of which can aid appreciation, but only when the level of meaningful content is engaged can full poetic appreciation begin. By embracing thought and imagination as well, aesthetic experience can move more comfortably into central literary terrain.

The trouble is that thought and imagination do not naturally fall under the heading "experience," and this is a major problem for aesthetic accounts of literature. The aesthetic realm is normally defined in terms of perception, or how things appear (not least through the etymology of *aisthesis*, meaning "sense perception" in Greek), yet perception is only incidental to literature, the art of language. Nevertheless, while it seems wrong to seek a distinct kind

---

[26] For a clear overview, see Noël Carroll, *Philosophy of Art* (London and New York: Routledge, 1999), ch. 4.

[27] The "classic" statement of this theory is Edward Bullough, "'Psychical Distance' as a Factor in Art and an Aesthetic Principle," *British Journal of Psychology*, vol. 5 (1912), pp. 87–117.

[28] Carroll, *Philosophy of Art*, p. 201.

[29] Livingston, "Literary Aesthetics and the Aims of Criticism," p. 660.

of phenomenology associated with reading literature, we should perhaps not too hastily throw out the notion of experience altogether. Reading is not characterized by any particular feeling or sensation, but there is a kind of "appreciation" involving directed attention to literary qualities that is at least analogous to "experience" and closely related to standard aesthetic considerations. That notion of appreciation will be explored in Chapter 4.

### Aesthetic qualities

Aesthetic qualities are those qualities toward which aesthetic experience is directed. But what are they, in either the narrow or broad conceptions? Do literary works possess aesthetic qualities of a kind recognizably similar to those of other art forms like music or painting? If so, are such qualities of significance in literary criticism? Or are they, as some critics suppose, merely peripheral to the critical enterprise?

It is to Frank Sibley's pioneering work on aesthetic concepts that one should first look for illumination. Sibley identified a range of concepts – *unified, balanced, integrated, lifeless, serene, sombre, dynamic, powerful, vivid, delicate, moving*, etc. – which serve to characterize aesthetic aspects of art or other objects. On first viewing, such a list might not appear of much interest to the critic. However, one benefit of Sibley's lists is to show that aesthetics is not exclusively confined to beauty. To speak merely of the "beauty" of literary works does indeed seem anodyne and outdated. Sibley showed that aesthetic appraisals, thus aesthetic interests, are considerably wider than that. Another benefit is his recognition of the subtly different ways in which descriptive and evaluative elements can interact in aesthetic concepts.[30] Aesthetic characterizations are not always or only ways of evaluating works; they also have implications for how the work *appears*, what *impact* it has, what is *salient* in it, what merits aesthetic *attention*. Aesthetic descriptions bring such matters to light.

There are also three more substantive theses in Sibley that seem especially significant in the literary context. The first is the view that aesthetic properties are "emergent" or *gestalt* properties that require something more than merely sensory perception for their discernment. Sibley maintains that only people possessing a certain kind of "sensitivity" or "taste," itself subject to training and improvement, will be able to apply aesthetic terms correctly and engage in aesthetic appreciation. Something parallel is true in the literary case, namely that mere grasp of the language is not sufficient to appreciate a work aesthetically. Whether or not a particular sensibility is called for

[30]  See Frank Sibley, "Particularity, Art, and Evaluation," in Lamarque and Olsen, eds., *Aesthetics and the Philosophy of Art*. Originally published in *Proceedings of the Aristotelian Society*, suppl. vol. 48 (1974), pp. 1–21.

might be open to question,[31] but that some skill is involved beyond linguistic competence seems certain. Literary appreciation is not a natural but a trained mode of discernment. To see how a literary work "hangs together," where its interest and literary quality resides, a reader must have a holistic grasp of its achievement, which exceeds a sentence by sentence understanding of its component parts.

The second Sibleyan thesis relates to this, namely that there is no logical or even inductive relation between an object's non-aesthetic properties and its aesthetic ones. No list of non-aesthetic properties – physical, structural, perceptual, grammatical – entails (or makes probable) the presence of an aesthetic property. The idea that aesthetic concepts are not condition-governed has been challenged,[32] but there is at least a case for saying in the literary application that a work's emergent aesthetic features, of a kind to be exemplified later, are not deducible from textual features alone. Merely noting the presence of metaphors, images, repetition, rhyme schemes, rhetorical devices of any kind, will not determine that a passage is effective or moving, any more than the use of a minor key in a musical work inevitably determines it as sad. It might be added too that the presence of such textual features is no guarantee that the work must count as "literature." The point takes us back to Danto, for whom how a work *appears* will never alone determine its art status.

Thirdly, Sibley's aesthetic "particularism" has an application in the literary context. This is the view that aesthetic judgments are not generalizable. If in this work this combination of non-aesthetic or textual features contributes to this aesthetic effect, it does not follow that there is a generalizable principle that states that whenever that or a similar combination occurs the same effect will follow.[33] For example, the use of the "same" poetic imagery – love as a rose, time as a tyrant – in different works never ensures sameness of aesthetic effect. The point might be put by saying that there are no hard and fast rules that connect linguistic features of syntax, rhetoric, or meaning to literary aesthetic achievement. There might be rules of thumb for would-be authors – do's and don'ts of composition – but no success is guaranteed by imitating bits and pieces from other writers. A device that works so well in novel A might be entirely out of place in novel B.

It might be thought that aesthetic qualities of literary works are closely linked to formal features, and thus that an aesthetic approach is a kind

---

[31]    It is explicitly rejected by Olsen in "Literary Aesthetics and Literary Practice," in *The End of Literary Theory*, p. 7.

[32]    E.g., Peter Kivy, *Speaking of Art* (The Hague: Martinus Nijhoff, 1973).

[33]    Frank Sibley, "Aesthetic Concepts," in Lamarque and Olsen, eds., *Aesthetics and the Philosophy of Art*, p. 133.

of formalism. Only a full analysis of literary appreciation will show why this need not be so. But a first step comes from pondering the idea of "fine writing." We all have a view about what counts as fine writing and could give our favorite examples. But in the literary context, matters are complicated because fine writing in literary art is seldom an end in itself, rather a means to some further end or effect. Mellifluous prose or delicately nuanced imagery will not always be appropriate in every context, say in a dialogue (in a novel) between drunken members of street gangs. Rhetorical or formal devices, like figurative language, imagery, alliteration, rhyme schemes, repetition, metre, do not have intrinsic aesthetic value but gain their effectiveness by the contribution they make to a desired end, be it emotional impact, realistic depiction, humor, or poetic insight. In the non-literary context, the use of alliteration, rhyming couplets, or enriched figuration might afford no aesthetic pleasure if used, for example, to convey bad news.[34]

The important theoretical point, though, is that formal or rhetorical devices are in themselves *textual* features, identifiable independently of discursive aims and often subject to learnable rules. They acquire aesthetic significance only when assigned a function within an artistic structure. Consider a critic's observations on certain rhetorical features in these well-known lines from Wordsworth's "Tintern Abbey":

> ... a sense sublime
> Of something far more deeply interfused,
> Whose dwelling is the light of setting suns,
> And the round ocean, and the living air,
> And the blue sky, and in the mind of man:
> A motion and a spirit, that impels
> All thinking things, all objects of all thought,
> And rolls through all things.

Some of the sweep of this passage is also to be explained by the repetition of 'and': '*And* the round ocean, *and* the living air, / *And* the blue sky, *and* in the mind of man'. In conventional prose 'and' would normally signal the end of a list, but here, no sooner has Wordsworth thought to end it than some other facet of nature's multitudinousness occurs to him. The list is apparently

[34]  Hume has noted the inappropriateness of powerful rhetoric on such occasions: "Who could ever think of it as a good expedient for comforting an afflicted parent, to exaggerate, with all the force of elocution, the irreparable loss, which he has met with by the death of a favourite child? The more power of imagination and expression you here employ, the more you encrease his despair and affliction." David Hume, "Of Tragedy," in *The Philosophical Works of David Hume*, ed. T. H. Green and T. H. Grose (London: Longman, Green, 1874–1875), vol. 3, p. 364.

endless, and Wordsworth's profligate way with connectives all adds to the sense of amplitude and prodigality. This impression is strengthened by a similarly extravagant use of 'all': '*All* thinking things, *all* objects of *all* thought, / And rolls through *all* things.' The omnipresence of the 'a'-sound is also worth noting. seven consecutive lines in this section begin with it, and all the singular elemental words — 'man', 'and', 'am', 'all', 'a' — contain it. When this ubiquitous sound is coupled with the way every aspect of the universe is merged together with connectives and embraced by repeated 'all's, we have the impression that man, language and the universe are merging together in a paean of ecstatic oneness.[35]

What is striking about this passage is that it highlights a textual feature – the repetition of "and" and "all" – which might in other contexts be thought a defect, far less a mark of fine writing. But the critic identifies an aesthetic function for this rhetorical feature and assigns both significance and value to it. The aesthetic significance of the repetition *emerges* from the particularities of the poetic context and the construction put upon it. The example demonstrates a fundamental aspect of literary aesthetic effect: the consonance of means to end. The critic's aesthetic appreciation of the passage lies in perceiving a consonance between the formal means and the further poetic purpose of expressing "nature's multitudinousness" and the "ecstatic oneness" of man and universe. The appreciation does not rest on the rhetorical feature (the *textual* feature) alone.

### Aesthetic pleasure

A third application of aesthetics is the idea of aesthetic pleasure. The association of pleasure with literature is, as we have seen, an ancient one. Horace's formula of *pleasure* and *usefulness* became standard and reverberated down the centuries, from Philip Sidney to Dr. Johnson to Percy Bysshe Shelley to Matthew Arnold. Sometimes the idea of usefulness is given substance in a theory of artistic truth; sometimes, though, it is just a way of emphasizing that the pleasures of poetry are not merely trivial but what John Stuart Mill called "higher pleasures."

Yet "pleasure," far less "aesthetic pleasure," is not a term that literary critics are comfortable with. A recent exchange between three prominent critics, Frank Kermode, Geoffrey Hartman, and John Guillory[36] shows not untypical

---

[35]   Mark Rowe, "Poetry and Abstraction," in *Philosophy and Literature: A Book of Essays* (Aldershot: Ashgate, 2004), pp. 174–175.

[36]   In 2004 Frank Kermode was emeritus professor of English at Cambridge, Geoffrey Hartman emeritus professor of English at Yale, and John Guillory chair and professor of English at New York University.

concerns. The latter two critics were invited to reflect on Kermode's Tanner Lectures at Berkeley[37] where his aim was precisely to relocate at least some notion of the aesthetic – specifically the idea of "aesthetic pleasure" – in the vacuum left by the demise of Theory from the turn of the twenty-first century. The ostensible focus is on canon formation and the extent to which judgments of aesthetic value, apart from what Kermode calls "collusion with the discourses of power," could validly be thought to underlie the shaping of the canon.

Although Hartman and Guillory are happy to move with Kermode beyond the simplistic ideological analyses of 1990s cultural critics, they both express skepticism about aesthetic pleasure. Guillory notes "the pervasive embarrass-ment with the subject of pleasure [in the critical community], and the ease with which pleasure has been neutralized as the merely contingent effect of reception."[38] His own unease with aesthetic pleasure stems from suspicion about "higher pleasures" and the traditional elevation of poetry among the literary arts. Although he accepts – more readily than Kermode himself – the specificity of aesthetic pleasure among other kinds of pleasures, he is inclined, against Kermode, to reject the link between pleasure and canonicity. Hartman finds the very concept of pleasure, in the literary context, "problematic" and "descriptively poor" and speaks of its "onomatopoeic pallor."

The skepticism voiced by Guillory and Hartman about the role of aes-thetic pleasure in criticism is probably widely shared, even if the extent to which this skepticism rests on an outdated or overly narrow conception of aesthetics deserves further investigation. However, Kermode is not entirely isolated. The critic Harold Bloom, for example, famously led an attack on fashionable Theory at its height in the 1990s in the name of the "autonomy of the aesthetic."[39] Like Kermode, Bloom defends the canon on the grounds of aesthetic value while recognizing that "the flight from or repression of the aesthetic is endemic in our institutions."[40]

The "flight from the aesthetic" among critics can probably be traced to several sources. In summary, these include: the politicization of criticism in the heyday of Theory and the thought that appeal to aesthetic value is reac-tionary and tainted with unwelcome ideological accretions;[41] a shying away

---

[37]　Frank Kermode, *Pleasure and Change: The Aesthetics of Canon* (New York: Oxford University Press, 2004).

[38]　Ibid., p. 66.

[39]　Harold Bloom, *The Western Canon: The Books and Schools of the Ages* (New York: Riverhead Books, 1994), p. 9.

[40]　Ibid., p. 22.

[41]　A view found, for example, in Pierre Bourdieu, *Distinction: A Social Critique of the Judgement of Taste* (London: Routledge, 1984) and Terry Eagleton, *The Ideology of the Aesthetic* (Oxford: Basil Blackwell, 1990).

from value judgments of any kind; a belief that any reference to pleasure or emotion or experience or indeed to a phenomenology of reading is marginal to the critical enterprise; and, by implication, the thought that the very vocabulary of aesthetics, as exemplified in Frank Sibley's list of aesthetic concepts, is itself peripheral to substantial critical discourse. If we are to find a place for aesthetics — in particular aesthetic appreciation, aesthetic qualities, and aesthetic pleasure – within the philosophy of literature, as it seems the subject demands, then we must show how this skepticism can be met.

What might be involved in supposing literary works to be proper objects of aesthetic attention and aesthetic appraisal? Kermode and Bloom are no doubt right that some conception of aesthetic pleasure is integral to such an approach, but their literary critical opponents are also right to be suspicious of this. Kermode gets off on the wrong foot by seeking to naturalize the pleasures of literature, via Sigmund Freud and Roland Barthes, identifying them with a heady mix of sexuality (Barthes's *jouissance*), transgression, and what he calls "dismay." This is psychologism of a highly simplistic variety and apart from being vague is open to counter-example. It also seems committed, again, to the implausible idea that there is a distinct phenomenology associated with reading literature. A characterization of the aesthetic pleasure that literature can afford is not some empirical datum with which the inquiry starts but at best a destination reached from quite other premises.

If aesthetics is to be at all relevant to literature it must deploy recognizable features of aesthetic appraisal as applied to the arts more widely, but it must also capture something distinctive about literature as an art form. To do that it must avoid reductionism in several areas.

## Avoiding Unhelpful Reduction

One of the principal lessons from the Sibleyan tradition is that aesthetic qualities, while related to textual qualities, are not reducible to them. The temptation to reduce literary works to instances of more familiar or more tractable kinds is the biggest obstacle to a successful characterization of literary appreciation conceived even partially in aesthetic terms. Only if literary works can be shown to be objects of a distinctive kind of aesthetic appraisal, and to promote and reward such appraisal, will it be possible to set apart the literary sphere as a subject worthy of its own treatment within aesthetics.

But the tendency to "naturalize" literature is strong, for example to see literary works as no more than pleasing pieces of language, or entertaining narratives, or utterances to be assigned meanings. If the philosophy of literature has any hope of offering a plausible characterization of literature as art and finding a coherent, central, and defensible place for aesthetic pleasure, for aesthetic features distinct from merely textual features, for a *sui generis* mode of aesthetic appreciation, and for some conception of aesthetic value, then it needs to avoid the temptation of reduction on several fronts.

(1) It must encompass all literary forms – lyric poetry, epic, drama, the novel, the short story – without giving implicit priority to one form over another (as New Criticism did to poetry, for example, and structuralism to narrative).

(2) It must avoid attempts to explain literature in terms of linguistic properties alone (semantic, syntactic, or rhetorical), for in doing so it is likely to miss those essential features of design and artifice that qualify literature as art.

(3) It must avoid pure formalism or "art for art's sake" aestheticism. In characterizing the "love of literature," for example, it should not seek to reduce the complex nature of a literary response to any one aspect of literary pleasure, such as poetic imagery or plot structure.

(4) In characterizing aesthetic pleasure it should not be narrowly *hedonistic*. There have been attempts to explain the pleasures of reading in purely "sensuous" terms, or even as "erotic": as with Roland Barthes, who distinguishes *plaisir* and *jouissance* to describe modes of reading,[42] and Susan Sontag, who argued that "[i]n place of a hermeneutics we need an erotics of art."[43] These ideas are playful and provocative, but neither is the basis for a *philosophical* account.

(5) It should not give priority to intuitive, "natural," or untutored responses to literary works. It should take seriously the Sibleyan idea (also found in David Hume) that artistic appreciation is a learned response, acquired through experience and training. We are not all equal as literary critics.

(6) On matters of perennial debate – the aims and constraints on interpretation, the place for cognition (or "instruction"), and the criteria of literary evaluation – it should as far as possible recognize the "autonomy" of literature as a human practice with its own traditions and conventions and concepts. It should not too readily abandon the idea that in that practice interpretation, cognition, and evaluation have their own standards and are to a large extent *sui generis*. The danger otherwise is to reduce literature to hermeneutics, or philosophy, or ethics.

---

[42] Roland Barthes, *The Pleasure of the Text* (*Le Plaisir du texte* [Paris: Seuil, 1975]); trans. R. Miller (London: Cape, 1976).

[43] Susan Sontag, "Against Interpretation," in *Against Interpretation* (New York: Farrar, Straus, and Giroux, 1961), p. 23.

Although these points will largely structure the inquiry to follow it should be acknowledged that they are by no means uncontroversial. Arguments are needed, and will be given, in their support. But if philosophy of literature is committed both to the idea of literature as art and literary works as having their own distinctive characteristics among art works, then some such framework seems a *prima facie* promising and substantial basis on which to proceed. It is also a framework that resists the reduction of literature to something else.

## Supplementary Readings

For classical approaches to philosophy of literature the best place to start is Aristotle's *Poetics*, of which there are many editions (e.g., *The Poetics of Aristotle: Translation and Commentary* by Stephen Halliwell, Chapel Hill: University of North Carolina Press, 1987). Another important historical source is David Hume's essay "Of Tragedy," in *Essays: Moral, Political and Literary* (New York: Cosimo Classics, 2006; first published in 1742). A "classic" from the twentieth century is René Wellek and Austin Warren, *Theory of Literature* (Harmondsworth: Penguin, 1973; originally published in 1949). More recent works covering basic issues in the philosophy of literature are: Stein Haugom Olsen, *The Structure of Literary Understanding* (Cambridge: Cambridge University Press, 1978); Peter Lamarque, *Fictional Points of View* (Ithaca, NY: Cornell University Press, 1996); Christopher New, *Philosophy of Literature: An Introduction* (London: Routledge, 1999); Ole Martin Skilleås, *Philosophy and Literature: An Introduction* (Edinburgh: Edinburgh University Press, 2001); Eileen John and Dominic McIver Lopes, eds., *Philosophy of Literature: Contemporary and Classic Readings: An Anthology* (Oxford: Blackwell, 2004); Mark Rowe, *Philosophy and Literature: A Book of Essays* (Aldershot: Ashgate, 2004).

On the idea of literature as an art form and the role of literature in aesthetics, see Monroe C. Beardsley, *Aesthetics: Problems in the Philosophy of Criticism*, 2nd ed. (Indianapolis, IN: Hackett, 1981). Another influential work from early in the development of analytical aesthetics is Morris Weitz, *Hamlet and the Philosophy of Literary Criticism* (Chicago: Chicago University Press, 1964). There are numerous encyclopedias, anthologies, companions, and handbooks on aesthetics, and most have sections on literature. Perhaps the most comprehensive is Michael Kelly, ed., *Oxford Encyclopedia of Aesthetics*, 4 vols. (Oxford: Oxford University Press, 1998). Also useful, in collecting core papers in analytical aesthetics, is Peter Lamarque and Stein Haugom Olsen, eds., *Aesthetics and the Philosophy of Art: The Analytic Tradition: An Anthology* (Oxford: Blackwell, 2003). Some overlap of topics in aesthetics from the "Continental" (i.e., French and German) tradition, can be found in Clive

Cazeaux, ed., *The Continental Aesthetics Reader* (London: Routledge, 2000). Readings on particular aspects of philosophy of literature and literary aesthetics will be given at the end of other chapters and in footnotes.

For an excellent overview of current issues in literary theory, comprising commissioned survey articles, see Patricia Waugh, ed., *Oxford Guide to Literary Theory and Criticism* (Oxford: Oxford University Press, 2006); a good collection of primary sources is Vincent B. Leitch, ed., *The Norton Anthology of Theory and Criticism* (New York: Norton, 2001). On philosophical reactions to literary theory, the following are useful (note that most are critical in one way or another): Stein Haugom Olsen, *The End of Literary Theory* (Cambridge: Cambridge University Press, 1987); David Novitz, *Knowledge, Fiction and Imagination* (Philadelphia, PA: Temple University Press, 1987); Raymond Tallis, *Not Saussure: A Critique of Post-Saussurean Literary Theory* (London: St Martin's Press, 2nd ed., 1995); D. Patai and W. Corral, eds., *Theory's Empire* (New York: Columbia University Press, 2005).

On aesthetic qualities and aesthetic experience, the classic papers in analytic aesthetics are by Frank Sibley, collected in Frank Sibley, *Approach to Aesthetics: Collected Papers on Philosophical Aesthetics* (Oxford: Clarendon Press, 2006). Sibley's work is debated in detail in Emily Brady and Jerrold Levinson, eds., *Aesthetic Concepts: Essays After Sibley* (Oxford: Clarendon Press, 2001). Two foundational works in early-twentieth-century aesthetics, which deal, among other things, with aesthetic experience, are John Dewey, *Art as Experience* (New York: Perigee Books, 2005; originally published in 1934) and R. G. Collingwood, *The Principles of Art* (Oxford: Clarendon Press, 1938). Further influential discussion is in Monroe C. Beardsley, *The Aesthetic Point of View*, ed. M. J. Wreen and D. M. Callen (Ithaca, NY: Cornell University Press, 1982). For contemporary treatment, see Noël Carroll, *Beyond Aesthetics* (Cambridge: Cambridge University Press, 2001) and Richard Shusterman and Adele Tomlin, eds., *Aesthetic Experience* (London: Routledge, 2007).

On the idea of the "pleasures" of literature, see Christopher Butler, *Pleasure and the Arts: Enjoying Literature, Painting, and Music* (Oxford: Oxford University Press, new ed. 2005); John Carey, *Pure Pleasure: A Guide to the 20th Century's Most Enjoyable Books* (London: Faber and Faber, 2000); Frank Kermode, *Pleasure and Change: The Aesthetics of Canon* (New York: Oxford University Press, 2004). For a rather different and provocative approach, see Roland Barthes, *The Pleasure of the Text* (Oxford: Blackwell, new ed. 1990).

# Chapter Two

# Literature

What is involved in conceiving literature as art, as a suitable subject for aesthetics? Clearly not all uses of the word "literature" are relevant. The term can mean, for example, any body of writing on a specified subject: the literature on laptop computers, a literature survey on Kant's Transcendental Deduction, etc. That usage is too broad for our purposes. But art-related conceptions, though narrower in scope, are still hard to pin down. The idea that writing and speaking are art forms is of great antiquity; for many centuries, going back to the ancient Greeks, rhetoric, imparting the skills of reasoning, persuasion, and self-expression, was a core subject in schools, later one of the Seven Liberal Arts. It has long been taken for granted that writing and speech can be beautiful as well as effective.

## Conceptions of Literature

There is, then, a generic conception of literature, relevant to aesthetics, which encompasses "fine writing" wherever it occurs. Literature as "belles lettres" (beautiful letters) looks like a specific application of the wider category of "beaux arts" (beautiful arts). Written works of any kind – philosophy, history, theology, personal memoirs, diaries, biographies, essays – that are well written, finely crafted, and with eloquent phrasing, could count as "literary" under this conception, as was recognized when Bertrand Russell and Winston Churchill each received the Nobel Prize for Literature. Both made a contribution to "letters." Literary qualities are also manifested in mere parts of works – individual passages or sentences – even where the works themselves might not be classified as literature (pieces of journalism, for example, even government reports). No doubt there is room for debate about criteria for judging aesthetic merit in writing (or speaking); the criteria are likely to be relativized to different discursive aims, they might be historically and culturally variable, and might to a certain degree be subjective. But this is a subject for rhetoric not philosophy.

Philosophers of literature are interested in the "art" of literature, its place in aesthetics, the kinds of pleasure it can afford, and the values for which it is acclaimed. It might seem natural, then, to give primacy to "fine writing" or "belles lettres" in characterizing the conception relevant to their inquiry. But in many ways this would be a mistake. It would tend, for example, to blur the distinction between the generic conception and a narrower conception of literary works of art. Fine writing might be a sufficient condition for literature in the generic sense but it is not sufficient for literature as art, and arguably not even necessary. Novels that are written in the first person through the narrative voice of a child (such as *Catcher in the Rye*) or someone uneducated (such as *True History of the Kelly Gang*, Peter Carey's novel) might not exemplify fine writing as that is normally understood, any more than does Philip Larkin's "This Be the Verse" or William Carlos Williams's "This is Just to Say," even if the writing is described as clever, direct, moving, or realistic. Other reasons altogether qualify the writing as literature or as art. It is important to distinguish "fine writing," with an emphasis on eloquence, from "well written," which emphasizes broader literary qualities including consonance of means to ends.

The narrower conception of literature as art is associated with imaginative or creative writing, the subject matter of "literary studies" or literary criticism. Can this conception be tied down as distinct from the generic belles-lettrist conception? Contentious matters are at stake, not least the very scope and ambition of literary criticism itself. If literature as art is the principal subject of literary criticism and yet the concept is vague and unspecified, then an important area of humanistic study has an inherent weakness at its heart. Philosophers interested in the arts could not view this with equanimity. So how might this narrower class of artistic or "creative" literature be characterized? Merely to use the label "imaginative literature" is not entirely satisfactory for it is not as if the imagination has no role in other discourses. If imaginative means fictional, then that seems to favor certain kinds of literary works, such as novels, over others, such as lyric poetry. The latter is seldom described as fiction.

Is there an "essence" of literature in the sense we are seeking? Is it possible to give a clear and uncontentious definition that sets apart the conception of literature at the heart of philosophy of literature or literary criticism? This chapter will explore various attempts to do this, but also various attempts to show that it cannot be done.

A major obstacle to the enterprise is the breadth of application in even the "narrow" conception of literature as art. Until the arrival of the novel and prose fiction, reflection on the literary arts was confined to poetry, conceived in a broad sense which, as well as the epic and short lyric, included drama, notably the great tragedies of Sophocles or Shakespeare. For many theorists poetry remains paradigmatically "literary" and "artistic" in its exemplification of language at its most intense and self-conscious. In spite of its diverse forms, poetry seems to have features that lend themselves to talk of an "essence":

> In general, the essence of poetry as an art is not so much that it is rhythmical (which all elevated language is) or that it is metrical (which not all poetry is, except by a considerable extension of the meaning of the word), as that it is *patterned* language. This is its specific quality as a 'fine art'. The essence of pattern (in its technical use, as applied to the arts) as distinct from 'composition' generally, is that it is composition which has what is technically called 'a repeat'; and it is the 'repeat' which technically differentiates poetry from non-poetry, both being (as arts) 'composition'. The 'repeat' may be obvious, as in the case of rhymed lines of equal length, or it may be more implicit, to any degree of subtlety; but if it doesn't exist, there is technically no poetry. The artistic power of the pattern-designer is shown in the way he deals with the problem of 'repeat'; and this is true of poetry likewise, and is probably the key (so far as one exists) to any technical discussion of the art.[1]

The emphasis on the "technical" nature of this definition shows that it is possible to conceive of poetry, properly so called, as something whose "essence" can be rigorously tied down. The point of course is debatable, as is the specific account given, but for many it will not seem surprising that there should be a "technical" or strict sense of the term. But whether the same can be said for "literature" generally is much more controversial.

As we observed in the last chapter, the notion that all the literary arts should be lumped together, including the novel, the short story, drama of all kinds, as well as poetry, is in many ways curious and makes the question of an "essence" of literature especially problematic. For what could poetry, seemingly with its own distinctive essence, have in common with prose fiction, on the face of it lacking all the features identified above? To suppose that the common feature is just "fine writing" is not only weak but also, as we have seen, fails to set apart the class of "imaginative or creative" writing that seems central to "literary studies." Even if we think of the literary arts in terms of artistic *forms* – poetry, the novel, drama, the short story – our task of capturing a single underlying conception seems daunting. For one thing, these forms are, for the most part, only loosely defined, but there also seem to be instances of each form which do not merit the title "literature." Not all novels or poems are "literary," and among genres

---

[1]  J. W. Mackail in a 1906 "communication" to the Oxford English Dictionary (*The Compact Edition of the Oxford English Dictionary*, volume II, Oxford: Oxford University Press, 1971, p. 2,220).

of novels recognized by publishers – science fiction, romance, horror, whodunit, spy, children's fiction – there is a separate category of "literary fiction." Presumably only the latter is "literature" in the sense we are exploring. It would be tendentious – and surely false – to suppose that being well written is all that sets "literary fiction" apart. Further qualities are needed: having a kind of moral seriousness, perhaps, or an aspiration to tackle broad human concerns.

## Anti-Essentialism about Literature

It is tempting to suppose that there is no "essence" of literature that binds together the literary arts and determinately sets them apart from other kinds of writing. Perhaps "literature" is too vague a term to be captured in a definition and we should rest content with recognizing multiple, loosely related usages of the term and a class of irreducibly varied objects.

A prominent literary theorist in the 1980s spoke of the "illusion that literature exists as a distinct, bounded object of knowledge,"[2] rejecting any timeless and objective essence of literature. Significantly, he proposed a return to rhetoric in place of literary criticism: "I wish to recall literary criticism from certain fashionable, new-fangled ways of thinking it has been seduced by — 'literature' as a specially privileged object, the 'aesthetic' as separable from social determinants, and so on — and return it to the ancient paths which it has abandoned."[3] For this critic there can be nothing more to literature than a "highly valued kind of writing," with the added proviso that the values involved are "notoriously variable."[4] Such radical anti-essentialism, though, seems far too reductive and in danger of losing altogether what intuitive grip we have on the notion of the literary arts. For unless the value is specified to be *literary* value – which seems patently circular – then all kinds of valued writing will turn out to be literature. The telephone directory is valuable if one wants a phone number but it would be absurd to class that as a "work of literature" in any recognizable sense of the term.

### *Family resemblances*

Within aesthetics an influential strand of anti-essentialist theory was advanced by the philosopher Morris Weitz in his seminal paper "The Role of Theory

---

[2]  Terry Eagleton, *Literary Theory: An Introduction* (Oxford: Blackwell, 1983), p. 205.

[3]  Ibid., p. 206.

[4]  Ibid., pp. 10–11.

in Aesthetics" from 1956.[5] Weitz argued that there can be no definition of concepts like "art," "literature," or even "novel" and "tragedy," because these are "open concepts," allowing for radically new kinds of instantiation. The most that could be sought are, using Wittgenstein's well-known terminology, "family resemblances" between instances of the concepts: a "complicated network of similarities overlapping and criss-crossing" but no defining conditions:

> Knowing what art is is not apprehending some manifest or latent essence but being able to recognize, describe, and explain those things we call "art" in virtue of these similarities.[6]

The same anti-essentialism would hold for "literature." Literary works, on this view, are a motley without any core essence but exhibiting overlapping similarities and resemblances. No determinate set of features is common to all poems, novels, dramas, sagas, epics, tragedies, etc., in virtue of which they are literature, but these and other kinds of works comprise a loosely knit "family." One reason Weitz gives for insisting on the openness of the concept of art is that a closed concept (one subject to defining conditions) would "foreclose on the very conditions of creativity in the arts."[7]

In fact Weitz does acknowledge what he calls "criteria of recognition" for works of art:

> Thus, mostly, when we describe something as a work of art, we do so under the conditions of there being present some sort of artefact, made by human skill, ingenuity, and imagination, which embodies in its sensuous, public medium—stone, wood, sounds, words, etc.—certain distinguishable elements and relations. ... If none of the conditions were present, if there were no criteria for recognizing something as a work of art, we would not describe it as one.[8]

However, he insists: "even so, no one of these or any collection of them is either necessary or sufficient."[9]

---

[5]  Morris Weitz, "The Role of Theory in Aesthetics," in Peter Lamarque and Stein Haugom Olsen, eds., *Aesthetics and the Philosophy of Art: The Analytic Tradition: An Anthology* (Oxford: Blackwell, 2003), pp. 12–18.

[6]  Ibid., p. 15.

[7]  Ibid., p. 16.

[8]  Ibid., p. 16.

[9]  Ibid., p. 17.

Initially, Weitz's anti-essentialism is appealing when applied to literature. The thought that we can have a perfectly viable concept of literature without pinning it down to any determinate conditions, far less some set of properties common to all works of literature which sets them apart, is attractive. The idea of an "open concept" hospitable to literary innovation meets the historical reality which has seen even in the past hundred years the creation of new literary genres, from stream of consciousness novels to absurdist drama to concrete poetry. And all this invites a relaxed attitude to the bounds between very generic and more restricted senses of "literature," even while retaining familiar "criteria of recognition" which stops complete arbitrariness in delimiting the literary realm.

But Weitz's position has come in for severe criticism. The idea of "family resemblance," it is often noted, is a poor analogy given prior genetic and legal ties between family members quite independent of looks, and in any case resemblances or similarities can hold between virtually any two items. Wordsworth's "Daffodils" and an entry in a plant catalogue are similar in being about daffodils, written in English, containing the definite article, and so forth. Textual similarities are easy enough to find; what is needed is a conception of *significant* similarities, but what those are seems to presuppose rather than illuminate the idea of literature. Also Weitz's point, that "art" must be an open concept otherwise creativity in the arts would be impossible, seems wrong. Part of the essence of art might be that it is creative and invites innovation. The game of chess is tightly constrained by rules but that doesn't mean there cannot be brilliantly creative strategies.[10]

A lesson often drawn from Weitz's anti-essentialism is that it is effective at best only against a certain kind of putative essential property of art, namely intrinsic perceptual properties, such as beauty or organization or expressiveness or imitation. Perhaps there are no such properties that all works of art have in common and that are necessary and sufficient for arthood. But, so the argument goes, there are other kinds of properties, notably *relational* ones, which might indeed provide such conditions. This is the source of institutional or historical accounts that seek to define art in terms of its role in human practices or in history. The point is of special relevance in attempts to define literature. If there is an essence of literature, is it to be found in inherent textual properties – formal or semantic or structural properties – or in relational properties of this kind? We shall return to this.

---

[10]  This along with other objections to Weitz is advanced by Stephen Davies in *Definitions of Art* (Ithaca, NY: Cornell University Press, 1991), ch. 1.

## Cluster theories

Another anti-essentialist view of art similar to Weitz's, yet distinct from it, is the "cluster account."[11] This account builds on Weitz's "criteria of recognition," none of which is sufficient or even necessary individually for an item to count as art but at least some of which need to be present. Berys Gaut has proposed the following such criteria "which count towards an object's being art":

> (i) possessing positive aesthetic qualities (I employ the notion of positive aesthetic qualities here in a narrow sense, comprising beauty and its subspecies); (ii) being expressive of emotion; (iii) being intellectually challenging; (iv) being formally complex and coherent; (v) having a capacity to convey complex meanings; (vi) exhibiting an individual point of view; (vii) being an exercise of creative imagination; (viii) being an artefact or performance that is the product of a high degree of skill; (ix) belonging to an established artistic form; and (x) being the product of an intention to make a work of art.[12]

Such a conception might well be adapted to the special case of literary art by applying the list specifically to linguistic items. What the list purports to capture are criteria for *art*, but if literature is art then they must apply here too.

Gaut's account has several advantages over Weitz's: it does not rest on the unspecified notion of "resemblances," far less family resemblances, it does not rely on the argument from creativity to the openness of the concept of art, and it spells out just how the criteria are to be applied: for example, no properties are individually necessary but there are disjunctively necessary conditions and there are also jointly sufficient conditions.

Gaut insists that his ten criteria are merely "candidates" and that other competent cluster accounts might come up with different criteria.[13] He claims that cluster accounts capture our intuitions about art, particularly the way that we appeal to different considerations in arguments about whether

---

[11] Berys Gaut, "'Art' as a Cluster Concept," in N. Carroll, ed., *Theories of Art Today* (Madison: University of Wisconsin Press, 2000), pp. 25–44; and "The Cluster Account of Art Defended," *British Journal of Aesthetics*, vol. 45, no. 3 (2005), pp. 273–288. For discussions, see Thomas Adajian, "On the Cluster Account of Art," *British Journal of Aesthetics*, vol. 43, no. 4 (2003), pp. 379–385; Stephen Davies, "The Cluster Theory of Art," *British Journal of Aesthetics*, vol. 44, no. 3 (2004), pp. 297–300; and Robert Stecker, "Is It Reasonable to Attempt to Define Art?" in Carroll, ed., *Theories of Art Today*, pp. 45–64.

[12] Gaut, "The Cluster Account of Art Defended," p. 274.

[13] For example, Denis Dutton offers his own list of eight criteria in "'But They Don't Have Our Concept of Art,'" in Carroll, ed., *Theories of Art Today*, pp. 217–238.

something is art or not. And he thinks it handles borderline cases well, not because it always settles borderline disputes but because it shows up where the disputes lie. If an item satisfies all the criteria then it is not borderline and is a clear case of art, but if it satisfies only some but not others then its borderline status is clear and the dispute comes down to how much weight should be given to individual criteria. Gaut rejects the notion that a cluster account must specify in advance precisely how many of the criteria must be satisfied and which ones are more significant than others.

There are two questions we can raise about the cluster account. Are the specified criteria relevant to an analysis of literature? And is the general format useful in exploring the nature of literature? The first question takes us into the details of what literature is: whether aesthetic, expressive, or formal qualities play an important role, what kind of meaning, intention, and creativity are exhibited in literary works, and how literary works relate to "established artistic forms." These are important issues that will arise as we proceed. We should, though, ponder the second question now, whether a cluster account is the right *kind* of account to illuminate what literature is.

Gaut insists that the cluster account is not a *definition* of art. That is what makes it anti-essentialist and affirms the influence of Wittgenstein, as found in Weitz. Wittgenstein held that concepts can be perfectly usable without being amenable to strict definition in terms of necessary and sufficient conditions. One might specify an "essence" for particular purposes, but empirical concepts mostly don't have essences and are employed in different contexts under much looser criteria. But this does raise the question of what counts as a definition and what is sought by those who insist on attempting to define art or literature.

## Disjunctive definitions

It has been argued, for example, that the cluster account is after all a kind of definition, a disjunctive definition.[14] A disjunctive definition of art takes the form: X is a work of art if and only if X is either F or G or H or … Note that this uses the terminology of necessary ("only if") and sufficient ("if") conditions but its peculiarity is that the conditions are a set of disjuncts (either/or). Gaut resists the invitation to recast his cluster account in this form on the grounds of the complexity of the disjunction and the inherent indeterminacy of the concept of "art."[15]

Disjunctive definitions seem to give with one hand and take away with the other. What they give is a neatly encapsulated set of conditions determining

---

[14] E.g., in Stephen Davies, "The Cluster Theory of Art" and Robert Stecker in "Is It Reasonable to Attempt to Define Art?"

[15] Gaut, "The Cluster Account of Art Defended," p. 287.

the extension of a concept, but what they take away is any thought that these conditions capture some determinate "essence" shared by all members of the extension. Monroe Beardsley puts the point nicely when he remarks, commenting on a disjunctive definition of his own:

> Unless we can demonstrate some connection between the two concepts included in this disjunctive predicate, the definition will seem as arbitrary and capricious as would a definition of "broose" as "anything that is either a broom or a moose."[16]

Indeed if there is no clear connection between the disjuncts in a disjunctive definition then it makes little sense to say that a single concept has been defined rather than two or more separate concepts. When dictionaries offer a series of definitions for a single term this is often because distinct concepts have developed in relation to that term. Gaut recognizes that the criteria in his own proposed cluster account are so distinct that they could barely amount to a coherent definition of a univocal term. But arguably this points to a weakness in the very notion of a cluster account. If the cluster is too "variegated" (Gaut's term) then it is hard to see what someone *understands* either in using or responding to the concept. What is it to *grasp* a concept of this kind? Has one grasped the concept if one only has knowledge of some of the criteria? Admittedly there are familiar cases where people only partially understand the concepts they use or only know a limited set of criteria for their application: natural kind terms (elm, mercury) or legal concepts (indemnity) or technical terms (microprocessor, analog). But if the cluster account of art is right there is an immense complexity to the concept, including ten broadly independent criteria, which makes it surprising that it has common currency at all.

Disjunctive definitions of literature have been advanced. Robert Stecker, for example, proposes the following:

> A work *w* is a work of literature if and only if *w* is produced in a linguistic medium, and,
>
> 1. *w* is a novel, short story, tale, drama, or poem, and the writer of *w* intended that it possess aesthetic, cognitive or interpretation-centered value, and the work is written with sufficient technical skill for it to be possible to take that intention seriously, or

---

[16] Monroe C. Beardsley, "The Concept of Literature," in Eileen John and Dominic McIver Lopes, eds., *Philosophy of Literature: Contemporary and Classic Readings: An Anthology* (Oxford: Blackwell, 2004), p. 57.

2. *w* possesses aesthetic, cognitive or interpretation-centered value to a significant degree, or
3. *w* falls under a predecessor concept to our concept of literature and was written while that predecessor concept held sway, or
4. *w* belongs to the work of a great writer.[17]

The first thing to note is that the definition is more disjunctive than implied by the four major disjuncts. The first two clauses each involve sub-disjuncts, between artistic forms – novel, short story, etc. – and between different kinds of value: aesthetic, cognitive, etc. There are, then, as with cluster accounts, multiple ways that the definition could be satisfied. A work, for example possessing cognitive value to a significant degree, would, according to the second clause, count as a work of literature. It need have no aesthetic value, nor need there be any intention of such. Thus any reasonably compe-tent article in a philosophy or medical journal becomes a work of literature. That might seem too inclusive. But inclusiveness is already accommodated in the fourth clause. Technical, mathematical, or scientific essays will be included as literature on the assumption that their authors are "great writers" (Newton, Leibniz, Russell). The third clause allows that instances of earlier concepts, like that of belles lettres, are included. So all instances of fine writing become literature and the subclass of the literary arts (introduced in clause 1) is not singled out. Indeed, given the inclusiveness of clauses 2, 3, and 4, it is hard to see that the more restricted clause 1, the only one to mention distinct literary forms, is doing much work. What cases could satisfy the latter (1) without satisfying the former (2, 3, or 4)? The only such cases would presumably be ones in which a serious intention to produce aesthetic, cognitive, or interpretation-centered value *fails*. But is a work, albeit produced with technical skill, which lacks any significant degree of the named values really a work of literature? The point is debatable, resting on the degree to which there can be works of literature that have virtually no literary value.

For the moment, though, it is worth reflecting on the status of highly dis-junctive definitions like Stecker's. Does it meet Beardsley's constraint that, to avoid arbitrariness, the disjuncts must be connected? The question is moot. By separating, as it does, the three kinds of values – aesthetic, cognitive, and interpretation-centered – Stecker's definition suggests that there need be no common value shared by literary works. This implies that there is no single "literary" value, and if literature is at least partially an evaluative term, then it might seem doubtful that there is any single conception hereby

---

[17] Robert Stecker, "What Is Literature?" in John and Lopes, eds., *Philosophy of Literature*, p. 71. Originally published in *Revue Internationale de Philosophie*, 50 (1996), pp. 681–694.

identified that binds together the different instantiations. It certainly could not be supposed that the definition picks out an "essence" of literature or indeed offers much illumination to what might be meant by the literary arts.

We might conclude that if the problem with the cluster theory is that it is too vague as to which criteria are sufficient, thus when something can count as literature, the problem with disjunctive definitions is they are too determinate with their sufficient conditions, allowing too many different ways of satisfying the definition.

## Different expectations

The question "what is literature?" is open to different kinds of answers. Not all of these involve the search for a hidden essence. Even those that do seek definitions can sometimes fall back on lexicography, well short of philosophy. A good dictionary definition can often satisfy a general curiosity as to how a word is used and clarify different uses of a single word. Philosophical analysis of a concept is usually thought to be different from mere lexicography in providing some insight into a concept that synonyms or summarized usages cannot afford. However, a "paradox of analysis" has been identified whereby philosophical analysis seems either to reduce to dictionary meanings, in which case it is trivial, or it goes beyond such meaning and is incorrect.[18] It is thus not a straightforward matter to determine what a philosophical analysis might offer. Wittgenstein's proposal, that we should be content with "family resemblances," is a salutary reminder that definition is not always either appropriate or possible as a philosophical ambition.

In some contexts an adequate answer to the question "What do you mean by literature?" might be "I mean works like *King Lear*, *Paradise Lost*, and *Little Dorrit*." This is definition by ostension. It is likely to be effective only where participants already know what the options are in talking about literature. In this case, for example, the questioner might recognize that works not of the imaginative/creative species are to be set aside. In effect an appeal is made in such a response to paradigm cases, but only someone who can, as it were, continue the list will find the response helpful. Again this takes us back to Wittgensteinian or Weitzian resemblances. Only those who can recognize that the works listed are similar in significant ways will be able to project the similarities to new cases. It does suggest, though, that philosophical analysis might at least aim to illuminate what the significant similarities are.

---

[18]   The paradox of analysis was first characterized by C.H.Langford in "The Notion of Analysis in Moore's Philosophy", in P. A. Schilpp, ed., *The Philosophy of G. E. Moore* (La Salle, IL: Open Court, 1942), p. 323.

Another way of determining what literature is, or at least responding to a request to that effect, is to determine what the relevant contrasts are. What is literature being contrasted with? Sometimes, for example, literature is contrasted with history or philosophy. When Aristotle explores the truth-telling capacity of poetry he famously locates poetry between these two modes of inquiry: "poetry is something more philosophic and of graver import than history, since its statements are of the nature rather of universals, whereas those of history are singulars."[19] If this is the contrast that matters then the conception of literature is narrower than implied in the more general contrast between the literary and the non-literary, on the assumption that historical and philosophical works can have literary qualities. Sometimes literature is contrasted with genre fiction or popular verse which is thought not to aspire to "literary" status. Some but not all fiction is literary fiction and, again, it is the job of conceptual analysis to identify the grounds of such a contrast.

It would be wrong to think that the question "What is literature?" is always raised by those who genuinely do not know what literature is and are seeking information. In fact philosophy of literature is not primarily (if at all) addressed to such people, rather to those already deeply immersed in literary culture:

> The question [What is literature?] is not a request for information about what texts are literary works. It is asked by those who know literature and know the literary canon. Nor does the question merely ask for a definition of literature. The motivation for asking and the interest in possible answers can only be understood against a cultural background where literature figures as an important cultural value. What is asked for is an account of the characteristic features and functions of literature. It is expected that in explaining these, the account should also explain why it is worthwhile to single out certain texts as literary works. It must display those features which define and justify that interest which members of the culture take in its literature. This is the setting which gives the question its point ....[20]

## Conceptions of Literature and Conceptions of Art

In the history of attempts to say what literature is, by far the most prominent approach has been to identify a feature of literary works that is thought to have overriding importance. This feature is then conceived as the very

---

[19]    Aristotle, *Poetics*, in *The Complete Works of Aristotle: The Revised Oxford Translation*, ed. Jonathan Barnes, vol. 2 (Princeton, NJ: Princeton University Press, 1984), p. 2,323.

[20]    Stein Haugom Olsen, *The End of Literary Theory* (Cambridge: Cambridge University Press, 1987), p. 1.

"essence" of the literary even if it is recognized that other features are probably needed as well. When J. Hillis Miller states that "an essential feature of literature [is] to hide secrets that may not ever be revealed" he is under no illusion that this *defines* literature.[21] To the extent that literature (or poetry broadly conceived) has been thought of as art then the kinds of features identified have been closely associated with prominent features of the arts in general. It is notable how these prominent features have been historically variable and have even come to characterize periods of history: classical, romantic, modern, and so on.

It is not necessary for our purposes to dwell on the historical details at length, but even the briefest survey reveals telling shifts of emphasis in how literature has been conceived. The critic M. H. Abrams in his much acclaimed book *The Mirror and the Lamp* (1953) sorts these historical shifts in an illuminating manner by postulating what he calls four "coordinates of art criticism": the universe, the audience, the artist, and the work.[22] Each of the four coordinates is given prominence in four corresponding critical theories that apply to art in general as well as to literature: mimetic, pragmatic, expressive, and "objective" theories.

### Mimetic theories

Classical "mimetic" theories, dating back to the ancient Greeks, focus on the relation of work to world (or "universe"). All the arts, including "poetry," have been associated with mimesis or the "imitation" of reality. Both Plato and Aristotle simply assumed that mimesis was the guiding principle of poetry, although famously they had different reactions to that fact, Plato objecting that mere appearance not reality was imitated, Aristotle holding that imitation could reveal something universal about human action. Aristotle thought of imitation as a natural disposition in humans and a source of pleasure. He also saw it as a way of distinguishing different literary forms. Tragedy differs from comedy according to the different kinds of characters imitated and it differs from the epic in the manner in which the imitation is presented; in tragic drama the poet is hidden behind his characters who, as it were, do the speaking for him.

Mimetic theories of poetry find in mimesis not only an essential aim of poetry but also its enduring and characteristic value. The value is not only that of instruction, where the emphasis is on a world or truth revealed, but

---

[21]  J. Hillis Miller, *On Literature* (London and New York: Routledge, 2002), p. 40.

[22]  M. H. Abrams, *The Mirror and the Lamp: Romantic Theory and the Critical Tradition* (Oxford: Oxford University Press, 1953), ch. 1.

also on pleasing an audience. Dr. Johnson, the quintessential neoclassical rationalist, locates the pleasure of poetry in mimesis: "Nothing can please many, and please long, but just representations of general nature." Johnson also uses the metaphor of a "mirror," which Plato himself had introduced to explain mimesis, although for Plato this showed only the vacuity of imitation. Johnson writes: "Shakespeare is above all writers … the poet of nature; the poet that holds up to his readers a faithful mirrour of manners and of life."[23]

The idea that literary works should "mirror" reality has had many incarnations. It was a strong motivation behind the realist novel of the nineteenth century, helping to determine even the subject matter of novels, encouraging individualized stories rather than conventional or epic plots, characters finely drawn and enmeshed in familiar domestic situations, and a narrative language that in many respects mimicked history or biography. Realism also surfaced as a value among Marxist critics for whom faithful depiction of social reality had a political as well as an aesthetic function.

### Pragmatic theories

Pragmatic theories promote a subtle shift from world to audience. They need not reject the mimetic function of poetry but they highlight another function and another value, that of bringing about some effect in readers. A characteristic effect is one we have seen already, namely pleasure. It is hardly surprising to associate pleasure with poetry but it is equally remarkable how often the aim of pleasure has been denigrated or played down. Perhaps the influence of Plato reverberates in the strictures on poetic pleasure. For Plato, the poet can all too easily use the seductive charm of language to undermine the course of reason, promote an unhealthy stimulation of emotion, and ultimately corrupt public morals. Sir Philip Sidney's *Defence of Poetry* (1579/80) sought to meet the Puritan charge, with its Platonist ancestry, that poetry was dangerous for its pleasurable effects. In fact Sidney resorted to a formula dating back at least to Horace that poetry served twin aims of instructing and pleasing. Dr. Johnson belonged to a long line of those who echoed Horace: "the end of writing is to instruct, the end of poetry is to instruct by pleasing."[24]

The emphasis on stirring pleasure in an audience recalls again the central aim of rhetoric, to use language and linguistic skills to bring about some effect. Pragmatic theories focus on the means to an end, the use of poetic

---

[23] Samuel Johnson, *Preface to Shakespeare* (1755), in *Johnson on Shakespeare*, ed. Arthur Sherbo, Volume VII, The Yale Edition of the Works of Samuel Johnson (New Haven, CT and London: Yale University Press, 1968), p. 62.

[24] *Preface to Shakespeare* (1755), in *Johnson on Shakespeare*, p. 67.

or narrative devices to move or affect an audience. But audience-centered approaches have gone well beyond rhetoric traditionally understood. They are anticipated in Aristotle's conception of the proper response to tragedy, as fear and pity, and the consequent "catharsis" of those emotions. In more modern times they have led into reader-response and reception theories which highlight the reader's role in constructing meaning. They relate to feminist criticism where gendered responses are incorporated into literary values. And they are manifest in psychological, psychoanalytical, and political theories of reader-response. If the essence of literature is sought in literary effects – pleasure, emotion, attitude – then arguably a different conception of literature emerges from that which underlies mimetic theories.

### Expressive theories

The third traditional theory of literature focuses not on the world depicted or the audience affected but the mind and "genius" of the poet. Abrams characterizes the expressive theory as follows:

> Poetry is the overflow, utterance, or projection of the thought and feeling of the poet; or else (in the chief variant formulation) poetry is defined in terms of the imaginative process which modifies and synthesizes the images, thoughts, and feelings of the poet.[25]

The notion of "overflow" comes from Wordsworth's much repeated dictum that "poetry is the spontaneous overflow of powerful feelings" (in the Preface to the *Lyrical Ballads*, 1800). As in all expressive theories of art the role of the artist is given prominence, along with creativity, imagination, and emotion. The contrast with mimetic theories is striking – emphasis on expression signals the move from the classical to the romantic and was a relatively late arrival among conceptions of the literary. With it comes a notion of poetic value that would have seemed quite alien to Dr. Johnson. Abrams again:

> The first test any poem must pass is no longer, 'Is it true to nature?' or 'Is is appropriate to the requirements either of the best judges or the generality of mankind?' but a criterion looking in a different direction; namely 'Is it sincere? Is it genuine? Does it match the intention, the feeling, and the actual state of mind of the poet while composing?'[26]

---

[25]  Abrams, *Mirror and the Lamp*, pp. 21–22.
[26]  Ibid., p. 23.

The shift to the poet's own sensibility and response to the world occasions a radical shift in the fundamental aims of poetry. The central aim is no longer to "imitate" the human world or please an audience but to express a state of mind. Shelley's poem "Mont Blanc," influenced by Wordsworth's "Tintern Abbey," as a personal reflection on a determinate location, illustrates the new ambition of romantic poetry. Shelley wrote of the poem:

> It was composed under the immediate impression of the deep and powerful feelings excited by the objects which it attempts to describe; and as an undisciplined overflowing of the soul, rests its claim to approbation as an attempt to imitate the untamable wildness and inaccessible solemnity from which these feelings sprang.[27]

What matters is less an accurate representation of the "wildness" of the scene as the corresponding "wildness" stirred in the poet's mind:

> Dizzy ravine! And when I gaze on thee
> I seem as if in a trance sublime and strange
> To muse on my own separate phantasy,
> My own, my human mind, which passively
> Now renders and receives fast influencings,
> Holding an unremitting interchange
> With the clear universe of things around.

The effect of all this on the reader is to some extent incidental, at least if John Stuart Mill's romantic conception of poetry is applicable. Mill wrote that "poetry is of the nature of soliloquy," and should it rest on a "desire of making an impression upon another mind, then it ceases to be poetry, and becomes eloquence";[28] in other words poetry that seeks to affect a reader is mere rhetoric.

Expressive theories of art, as with pragmatic theories, developed in different directions. They surfaced in the idealist aesthetics of Benedetto Croce and R. G. Collingwood, for whom the expression of an emotion was the aim of all art. They also found fertile ground in psychological and psychoanalytic theories of artistic creation. And they emerge in strong intentionalist conceptions of literary criticism where the primary aim of criticism is the recovery of an artist's inner thoughts and feelings.

---

[27]    Quoted in M. H. Abrams, E. T. Donaldson, et al., eds., *Norton Anthology of English Literature*, 4th ed., vol. 2 (New York: W. W. Norton, 1979), p. 684.

[28]    *Early Essays by John Stuart Mill*, ed. J. W. M. Gibbs (London: George Bell, 1897), pp. 208–209. Quoted in Abrams, *Mirror and the Lamp*, ch. 1.

## *Objective or autonomy theories*

Abrams's fourth category, which he calls "objective" theories, gives prominence to the work largely in isolation from the other three coordinates, universe, audience, and artist. Objective theories stress the "autonomy" of the work and are associated in an early incarnation with aestheticism or the "art for art's sake" movement of the late nineteenth century. Oscar Wilde contrasted his aestheticism with classical mimetic conceptions of poetry, often poking fun at the latter: "Life imitates art far more than Art imitates life" and "the more we study Art, the less we care for Nature." His preferred "principle [for a] new aesthetics" stated that "Art never expresses anything but itself."[29] A. C. Bradley wrote of poetry that it is "not a part, nor yet a copy, of the real world ... but ... a world by itself, independent, complete, autonomous," although he qualifies this by speaking of a "connection underground" between "life and poetry."[30] In turn T. S. Eliot insisted that "honest criticism and sensitive appreciation is directed not upon the poet but upon the poetry."[31] Autonomy conceptions of art are anticipated in the Kantian aesthetics of disinterestedness and Schiller's conception of art as "play," and find expression in formalist developments in the twentieth century. The aestheticist movement gave focus to autonomy sometimes in terms of the social isolation of the artist, sometimes, more philosophically, in terms of the intrinsic value of aesthetic experience.

"Objective" or autonomy theories of poetry (and the literary arts generally) were predominant in twentieth-century criticism. Many of the principal theories of criticism in that century, including formalism, New Criticism, structuralism, even post-structuralism, stressed the self-standing nature of the literary work cut off, more or less, from external reference, authorial control, and affective response. Correspondingly, a distinctive conception of poetry took shape, as a "verbal icon" or a "well-wrought urn," a linguistic entity that draws attention to its own artifice and fictionality. If this was the essence of poetry then it determined both the values of poetry and the very procedures of criticism for talking about poetry.

We shall be following up strands of these four theories in later chapters. For the moment it is worth reflecting on what they tell us about literature (or poetry) and how it can be conceived. Few proponents of these theories

---

[29]    Oscar Wilde, "The Decay of Lying," 1891, in *Complete Works of Oscar Wilde* (London and Glasgow: Collins, 1966), pp. 970, 982, 987.

[30]    A. C. Bradley, "Poetry for Poetry's Sake," in *Oxford Lectures on Poetry* (London: Macmillan, 1909), pp. 5–6.

[31]    T. S. Eliot, "Tradition and the Individual Talent," 1919, in David Lodge, ed., *20th Century Literary Criticism* (London: Longman, 1972), p. 73.

would have supposed they were offering a *definition* of literature (or poetry) in the strict philosophical sense of providing necessary and sufficient conditions. But they did think they were identifying an *essential* feature,[32] in other words a feature both necessary and important. This feature – imitation of nature, source of pleasure, expressiveness, or autonomy – would be shared with other arts but would have a distinctive manifestation in the literary arts. It would characterize a central *aim* of literature and also a central *value*. It would also provide a focus for literary criticism. A critic would seek out the feature concerned and would use it as a touchstone for literary value judgments.

It is striking how the four theories come to be associated – albeit loosely – with historical periods. Mimesis is associated with classical or neoclassical thought about the arts, originally manifest in ancient Greece, resurfacing both in the Renaissance and in the European eighteenth century. Expressive theories arise with Romanticism at the beginning of the nineteenth century, while autonomy theories are linked with aestheticism or formalism from the end of that century. The pragmatic theory, focusing on audience response and the pleasures of poetry, is the least easy to locate historically, not because of its rarity but because, as Abrams notes, it "has been the principal aesthetic attitude of the Western world." It is only when a strong shift occurs away from reader-response toward either the artist or the work itself that there appears a weakening in the grip of this aesthetic attitude. Finally, the different theoretical conceptions encourage a pre-eminence of different literary forms. Mimesis tends to promote those forms, like epic, narrative, and drama, where character, action, or plot are highlighted, whereas expressiveness finds its natural outlet in the lyric rather than the epic, and the poem rather than the novel. Autonomy theories, notably the New Criticism, also tend to give prominence to lyric poetry.

## Literary Language

The thought that literature might have an essence, albeit short of a strict definition, found expression, particularly in the twentieth century, in explorations of "the language of literature." This has taken many forms but starts with the entirely plausible premise that there is something special about literary uses of language. The plausibility resides partly, again, in the association of literature with "belles lettres" or fine writing. But it rests not just on

---

[32]   Not untypically Lessing writes that "imitation" for the poet "constitutes the essence of his art": *Laokoon*, ed. William G. Howard (New York: Henry Holt, 1910), p. 64.

a quality judgment. Poetry – some poetry at least – offers the very model of the specialness of literary expression. Lines like these, it seems, could only be "literary":

> I caught this morning morning's minion, king-
>> dom of daylight's dauphin, dapple-dawn-drawn Falcon in his riding
>> Of the rolling level underneath him steady air, and striding
> High there, how he rung upon the rein of a wimpling wing
> In his ecstasy! Then off, off forth on swing,
>> As a skate's heel sweeps smooth on a bow-bend: the hurl and gliding
>> Rebuffed the big wind. My heart in hiding
> Stirred for a bird,—the achieve of, the mastery of the thing!
>
> Brute beauty and valour and act, oh, air, pride, plume, here
>> Buckle! AND the fire that breaks from thee then, a billion
> Times told lovelier, more dangerous, O my chevalier!
>
>> No wonder of it: shéer plód makes plough down sillion
> Shine, and blue-bleak embers, ah my dear,
>> Fall, gall themselves, and gash gold-vermilion.
>> ("The Windhover," by Gerard Manley Hopkins)[33]

The dense and unusual syntax, the rhythm, the alliteration, the metaphors, the rhyming patterns, the striking imagery, and the sonnet form, all point to poetic usage. Such "devices" have been extensively studied and form the subject matter of stylistics. It is far from clear, though, that linguistic peculiarities of this kind can form the basis of a generalized account of literature as art. Poetic devices are not universal features of literary works and are not usual or mandatory in, for example, prose fiction. Nor, more interestingly, is their presence an automatic sign of the poetic. Individual instances of alliteration, metaphor, rhyme, and imagery occur in all kinds of context, by no means all "literary."

### Semantic definition

It is more promising to think of these surface features of poetry not as ends in themselves but as serving some further function, which might itself be "literary." A common proposal along these lines centers on the production of *meaning* in literary works, in particular stressing its complexity or density Monroe C. Beardsley's "semantic definition of literature" epitomized theorizing of this kind. What marked out literary

---

[33]   Gerard Manley Hopkins, *The Poetical Works of Gerard Manley Hopkins*, ed. Norman H. Mackenzie (Oxford: Clarendon Press, 1990), p. 144.

language, on this view, was "semantic density," or a high level of "implicit meaning." The "density" of lines like "shéer plód makes plough down sil-lion | Shine, and blue-bleak embers, ah my dear, | Fall, gall themselves, and gash gold-vermilion" is plain to see, the complexity and difficulty of meaning palpable. By no stretch of the imagination is this "ordinary" language.

Beardsley's conception grew out of an "interaction" theory of metaphor, formulated by I. A. Richards, according to which "when we use a metaphor we have two thoughts of different things active together and supported by a single word, or phrase, whose meaning is a resultant of their interaction."[34] Beardsley held that metaphorical meaning was a model for all poetic (liter-ary) meaning: "A metaphor is a miniature poem, and the explication of a metaphor is a model of all explication."[35] A poetic metaphor – like "king- | dom of daylight's dauphin, dapple-dawn-drawn Falcon" – contains not only an internal structure but an array of implicit meaning or connotation wait-ing to be explored. Many of the New Critics developed their own concep-tions of semantic density, as a kind of "tension" or "paradox" or "irony" at the heart of literary meaning. Cleanth Brooks wrote that "the structure of a poem resembles that of a ballet or musical composition. It is a pattern of resolutions and balances and harmonizations, developed through a temporal scheme."[36]

William Empson, whose favored concept was "ambiguity," illustrates the critic's exploration of semantic density in discussing some lines from *All's Well That Ends Well* (II iii 170):

> When I consider
> What great creation, and what dole of honour
> Flies where you bid it …

*What creation of honour* is courtly and reserved, but standing alone, as the intervening "*what*" may suggest, *creation* becomes more abject, and means "you make and break people according to your liking." On the other hand, taking *great creation* and *dole* together, and feeling for a connection, one passes from the idea of "doling out" to the idea of "doleful"; "how terribly the sort of honour you give people weighs them down"; he is overheard, as it were, muttering under his breath.[37]

---

[34]    I. A. Richards, *The Philosophy of Rhetoric* (New York: Galaxy Books, 1965), p. 93.

[35]    M. C. Beardsley, *Aesthetics: Problems in the Philosophy of Criticism*, 2nd ed. (Indianapolis, IN: Hackett, 1981), p. 144.

[36]    Cleanth Brooks, *The Well Wrought Urn*, 1947 (London: Methuen, 1968), p. 166.

[37]    William Empson, *Seven Types of Ambiguity* (London: Chatto and Windus, 2nd ed., 1947), p. 99.

What Empson sees himself as doing, apart from exemplifying a type of ambiguity, is uncovering the hidden connotations in the passage thereby revealing the complexity implicit in it. The idea that literary works have "layers" or "depths" of meaning to a greater degree than everyday or scientific language is familiar. The thought that one might analyse a neighbor's conversation or a scientific treatise along Empsonian lines is absurd. According to a modest version of the multiple meaning view: "a verbal structure is literary if it presents its topic at more than one level of presentation at the same time—or, alternatively, if one and the same utterance has more than one function in the structure of meaning in which it occurs."[38]

But there are equally familiar objections to finding the essence of literariness in textual semantic properties of this kind. For one thing, poetic "devices" are not universally present across all literary works and tend to be found only in certain kinds of finely wrought poetry. Narrative literary fiction need not exhibit complexity at this verbal level. Indeed, when we speak of complexity of meaning in narrative it is not complexity of connotation that is foremost so much as complexity of structure and theme. Then the analogy with metaphor begins to break down. A metaphor juxtaposes and creates a "tension" between two or more constitutive elements that themselves possess verbal meaning. But the elements making up a narrative include things like characters, incidents, background setting, and so forth, which do not seem to bear meaning in anything like this sense.[39]

Another objection to the semantic definition is that semantic properties like "implicit meaning," ambiguity, tension, or paradox cannot account for the *value* ascribed to literature. Colin Lyas makes the point:

> If someone cites *any* quality and argues that this quality is a defining condition of literature, then that quality must be a quality that will lead to a favourable evaluation of any work exemplifying the quality in question. It will, that is, be impossible to define literature unless we cite features the possession of which makes a piece of writing valuable in a certain way.[40]

It is far from clear what value semantic density could have in itself. In some areas of discourse – the law, philosophy, even conversation – too much ambiguity

---

[38] Winifred Nowottny, *The Language Poets Use* (London: Athlone Press, 1968), p. 2.

[39] The point is developed in detail in Stein Haugom Olsen, "The 'Meaning' of a Literary Work," in *The End of Literary Theory* (Cambridge: Cambridge University Press, 1987).

[40] Colin Lyas, "The Semantic Definition of Literature," *Journal of Philosophy*, vol. 66, no. 3 (1969), pp. 81–95 at p. 83.

or multiple connotation is a negative factor. Why should it be sought in literary works? If there is an answer it must lie, again, in some literary end, or value, to which these semantic features are merely a means.

The most telling objection to accounts of this kind is that they rest on a false assumption, namely that properties like semantic density are either present or not present in texts objectively, regardless of how they are read. The truth is that depths of meaning can be found in any texts if read with that notion in mind. Terry Eagleton has fun with his own example, the notice on the London Underground that states: "Dogs must be carried on the escalator." Even apart from its semantic ambiguity,

> One could let oneself be arrested by the abrupt, minatory *staccato* of the first ponderous monosyllables; find one's mind drifting, by the time it has reached the rich allusiveness of 'carried', to suggestive resonances of helping lame dogs through life; and perhaps even detect in the very lilt and inflection of the word 'escalator' a miming of the rolling, up-and-down motion of the thing itself.[41]

Virtually all words have connotations and associations that can be activated in juxtaposition with others. No doubt poets exploit this fact and are imaginative in finding the precise juxtapositions that work best for the effects they seek. But the idea that poetic language possesses densities of connotation unavailable elsewhere does not stand close scrutiny.

### Formalist theories

Similar problems can be found with all formalist theories of literary language. The Russian and Czech formalists from the early part of the twentieth century offered some of the most systematic and sophisticated attempts to capture, often in a quasi-scientific manner, what is distinctive about literature or "literariness." But as with the defenders of our earlier four theories – mimetic, pragmatic, et al. – they offer little more than isolated features that are recognizable in some but not all literary production. Viktor Shklovsky's notion of "making strange" (*ostranenie*) is a case in point. The idea that art, and poetry in particular, serves to shake us out of our "habituated" modes of perception and *defamiliarize* the banal realities we take for granted is a striking reminder of a feature of poetry that is immediately recognizable. Gerard Manley Hopkins certainly makes things strange in describing the flight of the "dapple-dawn-drawn Falcon." The very forms and patterns of poetic language remove us from humdrum utilitarian description. Although the formalists

---

[41] Eagleton, *Literary Theory*, p. 7.

put much store on the devices and techniques of poets to this end, they did not highlight any one manifestation, such as semantic density. Indeed, they gave equal attention to the novel, introducing another well-known distinction, between "story" and "plot" (a loose translation of the Russian *fabula* and *sjužet*); the story is the basic subject of the novel which is creatively "made strange" by the transformative structures of the plot. Shklovsky suggested that Laurence Sterne's novel *Tristram Shandy* was "the most typical novel in world literature" because it transformed its own story into its own plot.[42]

The kind of self-referentiality that Shklovsky finds in Sterne came, for some structuralist critics, to be another key feature of the literary:

> Every work, every novel, tells through its fabric of events the story of its own creation, its own history … the meaning of a work lies in its telling itself, its speaking of its own existence.[43]

Literary language on this conception is self-reflexive, its function again set apart from ordinary discourse whose characteristic aim is to convey thoughts about a world beyond itself. The notion is nicely encapsulated in Roland Barthes's essay title "To Write: An Intransitive Verb." Self-reflexivity here is derived from another recognizable feature of poetic language: its drawing attention to itself as an aesthetic object. Roman Jakobson promoted the idea of "the palpability of signs":

> The distinctive feature of poetry lies in the fact that a word is perceived as a word and not merely a proxy for the denoted object or an outburst of an emotion, that words and their arrangement, their meaning, their outward and inward form acquire weight and value of their own.[44]

A related notion is that of "foregrounding," defined by the Czech theorist Jan Mukarovsky as "the aesthetically intentional distortion of linguistic components."[45] "Any item in discourse that attracts attention to itself for what it *is*, rather than acting merely as a vehicle for information, is foregrounded."[46]

---

[42]  Viktor Shklovsky, "Sterne's *Tristram Shandy*," in Lee T. Lemon and Marion J. Reis, eds., *Russian Formalist Criticism: Four Essays* (Lincoln: University of Nebraska Press, 1965), p. 57.

[43]  Tzvetan Todorov, *Littérature et signification* (Paris: Larousse, 1967), p. 49; cited in Terence Hawkes, *Structuralism and Semiotics* (London: Methuen, 1977), p. 100.

[44]  See Victor Erlich, *Russian Formalism: History-Doctrine* (The Hague: Mouton, rev. ed., 1965), p. 183.

[45]  Paul L. Garvin, ed. and trans., *A Prague School Reader on Aesthetics, Literary Structure and Style* (Washington, DC: Georgetown University Press, 1964), pp. vii–viii; cited in David Lodge, *The Modes of Modern Writing: Metaphor, Metonymy, and the Typology of Modern Literature* (London: Edward Arnold, 1977), p. 2.

[46]  Lodge, *Modes of Modern Writing*, p. 2.

There is no denying that foregrounding is an important literary phenomenon, prominent in self-conscious writing of all kinds. However, it does not isolate the literary. Foregrounded language, as Mukarovsky himself realized, occurs outside the narrowly defined literary realm, in puns, obscenities, advertising slogans, even politicians' "soundbites," and there seem to be literary works where plain, "transparent" writing is prized. And it does not seem plausible to suppose that literariness resides just in the *degree* of foregrounding, or the degree of semantic density. A joke that consists of a whole string of puns is not more literary than a poem that consists of none. This then is the trouble with theories that try to capture the essence of literariness in formal linguistic properties. They cannot fit all cases of the recognizably literary and they do fit cases that are not recognizably literary. But these theories should not be dismissed out of hand. Any account of literariness needs to show how "fine writing" or being "well written" stands out or draws attention to itself and, indeed, why a search for layers of meaning is relevant.

## Literature and Fiction

The idea that literary language is self-referential, drawing attention to itself, rather than projecting outward to the world, is common among formalist and "autonomy" conceptions of literature. It also suggests a connection with fictionality. Exactly what fictionality is, when placed under the philosophical microscope, is a question we shall return to in Chapter 5. For the moment we should take note of various attempts to incorporate notions of fiction into definitions of literature. On the face of it this will not seem surprising since the literary arts are best exemplified by novels, plays, epics, and poems that characteristically have a high degree of imaginative invention in their content.

### Fictionality and foregrounding

David Lodge makes explicit the connection between fictionality and foregrounding:

> literary discourse is either self-evidently fictional or may be read as such, and … what compels or permits such reading is the structural organization of its component parts, its systematic foregrounding.[47]

The phrase "or may be read as such" attempts to accommodate the wider generic class of literary works that are not "self-evidently fictional," such

---

[47] Ibid., pp. 6–7.

as Boswell's *Life of Johnson* or Gibbon's *Decline and Fall of the Roman Empire*. For Lodge, to read Boswell *as literature* is to read his work *as fiction*, setting aside concerns with truth or falsity. A similar view is presented by Jonathan Culler: "Rather than say, for example, that literary texts are fictional, we might cite this as a convention of literary interpretation and say that to read a text as literature is to read it as fiction."[48] A consequence for Lodge is that "Boswell's Johnson then becomes something like a fictional character and his *Life* is read as if it were a kind of novel."[49] However, Lodge postulates a class of "axiomatically literary" works which directly exploit foregrounding for fictional ends. The Boswell and Gibbon would not belong in this class.

Unfortunately it is by no means clear what it means to read a work "as fiction." Must we suppose that all references in the work are fictional and not to real people? This is surprisngly difficult to do. Also, many novels make reference to real places and people, while still retaining their fictional status. So fictionality does not demand referential blocking. Must we suppose that all descriptive content is made up and not literally true? Yet, again, many novels contain accurate descriptions of real world settings. It would beg the question to suppose that reading "as fiction" consists entirely in attending to stylistic or formal or structural features as if that were not possible for non-fictional works. Obviously what is needed is a detailed exploration of fictionality. In the meantime, we can get some idea of what is behind certain claims for the fictionality of literary works by turning to applications of speech act theory to literature.

### Speech act theories

One prominent speech act account holds that:

> A literary work is a discourse whose sentences lack the illocutionary forces that would normally attach to them. Its illocutionary force is *mimetic* … a literary work *purportedly imitates* (or reports) a series of speech acts, which in fact have no other existence".[50]

Behind this line of thinking is an important, if unsurprising, observation about fictional works: in some sense they are not what they seem to be. An epistolary novel (like Richardson's *Clarissa*) appears to be a collection of letters but no such letters were ever sent. Sartre's *Nausea* appears to be a

---

[48]  Jonathan Culler, *Structuralist Poetics* (London: Routledge, 1975), p. 128.

[49]  Lodge, *Modes of Modern Writing*, p. 8.

[50]  Richard Ohmann, "Speech Acts and the Definition of Literature," *Philosophy and Rhetoric*, vol. 4 (1971), p. 14.

diary but it is not; it is only a pretend diary. A first-person novel (like Scott Fitzgerald's *The Great Gatsby*) appears to be an autobiography but it is no such thing. These are prime examples of "imitation." It looks as if statements are being made, questions are being asked, in a novel but in fact those illocutionary acts are only pretended. Even where it might look as if an author is speaking directly, we must, on this theory, attribute the apparent statement to a fictional narrator:

> Thus Jane Austen does not *make* the statement, "It is a truth universally acknowledged, that a single man ...." ... The making of the statement is an imaginary illocutionary act. But in order to do his part in the mimesis, the reader must nonetheless consider whether the statement is true or false. Its falsehood is one tip-off to the fact that the imaginary narrator of the story is being ironic.[51]

Readers have a crucial role because it is important that they recognize that the illocutionary acts are only "imaginary," not real. Indeed, this suggests what reading "as fiction" might amount to. A reader "constructs (imagines) a speaker and a set of circumstances to accompany the quasi-speech-act."[52]

Monroe Beardsley has advanced a similar view, also stressing the fictionality of the narrator: "the writing of a poem, as such, is not an illocutionary act; it is the creation of a fictional character performing a fictional illocutionary act."[53] Interestingly Beardsley attempts to combine his speech act conception with his earlier semantic density conception, offering a disjunctive definition:

> "literary discourse" might be defined as "discourse that is either an imitation illocutionary act or distinctly above the norm in its ratio of implicit to explicit meaning".[54]

Responding to the previously mentioned dangers of disjunctive definitions – failing to capture a unified concept – Beardsley draws a connection between the two disjuncts that alludes to features already noted in other formalist accounts:

[51]   Ibid., pp. 14–15.

[52]   Ibid., p. 14.

[53]   Monroe C. Beardsley, *The Possibility of Criticism* (Detroit, MI: Wayne State University Press, 1970), p. 59. He develops the view in several places: *Aesthetics: Problems in the Philosophy of Criticism*, 2nd ed. (Indianapolis, IN: Hackett, 1981), p. xliv; "Fiction as Representation," *Synthese*, 46 (1981); and "Aesthetic Intentions and Fictive Illocutions," in Paul Hernadi, ed., *What Is Literature?* (Bloomington: Indiana University Press, 1978).

[54]   Beardsley, "The Concept of Literature," in John and Lopes, eds., *Philosophy of Literature*, p. 57.

Both are forms of verbal play that set a discourse notably apart from pragmatic functions—one by deficiency of illocutionary force, the other by excess of semantic display. Both help to make a discourse self-centered and opaque, an object of attention in its own right.[55]

There are some intuitively attractive features of speech act accounts. They incorporate the standard literary critical postulate of a fictional narrator or persona and locate it in a theoretical context. They give a role to readers as well as authors. And they show how fictional discourse might be distinguished from non-fictional discourse without appealing directly to semantic notions like truth or reference.

However, there are problematic factors as well. It is questionable to what extent literary works, even those that have an overtly fictional content, should be distanced from their authors through, as it were, a veil of pretense. It does seem as if some works – for example, with a moral, political, or satirical import – can have a direct illocutionary force attributable to their actual authors and not merely to a fictional speaker: denouncing slavery, poking fun at pretentiousness, proposing reforms, affirming human rights. Are there not limits to the pretense attributable to literary works? Colin Lyas has argued that we should distinguish between the imaginative *world* of a literary narrative, which is a kind of pretense, and a "valuational response" to that world in the work which need not be a pretense and is often a genuine expression.[56]

More of course needs to be said about the role of an author's attitudes and intentions but to insist on a conceptual connection between literature and pretense early on in the discussion seems too strong and unmotivated. It might seem in general as if the conception of fiction implied by speech act accounts – and the corresponding conception of "autonomy" – cuts literary works off too much from the contexts in which they arise.

Even if fictionality comes to be closely *associated* with literature it should not be assumed that the concepts are the same. John Searle, among others, has insisted on the distinctness of the concepts.[57] Not all literary works are fictions (Searle cites Truman Capote's *In Cold Blood* and Norman Mailer's *Armies of the Night*) and not all fictions are literary (Searle offers comic books and jokes). Also the concepts seem to have different meanings: "'the Bible as literature' indicates a theologically neutral attitude, but 'the Bible as fiction' is tendentious."[58]

[55]    Ibid.

[56]    Colin Lyas, "The Relevance of an Author's Sincerity," in Peter Lamarque, ed., *Philosophy and Fiction: Essays in Literary Aesthetics* (Aberdeen: Aberdeen University Press, 1983), p. 45.

[57]    John Searle, "The Logical Status of Fictional Discourse," in *Expression and Meaning: Studies in the Theory of Speech Acts* (Cambridge: Cambridge University Press, 1979).

[58]    Ibid., p. 59.

To the extent that speech act accounts of literature – many of which have affinities to Searle's speech act theory of fiction – make fictionality a defining feature of literature they leave little room for keeping the concepts separate.

Another feature of literature that seems to get lost in speech act accounts is the very idea of an aesthetic interest. Why should the fact that literary works "purportedly imitate" speech acts give them any special status, make them stand out as objects of interest? Admittedly Aristotle thought that humans find imitation naturally appealing but this is not necessarily an aesthetic appeal, and in any case there are plenty of examples of imitation with no aesthetic merit. What gets lost in these accounts is the intuition that literary works are valued and sought after for their aesthetic quality and moral seriousness. The invocation of "mimesis" in the definition captures one aspect of "imitation" but not the traditional one of holding a "mirror" up to nature; indeed, there is nothing in the definition which alludes to any kind of representational content.

### "Literature" and "weed"

Another putative definition, proposed by John M. Ellis, draws on some of the underlying motivation behind speech act accounts but does so independently of speech act theory and anticipates the direction taken by institutional conceptions. Ellis rejects the formalist search for constitutive linguistic features common to literary works. Like Weitz and the anti-essentialists he holds that there are no such common features. But his Wittgensteinian stance involves not proposing family resemblances but looking to the uses to which the word "literature" is put, or the circumstances in which we describe a piece of writing as literature. In fact by appealing to "use" he sometimes runs together the use of a *word* in linguistic practices and the use of the *objects* (texts) themselves. His main interest is in the latter, the use to which texts are put.

He compares the logic of the concept of literature with the logic of the concept of a weed. The reason a plant is deemed a weed is that it is not wanted in the garden, the causes (as he puts it) of one plant's being included and not another might be various: being unsightly, rampant, poisonous, etc. By analogy texts with very little in common might be included as literature but what they share is an attitude taken to them. It is this shared attitude that serves to define literature:

> Literary texts are defined as those that are used by the society in such a way that the text is not taken as specifically relevant to the immediate context of its origin.[59]

[59]    John M. Ellis, *The Theory of Literary Criticism: A Logical Analysis* (Berkeley: University of California Press, 1974), p. 44.

When Shakespeare writes "Shall I compare thee to a summer's day?" we do not suppose that this question invites an answer, least of all from us. Here we have the intuition of the speech act theorist, that the illocutionary force is "drawn." We turn our attention to the aesthetic and thematic properties of the poem and set aside any immediate, contextually based communicative intention: "we no longer accept any information offered as something to act upon, nor do we act on its exhortations and imperatives."[60]

Ellis's definition shares many of the positive features of speech act accounts and is preferable for not tying literature so closely to fiction. Its main strength is its move away from any particular linguistic function or intrinsic property. The idea that what makes a text literary rests at least partially in the way it is used by relevant communities seems to point in the right direction, if only because it alleviates the problem of accommodating such a diversity of texts – novels, plays, poems, stories – under the single heading. And the definition finds a place for intuitions about the timelessness of literature and the autonomy of literary works.

But it also shares some of the weaknesses of speech act accounts. Perhaps it forces too much distance from the context of creation. Some literary works do seem to offer "exhortations and imperatives" to be acted on. Dickens might be dismayed to think that *Hard Times* no longer possessed its moral function in rousing awareness of harsh social conditions. Admittedly the conditions to which he was referring obtained in Victorian England but that fact should not be lost or sidelined in appreciating the novel as literature. Nor does it weaken the continuing relevance of the "exhortation." And must we really cut off the *Divine Comedy*, or Pope's satires, or even the novels of Trollope from their historical roots? Finally, what about jokes, catch-phrases, or epigrams whose origins have been lost? Do they become literary works?

## Institutional Accounts

We saw earlier that one response to Morris Weitz's anti-essentialism was the criticism that Weitz was concentrating on too narrow a band of properties that might serve to define art or literature. He should, so the objection goes, look at *relational* properties, those holding, for example, between works, artists, and audiences, to find the defining characteristics of art, and correspondingly between texts, authors, and readers in the case of literature. This line of thought leads to institutional theories of the arts which have had a dominant place in aesthetics since the 1960s. Admittedly some of our

[60] Ibid., p. 43.

earlier putative attempts to capture the essence of literature had appealed to relations: in the mimetic theory, between work and world; in the expression theory between work and author, and so on. But according to a prominent exponent of institutional theories these relations were always too "thin": "the institutional theory attempt[s] to place the work of art within a multi-placed network of greater complexity than anything envisaged by the various traditional theories."[61]

### Danto and Dickie

One of the early intimations of the institutional approach in aesthetics came from Arthur Danto, who introduced the idea of an "artworld." We noted in Chapter 1 Danto's startling claim that there might be no *perceptible* differ-ence between a work of art and an object that is not art, far less a difference in qualities like beauty or structure. His famous thought-experiments about "indiscernibles" are meant to show this.[62] Wherein can the difference lie? Danto's often quoted answer is: "To see something as art requires something the eye cannot descry—an atmosphere of artistic theory, a knowledge of the history of art: an artworld."[63]

The "theory" in which, for example, Andy Warhol's Brillo Box is embedded – in this case Pop Art and its underlying rationale – *makes possible* certain kinds of works. It also makes possible art-related properties attributable to the work, like being witty, ironic, a comment on the con-sumer society, and so forth. For Danto, then, there is something essential to all art – contra Weitz – namely embeddedness in an "artworld" with its supporting theories. The idea that works of art become art – and acquire their art-related properties – in virtue of their embeddedness in some kind of social institution will turn out to be of crucial significance in illuminating the concept of literature. But just what form this embed-dedness takes and how the institution should be characterized is far from determined. Arguably the notion of an "artworld" has more obscured than illuminated the debate.

George Dickie took over the idea of an artworld and developed it into one of the first systematically worked out institutional theories of the arts. In fact, Dickie has offered two versions, the later simpler than the earlier

[61] George Dickie, *Introduction to Aesthetics: An Analytic Approach* (Oxford: Oxford University Press, 1997), p. 82.

[62] See Arthur Danto, *The Transfiguration of the Commonplace* (Cambridge, MA: Harvard University Press, 1981).

[63] Arthur Danto, "The Artworld," in Lamarque and Olsen, *Aesthetics and the Philosophy of Art*, p. 32. Originally published in *Journal of Philosophy*, 61 (1964), pp. 571–584.

and, as he himself held, less subject to the criticisms directed at the first version.[64] The later version consists of five interlocking definitions:

A work of art is an artifact of a kind created to be presented to an artworld public.

This definition explicitly contains the terms "artworld" and "public" and it also involves the notions of *artist* and *artworld system*. I now define these four as follows:

An artist is a person who participates with understanding in the making of a work of art.

A public is a set of persons the members of which are prepared in some degree to understand an object which is presented to them.

The artworld is the totality of all artworld systems.

An artworld system is a framework for the presentation of a work of art by an artist to an artworld public.[65]

One striking difference between the later and earlier versions of Dickie's institutional theories is that only the earlier one makes reference to "appreciation." According to that version, a "set of aspects" of a work of art had "conferred on it the status of candidate for appreciation." Even then, the notion of appreciation is thin, making no commitment, for example, to aesthetic qualities or indeed to values of any kind. In the later version, which does away with appreciation, Dickie's theory has stripped the concept of art down to the barest minimum so it might seem to have little content left. Perhaps that is one of its strengths in allowing more or less anything to become art. No limit is placed on the forms that art might take or the attitudes or evaluations relevant to art or the role of art in human life. In its tight circle of defining concepts there is no indication of why there should even be a concept of art of this kind.

If we substitute "literary work" for "work of art" and "author" for "artist" in Dickie's definition we can see just how thin this definition is in application to a particular art form. Yet perhaps thinness alone is not the problem. More seriously, the definition still leaves the idea of an institution largely unexplained; if the philosophy of literature is to gain insights from the institutional approach then this must be clarified. The notions of a "framework for the presentation of a work of art" and a "public ... which are prepared in some degree to understand an object" will not shed much light on the nature of literature.

[64] The two versions appeared in George Dickie, *Art and the Aesthetic: An Institutional Analysis* (Ithaca, NY: Cornell University Press, 1974), and George Dickie, *The Art Circle* (New York: Haven, 1984).

[65] Dickie, *Introduction to Aesthetics*, p. 92.

## Sociological conception of institution

What is an "institution" in the sense that might apply to literature? It is important to distinguish two conceptions in this context. One is a sociological conception. Its characterization would make reference to a network of social relations which in some way or other comprise the "book industry," involving: writers, publishers, editors, book reviewers, academics, teachers, readers of all kinds, judges of literary prizes, bookshop owners, shareholders of publishing companies, designers, typesetters, and advertising executives. Anyone studying this complex network, from a sociological point of view, would need to take note of each group's interests, aspirations, social status, salaries, working relations, and working conditions; facts about sales, book distribution, readership patterns, means of communication, hierarchies, newspaper or journal reviewing policies, international connections, and advertising strategies would need to be collated; perhaps in the end hypotheses could be advanced about reading preferences, power relations, class biases, social and political trends, the influence of age, gender, or ethnicity on reading patterns and taste, and so on. A subclass of this sociological inquiry might examine the "institutionalization" of literary studies in universities and schools, how "English Literature" became established in tertiary education, what social pressures helped shape the form it took, and so forth.

There is no denying that there is a social institution of this kind – even if its boundaries are far from clear and it shades off on all sides into other areas of social life. Nor can it be denied that illuminating insights into a particular society over a particular period can be derived from its investigation. Given the complexity involved and the detail demanded, any such study is always likely to be a localized exercise; the social institution of literature will take different forms in different societies at different historical periods. For all its sociological interest, however, an inquiry of this kind is very limited in what it can do to clarify the *concept* of literature.

## Analytical conception of institution

A second conception of an institution is more relevant to philosophy of literature. This might be called an analytical conception. At the heart of this conception are not actual social relations between groups of people but rather principles and conventions governing social *roles*. A simple example might shed light on the difference.[66]

---

[66] I am indebted to Stein Haugom Olsen for this example and for the distinction among kinds of institution: see his "The Concept of Literature: An Institutional Account," in Stein Haugom Olsen and Anders Pettersson, eds., *From Text to Literature: New Analytic and Pragmatic Approaches* (Basingstoke: Palgrave Macmillan, 2005).

Take the position of a judge in a modern legal system. There is a sociological and an (as it were) analytical perspective. Under the former, facts about actual judges at specific periods will be adduced: how they are recruited, what social class they belong to, what attitudes to social and political issues they tend to exhibit, their salaries, their age, gender, social standing in the community, the extent to which they are subject to external influence, and so on. Yet none of this says much about the role of a judge, *qua* judge. To find this out one must look to the legal system itself: what duties judges, constitutionally, are obliged to fulfill, what constraints they operate under, what the limits of their powers are, how they are appointed and dismissed. The latter inquiry is "analytical," not sociological.

In parallel fashion it is possible to investigate the role of *authors* and *readers* and the nature of *literary works* within an institutional framework of this second kind without delving into sociology.

Part of the impetus behind analytical conceptions of institutions comes from Wittgenstein's notion of a rule-governed practice and his frequent analogies with games. Take the game of chess, an example that Wittgenstein uses.[67] Only within a game of chess is it possible to castle on the queen's side, take the bishop with the knight, checkmate. These are activities that could not exist independently of the rules of chess, just as the rules determine what can and cannot be done with each piece. Indeed, again, the very existence of chess pieces – pawn, bishop, knight, etc. – depends on the existence of the game and its rules. Certain social practices exhibit the same kinds of dependencies. Getting married, naming a child, and opening a bank account are likewise only possible given the relevant social conventions and "institutions." What counts as an item of currency depends not just on how something looks (it could be a perfect counterfeit or Danto-like "indiscernible") but on its legally sanctioned role in a banking system. Using the terminology of John Searle, there are "constitutive rules" underlying social practices that make possible constituent activities and objects of this kind.[68]

The claim of one version of institutional accounts of literature is that the very being and nature of literary works depend on an "institution" in a manner analogous to that in which a chess piece or an item of currency

[67] E.g., Ludwig Wittgenstein, *Philosophical Investigations*, trans. G. E. M. Anscombe (Oxford: Blackwell, 1968), §31.

[68] John R. Searle, *Speech Acts: An Essay in the Philosophy of Language* (Cambridge: Cambridge University Press, 1969), pp. 33–42; John R. Searle, *The Construction of Social Reality* (London: Allen Lane, 1995), chs. 1–6.

depends on a corresponding game or practice.[69] Certain consequences follow immediately. One is that there would be no literary works without the institution; literary works are not "natural kinds," just finely wrought stretches of language independent of specific purposes and actions. They are "institutional objects." Thus, secondly, the existence of literary works depends on a set of conventions concerning how they are created, appreciated, and evaluated; in other words, on attitudes, expectations, and responses found in authors and readers. A third point arises directly from the chess/currency examples. It is a feature of chess and currencies that there are multiple ways of instantiating the formal roles of the pieces in each case. The king in chess can not only be made of wood or plastic, be two inches or two feet high, take all kinds of stylized forms, but in fact it need have no physical manifestation at all. Chess can be played without a board, by just specifiying moves. Likewise, there are any number of forms in which a dollar or fifty pence can be manifested. The institutional account of literature places no restrictions on the form that literary works can take. Finally, there is nothing in the institutional account that implies restrictions on participants in the practice, their social class, age, gender, or ethnicity. To participate it is enough to know and conform to the conventions. The sociological account might notice features of the social or cultural background of authors and readers, but nothing in the analytical account presupposes this.

It does seem as if this is a promising framework for explaining what literature is, using resources that are well tested in other areas of philosophy. Of course there are plenty of questions still to be answered. One concerns the "conventions" that constitute the practice. These need to be specific enough to capture a substantial, recognizable, conception of literature – beyond the bare procedures offered by Dickie – yet not so specific that they apply only to some, not all, forms of literature, a problem faced by the formalists. But it is not too difficult to proceed, given the general assumption that the focus is on literature *as art*.

## *Two dimensions of literary art*

In common with all art, literary art can be characterized across two dimensions: an *imaginative/creative* dimension and a *content* dimension.[70] There is a

---

[69]    See Stein Haugom Olsen, *The Structure of Literary Understanding* (Cambridge: Cambridge University Press, 1978); Stein Haugom Olsen, *The End of Literary Theory* (Cambridge: Cambridge University Press, 1987); Peter Lamarque and Stein Haugom Olsen, *Truth, Fiction, and Literature* (Oxford: Clarendon Press, 1994).

[70]    For details, see Lamarque and Olsen, *Truth, Fiction, and Literature*, ch. 10.

conventional expectation that literary works of art will be creative, either through fictional invention or through the imposition of form on subject. In all cases, a central factor is the organization imposed on a complex of elements creating a unified whole. Even avant-garde works that reject "closure" or, like *Tristram Shandy*, revel in apparent disorder are still products of design and artifice.

The second dimension, content, raises an expectation of what might loosely be called moral seriousness, in the sense of some broad human interest raised and developed. A merely gripping story, meant to be read once and set aside, or a poem that adorns a birthday card, amusing but forgettable, do not even purport to have the status of literature. Their aims are different. Literary works invite multiple readings because they offer content with depth, inviting reflection. This might be called "mimesis" but without the connotation of realism or holding a mirror to life. It connects with the first dimension through the idea of "theme." A literary theme is a unifying element which orders the subject matter under general conceptions. Again, readers of literary works will have a conventional expectation that humanly interesting themes will be explored and developed through the subject presented, be it narrative content or poetic image.

On this conception, a complex interplay between authors, readers, and works is revealed. Authors present their works, not just, as Dickie has it, to an "artworld public ... prepared in some degree to understand an object ... presented to them" but under the constraints of an institutional practice where expectations are raised as to how the works are to be read and enjoyed *as literature*. Readers in turn come to works expecting to find the imaginative/creative and content criteria fulfilled. This determines how they appreciate the works and indeed what works they seek out to reward a literary interest. The works themselves come into being as objects of these intentions and expectations. In this way it seems that all four of Abrams's "coordinates" applied specifically to literature – work, world, author, reader – are accommodated without giving undue weight to the relations between any two, as found in traditional theories.

The institutional account also meets many of the intuitions of the formalists in insisting on the linguistic artifice of literary works and the ways that this can be exploited (through the imposition of form) for further ends, such as the consonance of subject and theme. What it emphasizes, though, is that formal and stylistic features – poetic "devices," narrative "techniques," uses of metaphor, imagery, and so on – can occur in any kinds of texts, and that rather than constituting the "essence" of the literary they are simply, in some cases, an effective means toward other distinctively literary ends. It even draws on some fundamentals of speech act theory in that it is possible to see an author's intention in producing a literary work as a "Gricean" intention (after H. P. Grice[71]) in the sense of having a reflexivity whereby the intended response (the "literary stance"[72]) is partially fulfilled by means of the recognition that that response is intended.

But there are potential objections. Perhaps the most persistent is that it is simply unrealistic to suppose that there is some single determinate institution underpinning the concept of literature. This objection breaks down into two strands. The first strand insists that literature is an ever evolving concept and there is little historical, far less inter-cultural, continuity.[73] In response it is important to identify exactly what has evolved over time. The use of the word "literature" has a clear history, and perhaps current usage is relatively modern. But the history of a word and the history of a concept should not be confused. The concept of literature captured by the institutional account encompasses what was called "poetry" by the ancient Greeks and up to the eighteenth century.

Also, literary forms have an evolving history. The novel was not a form known to the Greeks. The new term "literature" was useful in bringing the novel into the realm previously occupied by poetry alone. It is a clear benefit of the institutional view that it allows for new literary forms and genres. If one is looking for the empirical adequacy of the institutional account one must go deeper than lexicography. A study of the ways that the ancient Greeks saw poetry or the renaissance sonneteers or the neoclassicals like Dr. Johnson or the Romantics will reveal, as noticed, different emphases round the four coordinates but it does not seem to reveal much change at the fundamental level of imagination/creation and thematic content.

The second strand to the objection against a single institution is the existence of multiply varied "approaches" to literature. It seems obvious that critics – and other readers – often do more than look for thematic and aesthetic unity in a work, or for its moral seriousness and creative form. Of course that is right, but it does not weaken the institutional account. The account does not *prescribe* how to read, it seeks only to characterize constitutive principles governing what it is to identify a work *as literature* and to appreciate it as such. Not anything can count as adopting a *literary point of view* toward a work.[74] There might be other points of view that are equally valid; the focus

---

[71]  See H. P. Grice, "Meaning," *Philosophical Review*, vol. 66, no. 3 (1957), pp. 377–388; reprinted in *Studies in the Ways of Words* (Cambridge, MA: Harvard University Press, 1989).

[72]  Lamarque and Olsen, *Truth, Fiction, and Literature*, p. 256.

[73]  E.g., Robert Stecker, "What Is Literature?" p. 67: "it has evolved a great deal over the course of time (I would question whether the concept of literature extends back to ancient Greece)."

[74]  This idea is explored in Peter Lamarque, *Fictional Points of View* (Ithaca, NY: Cornell University Press, 1996), ch. 12.

might be on the author's biography, on the social conditions of the work's production, the effects it has on younger readers, the political consequences of its publication, and so on. Many of these aspects draw on facts about the sociological institution in which the work is embedded.

It should be emphasized as well that the institutional account has no implication that there should be some single correct interpretation, or reading, associated with each work. Perhaps the view even encourages a critical pluralism that allows for different thematic reconstructions of works and thus different ways in which they might be appreciated. These possibilities will be explored in Chapter 4.

### Interpretive communities

An influential example of the idea of multiple "approaches" to literary works is associated with the notion of "interpretive communities" advanced by the critic Stanley Fish. Fish's conception of literature is also a kind of institutional account, although a highly relativistic one. He shares the view of the analytical institutional conception that a work cannot count as a literary work independently of the institutional framework within which it is embedded:

> Thus the act of recognizing literature is not constrained by something in the text, nor does it issue from an independent and arbitrary will; rather, it proceeds from a collective decision as to what will count as literature, a decision that will be in force only so long as a community of readers or believers continues to abide by it.[75]

The very properties that constitute a work as a literary work are determined by the interpretive communities:

> Interpretive communities are made up of those who share interpretive strategies not for reading but for writing texts, for constituting their properties. In other words these strategies exist prior to the act of reading and therefore determine the shape of what is read rather than, as is usually assumed, the other way round.[76]

Not even formal features of literary works are independent of these frameworks: "formal units are always a function of the interpretative model one brings to bear; they are not 'in' the text."[77]

---

[75]  Stanley Fish, *Is There a Text in This Class? The Authority of Interpretive Communities* (Cambridge, MA: Harvard University Press, 1980), p. 11.

[76]  Ibid., p. 14.

[77]  Ibid., p. 164.

But the crucial difference with the analytical conception is that Fish holds that there are "multiple" communities of this kind. That notion is problematic. First of all, it is not clear what counts as a "community" or how these are to be individuated. To delineate them in terms of shared "interpretive strategies" only pushes the question a step back. What counts as an interpretive strategy? Are there different strategies, thus different communities, associated with "schools" of criticism such as New Criticism, structuralism, post-structuralism, psychoanalysis, cultural materialism, etc.? Or are the different communities even more narrowly circumscribed, identified simply with different interpretations, different readings of a single work?

Neither suggestion seems acceptable due to a second difficulty, the relativization of work-identity to communities. If a work's identity both as a literary work and as the particular work that it is depends on the community reading the work, then paradoxical consequences follow for both suggested glosses on "interpretive community." If communities are defined by different interpretations then it seems that no interpretation could ever be wrong (or fail to "fit"). The interpretation (with its underlying "strategy") would determine the identity of the work in question. There could be no disagreements about interpretations because each interpretation is paired with a unique work generated by it. Not only does that make for an arbitrary proliferation of works but it undermines the very point of interpretation, which is to countenance different perspectives on the same work.

On the other hand if the communities are identified with schools of criticism – New Criticism, structuralism, etc. – then there would seem to be no rational way of adjudicating between the schools, for each generates its own set of works (plus its own conception of literature) and it would make no sense to say that any one such "approach" gives a better or worse reading of any particular work. There is simply no single work that each "approach" addresses. Again, this makes debate about critical readings redundant.

We will be looking at questions about competing interpretations and the relations between interpretations and works in Chapter 4. For now, though, it should be noted that these problems do not arise for the overarching conception of an institution proposed on the analytical account. This conception, as we have seen, is hospitable to different perspectives, even different "approaches," taken to a single work, albeit marking general constraints on what counts as a literary work and on appreciation of a work *as literature*.

# Ontology

Before we turn to authors and interpretation there is another, somewhat more technical, issue about the nature of literature that needs to be addressed. This is related to, but distinct from, the definitional issue and concerns the "modes of existence" of the literary work. What kind of entity is a literary work? Where does it belong among the furniture of the world? Is it a physical object of some kind, an abstract object, a Platonist universal existing timelessly, a mental entity in the mind of its author or of its readers, or some more exotic variety like a "stratified system of norms"?[78] This is very much a philosopher's question but it is surprising how much attention has been given to it and, indeed, how difficult it is to resolve satisfactorily.

This ontological inquiry has parallels with other art forms. It is sometimes suggested that works of art fall into two broad ontological categories: physical objects on the one hand, encompassing paintings, sculptures, and buildings, and on the other hand abstract entities of some kind, to cover music, poetry, and drama. One difference between a painting and a poem can be brought out by an ambiguity in "copy." When we speak of a copy of a painting – say, a copy of the *Mona Lisa* – we mean something different from and no substitute for the original. But a copy of a poem – say, Wordsworth's "Tintern Abbey" – is not something less than the poem but simply the means by which we read the poem. To have read a copy of "Tintern Abbey" is to have read the poem, but to have seen only a copy of the *Mona Lisa* is not to have seen the *Mona Lisa*. The difference can be explained by taking paintings to be unique physical objects and taking poems to be abstract entities that allow for multiple instantiations. (Think of another kind of instantiated abstract quality: redness. You have experienced redness if you have experienced any instance of redness, i.e., any individual red thing.)

### Survival and destruction

Another way of approaching the ontological issue is to ask about survival and destruction conditions. Paintings and sculptures survive, it might seem, just as long as the physical objects that constitute them survive; they are destroyed if the objects are destroyed, perhaps by fire or earthquake. But with musical or literary works fires and earthquakes don't seem to have such a decisive effect. How can a poem be destroyed? Destroying the original manuscript is not sufficient – plenty of poems exist whose author's manuscripts are lost. Not even destroying all the printed copies (or scores in the case of music) is sufficient, for there might remain people who have memorized the poem. It looks as if we would have to get rid of all the copies and all the people who are able to read or recite the poem.

---

[78] The latter is a conception developed by René Wellek and Austin Warren in *Theory of Literature* (Harmondsworth: Penguin, 1973), ch. 12, "The Mode of Existence of a Literary Work," p. 153.

In fact even this account is oversimplified both about paintings and poems. Suppose a near perfect copy of the painting – a copy perhaps by the artist himself – had been made. Might we not say that the painting survived after all? And what about the gradual destruction of a painting or sculpture? When the paint begins to fade and the canvas crack, is there any definite moment when the painting ceases to exist? When the statue gets worn till its features are barely discernible, does it fade into oblivion? Suppose the paint on a painting is gradually replaced over the years – like Theseus's ship on which all the planks were replaced on a long voyage – is the end result the same work? As for musical and literary works, perhaps the destruction of all the scores and all the printed copies is not needed to destroy the work. Hasn't such a work ceased to exist if all the people competent to perform it or read it have disappeared? That suggests that the continued existence of a musical score or an intact copy of a poem need not, after all, be sufficient for a musical work or poem to survive. And couldn't there be a gradual loss of musical and literary works, as with paintings and sculptures? Suppose a few bars are lost or a few lines of a poem. Suppose some meanings in a poem are unrecoverable or some of the musical notation indecipherable. Would that be a partial but not complete loss?

### Poems as physical objects

The simplest ontological category is that of spatio-temporal physical objects. Give or take the worries just mentioned we have a fairly good idea of how they survive across time and are destroyed. Some works of art, notably paintings, sculptures, and buildings, seem to be unproblematically of this kind. However, there is little temptation to treat literary works as physical objects. Copies of poems and novels do, of course, occupy space and time but few would want to identify the *work* itself with any particular copy, even the author's manuscript. The work is not destroyed when any given copy is destroyed, so the work cannot be one of its copies. Also there are properties of a copy – the size of the font, the quality of the paper, its chemical composition – that are not properties of the work. Performances are physical events, yet works of drama are not identical with any given performance because the play still exists after any performance is over.[79] There can be multiple performances of a play, and even if we could identify an ideal performance that could not be equivalent to the play itself because then we would have to speak of some other performance as a performance of a performance.

[79]   There might be very special cases where a drama is identified with a particular, unique, one-off performance: i.e., a particular physical event. If so any recording of that performance would have the same status as a copy of a painting, rather than a copy of a poem.

And an ideal performance would also have properties, such as the actors, theater, and dates involved, that are not properties of the play. On the other hand if the ideal performance were merely described and not realized then we do not have an actual physical event. It is hard to find any other example of a physical object even remotely plausible as a candidate for the work itself. The sounds of a work being read aloud might be suggested – not forgetting the origins of poetry in oral traditions – but the same considerations that count against any given performance being identified with a work count here as well.

Some effort has been made by analytical philosophers to squeeze all forms of art into a single ontological category, rather than settling for a fundamental division between arts that are physical objects and arts that are not. This need not detain us, for most of the effort is toward seeing paintings as more like poems rather than poems as like paintings. P. F. Strawson, for example, has argued that "all works of art … are equally types and not particulars," on the grounds that it is "merely [a] contingent fact that we are, for all practical purposes, quite unable to make reproductions of pictures and statues which are completely indistinguishable, by direct sensory inspection, from the originals."[80] If Strawson is right then copies of paintings would, at least when the technology of reproduction is sufficiently advanced, have the same status as copies of poems. Gregory Currie takes a similar line: "No work of art is a physical object. … A work of art is rather an *action type*."[81] However, it is not easy to overcome the powerful intuition that paintings and (carved) sculptures are unique particulars, physical objects crafted by an artist at a specific time, and not multiply instantiable types, whose instances crop up in numerous locations and across time. Nor does there seem be any overwhelming reason to seek a unified ontology for all the diverse forms of art.

### Works as mental entities

Could a literary work be a mental rather than a physical event? Does it exist, for example, as a mental state or event in the mind of the author? Expressivist views of literature, as discussed earlier, might encourage such a line; idealist philosophers, like Croce and Collingwood, have worked out versions of it. For Collingwood a poem, like a tune or even a painting, is an "imaginary object." Speaking of music, he writes: the "tune is already complete and perfect when it exists merely as a tune in his [the composer's] head, that is, an imaginary tune. … The noises made by the performers,

---

[80] P. F. Strawson, "Aesthetic Appraisal and Works of Art," in Lamarque and Olsen, eds., *Aesthetics and the Philosophy of Art*, p. 240.

[81] Gregory Currie, *An Ontology of Art* (Basingstoke: Macmillan, 1989), p. 7.

and heard by the audience, are not the music at all; they are only means by which the audience, if they listen intelligently, … can reconstruct for themselves that imaginary tune that existed in the composer's head."[82] By parity of reasoning we might infer that a copy of a poem (or a reading of a poem) is merely a means by which readers can reconstruct the "imaginary object" in the author's mind. Such a thought might lie behind Shelley's remark that "the most glorious poetry that has ever been communicated to the world is probably a feeble shadow of the original conception of the poet."[83]

But this idealist and mentalistic theory has little to commend it. Perhaps the author of a short lyric might hold the work complete in his or her mind at some moment before transcribing it – although facts about how poets actually compose suggest even that it is uncharacteristic[84] – but it seems impossible to suppose that the author of a lengthy novel could retain in mind some unitary "imaginary object" comprising the complete work. Even if that were the case, what form would this imaginary object take? Is it a linguistic structure or not? If it is, then it must be in some language or other, but if it is in any natural language then whether it is lodged in the mind or manifested in public on a page makes no essential difference to its status.[85] If it is not linguistic but merely, say, an experience or sensation of some kind, then we could not say it is a *literary work* (although the experience might be the subject of the work).

Perhaps it is a *thought* or a complex of thoughts? But again, we must ask if these thoughts are or are not linguistically expressed, with the same consequences as before. Thoughts in the mind can be conceived in two ways: as occurrent and unique states, probably of the brain, taking place at a particular time in an individual, or as intentional (representational) contents which in principle can be shared and repeated. Under only the second, not the first, conception can I have the "same thoughts" as you. If literary works are of the first kind then they are fleeting physiological occurrences, accessible at best to neuroscientists, only indirectly accessible (through their "content") even to their owners. If they are of the second kind then they are representational entities in principle capturable in a public medium like a language or picture. If the mentalistic theorist settles, as surely he must, for the second, then the occurrent, purely mentalistic, element seems to lapse into irrelevancy.

---

[82]   R. G. Collingwood, *The Principles of Art* (Oxford: Clarendon Press, 1938), p. 139.

[83]   Percy Bysshe Shelley, "A Defence of Poetry," in *Percy Bysshe Shelley: The Major Works*, ed. Zachery Leader and Michael O'Neill (Oxford: Oxford University Press, 2003), p. 697.

[84]   Andrew Motion describes the lengthy process of composition of even short poems by Philip Larkin: *Philip Larkin: A Writer's Life* (London: Faber, 1993).

[85]   Wittgenstein, *Philosophical Investigations,* §243, §§256–261, §293.

It is important to note that the issue of whether a literary work like a poem fundamentally exists as an "object" in the mind of the author is distinct from the issue of what it is for a reader to acquire a legitimate understanding of a work. The debate over whether this understanding rests on a reconstruction of an author's intentions is not foreclosed by establishing independent reasons why a work cannot be a purely mental entity. For one thing, there are different ways of determining intentions than examining someone's mind; for another, the intention debate is about meaning not about modes of existence. Even on the view that literary works are essentially linguistic entities of some kind there is room for debate about how their meanings are arrived at.

A different mentalist theory locates the work in the minds of readers rather than authors. This is a shift from expressivism to reader-response theories. Although it is commonly supposed that readers of literary works have some role in determining the nature of the works read, it is hard to find a convincing version that holds that works just are mental states or experiential states of readers. The obvious question to ask is: which readers? If Jim and Jill read a novel is it their experiences in reading that give the novel its existence? Surely not. It can only be a contingent fact that any particular reader (setting aside the author) reads a work. Any work, we feel, could continue to exist whether or not it has been read by X or Y. It would seem equally absurd to suppose that every reading generates a unique work. That would imply that no two readers ever read the same work – making discussion of works impossible.

More promising is to allude to a class of readers, rather than individual readers. It was suggested earlier that a work can only survive if there are readers competent to read it. Even if written texts survive it seems that if no one can decipher them then the works they embody are lost. It also seems to be an implication of the analytical institutional view that literary works are in some way dependent on the existence of a practice involving competent readers. The point is important but it does not imply that the works somehow exist in the minds of readers. A class of readers with requisite competencies might be necessary for the continued existence of literary works but we still need to retain a distinction between the works themselves and readers' responses to them.

### Work and text

If literary works are neither physical nor mental, what kind of entities could they be? A prominent and perfectly intuitive answer is that they are *texts*. The thought is not that they are physical texts, as sold in bookshops, but rather text-*types* of which individual physical texts, or copies, are *tokens*.

The type/token distinction, which derives from C. S. Peirce, is easily illustrated with the following example. If I ask how many words there are in the sentence "The cat sat on the mat" the answer could either be six, if we count word tokens, or five if we count word-types. The word-type "the" occurs twice so there are only five distinct word-types: "the," "cat," "sat," "on," and "mat." There are interesting relations that tokens have to types. Many, but not all, properties of a token are also possessed by the type of which it is a token. Containing the letter "t" and having precisely three letters are properties that the word-type "the" possesses in common with all its tokens. But being in Times Roman font might be a property of a token although it is not a property of the type. Richard Wollheim has suggested that "all and only those properties that a token of a certain type has necessarily, i.e., that it has in virtue of being a token of that type, will be transmitted to that type."[86] The point is of significance because if we take individual copies of a literary work to be tokens of a type which is the work itself then we have a principled way of marking off merely contingent properties possessed by the copy – its physical form, size, chemical composition, etc. – from those properties it possesses in virtue of being a copy of the work. We can ask what properties all tokens must possess in order to be tokens of such-and-such a type.

The view that copies of literary works are tokens and the works themselves types is widely endorsed, although the question of what these types are is more controversial. Thus the view just propounded, that works are text-types, is disputed. There are several points of disagreement, notably, what the identity conditions are for texts (i.e., text-types), whether works really are just texts, and whether there could be distinct works with the same text.

Under what conditions can we speak of the *same* text? (For simplicity I will use "text" in this discussion to mean "text-type" – where text-tokens are concerned that will be made explicit.) One possibility is to use a purely syntactic criterion, regardless of meaning, so a text consists simply of syntactically ordered strings of words. Wherever precisely that string of words occurs there is a token of that text-type. Nelson Goodman, who proposes this criterion, has spoken of "sameness of spelling" as the criterion,[87] although he also relativizes text-identity to languages, allowing that there could be distinct texts in different languages with identically spelt word-strings.[88]

---

[86]    Richard Wollheim, *Art and Its Objects*, 2nd ed. (Cambridge: Cambridge University Press, 1980), p. 77.

[87]    Nelson Goodman, *The Languages of Art* (New York: Bobbs-Merrill, 1968), p. 115.

[88]    Nelson Goodman and Catherine Elgin, "Interpretation and Identity: Can the Work Survive the World?" in John and Lopes, eds., *Philosophy of Literature*, p. 95. Originally published in *Critical Inquiry*, 12 (1986), pp. 567–574.

A further restriction on text-identity might build in some semantic elements: "they should consist of words, in the same order, that mean the same thing and are spelled the same way."[89]

It is probably not important for our purposes to choose between these criteria, although it does not seem desirable to build into text-identity fine differences of meaning. It seems unsatisfactory to say, for example, that the sentence "He has lost his case" yields (at least) two distinct texts when used to refer to the misfortunes of a lawyer and those of a traveller. It is better to say that the sentence represents a single text open to different interpretations.

The more pressing and difficult issue is what relation a text – defined as a string of word-types in a particular language – bears to a literary work. The simplest position is to identify work and text such that where there is sameness of text there is sameness of work and where there is difference of text there is difference of work.[90] We can call this the *textualist* conception of works.[91] But several factors make this problematic.

The first is translation. An English translation of *War and Peace* is a different text from the Russian original so, on this criterion, the translation could not be the same work as the original. Strictly speaking, no one reading only the translation has read the work. This might seem counterintuitive and would have the consequence that far fewer people have read Tolstoy's novel than is normally supposed. But this is not a fatal weakness of the textualist view, as it is often pointed out that translations have distinct qualities of their own.

A second problem is that of untokened types. If a text is a mere word-structure-type then it could be argued that the abstract type exists whether or not there are any actual tokens of it. The sentence "Elephants and kangaroos enjoy cucumber sandwiches" has probably never been tokened before but, given English vocabulary and syntax, the fact that it is a well-formed abstract structure in the English language is derivable from the language itself. In that sense, the sentence-type pre-exists the production of this token. But if we generalize from the example it seems that every text in a language already exists as an abstract structure before a token of it is produced or written down. So the text of *Pride and Prejudice* – as an abstract string of sentence-types – pre-dated its publication in 1813. And if the text is the work then the work too existed long before Jane Austen wrote it. Austen, it might even be said, "discovered" the work (as an abstract structure) rather than created it, in much the same way that Pythagoras discovered his famous mathematical theorem about right-angled triangles. Similar issues arise for music. If musical works are abstract sound-structure-types then composers discover,

[89]   Gregory Currie, "Work and Text," *Mind*, vol. 100, no. 3 (1991), p. 325.
[90]   This is roughly the view of Goodman and Elgin, "Interpretation and Identity."
[91]   Following Currie in "Work and Text."

but do not create, them. This is a view, sometimes called Platonism, that has been defended,[92] although Platonistic conceptions of literary works, i.e., the view that authors discover abstract linguistic structures, are not common, perhaps unsurprisingly given (again) how counterintuitive they seem.

Another problem for the identity of work and text is the problem of eerie coincidences. Suppose that marks are discovered on a rock face from the Palaeozoic period that, through the action of wind and water erosion, spell out the text of Wordsworth's short lyric "A Slumber Did My Spirit Seal." Vastly incredible, of course! But not theoretically impossible. What should we say? If the text just is the work then it seems we must say that the poem is not original to Wordsworth and existed millions of years before he was born. Again, but for different reasons from the untokened type case, Wordsworth could not be credited with creating one of his best known works, and all because of an accident of nature. One way of resisting this conclusion would be to deny that the rock-eroded inscription is strictly a *text* at all. The marks might look like words but they are not words because there is no appropriate intention behind them.[93] If we accept this approach then we must either build intentionality into text-identity or pull text-identity apart from work-identity. While it seems quite legitimate to introduce intentions into work-identity it seems less so for text-identity. Doing so would imply that a text is more than an abstract structure and is of necessity *authored*. That detracts from the purely syntactic conception of text.

Suppose that the text crops up twice but there is an intention in both cases. This is an extension of the eerie coincidence case and brings us to our third question, whether there could be two distinct works associated with a single text. What if two authors quite independently produced identical texts? If textualism is true then it follows that the two authors have produced the same work. Yet there are reasons for thinking that this isn't right and that work-identity must be tied to individual creative acts.

---

[92]　Peter Kivy, "Platonism in Music: A Kind of Defense," *Grazer philosophische Studien*, vol. 19 (1983), pp. 109–129, reprinted in Peter Kivy, *The Fine Art of Repetition: Essays in the Philosophy of Music* (Cambridge: Cambridge University Press, 1993), pp. 35–58. See also Peter Kivy, "Platonism in Music: Another Kind of Defense," *American Philosophical Quarterly*, vol. 24, no. 3 (July 1987), pp. 245–252 (reprinted in Kivy, *The Fine Art of Repetition*, pp. 59–74); Julian Dodd, "Musical Works as Eternal Types," *British Journal of Aesthetics*, vol. 40, no. 4 (October 2000), pp. 424–440; Julian Dodd, "Defending Musical Platonism," *British Journal of Aesthetics*, vol. 42, no. 4 (October 2002), pp. 380–402.

[93]　This is the line taken by Steven Knapp and Walter Benn Michaels in "The Impossibility of Intentionless Meaning," in Gary Iseminger, ed., *Intention and Interpretation* (Philadelphia, PA: Temple University Press), pp. 54–55. Originally published as "Against Theory," in W. J. T. Mitchell, ed., *Against Theory: Literary Studies and the New Pragmatism* (Chicago: University of Chicago Press, 1985).

Jorge Luis Borges's witty short story "Pierre Menard, Author of the *Quixote*"[94] has come to epitomize, for philosophers, thought-experiments about works and texts, supposedly offering a powerful fictional exemplification of the view that distinct works can have identical texts. In the story, Menard, a fictional early-twentieth-century Symbolist poet, has the ambition to write *Don Quixote*, not by merely copying the original, but by a fully inspired act of literary creation. Here is a key, and often quoted, passage from the story:

> It is a revelation to compare Menard's *Don Quixote* with Cervantes's. The latter, for example, wrote (part one, chapter nine):
>
>> ... truth, whose mother is history, rival of time, depository of deeds, witness of the past, exemplar and adviser to the present, and the future's counsellor.
>
> Written in the seventeenth century, written by the "lay genius" Cervantes, this enumeration is a mere rhetorical praise of history. Menard, on the other hand, writes:
>
>> ... truth, whose mother is history, rival of time, depository of deeds, witness of the past, exemplar and adviser to the present, and the future's counsellor.
>
> History, the *mother* of truth: the idea is astounding. Menard, a contemporary of William James, does not define history as an inquiry into reality but as its origin. Historical truth, for him, is not what has happened: it is what we judge to have happened. The final phrases—*exemplar and adviser to the present, and the future's counsellor*—are brazenly pragmatic.
> The contrast in style is also vivid. The archaic style of Menard—quite foreign after all—suffers from a certain affectation. Not so that of his forerunner, who handles with ease the current Spanish of his time.[95]

There is no doubt that Borges is having fun. There is something intuitively absurd about quoting two identical passages while insisting on their profound differences. But serious matters are at hand. Philosophers have drawn out the following features of the example:

1  that although the quoted segments of text are identical they nevertheless have different stylistic and connotative properties in the context of their origins;

---

[94]  Jorge Luis Borges, "Pierre Menard, Author of the *Quixote*," in *Labyrinths* (Harmondsworth: Penguin, 1971), pp. 62–71.

[95]  Ibid., p. 69.

2   that the text-segments are products of distinct acts of creation, not pro-
    duced by copying or quoting;
3   that they therefore belong to different imaginative and creative *works*
    even while constituted by type-identical texts
4   thus that works cannot be identical to texts.

In fact there is much disagreement as to whether the story really does
establish – or even try to establish – the conclusion in (4). There is some
doubt, even internal to the story, whether the creative acts of Pierre Menard
really are distinct from those of Cervantes, or at least sufficiently distinct
to meet the criterion of a separate work.[96] As for (3) we are explicitly told
that Menard's ambition is not to create a *different* work but "to compose *the
Quixote*" ("he did not want to compose another *Quixote*—which is easy—but
*the Quixote* itself"). Nor is it clear what consequences we are to draw from
the different properties alluded to in (1). It has been argued that at most
Menard can be credited with "having produced a replica of the text without
copying it; and having formulated or inspired a new interpretation of the
work—a way of reading it as a contemporary story in an archaic style."[97]
According to this view – a version of textualism – there is only one work
here, identical with the text, admitting of two different readings. Borges
himself encourages the thought that what is at issue is a new way of reading, involving "deliberate anachronism and … erroneous attribution," rather
than an ontology of literature.

Whether or not Borges's story in itself provides adequate grounds for distinguishing work from text, it shows in effect the way that distinction could
be maintained. A single text could be shared by two distinct works if certain
conditions are in place: at the least, the works must have different properties
and the texts be produced by independent creative acts.

Here is a putative, though again manufactured, example that perhaps does
not share the problems of the Borges case:

> Jane Austen wrote *Northanger Abbey* in 1803 as a burlesque on the Gothic
> novel. Imagine that a hitherto unknown manuscript by Anne Radcliffe, enti-
> tled "Northanger Abbey" (circa 1793), and word for word the same as
> Austen's, turns up in the attic, that we conclude … that this is a coincidence,

---

[96]   Michael Wreen, in "Once Is Not Enough?" *British Journal of Aesthetics*, vol. 30, no. 2
(1990), pp. 149–158, argues that to all intents and purposes Menard's work is a copy of
Cervantes' and thus is not distinct. Christopher Janaway, in "Borges and Danto: A Reply to
Michael Wreen," *British Journal of Aesthetics*, vol. 32, no. 1 (1992), pp. 72–76, rejects this on
the grounds that some crucial conditions for copying are missing in the Menard case.

[97]   Goodman and Elgin, "Interpretation and Identity," p. 96.

that Austen had no knowledge of Radcliffe's work, and that, far from being a satire, Radcliffe's *Abbey* was meant as a serious contribution to the genre. … [T]here's a word-for-word match between them for semantics as well as for syntax, and these are works with the same text …. But, so the argument goes, it is not plausible to say they are the same work; there are so many judgements appropriate to the one but not to the other. There are implicit references in Austen's *Abbey* to certain other works in the genre …. But it would be anachronistic to see implicit references to Radcliffe to these other works, since … she did her writing before those other works were composed. Austen's work is suffused with an irony not to be found in Radcliffe's.[98]

The case for distinguishing work from text rests on noting significant differences between the two works – one is ironic, the other could not be, etc. – differences that are not explicable simply as alternative interpretations of a single work. The pattern of argument is familiar from other areas of aesthetics, notably philosophy of music, where similar thought-experiments are proposed for the independent creation of works which are notationally identical (having identical scores) but, arguably, distinct in virtue of different aesthetic and art-related qualities.[99] The underlying thought in all such cases is that facts about the origin or provenance of a work are crucial to its identity.

In contrast to *textualism*, which grounds work-identity in text-identity quite apart from facts about provenance, the view under discussion, sometimes called *contextualism*, grounds work-identity in the historical context of production. So identical texts grounded in different historical contexts will constitute different works.

The argument for a work/text distinction does not involve denying that works are, or are associated with, texts. Clearly Wordsworth's lyric "A Slumber Did My Spirit Seal" has a text-type – a linguistic structure – associated with it. Its first line is "A slumber did my spirit seal"; it possesses that first line essentially, such that any proper token (copy) of the poem must also contain the line, and the token shares that line with the type. But contextualism requires more of the text-type. Wordsworth's poem (the work) is not the text-type *simpliciter* but the text-type *as embedded in a historical context*.[100] Now we can see that an identical text-type arising in a different context – on a Palaeozoic rock-face or independently composed at a different time by a

---

[98] Currie, "Work and Text," pp. 328–329.

[99] The most well known examples are in Jerrold Levinson, "What a Musical Work Is," reprinted in Lamarque and Olsen, eds., *Aesthetics and the Philosophy of Art*.

[100] For a similar account, see Jerrold Levinson, *The Pleasures of Aesthetics* (Ithaca, NY: Cornell University Press, 1996), p. 195.

different poet – cannot be the identical work. This poem twin might, as the Menard example showed, have different stylistic or connotative properties.

If we combine contextualism, as roughly outlined, with the earlier institutional conception of literature we can note a double embeddedness of works. There is the *historical* embeddedness which finds an essential connection between the identity of a work and its origins in a historical act of creation. And there is the additional *institutional* embeddedness according to which a work only counts as literature within a cultural practice of intention, expectation, and reception. In fact these are closely intertwined. The historical context of origin determines the particular identity of a work – that which makes this work distinct from any other – and the institutional context determines the work's identity as of one kind rather than another. No work would be a unique work of literature if it were not grounded in both kinds of context.

## Contextualism

A clearer picture is now beginning to emerge of the ontological status of a literary work. Such a work is an *institutional object*, governed by social conventions of production and reception. Without the operative conventions, determining expectations and responses of appropriately competent participants, there would be no literary works. What kind of institutional object? An abstract and complex linguistic structure consisting of a *text-type* (strictly a word-sequence-type) tied to a specific *context of origin*. What the account serves to emphasize, which is in jeopardy under minimal textualism, is the importance of the creation of works under determinate conditions. Mere "found" texts or even texts produced by the proverbial typing monkeys will not satisfy this requirement. More pertinently for literary criticism, the account emphasizes that a work is always and necessarily "of its time," however much its thematic content might reach out timelessly.

The idea that literary works are institutional objects of this kind and distinct from mere texts *simpliciter* is parallelled in other art forms. Musical works are sound-structure types also embedded in historical and institutional contexts. If the sounds of the Moonlight Sonata were eerily conjured by wind effects in the Palaeozoic swamps they would not *be* Beethoven's sonata, nor would their existence detract from Beethoven's creativity. Pictures and sculptures in turn invite a distinction between the material that constitutes them – paint and canvas for pictures, marble or bronze for sculptures – and the works themselves.[101] In all these cases there are different identity conditions

---

[101]    See Peter Lamarque, "Work and Object," *Proceedings of the Aristotelian Society*, vol. CII, pt. 2 (2002).

and survival conditions for the works themselves, as cultural objects, and the materials (including sound or word-types) that constitute them. The atoms of the physical bronze could survive, but if the material has been melted down then the statue is lost, so the statue cannot be identical with the lump of bronze *simpliciter*. Similarly, as suggested earlier, the text of a poem might survive, but if there is no one competent to understand it or appreciate it, then the work itself has ceased to exist.

Contextualism is an appealing account of art ontology but it is not without controversy, and several questions remain. For example, how finely delineated should the historical context be? According to one view the context is "anchored to a particular person, time, and place."[102] What this means is that any given literary work could not, as a matter of necessity, have been produced by a different author at a different time in a different place. This is a metaphysical thesis concerning essential (relational) properties. Is it too strong? Might not an author have finished his poem a week earlier than he did, or ten minutes? Should the precise time of composition (start to finish) be *essential* to the identity of a work? And if the author was in Paris rather than London, or in the kitchen rather than the garden, does that affect the identity of the work?[103] Any reasonable contextualist must allow for accidental as well as essential spatio-temporal relational properties of a work, but it might seem difficult to say precisely where that line is drawn without begging the question in favor of contextualism. It is clearly not enough to claim that only those features of the spatio-temporal context that determine work-specific properties are essential.

What about the necessity of the author? Might not a work have been written by a different author? The point is not that misattribution is impossible. Perhaps Bacon wrote the plays now attributed to Shakespeare. That indeed is possible. But for the strict contextualist, a Bacon-authored *King Lear* could not be the same work as a Shakespeare-authored *Lear*. They would have different aesthetic and artistic properties. If Francis Bacon, aristocrat, political manipulator, scientist, and philosopher, author of the *Novum Organum*, had written *Lear* the play might well yield quite different allusions and meanings from the textually identical but arguably distinct play written by the more humble Shakespeare. However, it seems less plausible to suppose that every work should, of necessity, have precisely the author it does. An anonymous medieval ballad might, it seems, have been written by any number of balladeers without losing its unique identity.

---

[102] Levinson, *Pleasures of Aesthetics*, p. 197.

[103] Similar questions about fine individuation conditions applied to music are raised by David Carrier in "Art without Its Artists," *British Journal of Aesthetics*, vol. 22, no. 3 (1982), pp. 233–244.

None of this is seriously damaging to the contextualist. What is needed is a more flexible view of context-specification, what has been called the "work-relativity of modality."[104] Rather than specifying in advance all the features of context that determine the identity of a work, a flexible contextualism will allow that cases will differ, perhaps relative to the demands the works make on readers for their comprehension and evaluation.[105] But the central claim of contextualism, that work-identity is bounded by historical conditions of production (and institutional conventions), remains intact.

Another concern with contextualism is the extent to which contexts constrain meanings. One of the reasons for supposing that Menard's *Don Quixote* is a different work from Cervantes' is that certain meanings or connotations in the two texts are different (their discussions of history, for example, have different implications); similar observations arose about the Austen *Northanger Abbey* and the Radcliffe. But how determinate in meaning is a work, as opposed to a text? Is difference of meaning sufficient for difference of works? There are those for whom work-identity is closely bound up with meaning-identity. Anthony Savile, for example, in defending a view he calls "historicism," believes that a work only survives the test of time – and survives across time – if it "survives in our attention under an appropriate interpretation in a sufficiently embedded way."[106] This involves rejecting the notion that one and the same work might acquire different interpretations at different times. The work and its canonical interpretation are bound together. But it should not be a commitment of contextualism that the context of production fixes meaning. It should allow for works to be open to different readings and interpretations consistent with its identity conditions. Once again this will be a topic for Chapter 4.

There is another kind of contextualism which agrees that works are culturally and contextually embedded, indeed are "culturally emergent" entities, but which holds that contexts themselves change, thereby changing the identity of works.[107] *King Lear* might be bound in its origins to the early seventeenth century (the *same* work could not have been written two hundred years before) but, on this view, the play itself has no core of meaning or aesthetic qualities that remain unchanged over time but can radically change its nature as it is performed and interpreted in different eras. Even the text, which is its constitutive base, is radically underdetermined in meaning.

104  David Davies, *Art as Performance* (Oxford: Blackwell, 2004), ch. 5.

105  This is developed in Lamarque, "Work and Object," pp. 157–158.

106  Anthony Savile, *The Test of Time: An Essay in Philosophical Aesthetics* (Oxford: Clarendon Press, 1982), p. 11.

107  Joseph Margolis, *What, After All, Is a Work of Art?* (University Park, PA: Penn State Press, 1999).

This is at the opposite extreme of Savile's "historicist" conception, although both are kinds of contextualism. A sensible compromise would seem to lie somewhere between the two.

The distinction between text and work that has been central to the account developed here about the ontology of literature is not always acknowledged. It is common to find literary works simply described as "texts," although this is often not meant to bear ontological significance. Sometimes "text" is used very broadly, designating anything that is an object of interpretation.[108] Roland Barthes, in an acclaimed essay from the 1960s, popularized a distinction between "text" and "work," similar, but not identical, to that advanced above, although his insistence on prioritizing text over work is the opposite of the contextualist position.[109] For Barthes a work is "a fragment of substance," "occupying a part of the space of books (in a library, for example)" while a Text (Barthes capitalizes the first letter of "Text") is "a methodological field." On the contextualist view, in contrast, both works and texts are abstract entities. What occupies space on a shelf might be copy or instance of a work but cannot be the work itself, for a work, as we have seen, can outlive any particular copy. Barthes's "Text" is an instance of *écriture* (writing in general); it is "always *paradoxical*"; it "practises the infinite deferment of the signified," "it answers not to an interpretation, even a liberal one, but to an explosion, a dissemination," "it cannot be contained in a hierarchy, even in a simple division of genres." Under this conception it is hard to see what semantic constraints operate on a Text, there being virtually no limits on what a Barthesian Text can mean, nor what its identity conditions are. A text-type of the kind associated with a work on the contextualist view is a much more familiar item – a string of sentences in a language, bearing the meanings that the language prescribes.

Barthes's recommendation to move from work to text seems an unpromising start in trying to understand the literary realm. Indeed, in emphasizing the undifferentiated text, it undermines the very notion of the literary. It affords no room for value and little for informed interpretation. A text that can mean anything means nothing in particular.

---

[108]  E.g., Joseph Margolis, "Reinterpreting Interpretation," in John W. Bender and H. Gene Blocker, eds., *Contemporary Philosophy of Art: Readings in Analytic Aesthetics* (Englewood Cliffs, NJ: Prentice Hall), p. 456. He also speaks of "text or artwork," p. 459. Originally published in *Journal of Aesthetics and Art Criticism*, vol. 47, no. 3 (1989), pp. 237–251.

[109]  Roland Barthes, "From Work to Text," in *Image-Music-Text*, Essays Selected and Translated by Stephen Heath (London: Fontana/Collins, 1977).

## Supplementary Readings

The best book-length survey and discussion of philosophical attempts to define art is Stephen Davies, *Definitions of Art* (Ithaca, NY: Cornell University Press, 1991). Also useful are Robert Stecker, *Artworks: Definition, Meaning, Value* (University Park, PA: Penn State University Press, 1997); Joseph Margolis, *What, After All, Is a Work of Art?* (University Park, PA: Penn State University Press 1999); and Noël Carroll, ed., *Theories of Art Today* (Madison: University of Wisconsin Press, 2000). George Dickie's (later) institutional account is in George Dickie, *The Art Circle: A Theory of Art* (New York: Haven, 1984) and is discussed in Robert J. Yanal, ed., *Institutions of Art: Reconsiderations of George Dickie's Philosophy* (University Park, PA: Penn State University Press, 1994).

On the idea of defining literature, from a philosophical point of view, see Paul Hernadi, ed., *What Is Literature?* (Bloomington: Indiana University Press, 1978); Anthony J. Cascardi, ed., *Literature and the Question of Philosophy* (Baltimore, MD: Johns Hopkins University Press, 1987); Stein Haugom Olsen, *The End of Literary Theory* (Cambridge: Cambridge University Press, 1987); and Peter Lamarque and Stein Haugom Olsen, *Truth, Fiction, and Literature: A Philosophical Perspective* (Oxford: Clarendon Press, 1994). More recent essays on the analytic conception of literature are in: Stein Haugom Olsen and Anders Pettersson, eds., *From Text to Literature: New Analytic and Pragmatic Approaches* (Basingstoke: Palgrave Macmillan, 2005). For a more polemical outlook, with a political edge, see Jean-Paul Sartre, *What Is Literature?* (London: Routledge, 2001; originally published, in French, in 1948).

Literary critical perspectives on the concept of literature can be found in M. H. Abrams, *The Mirror and the Lamp: Romantic Theory and the Critical Tradition* (Oxford: Oxford University Press, 1953); John M. Ellis, *The Theory of Literary Criticism: A Logical Analysis* (Berkeley: University of California Press, 1974); Terry Eagleton, *Literary Theory: An Introduction* (Oxford: Blackwell, 1983); W. W. Robson, *The Definition of Literature and Other Essays* (Cambridge: Cambridge University Press, new ed. 1984); and Derek Attridge, *The Singularity of Literature* (London: Routledge, 2004).

On the ontology of literature (the "mode of existence" of the literary work), a seminal text is Roman Ingarden, *The Literary Work of Art: An Investigation of the Borderlines of Ontology, Logic, and Theory of Language* (Evanston, IL: Northwestern University Press, 1979; originally published, in German, in 1931). Another classic discussion, René Wellek and Austin Warren, *Theory of Literature* (Harmondsworth: Penguin, 1973), is helpful in laying out alternative points of view.

Key texts in analytic aesthetics on the ontology of art include: Richard Wollheim, *Art and Its Objects* (Cambridge: Cambridge University Press,

2nd ed., 1980); Nelson Goodman, *Languages of Art* (Brighton: Harvester, 2nd ed., 1981); Nicholas Wolterstorff, *Works and Worlds of Art* (Oxford: Clarendon Press, 1980); and Arthur Danto, *The Transfiguration of the Commonplace* (Cambridge, MA: Harvard University Press, 1981). More recent, also influential, treatments which have things to say about the ontology of literature as well as art in general, are Gregory Currie, *An Ontology of Art* (London: Macmillan, 1989); Jerrold Levinson, *Music, Art & Metaphysics* (Ithaca, NY: Cornell University Press, 1990) (whose focus is mostly on music); Amie Thomasson, *Fiction and Metaphysics* (Cambridge: Cambridge University Press, 1999); and David Davies, *Art as Performance* (Oxford: Blackwell, 2003).

# Chapter Three

# Authors

Behind any serious reflection on works or texts or meaning there looms the enigmatic figure of the author. While it might seem obvious what an author is and why authorship matters in literature, in fact the issues are complex and controversial. In different guises these issues assume a pivotal role in philosophy of literature.

## Authors and Conceptions of Literature

We have already made brief reference to expressive theories of literature, associated with Romanticism, which give central place to the author in the very conception of literature. For the Romantic, the lyric poem is the paradigmatic literary product where the author expresses a deeply personal response to a place, event, or predicament. To appreciate the poem is to grasp what it is that the poet feels. Yet the idea of poetry as personal expression, particularly when taken to the extremes of idealism, where the poem becomes identified with the inner feelings themselves, is highly problematic. Dominant currents of thought in the twentieth century sought to expose the contradictions in Romantic conceptions of authorship. New Criticism, structuralism, Marxism, and psychoanalysis in their different ways eroded the vision of the author as autonomous expressive self.

The institutional and contextualist conceptions of literature that emerged in the previous chapter reveal quite complex connections with authors. For the contextualist the literary work is essentially embedded in the historical context of its creation: without that context it would not be the work it is. Strong versions of contextualism tie a work essentially to its author: different author, different work, even in cases where two texts are identical. But arguably such versions are too strong, for it seems not metaphysically inconceivable that a specific work might have been created by a different author, albeit in a broadly similar historical context. The institutional account sees works as embedded not merely in a historical context but in the context of a "practice," involving author-roles and reader-roles. These conventional roles help to determine what it is to create and respond to a work as literature rather than as, say, philosophy, biography, or history. In both theories the author figures large. Yet neither theory is committed to expressivism.

Another prominent debate in philosophy of literature regarding authors concerns meaning and the extent to which an author is the source of meaning. While it might seem obvious that this is so – given that the author creates the work in the first place – it is a matter of contention how much "authority" an author has over legitimate interpretations of a work. It remains a vexed and persistent question in literary criticism to what extent a critic's explorations are constrained by what an author "had in mind." No doubt a critic who willfully ignored an author's intentions would have some explaining to do. On the other hand, intentions are elusive entities. Sometimes they are simply manifested in the words the author has chosen; sometimes they seem to make no appearance in the work and have to be dug out from independent sources; sometimes they don't seem to matter at all, as when authors are pleasantly surprised at imaginative readings of their own work by perceptive critics.

The intention debate is a manifestation of deep divisions over the very nature of literature, arising at a fault-line between two powerful but conflicting conceptions: the romantic conception, as noted, which sees literature as a vehicle for personal expression, and the modernist "autonomy" conception which sees literature as pure linguistic artifact. There are correspondingly different conceptions of the critic's task: to explore a personality expressed in a work or to explore intrinsic properties of a "verbal icon" (to use W. K. Wimsatt's phrase[1]). Pressures toward one or other of these conceptions have resisted satisfactory resolution or balanced equilibrium.

There are questions too about what makes someone an author in the first place. "Author" is an honorific term. Someone who merely writes emails, text messages, and grocery lists is not deemed to be an author: writing is not enough. An author is in some manner creative, a designer, a source of something valued. But being created, designed, and valued are properties integral to literature, which suggests there is more than just a causal relation between author and work. Is there not also an "internal," even conceptual, relation between the two, in the sense that someone who writes a literary work (a work acknowledged as such) thereby becomes an author, and a literary work could not be "literary" without being "authored"?

Yet just how creative are authors? Unlike God, they do not create *ex nihilo*. They have to use, and are constrained by, the resources available to them,

---

[1]   W. K. Wimsatt, *The Verbal Icon: Studies in the Meaning of Poetry* (Lexington: University Press of Kentucky, 1954).

linguistic and cultural. They do not (for the most part) create the language they use; the meanings they express must already be, in some sense, embodied in the language itself. Nor do they create the institution whose conventions they are following or the historical circumstances or literary tradition within which they work. A poet who writes a sonnet has not created the sonnet form. To grasp what's going on in a poem, facts about the author can come to seem less important than facts about the tradition, the culture, and the historical setting in which the author writes. Such is the path to the "depersonalization" of poetry, even to the "death of the author," that characterized twentieth-century criticism and seemed to arise inevitably from serious tensions already present in the very idea of an author.

## The Poet as Sage

One of the targets of the New Criticism that developed in the 1930s and 1940s was the cult of the author, or what C. S. Lewis called "Poetolatry," idolatry toward the poet.[2] The New Critics saw this as directing attention away from the work itself. There is no denying, though, how deep is the fascination with the personality of famous authors, a fascination that has a strong hold on the kinds of *interests* that readers have in literary works. As Roland Barthes writes,

> The image of literature to be found in ordinary culture is tyrannically centred on the author, his person, his life, his tastes, his passions, while criticism still consists for the most part in saying that Baudelaire's work is the failure of Baudelaire the man ...[3]

The personality cult of the poet flourished in the early nineteenth century with the Romantics. Wordsworth, in his ground-breaking Preface to the *Lyrical Ballads* (1800), grandly pronounced the elevated qualities of the poet, compared with ordinary people:

> more lively sensibility, more enthusiasm and tenderness, who has a greater knowledge of human nature, and a more comprehensive soul ...; a man pleased with his own passions and volitions, and who rejoices more than other men in the spirit of life that is in him; delighting to contemplate similar

---

[2]   E. M. W. Tillyard and C. S. Lewis, *The Personal Heresy: A Controversy* (London: Oxford University Press, 1939), p. 104.

[3]   Roland Barthes, "The Death of the Author," in *Image-Music-Text*, Essays Selected and Translated by Stephen Heath (London: Fontana/Collins, 1977), p. 143.

volitions and passions as manifested in the goings-on of the universe, and habitually impelled to create them where he does not find them.[4]

Here is the image of the poet as sage, someone not only with heightened responses to the world but possessed of a "greater readiness and power in expressing what he thinks and feels."[5] "Poetry," Shelley writes, in a similar vein, "is the record of the best and happiest moments of the happiest and best minds." Furthermore, "To be a poet is to apprehend the true and the beautiful."[6] Wordsworth's own poetry is often strongly autobiographical, not least the monumental *Prelude* (1850), subtitled "or Growth of a Poet's Mind: an autobiographical poem," and readers came to expect of poetry that it would reveal not just a poet's personality but also the outlook of a visionary.

Related to the idea of the poet as sage or as having special gifts is the idea of genius. Versions of the idea go back to the ancient Greeks. Long before the advent of Romanticism, early in the eighteenth century, Joseph Addison, for example, extolled artistic genius in these terms: "Among great geniuses those few draw the admiration of all the world upon them, and stand up as the prodigies of mankind, who by the mere strength of natural parts, and without any assistance of art and learning, have produced works that were the delight of their own times, and the wonder of posterity."[7] It was later in the century when Kant offered his definitive account of genius as "the exemplary originality of the natural endowments of an individual in the *free* employment of his cognitive faculties."[8] For Kant a genius is governed not by pre-existing rules, but by "natural endowments," and becomes an "example" for others.

The line between taking an interest in the *personality* of a genius and the *work* of a genius is often a narrow one. Contemporary responses to the poet Lord Byron provide a good example of how narrow this line can be. Bryon's reputation was established by the publication of his thinly disguised autobiographical poem *Childe Harold's Pilgrimage* (1812).[9] Here was born the myth

---

[4]  William Wordsworth, Preface to *Lyrical Ballads*, in M. H. Abrams, E. T. Donaldson, et al., eds., *The Norton Anthology of English Literature*, 4th ed., Vol. 2 (New York: W. W. Norton, 1979), p. 168.

[5]  Ibid., p. 169.

[6]  Percy Bysshe Shelley, "A Defence of Poetry," in *Percy Bysshe Shelley: The Major Works*, ed. Zachery Leader and Michael O'Neill (Oxford: Oxford University Press, 2003), pp. 697, 677.

[7]  Joseph Addison, *The Spectator*, no. 160, Monday, September 3, 1711.

[8]  Immanuel Kant, *Critique of Judgment*, trans. James Creed Meredith (Oxford: Clarendon Press, 1952), §49.

[9]  Lord Byron, *The Poetical Works of Lord Byron* (London: Oxford University Press, 1928), pp. 174–244. Four cantos were published between 1812 and 1818. "Childe" is an archaic term for a young nobleman awaiting knighthood.

of the Byronic hero, dark, passionate, seductive, melancholic, "dangerous to know," a social outcast. It was all too easy for readers to identify Byron with Childe Harold, and as he added new cantos in subsequent years so the identification seemed to become ever closer, with his continuing – well publicized – "pilgrimage" round Europe.

But the example soon begins to turn against itself. The identification of Byron with his poetic persona is not as secure as it at first seems. As one biographer of Byron has written,

> he was emphatically not Childe Harold. "I would not be such a fellow", he wrote, "as I have made my hero for all the world." Many of his qualities were very unChilde-like indeed. Far from being habitually secretive, he could be totally uninhibited. His friends revelled in him as a boon companion, spirited, playful, mischievous, witty, often convulsed not with "strange pangs" but uproarious laughter.[10]

And as the sales of *Childe Harold* escalated, Byron was fêted at all the best dinner tables in London.

Some preliminary points of philosophical interest start to emerge. The first is that the expression "work of genius" has a double connotation that should not be blurred into one: it can mean "produced by a genius" or it can mean "of exemplary quality." The former is a claim about cause, about the nature of the author as a person, a sage, one who "draw(s) the admiration of all the world." The latter is about the work itself, not directly about its cause, but about its merits. Usually, the explanatory path is from the latter to the former, in other words from a judgment about literary quality to a judgment about the author's genius. After all, being written by a genius is not in itself a guarantee of literary quality. Logically speaking the literary judgment, the province of the critic, comes before the personal judgment, the province of the biographer.

The second point, which will need elaboration, is that a personality portrayed in a literary work, however autobiographical the work purports to be, is never to be *simply* projected onto the author. Authors hide behind "masks," they adopt personae, they engage in myth-making. Byron, as he himself noted, created Childe Harold "for all the world," i.e., for universal appeal. It is an often repeated – and important – critical principle that however close a work might be to the personality and attitudes of its author, it is never legitimate merely to substitute one for the other, to suppose that in studying the work one is *thereby* studying the poet, or in knowing the poet one is *thereby* grasping the work.

[10]   Elizabeth Longford, *Byron* (London: Arrow Books, 1976), p. 52.

# Biography and Criticism

Poets writing about themselves were not an invention of the Romantics. Dante did so in the *Divine Comedy* five hundred years before Wordsworth. What perhaps was new was the attitude of readers nurtured on Romanticism that authors inevitably *expressed* their innermost feelings in their works. But, as already intimated, the relation of authors' lives (including their feelings, attitudes, or desires) and their works is far from straightforward. The relation can be invoked in two directions: the works might be used to illuminate the lives, the lives to illuminate the works.

*From works to lives*

Biographers of poets, novelists, or dramatists will quite properly want to incorporate the works, and what they contain, into the life story. To the extent that "literary biography" is simply the biography of literary authors it raises no contentious issues about literary criticism. However, it is worth noting obvious and well-rehearsed dangers in using works to supplement details of lives when the details are not documented independently. These dangers do bear on the nature of criticism. The case of Shakespeare stands out. Little is known of his life, even less of his beliefs or attitudes; there are no diaries, letters, or autobiographical fragments to call on. Yet there is endless speculation in Shakespearean biography as to what Shakespeare *really* thought: about immortality, love, marriage, kingship, religion, power, wealth, the theater, his family, or a hundred other things. Speeches from his plays are cited as evidence of his true beliefs, although more often than not other passages appear to take a contradictory stance. Ben Jonson's warning in the First Folio "Reader, looke | not on his Picture, but his Booke" has not stopped biographers trying to form a picture of the man from his books.

Stephen Greenblatt's ingenious *Will in the World* (2004) is a recent addition to this genre, scouring the works for evidence of the man, but carried out with an unusual degree of sensitivity to the dangers of the enterprise. What were Shakespeare's true feelings for his wife? Facts are scarce. Shakespeare married Anne Hathaway when he was 18, she 26, already three months pregnant. They were married for 32 years yet most of that time Shakespeare was away from home (in Stratford), living and working in London. As Greenblatt notes: "[f]rom this supremely eloquent man, there have been found no love letters to Anne, no signs of shared joy or grief, no words of advice, not even any financial transactions."[11] He left her nothing in his will, except, famously,

---

[11]  Stephen Greenblatt, *Will in the World: How Shakespeare Became Shakespeare* (New York: W. W. Norton, 2004), p. 125.

in a later amendment, his "second best bed." Can we infer that the marriage was a "disaster"? Greenblatt explores in detail the treatment of marriage in the plays to try to find an answer. What he finds in the works is an "unwillingness or inability to imagine a married couple in a relationship of sustained intimacy," with the surprising exception of Gertrude and Claudius in *Hamlet* and the Macbeths, whose marriages are "powerful, in their distinct ways, but ... also upsetting, even terrifying, in their glimpses of genuine intimacy."[12]

Greenblatt notices in several plays the "intensity of the dire visions of pre-marital sex and its consequences." For example, in *The Tempest* (IV i 15–22), Prospero warns Ferdinand about marrying his (Prospero's) daughter:

> If thou dost break her virgin-knot before
> All sanctimonious ceremonies may
> With full and holy rite be ministered,
> No sweet aspersion shall the heavens let fall
> To make this contract grow; but barren hate,
> Sour-eyed disdain, and discord, shall bestrew
> The union of your bed with weeds so loathly
> That you shall hate it both.

Greenblatt comments: "These lines — so much more intense and vivid than the play calls for — seem to draw upon a deep pool of bitterness about a miserable marriage. Instead of a shower of grace ('sweet aspersion'), the union will inevitably be plagued, Prospero warns, if sexual consummation precedes the 'sanctimonious ceremonies.' That was precisely the circumstance of the marriage of Will and Anne."[13]

It is notable in this example how close the biographical comes to the literary critical. Exploration of the theme of marriage in Shakespeare's plays is paradigmatically a literary concern. The comment that the quoted lines from *The Tempest* are "more intense and vivid than the play calls for" is itself a literary critical observation. Only the additional comment that they "seem to draw upon a deep pool of bitterness about a miserable marriage" is biographical.

Nevertheless the role of the biographer should be distinguished from that of the critic. The biographer reads with different interests in mind. There is no objection to reading works to draw inferences about their author, with the reservations noted. It might be thought, though, that Shakespeare is too easy an example to encourage a distance between work and biography. Because we know so little of Shakespeare, attempts to infer personal beliefs from his works will always seem speculative. What of writers whose lives we

---

[12] Ibid., p. 137.
[13] Ibid., p. 142.

*do* know much about and whose works seem deliberately to speak of their personal concerns?

Again the Romantic poets come to mind. Can we not learn about Wordsworth from *The Prelude* or from his Ode "Intimations of Immortality from Recollections of Early Childhood"? It would be perverse to insist otherwise. On the latter poem, for example, Wordsworth offers a gloss revealing the "particular feelings or *experiences* of my own mind on which the structure of the poem partly rests," including a strong sense of solipsism felt in his youth: "I was often unable to think of external things as having external existence, and I communed with all that I saw as something not apart from, but inherent in, my own immaterial nature."[14] Interestingly, though, also in his gloss Wordsworth pulls back from a full commitment to the neo-Platonist view, apparently explicit in the poem, about the pre-existence of the soul ("Our birth is but a sleep and a forgetting"). He tells us: "I took hold of the notion of pre-existence as having sufficient foundation in humanity for authorizing me to make for my purpose the best use of it I could as a Poet."[15] The disclaimer is significant, however hard to interpret, for it reminds us that Wordsworth, in his poetry, is first a poet, only second an autobiographer.

Even in *The Prelude*, subtitled "autobiography," the artistry of the whole seems to take precedence over the faithfulness of record-keeping. As one critic has noted, "although the separate episodes are events from Wordsworth's own life, he does not describe these events as they had seemed to him at the time, but as they are interpreted in distant retrospect, re-ordered in sequence, and shaped into the inherited design of crisis and recovery, from which the author emerges as a different self in a transformed world."[16] Again, the lesson is clear – a lesson for both biographer and critic – namely that art always transforms and shapes its material even where that material is overtly autobiographical.

### From lives to works

For the critic the move in the opposite direction, from life to work, is closer to home. There are untold cases where background knowledge about an author's life can affect a reader's response to the work. Returning to Byron, in Canto III of *Childe Harold* he refers to his own daughter (Augusta Ada) by name:

> Is thy face like thy mother's, my fair child!
> Ada! Sole daughter of my house and heart?

[14] M. H. Abrams, E. T. Donaldson, et al., eds., *The Norton Anthology of English Literature*, 4th ed., Vol. 2 (New York: W. W. Norton, 1979), p. 212.

[15] Ibid.

[16] Ibid., p. 256.

> When last I saw thy young blue eyes they smiled,
> And then we parted — not as now we part,
> But with a hope —
>
> (stanza 1)

Biography tells us not only that Byron's daughter was named "Ada" – confirming the direct reference – but also, more poignantly, that he was never to see her again after his separation from his wife and self-exile in 1816 (the year Ada was born). The "hope" of reconciliation was never realized. Throughout his life Byron sought news of Ada, and shortly before his death received a pen-portrait of her. Does this not add poignancy to the lines? Should we read the lines with this information in mind (note that the point is independent of intention, as Byron did not know when he wrote the lines what fate would befall him)?

Similarly, consider these lines in Canto III, stanza 53:

> For there was soft remembrance, and sweet trust
> In one fond breast, to which his own would melt,
> And in its tenderer hour on that his bosom dwelt.

Biographers tell us the lines refer to Byron's own feelings for his half-sister Augusta Leigh to whom he was emotionally – in the eyes of many, scandalously – attached. Is not a prurient interest raised? Isn't the mask of Childe Harold lifted? Does the specter of incest color our response?

It is not only our affective attitudes that are influenced by biographical knowledge. Sometimes biography can guide understanding. Philip Larkin's poem "Dockery and Son" (1964)[17] is about a visit Larkin made to his old Oxford college, which prompted reflections on having children (Dockery, a contemporary, had them, Larkin did not) and being settled in one's ways ("a style | Our lives bring with them"). The poem begins:

> "Dockery was junior to you,
> Wasn't he?" said the Dean. "His son's here now."
> Death-suited, visitant, I nod.

Why "death-suited"? Nothing in the poem itself makes this clear. But Larkin's biographer explains the background: Larkin was "on the way back from the funeral of Agnes Cuming, his predecessor as librarian at Hull."[18] Not only

---

[17] Philip Larkin, "Dockery and Son," *Collected Poems* (London: Faber and Faber, 1988), pp. 152–153.

[18] Andrew Motion, *Philip Larkin: A Writer's Life* (London: Faber and Faber, 1993), p. 333.

does this explain his attire but also, the biographer claims, it helps illuminate "larger questions of theme and mood." The fact that Larkin was returning from a funeral perhaps gives a biographical explanation for the somber tone at the end of the poem, with its reflection on death:

> Life is first boredom, then fear.
> Whether or not we use it, it goes,
> And leaves what something hidden from us chose,
> And age, and then the only end of age.

Another kind of example is where authors draw on real people in their fictional characterization. Returning to Shakespeare, Greenblatt expounds at length the role of Robert Greene, a seedy but colorful contemporary of Shakespeare's, and the characterization of Falstaff (Greene had mocked Shakespeare as "an upstart Crow, beautified with our feathers"[19]). "Shakespeare seized upon the central paradox of Greene's life – that this graduate of Oxford and Cambridge hung out in low taverns in the company of ruffians – and turned it into Falstaff's supremely ambiguous social position, the knight who is intimate with both the Prince of Wales and a pack of thieves."[20] But in making the Falstaff/Greene identification, Greenblatt takes care "not to strip away the reimagining, as if the life sources were somehow more interesting than the metamorphoses but, rather, to enhance a sense of the wonder at Shakespeare's creation … that took elements from the wasted life of Robert Greene and used them to fashion the greatest comic character in English literature."[21] The caution is well expressed and the moral well drawn. It is one thing to surmise Shakespeare's attitude to Greene by observing his handling of Falstaff, quite another to appreciate Falstaff as a literary creation by appealing back to Greene.

Such examples, which could be multiplied at will, are not primarily about authorial intention but about the role that biographical knowledge plays in our appreciation of poetry (or literature in general). It seems inevitable that facts we happen to know about the lives of authors will impinge in these different kinds of ways on our responses. What should be the attitude of the literary critic?

Although the area is fraught with controversy, there do seem to be cases where biographical facts, even where superficially relevant, seem to have little impact on literary responses. It is well known, for example, that Daniel Defoe based his novel *Robinson Crusoe* (1719) very loosely on the celebrated story of Alexander Selkirk who had been stranded on a remote uninhabited

---

[19]   Greenblatt, *Will in the World*, p. 213.
[20]   Ibid., p. 219.
[21]   Ibid., p. 220.

island off Chile in 1704 and not rescued till 1709. Do we need to find out about Selkirk to appreciate the novel? Or what Defoe knew about Selkirk? Surely not. Robinson Crusoe's adventures have virtually nothing in common with Selkirk's, and the latter's story was a mere "proximate cause" for the plot. Is this example significantly different from the Falstaff/Greene example? To appreciate Shakespeare's genius in creating the comic character of Falstaff, do we need to investigate Robert Greene? Or Shakespeare's relations to Greene? Again, it would seem not. The character has "broken free" from its causal roots and exists as an autonomous creation. Similarly, however fascinating it might be from a biographical point of view, no amount of speculation on the identity of the Dark Lady or Mr. WH will help us appreciate the literary achievement of the Sonnets.

However, the line between relevant and irrelevant background knowledge is not always easy to draw. When it comes to an author's use of source material, there is a continuous scale, no sharp lines, between the Selkirk/Crusoe cases, through the source texts of Shakespeare's plays, to, say, the deliberate allusions in T. S. Eliot's *The Waste Land*. In practice, many critics, setting aside any theoretical stance, call on whatever resources come to hand to aid comprehension. It might be argued that there is no difference in principle between personal information about authors and more general kinds of knowledge. To understand the lines in *Childe Harold* (Canto III, stanza 41), "The part of Philip's son was thine, not then | … Like stern Diogenes to mock at," a reader is expected to know that the first reference is to Alexander the Great, son of Philip of Macedon, and the second to the Greek philosopher of Cynicism, a contemporary of Alexander's. This is part of a shared stock of beliefs that Byron could assume his readers possessed. Is this so different from knowing that Byron's daughter was named "Ada" and indeed what became of her? Details of Byron's personal life were in the public domain even in his lifetime; they certainly are now.

However, even those who encourage permissiveness of background might acknowledge a distinction, however vague its bounds, between a recognized stock of common knowledge (cultural, historical, mythical, literary), which a critic draws on unhesitatingly, and very specific facts about an author's private life, which can seem remote to literary appreciation. What makes Byron an interesting case (though surely not unique) is that he sometimes seems to be writing for two audiences, the general public and his own close associates. In *Don Juan*, for example, his friends would have had no difficulty picking up the personal references:

> For Inez called some druggists and physicians,
> And tried to prove her loving lord was *mad*
>
> (Canto I, stanza 27)

> Some play the devil, and then write a novel
>
> (Canto II, stanza 201)

The first alludes to just such an action (calling physicians to try to certify him as mad) taken by Byron's wife; the second alludes to Lady Caroline Lamb, whose advances he rejected, and who incorporated scenes of their relationship in her novel *Glenarvon* (1816). Such knowledge seems of a different order from knowledge of Diogenes and Alexander. Admitting the latter does not force one to admit the former, even if some critics are happy to do so.

A different line, though, insists on just such a distinction. From this point of view the work must "speak for itself" as far as possible so that responses – particularly affective responses – that depend exclusively on external information about the circumstances of the author should not be deemed appropriate as distinctly "literary" responses. Details that intrigue the biographer or the gossip are irrelevant to an *artistic* assessment. This line stresses the "autonomy" of the work and, again, is the characteristic stance of the New Critics. Thus Cleanth Brooks, in his celebrated essay of 1947 on Wordsworth's Ode "Intimations of Immortality," exhibited the New Critical methodology by emphasizing that he would treat the Ode "as a poem, as an independent poetic structure, even to the point of forfeiting the light which [Wordsworth's] letters, his notes, and his other poems throw on difficult points."[22] But it is noteworthy that Brooks is cautious rather than dogmatic in adopting this approach. He states that his purpose is "not to condemn the usual mode of procedure" (i.e., treating the poem as autobiographical) and that "the forfeiture … need not, of course, be permanent."

Perhaps the sensible route between the two stances is the pragmatic one which says look at cases as they arise and judge the relevance or otherwise of biographical information case by case. In the end it is a literary critical judgment whether or how such information can enhance literary appreciation. A literary critical argument has to be made for utilizing little known facts to illuminate a work; like all such arguments it is answerable to the work itself and the aims of reading. But to make the pragmatic approach viable requires some sense of what the pitfalls are in either direction. So attention should be given to the rationale behind the two extreme views, that which stresses "autonomy" and seeks to distance the poem from the poet, and that which highlights the poet's personality, states of mind, or biography.

---

[22] Cleanth Brooks, *The Well Wrought Urn: Studies in the Structure of Poetry* (London: Methuen, 1968), p. 101.

# The Paradoxes of Inspiration and Expression

The idea of "inspiration" holds an intriguing, if unstable, place between personal and impersonal conceptions of poetic composition. According to Plato's idea of "divine inspiration," as developed in the *Ion*, a poet has little control over the creative process and is "possessed" by a Muse: "all good poets, epic as well as lyric, compose their beautiful poems not as works of art, but because they are inspired and possessed … they are inspired to utter that to which the Muse impels them."[23] In some way the Muse, an external force, takes over the poet and "breathes in" ("inspires") the beautiful lines which flow forth. Taken literally, such a view seems to undermine the "authority" of the author and the personal nature of composition. The conception that poetic creation is outside the conscious control of the artist also reappears in the Freudian or psychoanalytic view that the creative force comes from unconscious elements in the mind.

A more downbeat version of a not dissimilar kind of "impersonal" inspiration is offered by the twentieth-century poet A. E. Housman:

> Having drunk a pint of beer at lunchtime — beer is a sedative of the brain, and my afternoons are the least intellectual portion of my life — I would go out for a walk of two or three hours. As I went along, thinking of nothing in particular, only looking at things around me and following the progress of the seasons, there would flow into my mind, with sudden and unaccountable emotion, sometimes a line or two or verse, sometimes a whole stanza at once.[24]

Inspiration was a central notion for the Romantics but the tensions are already apparent in their efforts to combine it with a view of poetry as intensely personal. In *The Prelude*, Wordsworth also uses the motif of the poet walking in the countryside awaiting inspiration:

> To the open fields I told
> A prophecy: poetic numbers came
> Spontaneously, and clothed in priestly robe
> My spirit, thus singled out, as it might seem,
> For holy services. Great hopes were mine!
> My own voice cheered me, and — far more — the mind's

---

[23] Plato, *Ion*, in *The Works of Plato*, trans. with analysis and introductions by Benjamin Jowett, Four Volumes Complete in One (New York: Tudor Publishing, 1937), vol. 4, p. 287.

[24] A. E. Housman, *The Name and Nature of Poetry* (Cambridge: Cambridge University Press, 1933), p. 49.

Internal echo of the imperfect sound.
To both I listened, drawing from them both
A cheerful confidence in things to come.

*The Prelude* (1805), book I, ll. 59–67

Commenting on the idea of authorship implicit in this passage, a critic writes:

> The poet speaks poetry. Poetry is unmediated by the delay of writing. The poet addresses "the open fields", and his self-communion is not therefore compromised by any sense of an audience. Poetry ("poetic numbers") arrives "spontaneously": there is no work of writing, no effort of composition. The experience that the poem describes and the poem itself are identical: the poem *is* the experience of writing a poem. And the inspired poet is like a priest, "singled out" as he is for a "holy" function.[25]

Yet paradoxes set in when we ask in what exactly composition consists. It might seem to be the expression, or putting into words, of a private experience. But the experience seems already to be articulated in words, albeit through an "imperfect sound," echoed in the mind. If the poem and the experience really are identical and the poem is a linguistic expression, then so too must the experience be. What role is there for the poet's "own voice"? It is not clear whether the poet is discovering an experience through introspection or discovering a poem. The problem is one we have seen already: the tension between the immediacy and privacy of an experience and its formal linguistic expression. If they are fused into one, then what interest is there in the former when the latter is publicly available? As Wittgenstein said: "the [private] object drops out of consideration as irrelevant."[26]

## "Impersonality" of Poetry

The idea that poetry (literature) is "impersonal" is quintessentially a modernist notion, in reaction to Romanticism. Intimations are already present in the *fin-de-siècle* art-for-art's sake movement, as when Oscar Wilde writes, in *The Picture of Dorian Gray* (1891), albeit with an air of paradox given his own flamboyant personality, "To reveal art and conceal the artist is art's aim."

---

[25] Andrew Bennett, "Expressivity: The Romantic Theory of Authorship," in Patricia Waugh, ed., *An Oxford Guide to Literary Theory and Criticism* (Oxford: Oxford University Press, 2006), p. 55.

[26] Wittgenstein, *Philosophical Investigations*, §293.

## *T. S. Eliot and the doctrine of depersonalization*

The distinctly modernist version was first and influentially expressed by
T. S. Eliot in his essay "Tradition and the Individual Talent," from 1919, an
essay that arguably launched the New Criticism. What Eliot calls "depersonalization" has several interlocking strands.

The first concerns the idea of "tradition" and anticipates the later critical
concept of "intertextuality:" in brief, the idea that what matters in poetic
appreciation is not how poems relate to their authors but how they relate to
other poems. Eliot speaks of "the conception of poetry as a living whole of
all the poetry that has ever been written" and makes the striking suggestion
that each genuinely new work not only arises out of the past (the tradition)
but serves to modify or alter the past, readjusting "the whole existing order,"
the "relations, proportions, values."[27]

A second, related, strand concerns the creative process. The poet's mind,
for Eliot, is like a catalyst or a medium, a "receptacle for seizing and storing
up numberless feelings, phrases, images, which remain there until all the
particles which can unite to form a new compound are present together."[28]
This might be seen as a quasi-scientific version of Platonic inspiration; the
poet's mind acting as both storage and catalyst for unbidden inputs from the
world beyond.

This notion in turn connects to a view about poetic expression. Gone is
the Wordsworthian ideal of a "spontaneous overflow of powerful feelings"
and in its place is "a continual extinction of personality":

> the poet has, not a "personality" to express, but a particular medium, which is
> only a medium and not a personality, in which impressions and experiences
> combine in peculiar and unexpected ways. Impressions and experiences which
> are important for the man may take no place in the poetry, and those which
> become important in the poetry may play quite a negligible part in the man,
> the personality.[29]

Eliot draws a distinction between the emotions felt by the poet and emotions
in the work, stressing that only the latter are either relevant or remarkable:

> It is not in his personal emotions, the emotions provoked by particular events
> in his life, that the poet is in any way remarkable or interesting. His particular
> emotions may be simple, crude, or flat. The emotion in his poetry will be a

[27] T. S. Eliot, "Tradition and the Individual Talent," in David Lodge, ed., *20th Century Literary Criticism* (London: Longman, 1972), p. 74.
[28] Ibid.
[29] Ibid., p. 75.

very complex thing, but not with the complexity of the emotions of people who have very complex or unusual emotions in life. … Poetry is not a turning loose of emotion, but an escape from emotion: it is not the expression of personality but an escape from personality.[30]

What emerges, in a fourth and final strand, is a doctrine about criticism: "Honest criticism and sensitive appreciation are directed not upon the poet but upon the poetry." This is the heart of the "autonomy" conception, and the doctrine helped move criticism on decisively from its earlier emphasis on literary biography. The emotions that matter in poetry are now those that are expressed in the poetic language, not those attributable directly to the poet. That there is a valid distinction here is easily grasped when we think of drama. King Lear's anguished speech at the death of Cordelia ("Oh you are men of stones! | Had I your tongues and ears, I'd use them so | That heaven's vault should crack") displays intense emotion but it is not Shakespeare's emotion. The critic is concerned not with the source of the emotion but with the mode of its expression. What matters is the "medium" in which the emotion is embodied and which gives it both its character and its identity.

Even in the apparently hardest cases for the "impersonal" theory of poetry, where a poem seems to spring directly from a personal emotion, it is evident that the "medium" is inescapable and foremost. Returning once more to the Romantics, consider Shelley's "Stanzas Written in Dejection — December 1818, Near Naples," a poem composed after Shelley's baby daughter Clara had just died, his first wife, Harriet, had drowned herself, and he himself was in ill-health, worried about money, and sensing he had failed as a poet. The poem begins:

> The Sun is warm, the sky is clear,
> The waves are dancing fast and bright,
> Blue isles and snowy mountains wear
> The purple noon's transparent might,
> The breath of the moist earth is light
> Around its unexpanded buds;
> Like many a voice of one delight
> The winds, the birds, the Ocean-floods;
> The City's voice itself is soft, like solitude's.

Later in the poem Shelley turns to himself:

> Alas, I have nor hope nor health
> Nor peace within nor calm around,
> Nor that content surpassing wealth

---

[30] Ibid, p. 76.

> The sage in meditation found,
> And walked with inward glory crowned;
> Nor fame nor power nor love nor leisure —
> Others I see whom these surround

Facts about the "medium" are immediately striking: the setting in nature (tranquil and benign in this case) locating the poem firmly in the Romantic lyric "tradition," the formal structure of the stanzas with a conventional rhyme scheme, the measured list of woes, the carefully controlled tone of resignation. At the end of the poem, as is traditional, Shelley offers a generalized reflection:

> They might lament – for I am one
> Whom men love not – and yet regret,
> Unlike this day, which, when the sun
> Shall on its stainless glory set,
> Will linger, though enjoyed, like joy in memory yet.

The sense of working in a tradition is palpable. Not just the title but the content itself has echoes of Coleridge's well-known "Dejection: An Ode" (1802), which also evokes the natural setting:

> All this long eve, so balmy and serene,
> Have I been gazing on the western sky,
> And its peculiar tint of yellow green:
> And still I gaze – and with how blank an eye!

M. H. Abrams has delineated the genre in which both poems fit, in characterizing Romantic odes in general:

> They present a determinate speaker in a particularized, usually localized, outdoor setting whom we overhear, as he carries on, in a fluent vernacular which rises easily to a more formal speech, a sustained colloquy, sometimes with himself or with the outer scene, but more frequently with a silent human auditor, present or absent. The speaker begins with a description of the landscape; an aspect or change of aspect in the landscape evokes a varied but integral process of memory, thought, anticipation, and feeling which remains closely intervolved with the outer scene. In the course of this meditation the lyric speaker achieves an insight, faces up to a tragic loss, comes to a moral decision, or resolves an emotional problem. Often the poem rounds upon itself to end where it began, at the outer scene, but with an altered mood and deepened understanding which is the result of the intervening meditation.[31]

---

[31]  M. H. Abrams, "Structure and Style in the Greater Romantic Lyric," in *Sensibility to Romanticism: Essays Presented to Frederick A. Pottle*, ed. Frederick W. Hilles and Harold Bloom (New Haven, CT: Yale University Press, 1965), pp. 527–528.

Note how the convention lives on in Matthew Arnold's "Dover Beach" (1867), with its own echoes of both Coleridge and Shelley, beginning:

> The sea is calm to-night.
> The tide is full, the moon lies fair
> Upon the straits;

And later reflecting, like Shelley, on a string of negatives:

> the world ...
> Hath really neither joy, nor love, nor light,
> Nor certitude, nor peace, nor help for pain;

Shelley's poem sits squarely in this mode. It exhibits a tight control of form and subject, and far from standing as a counter-example to Eliot's position can be seen to endorse it. For here we find, indeed, not a "turning loose of emotion" (a mere uncontrolled outpouring) but something like "an escape from emotion," an artistic attempt to characterize, understand, and regulate it. Furthermore, to appreciate the expressed emotion a reader need know little of Shelley's own plight (beyond, of course, what the title and poem suggest). The enduring interest of the poem is its timeless exploration of an experience (dejection), not merely a snapshot of a person at a time.

In defending a view similar to Eliot's, attacking the "Personal Heresy," the critic C. S. Lewis insists that "when we read poetry as poetry should be read, we have before us no representation which claims to be the poet, and frequently no representation of ... a personality at all."[32] Even when we do, as he puts it, "approach the poet," we do it "by sharing his consciousness, not by studying it. I look with his eyes, not at him."[33]

### Dramatic speakers

A further familiar move for the "impersonality" theorist is to postulate a "dramatic speaker" in a work, distinct from the actual author. Just as we do not always take the "I" in a first person narrative to refer to the author, so, on this view, we should *never* do so: "clearly Conan Doyle's use of the word 'I' in the Sherlock Holmes stories does not give this pronoun a reference to an actual person. ... Why then must we assume that when Keats or Shelley uses the pronoun he is always referring to himself?"[34] It is now a commonplace in critical discourse to refer to a poem's dramatic speaker. This is partly to acknowledge

[32] C. S. Lewis in Tillyard and Lewis, *The Personal Heresy*, p. 4.
[33] Ibid., p. 11.
[34] Beardsley, *Aesthetics*, pp. 239–240.

the psychological fact that authors frequently present "masks" when writing poetry, even ostensibly about themselves, also partly to allow for the attribution of attitudes or emotions to a speaker without commitment to direct biographical or psychological assertion. This leaves room for personal qualities in a work while maintaining a distance from the personality of the author:

> The meaning of a poem may certainly be a personal one, in the sense that a poem expresses a personality or state of soul. ... But even a short lyric poem is dramatic, the response of a speaker ... to a situation. ... We ought to impute the thoughts and attitudes of the poem immediately to the dramatic speaker and if to the author at all, only by an act of biographical inference.[35]

The view is sometimes supported by appeal to a speech act conception of literature of the kind discussed in Chapter 2: the idea that literary works by their very nature are a kind of pretense or imitated illocutionary act:

> It does not matter how sincerely the poet believes his doctrines, or how fondly he hopes to persuade others. If he goes about making speeches, writing letters and distributing textbooks, then he is indeed arguing. But if he embodies his doctrines in a discourse that flaunts its poetic form ... and directs attention to itself as an object of rewarding scrutiny, then, so to speak, the illocutionary fuse is drawn. His utterance relinquishes its illocutionary force for aesthetic status and takes on the character of being an appearance or a show of living language use.[36]

An objection to this view as applied to personal qualities is that there are limits to the scope of "pretense" possible for literary works.[37] Certainly an author might create a persona far different from his own: an extreme case might be Robert Browning's famous soliloquies – "My Last Duchess," "Soliloquy of the Spanish Cloister" – with their sinister and malevolent speakers. But could a work that exhibits positive personal qualities, such as perceptiveness, sincerity, maturity, or sensitivity, be a mere pretense bearing no implications about the actual author? Arguably, if such qualities are present they must reflect qualities of the author. It is useful to introduce another notion, not equivalent to dramatic speaker, namely, that of a *controlling intelligence* detectable, in at least some works, as an evaluative response to the world of the work as a whole:

---

[35] W. K. Wimsatt and M. C. Beardsley, "The Intentional Fallacy," in Lodge, ed., *20th Century Literary Criticism*, p. 335.

[36] Beardsley, *The Possibility of Criticism*, p. 60.

[37] Colin Lyas, "The Relevance of the Author's Sincerity," in Peter Lamarque, ed., *Philosophy and Fiction: Essays in Literary Aesthetics* (Aberdeen: Aberdeen University Press, 1983).

If the kind of quality of response shown by the controlling intelligence of a work, and hence by the work itself, is perceptive, sensitive, emotionally mature and the like, there seems to be little sense in the supposition that the artist has, by an act of pretence, embodied these characteristics in a work although he himself was not possessed of them. The judgment that the work *is* these things is the judgment that the author *there* exhibited those qualities (though he might not otherwise exhibit them in the responses of his or her non-literary life).[38]

The idea is that even though the world of the work is a fictional construct, and even if the apparent assertions are only pseudo-assertions, there is often an informing spirit in a work which it is impossible to see as mere invention. Colin Lyas offers these examples: "If we discovered that Pasternak did not have the kinds of attitudes expressed by the controlling intelligence of *Dr Zhivago*, or that Solzehnitsyn did not have those expressed in *The Gulag Archipelago* this would not be a matter of indifference."[39]

The argument might apply also to non-positive qualities. The critic F. R. Leavis, in *The Great Tradition* (1962), finds an inadequacy in George Eliot's characterization of Maggie Tulliver in *The Mill on the Floss*: "in George Eliot's presentiment of Maggie there is an element of self-idealisation … [and] an element of self-pity. George Eliot's attitude to her own immaturity as represented by Maggie is the reverse of a mature one."[40] Here Leavis derives a criticism of the author directly from a feature of the work. No doubt the inference would be rejected by the depersonalization theorist but it is hard to see how such judgments, if correct, can fail to reflect back to the author in some such way.

### Style

One manifestation of such a spirit or intelligence is a work's *style*. "'Style,'" writes E. M. W. Tillyard, in response to the "impersonality" view of C. S. Lewis, "readily suggests the mental pattern of the author, the personality realized in words."[41] If style is thought of as *a way of doing something*, rather than merely as a set of formal features, then it seems to be closely related to the expression of personality.[42] It has been argued, for example, that

---

[38]  Lyas, "The Relevance of the Author's Sincerity," p. 22.

[39]  Ibid., p. 33.

[40]  F. R. Leavis, *The Great Tradition* (Harmondsworth: Penguin, 1962), p. 54.

[41]  Tillyard and Lewis, *Personal Heresy*, p. 35.

[42]  This is the view of Jenefer Robinson in "Style and Personality in the Literary Work," *Philosophical Review*, vol. 94 (1985), pp. 227–247; reprinted in Lamarque and Olsen, eds., *Aesthetics and the Philosophy of Art*. Page references are to the latter.

literary style is a way of performing "artistic acts," describing a setting, portraying character, manipulating plot, and so on and it is the writer's way of performing these acts which is expressive of all those standing traits, attitudes, qualities of mind and so on that together form her personality.[43]

Thus the "judicious mixture of irony and compassion" evident in the way that Jane Austen portrays her characters in *Emma*, along with other "artistic acts" performed in writing the novel, partly expresses a personality. But is it Jane Austen's own personality? In fact Jenefer Robinson, who advances this conception of literary style, pulls back from that conclusion, allowing only that the personality of the *implied author*, "the author as she seems to be from the evidence of the work," is thereby revealed.[44] It then remains a further, biographical, question whether an inference from implied to real author is legitimate. This concedes much to the "impersonality" theory, perhaps more than strictly necessary. If the earlier argument about the limits of pretense is correct, then it could be invoked to show that the inference in some cases *must* be drawn, for no author could project a personality showing, for example, compassion or perceptiveness without, at least on that occasion, actually possessing those qualities.

## The Death of the Author

A far more radical rejection of the personality of the author arises in poststructuralist literary theory, associated with the doctrine of the "death of the author." There are two broad strands to this constellation of ideas. The first is a metaphysical thesis about the self, in effect that there is no such thing, at least conceived as an autonomous, unified subject of experience. For poststructuralists the self is a complex social construction – a "site" of multiple "discourses" – not a given inner ego; it is fragmented, shifting, decentered.[45] Many consequences are drawn from the disintegration of the self, including the rejection of the author as a source of meaning and a general suspicion about all forms of "humanist" criticism that seem to rely on "human nature," "character," or "identity."

---

[43] Robinson, "Style and Personality in the Literary Work," p. 413.

[44] Ibid., p. 414.

[45] See, e.g., Catherine Belsey, *Critical Practice* (London: Methuen, 1980). Or "The notion of the 'self'—so intrinsic to Anglo-American thought—becomes absurd. It is not something called the self that speaks, but language, the unconscious, the textuality of the text": Alice A. Jardine, *Gynesis: Configurations of Woman and Modernity* (Ithaca, NY: Cornell University Press, 1985), p. 58.

The second is related to the first but more directly concerns meaning and writing, and is therefore more relevant for our purposes. This is the notion, in Roland Barthes's words, that "it is language which speaks, not the author," a notion perhaps not too far removed from that of T. S. Eliot's "the poet has, not a 'personality' to express, but a particular medium."

The conception of the "death of the author" specifically related to literature is developed in two seminal papers: Roland Barthes's "The Death of the Author" and Michel Foucault's "What Is an Author?"[46] These papers present the key underpinnings of post-structuralism (as applied to literature) and as such have been highly influential. They contain a complex web of ideas and arguments that are worth unraveling and analyzing. In what follows four prominent theses will be identified, which I shall label the author-is-modern thesis, the author-is-dead thesis, the author function thesis, and the *Écriture* thesis.

### The author is modern

According to Barthes, "The author is a modern figure, a product of our society" (p. 142). Foucault speaks of the "coming into being of the notion of 'author'" at a specific "moment ... in the history of ideas" (p. 101). Both he and Barthes locate the birth of the author in post-medieval times, a manifestation of the rise of the individual from the Reformation through to the philosophical Enlightenment. The idea that written works only acquired authors at a specific time in history is striking but in need of explanation. Three principal explanations, not mutually exclusive, seem available, and they will have a bearing on how to interpret the other theses in the overall argument.

The first interpretation, then, is this: *A certain conception of a writer (writer-as-author) is modern*. For Foucault this conception is highly specific; in effect it is a legal and social conception of authorship. The author is seen as an owner of property, a producer of marketable goods, as having rights over those goods, and also responsibilities: "Texts, books, and discourses really began to have authors ... to the extent that authors became subject to punishment" (p. 108). In a similar vein Barthes identifies the author with "capitalist ideology" (p. 143). The central point is that at a determinate stage in history, according to this thesis, writers (of certain kinds of texts) came to acquire a new social status, along with a corresponding legal and cultural recognition.

---

[46] Roland Barthes, "The Death of the Author," in *Image-Music-Text*, Essays Selected and Translated by Stephen Heath (London: Fontana/Collins, 1977); Michel Foucault, "What Is an Author?" in *The Foucault Reader*, ed. Paul Rabinow (Harmondsworth: Peregrine Books, 1986). All citations and page references are from these editions.

The distinction between a writer and an author is useful, as mentioned earlier, in showing that the mere act of writing (text messages, grocery lists) does not make an author. An author so designated is a weightier figure with legal rights and social standing, a producer of texts deemed to have value. Authors on this conception come into being when things like copyright and ownership obtain legal sanction. This conception is not about a persona, a dramatic speaker, or a construct of the text.

The second interpretation of the author-is-modern thesis is about criticism: *A certain conception of criticism (author-based criticism) is modern*. Here the idea is that it is only at a certain stage of history that the focus of criticism turned to the personality of the author. According to Barthes, this occurred after the bourgeois revolution which gave prominence to the individual. Although the author as person (writer, cause, origin, etc.) is again evoked in this interpretation, it is nevertheless distinct from the social and legal conception. No direct implications about criticism follow from the fact that the author comes to be viewed as having rights over a text. Purely formalist criticism is compatible with a state of affairs where an author is accorded a secure legal and social identity.

The third interpretation is the most controversial but also the most interesting: *A certain conception of a text (the authored-text) is modern*. At a certain point in history, (written) texts acquire significance in virtue of being "authored." "There was a time," Foucault writes, "when the texts which we today call 'literary' (narratives, stories, epics, tragedies, comedies) were accepted, put into circulation, and valorized without any question about the identity of their author" (p. 109). Many after all were anonymous. Foucault contrasts this with the case of scientific discourses which, in the Middle Ages, owed their authority to a named provenance (Hippocrates, Pliny). A radical change occurred, so Foucault claims, in the seventeenth and eighteenth centuries when literary texts came to be viewed as essentially "authored," while scientific writing could carry authority even in anonymity.

In effect this conception of an *authored-text* is close to that of a *work* as characterized in Chapter 2. The authored-text is viewed as the product of a creative act, but what is important is that this instills or makes accessible a distinctive kind of unity, integrity, meaning, interest, and value. For Foucault it is works of this kind that exhibit what he calls the "author function," which we shall come to later. The idea that works in this sense are a modern phenomenon is intriguing.

## The author is dead

The meaning of the claim *The author is dead*, and assessment of its truth, can only be determined relative to the author-is-modern thesis, under its different interpretations. The underlying thought is this: if a certain conception (of an author, a text, etc.) has a definite historical beginning, i.e., arises under determinate historical conditions, then it can in principle come to an end, when the historical conditions change.

One complication is that the author-is-dead thesis can be read either as a statement of fact or as wishful thinking, i.e., either as a description of the current state of affairs (we simply no longer *have* authors conceived in a certain way) or as a prescription for the future (we no longer *need* authors so conceived, we can now get by without them).[47] Both Barthes and Foucault seem to waver on the question of description and prescription. Barthes, for example, admits that "the sway of the Author remains powerful" (p. 143), yet in speaking of the "modern scriptor," in contrast to the Author (pp. 145, 146), he suggests that (modern) writing is no longer conceived as the product of an author. Similarly, Foucault tells us "we must locate the space left empty by the author's disappearance" (p. 105), the latter thus taken for granted, yet makes a prediction at the end of his paper that the author function, which is his own conception of the author, "will disappear," i.e., sometime in the future, "as our society changes" (p. 119).

To see what the author-is-dead claim amounts to, we can run through the different permutations. The first claims: *the writer-as-author is dead, or should be*. Does the conception of writer-as-author, with a certain social and legal status, still obtain? Surely it does. Authors are still, in Foucault's words, "subject to punishment"; there are copyright laws and blasphemy laws; authors can be sued for libel or plagiarism; they attract interest from biographers and gossips. Authors under this conception are certainly not dead. But should they be killed off? Should we try and rid ourselves of this conception? In the extreme case it would be hard to imagine a world where writers have no legal status and no rights over their work or where all writing is anonymous. Perhaps the internet is moving in that direction. However, it might be argued that the world of letters would be better off without the celebrity cult of authors. These, though, are more political or social than philosophical judgments.

According to the second permutation, *author-based criticism is dead, or should be*. Here the author-is-dead thesis comes closest both to the kind of depersonalized theory of literature already considered and also to the Intentional Fallacy, to be examined later. In fact the views of Barthes and Foucault are more radical than those of T. S. Eliot and the anti-intentionalists. The context of their discussion is broader and more politically charged.

---

[47] A similar ambiguity lies in the origin of the author-is-dead thesis, namely Nietzsche's proclamation that "God is dead." Was Nietzsche describing a new human consciousness already in evidence or was he heralding a radical break with the past?

Their attack on the author is not just a prescription for literary criticism but a challenge to the status of the individual per se and, indeed, a challenge to the very idea of "literature" as commonly conceived. The death of author-based criticism is a consequence of these ideas not a central focus for them.

The third interpretation of the death of the author concerns the authored text: *the authored-text is dead, or should be*. This is where the attack on *works* gets started. But it is surely not a *fact* that texts conceived as having determinate meaning and as the manifestation of creative acts no longer exist. At best this can only be a prescription of the post-structuralists. Indeed, Foucault would accept that literary criticism still retains its conception of the authored-text: he perceives this conception as the foundation of literary criticism. His project is to move beyond the authored-text itself (along with its concomitant notions of meaning, interpretation, unity, expression, and value). The so-called "author function," which is the defining feature of an authored-text, is, according to Foucault, "an ideological product" (p. 119), a repressive and restricting "principle of thrift in the proliferation of meaning" (p. 118). In effect Foucault's death prescription is aimed at the very concept of a literary work which sustains the practice of literary criticism (it is also aimed, more broadly, at any class of work subject to similar interpretive and evaluative constraints).

### The author function

Elaboration on the author function is intended to provide further support for the attack on the authored-text. Although the notion is never explicitly defined by Foucault, the central idea is that the author function is a property of a discourse (or text) and amounts to something more than it just having been written or produced by a person (of whatever status): "there are a certain number of discourses that are endowed with the 'author function', while others are deprived of it" (p. 107).

Foucault's notion is important and subtle, justifying a closer look. There seem to be a number of separate claims associated with the "author function." The first involves its relation to the author as person:

(i) *The author function is distinct from the author-as-person.*

Foucault makes it clear that the author function "does not refer purely and simply to a real individual" (p. 113). He complicates the exposition by often using the term interchangeably with "the author"; however, the term "author" itself is not intended as a direct designation of an individual. He says that "it would be … wrong to equate the author with the real writer" (p. 112), and he speaks of the author as "a certain functional principle" (p. 119).

What are the grounds for postulating an impersonal conception of an author as distinct from a personal conception? Foucault does not simply have in mind the literary critical notions of an "implied author" or dramatic speaker, a set of attitudes informing a work that might or might not be shared with the real author. For one thing Foucault's author function is not a construct specific to individual works but may bind together a whole oeuvre; and whereas an implied author is, as it were, just one fictional character among others in a work, the author function is more broadly conceived as determining the very nature of the work itself.[48]

One of the arguments that Foucault offers for the distinctness claim (i), indeed it is also his justification for describing the author as an "ideological product," rests on a supposed discrepancy between the way we normally conceive the author as a person (i.e., as a genius, a creator, one who proliferates meaning) and the way we conceive texts which have authors (i.e., as constrained in their meaning and confined in the uses to which they can be put). But whether there is such a discrepancy is questionable. To the extent that we conceive of an author as offering "an inexhaustible world of significations" (p. 118), as a proliferator of meaning, then we expect precisely the same of the work itself.

It is more promising to read Foucault as proposing a semi-technical sense of the term "author," one which conforms to the following principle:

(ii) *"Having an author" is not a relational predicate (characterizing a relation between a work and a person) but a monadic predicate (characterizing a certain kind of work).*

This principle signals the move from "X has an author" to "X is authored" or, more explicitly, from "X has Y as an author" (the relational predicate) to "X is Y-authored" (the monadic predicate). The author function becomes a property of a text or discourse, not a relation between a text and a person. We need to ask what the monadic predicate "being authored" or being "Y-authored" actually means in this special sense.

First, though, it might be helpful to offer a further elaboration of (ii) in terms of paraphrase or reduction:

(iii) *All relevant claims about the relation between an author-as-person and a text are reducible to claims about an authored-text.*

In this way the author disappears through a process comparable to reduction by paraphrase. In place of, for example, "The work is a product of the

[48] See Alexander Nehamas, "Writer, Text, Work, Author," in Anthony J. Cascardi, ed., *Literature and the Question of Philosophy* (Baltimore, MD: Johns Hopkins University Press, 1987).

author's creative act" we can substitute "The work is an authored-text" and still retain the significant cognitive content of the former. Such a semantic maneuver is not intended, of course, to show that authors (as persons) are redundant. At best its aim is to show that *relative to critical discourse* references to an author can be eliminated without loss of significant content. It seems that some such thesis underlies Foucault's statement that the

> aspects of an individual which we designate as making him an author are only a projection, in more or less psychologizing terms, of the operations that we force texts to undergo, the connections that we make, the traits that we establish as pertinent, the continuities that we recognize, or the exclusions that we practice. (p. 110)

Foucault is thinking of such aspects as an author's "design" and "creative power," as well as the meaning, unity, and expression with which the author informs the text. He believes, as we have seen, that these features can be attributed directly to an authored-text without reference back to the author-as-person. This is the heart of the author function thesis.

What support can be offered for propositions (ii) and (iii)? After all, they are not obviously true and they depart from the more familiar meaning of "author." The main logical support that Foucault offers is an argument about authors' names. An author's name, he suggests, does not operate purely referentially. Rather than picking out some individual person, it has, he says, a "classificatory function," it "serves to characterize a certain mode of being of discourse" (p. 107). He seems to have something like the following in mind:

(iv) *(Some) author attributions (using an author's name) are non-extensional.*

If we say that a play is by Shakespeare we mean, or connote, more than just that the play was written by a particular man (Shakespeare); for one thing we assign a certain honorific quality to it (it is likely to be a play worthy of our attention); also we relate the play to a wider body of work, to *Hamlet, King Lear, Twelfth Night*, and so on. Being "by Shakespeare" signals not just an external relation but an internal characterization. We move from "X is a play by Shakespeare" to "X is a Shakespeare play" or even "X is Shakespearean." The latter formulations are non-extensional, or at least have non-extensional readings, in the sense that substitution of co-referential names is not always permissible (does not preserve truth). If Shakespeare turns out to be Bacon it does not follow that the plays become Baconian, where that has its own distinctive connotations.

This argument is perceptive, showing subtle nuances underlying the innocent-seeming expressions "by Shakespeare" and "Shakespearean." Of course it doesn't follow that "X has Shakespeare as an author" *only* has a non-extensional, classificatory meaning because a fully extensional, relational meaning, where reference to Shakespeare the person is maintained, is still possible. It would be wrong to suppose that Foucault's argument eliminates the referential function altogether.

What about the move, in (ii), from "X has an author" to "X is authored"? This move is not directly supported by the argument from authors' names but hangs on a distinctive conception of an "authored-text." This takes us back to the author-is-modern thesis. Foucault, as we saw, has in mind not just the attribution of an author to a text, nor in the more sophisticated version of (iv) a text classified through a non-extensional attribution, but rather a notion of an authored-text conceived more broadly:

> (v) *An authored-text is one that is subject to interpretation, constrained in its meaning, exhibiting unity and coherence, and located in a system of values.*

It is precisely this notion he is attacking when he attacks the author function. But the attack has moved beyond any simple, perhaps Barthesian, repudiation of the author as creator. The power of Foucault's position is that in effect he has recognized, in postulating the author function and the notion of an authored-text, that the qualities in (v) are *institutionally based* qualities, i.e., part of the conception of literature, and not *individualistically based*, i.e., formulated in terms of individual psychological attitudes. There is no need to see the constraints on interpretation, nor the source of unity and coherence, nor the criteria of value, as directly attributable to an individual (the author-as-person).

Literary works have authors, of course; they are the product of a creative act (a real act from a real agent) but the constraints on interpretation, and the determination of coherence and value, that serve to characterize the literary work, are independent of the individual author's will. That is the lesson of the author-is-dead thesis in its more telling versions and the lesson too of the author function thesis.

## Écriture

Barthes's version of the author function is what he calls the "modern scriptor" who is "born simultaneously with the text" (p. 145). But Barthes bases his move from the relational author to the non-relational scriptor – i.e., his version of the author function thesis – on a conception of writing (*écriture*). The basic claim of the *Écriture* thesis is this (in Barthes's words): *writing [écriture] is the destruction of every voice, of every point of origin* (p. 142). The implication is that the very nature of writing makes the author – i.e., the author-as-person – redundant. How does Barthes support this thesis? Unlike Foucault, Barthes is not strictly a philosopher, and his essay "The Death of the Author" is more a spirited polemic than a closely reasoned argument. But he does offer reasons.

First of all there is an argument from narration:

> As soon as a fact is *narrated* no longer with a view to acting directly on reality but intransitively, that is to say, finally outside of any function other than that of the very practice of the symbol itself ... the voice loses its origin. (p. 142)

The difficulty is to conceive of any act of narration that in fact satisfies the condition of having no other function than the "practice of the symbol itself." Nearly all narration has some further aim, indeed the aim in some form or other to "act ... directly on reality": be it to inform, entertain, persuade, instruct, or whatever. Narration is by definition an act and no acts are truly gratuitous.

Perhaps Barthes might respond to this difficulty in several ways. When the context in which a written narrative is read is totally different from that of the original writing – think of reading Thucydides or a medieval chronicle – then the original aims, however clear their initial focus, get lost or blurred or become irrelevant. Also certain kinds of fictional narrative come close to Barthes's specification: narratives where playfulness is paramount. It is a convention of some kinds of fiction that they draw attention to their own fictional status, that they point inward rather than outward, that they teasingly conceal their origin. It is sometimes thought to be a convention of literary fiction in general, as we saw in discussing speech act theories and, in particular, the theory of John M. Ellis in Chapter 2, that the original context of utterance is set aside. There is also a familiar convention in literature of embedding narrative voices – think of Joseph Conrad's *Heart of Darkness* or Emily Brontë's *Wuthering Heights* – such that a narrator might recount another story-teller's memory of what some third character once said. Any original "authorial" voice (e.g., attitude) is lost or hidden. Such examples draw attention to important facts about narration but perhaps fall short of supporting any universal thesis about writing (or authors). Not all writing is in narrative form and some narratives make their voice of origin manifest.

A second argument for the *Écriture* thesis rests on the characterization of writing as performative:

> *writing* can no longer designate an operation of recording, notation, representation, "depiction" ...; rather, it designates ... a performative ... in which the enunciation has no other content ... than the act by which it is uttered. (pp. 145–146)

But the claim that writing has the status of a performative utterance, instead of supporting the *Écriture* thesis, seems instead to contradict it. A performative utterance only counts as an act – a promise, a marriage, a declaration of war – under precisely specified contextual conditions; and one of those conditions, essential in each case, is the speaker's having appropriate intentions. Far from being the destruction of a "voice of origin," the successful performative relies crucially on the disposition and authority of the speaker.

Clearly what impressed Barthes about the performative utterance is another feature: that of self-validation. If I say "I promise" I am not reporting some external fact but, under the right conditions, bringing a fact into existence. However, even if we set aside the requirement of the speaker's authority, and focus only on the feature of self-validation, the analogy with performatives is still questionable. It seems to rest on taking a certain kind of fictive utterance, which creates its own facts or world, as paradigmatic. Fictional writing does have a kind of self-validation but for that reason it is precisely contrasted with writing that has an overt referential function. It is not clear, though, that Barthes is even right about fiction. Knowing that a stretch of writing is fiction, rather than fact, or is playfully referring to itself, rather than reaching out to reality, already seems to imply knowledge of its origins, the intentions behind it.

The third argument is about meaning and is probably the most powerful, getting to the heart of Barthes's view of *écriture*. The thought is this, that writing per se, in contrast to the constrained authored-text, does not yield any determinate meaning:

> a text is not a line of words releasing a single 'theological' meaning (the 'message' of the Author-God) but a multi-dimensional space in which a variety of writings, none of them original, blend and clash. (p. 146)

We find the same idea in Foucault, even though he voices some skepticism later on about *écriture*: "today's writing has freed itself from the dimension of expression," "it is an interplay of signs," it "unfolds like a game" (p. 102). How does this support the thesis that writing has destroyed the voice of origin? The idea seems to be that determinate meaning is always an imposition from the outside, even an "arbitrary" imposition, while writing itself, conceived as pure text, is unconstrained: "writing ceaselessly posits meaning ceaselessly to evaporate it." Strings of sentences in a written text mean *all they can possibly mean*, given the history of the language or usage or culture. They are constituted by "a tissue of quotations drawn from the innumerable centers of culture." Every word has a vastly rich history of connotation, and in the written text these are all alive and accessible.

In many ways this idea is exciting and compelling. The possibilities of textual meaning do seem almost infinitely rich. And Barthes's seductive challenge to shift the delimitation of meaning from the author to the reader offers new powers to readers who might well think of themselves as merely passive receivers:

> a text is made of multiple writings, drawn from many cultures and entering into mutual relations of dialogue, parody, contestation, but there is one place

where this multiplicity is focused and that place is the reader, not, as was hitherto said, the author. The reader is the space on which all the quotations that make up a writing are inscribed without any of them being lost; a text's unity lies not in its origin but in its destination. ... [T]he birth of the reader must be at the cost of the death of the Author. (p. 148)

It is heady stuff and has been rightfully influential. But the crucial question remains what priority should be given to "text." Barthes's notion of a Text, which we looked at in Chapter 2, is a specific manifestation of *écriture*. It is to be contrasted with a "work"; a work belongs in a genre, its meaning is constrained, it has an author, it is subject to classification. A Text for Barthes, as we recall, "practises the infinite deferment of the signified";[49] "no vital 'respect' is due to the Text: it can be *broken*" (p. 161).

Perhaps the disagreement between the contextualist described in Chapter 2 and the Barthesian textualist is not over the god-like status of the author – both are happy to cede rights to the reader – nor over whether there is such a thing as an undifferentiated Text, but over priorities. For the contextualist the starting point for grasping the concept of literature is the authored work, constrained by institutional conventions and historical context. Once that conception is in place there is no need for the contextualist to deny that it is possible to read a work in a Barthesian manner *as if* it were an undifferentiated Text. But a pure Text or *écriture* is always an abstraction from a work. Works come before Texts because any text must be a product of an intentional act. For Barthes the opposite is the case. All texts are initially undifferentiated Texts whose origins are irrelevant just in virtue of being *écriture*. They could, no doubt, always be read *as if* they are works with meaning imposed on them. The Author could be searched out and interrogated. To do so, though, would be limiting and would, unnecessarily, remove the "play" from the signifier, denying something fundamental to the nature of writing itself.

For some the choice between the positions might seem evenly balanced. The differences, though, are profound in their consequences, not just in styles of reading and in practices engaged, but in the very future of "literary studies." In favor of the contextualist it seems hard to deny that writing, like speech, or any language "performed," is inevitably, and properly, conceived as purposive. Just as it seems perverse to try to listen to a Mozart symphony as a mere string of unstructured sounds so it seems not just pointless but misguided to try to read works by Dante or Dickens, Allen Ginsberg or Adrienne Rich as undifferentiated Texts cut off from their historical origins and not anchored in the genres, traditions, and religious, social or political contexts to which they belong.

What the discussion has shown are the radical repercussions of the death-of-the-author movement, but also the considerable sophistication lying behind

---

[49]   Barthes, "From Work to Text," in *Image-Music-Text*, p. 158.

reflections on the author function and the distinction between texts and works. Only when we look in detail at the practices of reading literature will the constraints on the theoretical decisions become clearer.

## Anti-Intentionalism

No discussion of the author, however, would be complete without consideration of intention. A great many of the issues already raised come sharply into focus in this context. In their acclaimed article "The Intentional Fallacy" (1946) the literary critic William K. Wimsatt and the philosopher Monroe C. Beardsley argued that it is fallacious (i.e., an invalid form of reasoning) to base a critical judgment about the "meaning or value" of a literary work on "external evidence" concerning the author's intentions. To do so, they claimed, involves "a confusion between the poem and its origins." As with T. S. Eliot and C. S. Lewis, their target was not merely intention but also a certain kind of "romanticism" (a concept they deploy several times), along with other notions associated with an author's "personality," such as "sincerity," "fidelity," "spontaneity," "authenticity," "genuineness," "originality."

The Wimsatt and Beardsley article stirred up an immense amount of debate which, perhaps distortingly, came to dominate philosophy of literature and which still rumbles on. Arguably what is most important about the debate is how it impacts on actual critical practice, something we shall examine in the next chapter. To bring the debate as sharply as possible into focus it is worth laying out in a systematic way the central claims and central arguments on both sides.

Let us begin with the anti-intentionalist case, as defended by Wimsatt and Beardsley, the principal theses of which will be listed and analyzed. [50]

1. *"The design or intention of the author is neither available nor desirable as a standard for judging the success of a work of literary art."* [51]

---

[50]    Some of these arguments appear in the original article "The Intentional Fallacy," some are developed in later writings by both Wimsatt and Beardsley separately, some come from independent sources, as noted. Beardsley returned to the topic on numerous occasions, most prominently in *Aesthetics: Problems in the Philosophy of Criticism*, 2nd ed. (Indianapolis, IN: Hackett, 1981), originally published in 1958; *The Possibility of Criticism* (Detroit, MI: Wayne State University Press, 1970); and "Intentions and Interpretations: A Fallacy Revived," in *The Aesthetic Point of View*, ed. Michael J. Wreen and Donald M. Callen (Ithaca, NY: Cornell University Press, 1982). Wimsatt's most notable reassessment is "Genesis: A Fallacy Revisited," which appeared in the influential anthology *On Literary Intention*, ed. David Newton-de Molina (Edinburgh: Edinburgh University Press, 1976).

[51]    Wimsatt and Beardsley, "The Intentional Fallacy," p. 334.

To say that an author's intentions are not *available* to the critic looks like a claim of fact, to say that they are not *desirable* looks like a claim about norms or principles. The principle that it is not *desirable* to appeal to intention "as a standard for judging ... a work of literary art" rests on a conception of criticism, in particular concerning the kinds of evidence that it is legitimate to cite in support of a critical judgment. That will be discussed later. The *availability* of intentions looks differently grounded. Indeed, sometimes little is known about the thoughts or intentions of authors independent of their work (think of Homer or the authors of the Psalms). Sometimes, though, authors self-consciously record their intentions (T. S. Eliot wrote notes on *The Waste Land*, W. B. Yeats discussed his own poetic symbolism) and living authors can always be asked what they intended. So either the anti-intentionalist's claim about availability is just a contingent fact, with few implications for critical method, or it points to something deeper about the nature of literary intention.

Thus, first, if it is true that in some cases the lack of independent access to intentions does not pose an insuperable barrier to interpretation, then it follows that in principle appeal to such independent access cannot be *necessary* for criticism. Of course that does not entail it might not be helpful in some cases. Second, though, it might be argued that in every case – even that of the cooperative living author – the author's fine-grained mentalistic states that gave rise to the work are inaccessible after the event. Wimsatt writes: "the closest one could ever get to the artist's intending or meaning mind, outside his work, would be still short of his *effective* intention or *operative* mind as it appears in the work itself." [52]

The anti-intentionalist need not deny the existence of intentions. Indeed Wimsatt and Beardsley readily admit that an author's "designing intellect" might be "the *cause* of a poem"; they deny only that it is a *standard* for judging the poem. Also they are happy to acknowledge intentions *realized in* a work. According to the anti-intentionalist, however, if an intention is realized in a work then it is not necessary to consult the author, but if it is not realized then it cannot be relevant to the work itself.

*2. Intention is not a standard for evaluation.*

In "The Intentional Fallacy," Wimsatt and Beardsley do not make a clear distinction between the role of authorial intention in evaluation and its role in interpretation. Wimsatt, in "Genesis: a Fallacy Revisited," sought to sharpen that distinction, showing that different kinds of arguments

---

[52]  Wimsatt, "Genesis: A Fallacy Revisited," p. 136.

might be adduced relating intention to value and to meaning. Let us take value first. Suppose an artist's sole aim in producing a work was to make money or seek fame. Should that intention bear on the value of the work produced? The anti-intentionalist insists it should not and that the work must be valued on its merits. And clearly an author's intention to produce a masterpiece cannot be evidence that a masterpiece has been produced.

Even where a work does perfectly capture what the author aimed to achieve – perhaps the expression of an emotional response – there still seems room for independent assessment of the work itself. Here the anti-intentionalist clashes with the Romantic expressivist, such as the philosophers Croce and Collingwood, for whom artistic success rests with successful expression. The anti-intentionalist, though, can argue that while a skillfully executed murder might attest to the murderer's imaginativeness or ingenuity, the latter has no bearing on the moral worth of the act itself.

Finally, the intentionalist might propose another kind of case where intention does seem relevant to literary value, namely the intention to parody or lampoon. Take, for example, William McGonagall's best known poem "The Tay Bridge Disaster" (1879), which begins as follows:

> Beautiful Railway Bridge of the Silv'ry Tay!
> Alas! I am very sorry to say
> That ninety lives have been taken away
> On the last Sabbath day of 1879,
> Which will be remember'd for a very long time.
>
> 'Twas about seven o'clock at night,
> And the wind it blew with all its might,
> And the rain came pouring down,
> And the dark clouds seem'd to frown,
> And the Demon of the air seem'd to say –
> "I'll blow down the Bridge of Tay."

On the face of it this is a piece of entirely artless doggerel. However, if the poem had been intended as a parody of sentimental poetry, i.e., to be deliberately bad and exaggerated, it might be reassessed as witty and amusing and be anthologized in collections of comic verse. Thus the pro-intention argument would be that only when we know what kind of work is intended can we evaluate it. These are difficult cases for the anti-intentionalist, who must insist that any parodic quality would show itself in the work and not rest entirely on independent intention.

3. *Intention is not a standard for literary meaning.*

The focus for the anti-intentionalist case is usually more on *meaning* than on evaluation. The job of the critic, it is said, is to explore a work's meaning; meaning, for the anti-intentionalist, is recoverable through purely linguistic, historical, and broadly cultural resources, not through author psychology. At root are deep issues about not just the nature of meaning itself but also the nature of literature. Even if it could be established that in some cases of meaning – for example, conversational meaning – knowledge of what is *in the speaker's mind* is essential, it would not follow that literary meaning is itself mentalistic in this way.

Beardsley characterizes an Identity Thesis about literary meaning, which he rejects: "what a literary work means is identical with what its author meant in composing it."[53] He believes the thesis can be "conclusively refuted." First, he argues, there are "textual meanings without authorial meanings," as when a printer's error changes the sense of a sentence. Second, the "meaning of a text can change after its author has died," exemplified, for Beardsley, by a line from Mark Akenside's poem *The Pleasures of the Imagination*, published in 1744: "he rais'd his plastic arm" (Bk. II, line 313).[54] The word "plastic" now has a meaning that it could not have when it was written. Whether or not the new meaning is active in the poem, the example shows that textual meaning is not always identical with intended meaning. Third, "a text can have meanings that its author is not aware of."[55] Meanings might be unconscious or connotations unnoticed.

The distinction between "textual meaning" and "authorial meaning" is an instance of a distinction that the philosopher H. P. Grice introduced into philosophy of language, between "sentence meaning" and "speaker's meaning" (sometimes called "utterer's meaning").[56] The distinction is simply illustrated by the case of sarcasm. By uttering the sentence "That was clever" in the context of someone knocking over a priceless vase, a speaker can mean "That was stupid." It does not follow that one of the meanings of "clever" is "stupid"; the word retains its original semantic meaning but the speaker can convey the opposite meaning. However, merely distinguishing sentence meaning and speaker's meaning does not establish the anti-intentionalist case. A further argument is needed to show that only sentence meaning (or textual meaning) is relevant in literary interpretation. There is a crucial slippage in Beardsley's argument from "what a literary work means" to "textual meaning." The latter might well be distinct from an author's intended

---

[53]   Beardsley, *The Possibility of Criticism*, p. 17.

[54]   Ibid. p. 19.

[55]   Ibid. p. 20.

[56]   See H. P. Grice, *Studies in the Way of Words* (Cambridge, MA: Harvard University Press, 1989), pp. 86–117.

meaning but it does not follow that what a literary work means is identical with textual meaning.

Anti-intentionalists sometimes argue that giving ultimate authority to private intention collapses into the so-called "Humpty Dumpty theory" of meaning, after the character in Lewis Carroll's *Through the Looking Glass* who claimed that when he said "There's glory for you" he meant "There's a nice knock-down argument for you." Contrary to Humpty Dumpty, intentions alone cannot determine meaning, which must rely to a large extent on publicly accepted linguistic convention. The retrievability of meaning through knowledge of convention is at the heart of the anti-intentionalist case. Of course the intentionalist might accept a role for convention but still insist that what makes an utterance of "That was clever" mean "That was stupid" must rest partially on what the speaker intended. The matter is complicated by the fact that sarcasm – when and how it occurs – is itself highly conventionalized.

Beardsley's argument that texts can have meanings not acknowledged by an author, through linguistic change or through unnoticed connotations, raises an important issue about the fallibility of the author as a guide to interpretation. The anti-intentionalist in principle treats an author's own interpretation of a text as one among others, itself calling for textual justification. Cases of critics directly repudiating an author's own reading are rare, but Wimsatt gives the example of "Chekhov's desire (revealed in his letters) to have his *Seagull* and *Cherry Orchard* produced as comedies." This, Wimsatt says, was "doomed to defeat … resulting only in Stanislavsky's successful and well-established interpretation of them as tragedies."[57] For the anti-intentionalist, even if biographical facts point toward one reading, the legitimacy of that reading must be established with relation to the work itself. This brings us to the question of kinds of evidence for interpretation.

4. *"External" evidence for the meaning of a poem is irrelevant to literary criticism.*

Underlying anti-intentionalism, at least in Wimsatt's and Beardsley's formulation, is a conception of critical practice. In the final paragraph of "The Intentional Fallacy," discussing how to settle the question of whether there is an allusion to John Donne in T. S. Eliot's "Love Song of J. Alfred Prufrock," Wimsatt and Beardsley describe two fundamentally different approaches: "the way of poetic analysis and exegesis" which is "the true and objective way of criticism," and "the way of biographical or genetic enquiry." The difference lies in what is admitted as evidence for a claim about a work's meaning.

---

[57] Wimsatt, "Genesis: A Fallacy Revisited," p. 131.

Some evidence – for the anti-intentionalist this is the most relevant – is "internal" to the work: "it is discovered through the semantics and syntax of a poem, through our habitual knowledge of the language, through grammars, dictionaries, and all the literature which is the source of dictionaries, in general through all that makes a language and culture." In contrast, some evidence is "external": this is "private or idiosyncratic; not a part of the work as a linguistic fact," coming from "journals, for example, or letters or reported conversations." Then there is an "intermediate kind of evidence": "about the character of the author or about private or semiprivate meanings attached to words or topics by an author or by a coterie of which he is a member."[58]

Wimsatt and Beardsley admit there is not a sharp line between these kinds of evidence, pointing out, for example, that an author's own idiosyncratic meanings can become incorporated into the language and thus move from the third to the first category of evidence. Their point is only to promote "internal" evidence over the other two as a working methodological principle. The principle arises as a consequence of the "autonomy" of the literary work and the independence of cause and meaning. Nor is it reasonable to charge anti-intentionalists – a charge often made – with proposing a sharp distinction between what is "in" a work (or text) and what is "outside" it. After all, if "internal" evidence for a work's meaning covers the whole of the language, most literature, and "all that makes a language and culture," then the distinction between "inside" and "outside" becomes pretty tenuous. But that does not weaken anti-intentionalism which is committed only to rejecting a narrowly defined class of "external" evidence, that of a psychological or "private" nature. It should be added that anti-intentionalism does not entail that inferences cannot be drawn from works to authors. Biographers can legitimately look to works to illuminate their subjects – with the provisos noted earlier – even if critics should be wary of drawing on biography to explain meaning.

The rejection of private external evidence has some affinities to the death-of-the-author doctrine that "writing [écriture] is the destruction of every voice, of every point of origin." Wimsatt and Beardsley state that a "poem … is detached from the author at birth … belongs to the public … [and] is embodied in language." A connection might be drawn between the notion of "internal evidence," where only the language itself and other texts are deemed legitimate sources for interpretation, and the Barthesian view of a text as "a multi-dimensional space in which a variety of writings, none of them original, blend and clash." If each text can be understood only in relation to another text (not grounded in a "point of origin") then the end result for Barthes is "the infinite deferment of the signified." This not only offers a new creative freedom for the reader but encourages criticism based on

[58] Wimsatt and Beardsley, "The Intentional Fallacy," p. 339.

"intertextuality," i.e., a juxtaposition of texts, and away from author-based psychology and biography. However, Wimsatt's and Beardsley's anti-intentionalism is not identical to Barthes's: the former applies exclusively to literary works, in virtue of an "autonomy" that sets literary discourse apart from ordinary discourse; the latter holds, indiscriminately, for all texts.

Poetic allusion is often thought to pose a problem for anti-intentionalism. To say that the line "Sweet Thames, run softly till I end my song" in *The Waste Land* alludes to Spenser's "Prothalamion" (Beardsley's example in "Intentions and Interpretations: A Fallacy Revived") seems to imply that T. S. Eliot intended to make this connection. Evidence that Eliot knew and admired Spenser's poetry would seem to count in favor of the allusion, whereas evidence that he knew nothing of Spenser would seem to count against it. However, the relation between allusion and intention is keenly debated. Could not an intended allusion *fail*, if no readers pick it up or it plays no significant or relevant role? Might not some allusions occur that are unknown to an author, grounded in a wider fabric of "intertextuality"? Is there not a distinction between an *author's* allusions and a *work's* allusions?

Take another example from Eliot, the opening of *The Waste Land*: "April is the cruelest month, breeding | Lilacs out of the dead land." For those with even a modest knowledge of English literature, the reference to April will resonate with another famous opening, that of Chaucer's *Canterbury Tales*: "Whan that April with his showres soote | The droughte of March hath perced to the roote." The resonance is present, a poignant contrast between the optimism of Chaucer and the gloom of Eliot, whatever is known about conscious intentions. It is, as it were, embedded in what Eliot calls the "tradition." The fact that the poem goes on to speak of "stirring | Dull roots with spring rain" reinforces the Chaucerian connection. In "The Intentional Fallacy" Wimsatt and Beardsley discuss at length the status of T. S. Eliot's notes to *The Waste Land*, where Eliot spells out his allusions (although not this one). Wimsatt and Beardsley argue that far from supporting simple intentionalism the case is complex and such notes "ought to be judged like any other parts of a composition."

    *5. Authors should not be confused with dramatic speakers.*

A central tenet of anti-intentionalism, as we saw earlier in relation to the depersonalization theory, is that even where a poem expresses personal emotions "we ought to impute the thoughts and attitudes of the poem imme-diately to the dramatic *speaker*, and if to the author at all, only by an act of biographical inference."[59] A claim about what a dramatic speaker in a poem feels or thinks, supported by poetic analysis, is fundamentally different from a claim about what the actual author feels or thinks, supported by "external

---

[59] Wimsatt and Beardsley, "The Intentional Fallacy," p. 335.

evidence." It is no part of literary criticism, according to the anti-intentionalist, to move from one to the other. Beardsley invokes the distinction between the *performance* of an illocutionary act (such as stating, questioning, commanding) and the *representation* of an illocutionary act. Lyric poems, he argues, are representations not performances. So when Wordsworth writes of England:

> she is a fen
> Of stagnant waters: altar, sword, and pen,
> Fireside, the heroic wealth of hall and bower,
> Have forfeited their ancient English dower
> Of inward happiness,

we should, on Beardsley's view, think of Wordsworth as "representing an illocutionary action of castigating England."[60] Whatever Wordsworth's actual feelings about England in 1802, the critic should concentrate on the feelings represented in the poem and attribute them to the speaker in the poem. While we might need to know that Wordsworth intended the lines to be a representation and not a performance, we do not need to know whether he intended to endorse the sentiments expressed.

6. *The literary work is a self-sufficient linguistic entity.*

Anti-intentionalism is often associated with a specific conception of the literary work. Beardsley postulates a Principle of Autonomy, according to which "literary works are self-sufficient entities, whose properties are decisive in checking interpretations and judgments."[61] These properties are essentially linguistic, not psychological. The poem is a "verbal icon," in the public realm, explicable exhaustively through the resources of "internal evidence." This is a clear example of how a theory of criticism connects with a theory of ontology (i.e., the mode of being of a work). However, there is nothing in the conception of literature as an institutional object that promotes a strong anti-intentionalism. Indeed, the idea that an author *invites* a certain kind of response in a reader is already a commitment to a version of intentionalism.

## The Intentionalist Response

Anti-intentionalism, of different strengths, became the unquestioned norm for a generation of critics after the publication of "The Intentional Fallacy," at

---

[60] Beardsley, "Intentions and Interpretations: A Fallacy Revived," p. 193.
[61] Beardsley, *Possibility of Criticism*, p. 16.

least to the extent that "poetic analysis" took precedence over biographical criticism. Curiously, though, whenever the theoretical issue came up, defenses of intentionalism would outnumber those of anti-intentionalism, at least among philosophers, as is evident from the two prominent anthologies on the topic, those of Newton-de Molina (1976) and Iseminger (1992).[62]

We should turn now to the pro-intention arguments, which again support a range of central claims:

A. *Intentions are not private and inaccessible.*

After the publication of Ludwig Wittgenstein's *Philosophical Investigations* (1953) and Gilbert Ryle's *Concept of Mind* (1949), philosophers became increasingly skeptical of mind – body dualism, epitomized by the writings of René Descartes, which postulated an elusive private domain of mental life. Description of a person's thoughts, desires, and intentions, on the preferred view, was not a guess at a mysterious inner world to which only that person had direct access but a complex judgment about the person's social interactions and observable responses.[63] Intentions became part of the publicly accessible realm, with the consequence, in the literary application, that to study the work was precisely to study the intention:

> The intention is evident in the work itself, and, insofar as the intention is identified as the purposive structure of the work, the intention is the focus of our interest in and attention to the artwork.[64]

Thus literary works were deemed as good an indicator of intention as any other manifest behavior. Rather than insisting on a sharp divide between the work and, in Wimsatt's and Beardsley's terms, "the design or plan in the author's mind," it was now possible to see the work as a manifestation of a complex intentional act. Just as we can observe in someone's action an intention to run away or to hit someone, so we can observe an intention to say or convey something in a poet's choice of words.

---

[62] Newton-de Molina, ed., *On Literary Intention*; Gary Iseminger, ed., *Intention and Interpretation* (Philadelphia. PA: Temple University Press, 1992).

[63] The first attempt to apply the view systematically to intentions comes in G. E. M. Anscombe, *Intention* (Oxford: Blackwell, 1959). Arguments applying it to literary criticism can be found in Frank Cioffi, "Intention and Interpretation in Criticism," in Newton-de Molina, ed., *On Literary Intention*; and in Colin Lyas, "Wittgensteinian Intentions," in Iseminger, ed., *Intention and Interpretation*.

[64] Noël Carroll, "Art, Intention, and Conversations," in Iseminger, ed., *Intention and Interpretation*, pp. 97–131. Reprinted in Carroll's *Beyond Aesthetics: Philosophical Essays* (Cambridge: Cambridge University Press, 2001), pp. 157–180 at p. 160.

Undoubtedly this behavioristic conception of the mind weakens anti-intentionalist claims about the unavailability of intention (see 1 above). But it does not in itself refute anti-intentionalism per se, for the further claims about kinds of evidence (4 above) and about the autonomy of the text (6 above) are unaffected. Also it might be argued that intention is not always observable in a work. The McGonagall case (in 2 above) might suggest that the text of a work could be neutral as to the kind of work it is. To discover the relevant kind we need to know external facts about its production.

B. *Meaning and intention are inseparable.*

Intentionalism has received support from developments in philosophy of language, as well as from philosophy of mind. Two philosophical views of language promote connections between meaning and intention: H. P. Grice's theory of "non-natural meaning" and J. L. Austin and J. R. Searle's speech act theory.[65] According to the former, all linguistic meaning must ultimately be explicable in terms of intention; according to the latter, intention has an essential role in the analysis of individual speech acts (such as promising, asserting, or questioning).

However, although these theories make it more acceptable to invoke intention in explanations of meaning, they do not in themselves resolve the debate about intention in literary criticism. At the heart of that debate is the question whether semantic or conventional meaning (bolstered by historical and literary resources) is *sufficient* to ground literary interpretation. Grice's distinction between sentence meaning and speaker's meaning (3 above) does not answer that question for it remains to be established whether interpretation is aimed at the former or the latter. And if Beardsley is right that authors do not perform speech acts but only represent the performance of speech acts (5 above) then the intentional nature of speech acts will again not be decisive.

The critic E. D. Hirsch in *Validity in Interpretation* (1967) offers one of the most systematic defenses of intentionalism[66] and addresses the sufficiency question head-on. His view, in direct opposition to Wimsatt and Beardsley, is that "a text means what its author meant." His argument rests on the

---

[65]   Grice, *Studies in the Way of Words*; Austin, *How to Do Things with Words*; J. R. Searle, *Speech Acts: An Essay in the Philosophy of Language* (Cambridge: Cambridge University Press, 1969).

[66]   Perhaps Hirsch's defense is the best known because it was the first. Other full-length defenses of intentionalism include P. D. Juhl, *Interpretation: An Essay in the Philosophy of Literary Criticism* (Princeton, NJ: Princeton University Press, 1980) and W. Irwin, *Intentionalist Interpretation: A Philosophical Explanation and Defense* (Westport, CT: Greenwood, 1999).

determinacy of meaning and the difference between what a text *can* mean and what it *does* mean. "Almost any word sequence can, under the conventions of meaning, legitimately represent more than one complex of meaning. A word sequence means nothing in particular until somebody means something by it."[67] He goes on:

> A determinate verbal meaning requires a determining will. Meaning is not made determinate simply by virtue of its being represented by a determinate sequence of words. … [U]nless one particular complex of meaning is *willed* … there would be no distinction between what an author does mean by a word sequence and what he could mean by it. Determinacy of meaning requires an act of will.[68]

Hirsch allows that a determinate meaning might nonetheless be ambiguous, where two meanings are simultaneously willed, and he insists on a distinction between meaning and *significance*, illustrating the latter by the well-known critical claim that Milton was "of the devil's party without knowing it," which, Hirsch believes, is not part of the meaning of *Paradise Lost* but has significance in relation to Milton's personality.[69] Significance is always significance *for* someone; it presupposes verbal meaning, and while the latter stays constant across readings, significance can change in different contexts.

Anti-intentionalists, however, question several of Hirsch's premises, notably the premise that there can be no determinate meaning without an act of will, and also the premise that for each work there is a "particular, self-identical, unchanging complex of meaning." Beardsley, for example, holds that textual meaning can change (3 above); he and Wimsatt contend that textual meaning can attain a degree of determinacy on its own. Barthes and the post-structuralists would view the very idea of determinate meaning with suspicion.

An even more radical form of intentionalism has been espoused by the critics Steven Knapp and Walter Benn Michaels in *Against Theory* (1985).[70] They have argued that there can be no "intentionless meaning," so Hirsch is wrong to imagine "a moment of interpretation before intention is present," i.e., a range of meanings (what a text *can* mean) waiting for an author's act of will (to generate what the text *does* mean). Even for a sequence of words to count

---

[67] E. D. Hirsch, Jr., *Validity in Interpretation* (New Haven, CT: Yale University Press, 1967), p. 4.

[68] Ibid., p. 47.

[69] Ibid., p. 63.

[70] Steven Knapp and Walter Benn Michaels "Against Theory," in W. J. T. Mitchell, ed., *Against Theory: Literary Studies and the New Pragmatism* (Chicago: University of Chicago Press, 1985).

as a sentence in a language, claim Knapp and Michaels, it must already have been produced by an agent with an intention. It is not clear how far this amounts to a rejection of the idea of semantic meaning or meaning in a language but it is hard to see how speakers could communicate without relying on some shared linguistic conventions (over and above intention). Without such reliance it is a short step from Knapp and Michaels back to Humpty Dumpty.

C. *Intentionalism rests on a distinction between sentence meaning, utterer's meaning, and utterance meaning.*

Conceptions of meaning in the literary context can sometimes seem too expansive, sometimes too arbitrary. On the Barthes/Foucault view, a "text" seems to have too much meaning, too many possible connotations. The interpreter has too many options and no constraints in narrowing them down. On the other hand, on the Knapp/Michaels view, the overriding control proposed for authorial intention seems to allow an author to mean anything at all. Using terminology from Grice (see 3 above) we might associate the former kind of meaning with "sentence meaning," the latter with "utterer's (or speaker's) meaning." The former leaves out intention altogether (except in the broader Gricean context of explaining how sentences come to have meaning in the first place), the latter makes intention paramount. Sentence meaning is determined by the semantics and syntax of a language, utterer's (or speaker's) meaning is whatever meaning a speaker intends to convey on a specific occasion (like the sarcasm case in 3 above).

Many intentionalists prefer to appeal to "utterance meaning," which lies somewhere in between. Although construed in slightly different ways by different theorists, the basic idea is that utterance meaning is contextualized meaning, a combination of what a speaker intended and linguistic conventions.[71] With semantically or syntactically ambiguous sentences – "flying

---

[71] Robert Stecker: "work meaning [i.e., utterance meaning] is a function of both the actual intentions of artists and the conventions in place when the work is created": in R. Stecker, *Interpretation and Construction: Art, Speech, and the Law* (Oxford: Blackwell, 2003), p. 42. Jerrold Levinson: "the meaning a linguistic vehicle has in a given context of presentation or projection, a context that arguably includes, in addition to directly observable features of the act of utterance, something of the characteristics of the author who projects the text, something of the text's place in a surrounding oeuvre and culture, and possibly other elements as well": in "Intention and Interpretation in Literature," in *The Pleasures of Aesthetics: Philosophical Essays* (Ithaca, NY: Cornell University Press, 1996), p. 178. William Tolhurst: "utterance meaning is to be construed as that hypothesis of utterer's meaning which most justified on the basis of those beliefs and attitudes which one possesses qua intended hearer or intended reader": in "On What a Text Is and How It Means," *British Journal of Aesthetics*, vol. 19, no. 1 (1979), p. 13.

planes can be dangerous" – utterance meaning selects from one of the standard meanings, determined by context. But utterance meaning can never be as permissive as utterer's meaning, at least in blocking the Humpty Dumpty option whereby someone can mean "There's a nice knock-down argument for you" in saying "There's glory for you."

The anti-intentionalist is not too remote from the intentionalist who appeals to utterance meaning. Both hold that literary meaning is contextualized and both can maintain determinacy of meaning, rejecting the extreme "free-for-all" anti-intentionalism of Barthes and Foucault. For the (modest) anti-intentionalist the literary context is itself rich enough to select relevant meanings without needing to appeal to external evidence of an author's intentions. Even Wimsatt and Beardsley admit that intentions can be realized in works; those intentions are admissible, being revealed through internal evidence. The issue between the two camps comes down to how to handle the relatively rare cases where the internal evidence is neutral as to alternative readings. The intentionalist looks for evidence elsewhere for what was in the author's mind; the anti-intentionalist settles, in such cases alone, for indeterminacy.

D. *Intentionalism admits of two varieties: actual intentionalism and hypothetical intentionalism.*

A recent debate among philosophers (prominent in Iseminger's anthology *Intention and Interpretation*) pits "hypothetical intentionalism" against the "actual intentionalism" of writers like Hirsch and Knapp and Michaels. The philosopher Noël Carroll defends a "modest" version of "actual intentionalism," one that is distanced from Humpty Dumpty-ism, arguing that "the correct interpretation of a text is the meaning of the text that is compatible with the author's actual intentions."[72] This looks like a version of utterance meaning, not least in stressing the important role of standard textual meanings. The principal support for "modest actual intentionalism" is the thought that readers have a "conversational interest" in literary works and quite properly seek to grasp what the author aims to communicate. Setting aside obvious differences between two people in a conversation and a reader engaging with a text, there is a core of commonality, on this view, in the shared idea of a "prospect of community."[73]

"Hypothetical intentionalism," notably defended by the philosophers William E. Tolhurst and Jerrold Levinson, challenges even Carroll's "modest"

---

[72] Noël Carroll, "Interpretation and Intention: The Debate between Hypothetical and Actual Intentionalism," in *Beyond Aesthetics*, p. 198.

[73] Carroll, "Art, Intention, and Conversation," p. 174.

position by associating literary meaning with a kind of "utterance meaning" at one remove from an author's actual intentions and defined as "our best appropriately informed projection of [an] author's intended meaning from our positions as intended interpreters."[74] In other words a critic's task is to *hypothesize* an author's intention from the point of view of an ideal member of the intended audience fully informed about "the work's internal structure and the relevant surrounding context of creation." Of course, most of the time these hypothesized intentions will coincide with actual intentions, but they need not: "if we can make the author out to have created a cleverer or more striking or more imaginative piece, without violating the image of his oeuvre underpinned by the total available textual and contextual evidence, we should perhaps do so."[75] Hypothetical intentionalism is offered as a compromise between intentionalism and anti-intentionalism, capturing important features of both. However, to the extent that hypothesized intentions might pull apart from actual intentions it seems questionable whether hypothetical intentionalism really is a version of intentionalism at all.

The strength of hypothetical intentionalism is that it acknowledges something distinctive about literary interpretation as not simply a more complex instance of grasping someone's meaning in a conversation. Here is Levinson, in defense of hypothetical intentionalism:

> Although in informative discourse we rightly look for intended meaning first ..., in literary art we are licensed, if I am right, to consider what meanings the verbal text before us, viewed in context, *could* be being used to convey, and then to form, if we can, in accord with the practice of literary communication to which both author and reader have implicitly subscribed, our best hypothesis of what it is being used to convey ...[76]

Levinson is appealing to a practice associated with the reading of literature which he believes differs, with regard to the role of intentions, from the practice of ordinary conversations. Carroll's objection is that in characterizing this practice Levinson is "making some extremely substantial empirical claims about the nature of our literary practices," and he, Carroll, is "not convinced that the evidence will bear out these claims."[77]

However, even if the evidence from critical practice is inconclusive as between the two kinds of intentionalism, the evidence is surely overwhelming in another respect, namely that literary works, apart from the question of

---

[74] Jerrold Levinson, "Intention and Interpretation in Literature", p. 178.

[75] Ibid., p. 179.

[76] Ibid., p. 198.

[77] Carroll, "Interpretation and Intention," p. 207.

intention, are *not* treated as though they were contributions to a conversation. The kinds of comments that are standard in literary interpretation, the kinds of interest taken, the focus of attention, are radically different from those common among participants of conversations. Also, it is odd even to speak of *interpretation* in a conversational context. Only exceptionally would interpretation be necessary or appropriate for a remark in a conversation and would be called for only on occasions when conversations break down (with the suspicion, for example, that things are being hinted at, not honestly or straightforwardly spoken). Normally conversational remarks are grasped (their meaning grasped) and responses elicited without any deep reflection, and without any need for *interpreting*.

The critic Umberto Eco defends a position comparable to hypothetical intentionalism in proposing what he calls the *intentio operis*, or intention of the work. "The intention of the text," he writes, "is basically to produce a model reader able to make conjectures about it."[78] On Eco's view, the criterion for checking conjectures is grounded in holism or coherence, as derived from Augustine's *De doctrina christiana*: "any interpretation given of a certain portion of a text can be accepted if it is confirmed by, and must be rejected if it is challenged by, another portion of the same text. In this sense the internal textual coherence controls the otherwise uncontrollable drives of the reader."[79]

E. *Connections between a work and its author are ineliminable.*

Intentionalists will often insist that however much the literary work is viewed as an "autonomous" verbal structure, and however desirable or otherwise that might be, nonetheless in certain aspects the presence of the actual, as opposed to "implied," author is ineliminable. A distinction is sometimes drawn between an author's "categorial" intentions and his or her "semantic" intentions.[80] The latter concern textual meaning at a sentential or work-wide level, and much of the debate over the Intentional Fallacy has focused on them. The former are not strictly *meaning* intentions at all but involve the very categories into which texts are placed. While arguably an author's semantic intentions might fail (through linguistic misuse or clumsy expression) or might not adequately determine textual meaning, more basic categorial intentions, determining what *kind* of work it is, do seem definitive. Whether a work is fiction or non-fiction, a poem or an entry in a diary, is determined by an author's categorial intentions; these intentions must be

---

[78]  Umberto Eco et al., *Interpretation and Overinterpretation*, ed. Stefan Collini (Cambridge: Cambridge University Press, 1992), p. 64.

[79]  Ibid., p. 65.

[80]  See Levinson, "Intention and Interpretation in Literature," pp. 188–189.

known, according to the intentionalist, before interpretation can proceed. Perhaps the William McGonagall case (2 above) should be treated as an example of categorial intentions. We must know, arguably, what category – serious verse, parody, humor – McGonagall intended for his lines before we are in a position to judge them.

There seems no easy way to resolve the debate between intentionalists and anti-intentionalists. This is partly, as noted, because the debate involves deep disagreements about the nature of literature and of criticism. But it is partly because there is uncertainty about where the nub of the debate lies. Is it primarily about *meaning*? Is it about the nature of *intention* – for example, how mentalistically it should be conceived? Is it about the *autonomy* of the work? Is it about the kinds of *evidence* that a critic can legitimately call on in critical judgments? It just seems obvious to the intentionalist that *what the author intended*, however that is determined, is a crucial constraint in our understanding of a literary work. Equally, it seems obvious to the anti-intentionalist that *the work must speak for itself*, that if an author's intentions are not recoverable from the work and need to be discovered independently then they cannot be relevant to our understanding and will distract us into biography and gossip.

It should be noted that most of the time this theoretical issue need not impinge on critical practice. For most of the time what the author intended coincides with what is recoverable from the work. It is only in rare cases where these pull apart. If we take intention to be literally "what was in the author's mind" (however that might be construed) then there are two eventualities:

I. A thought or idea or meaning might have been in the author's mind but there is no independent evidence for this in the work, or

II. A thought or idea or meaning might appear to be in a work but there is no independent evidence that this had ever been in the author's mind.

Critics' attitudes to these two possibilities tend to indicate their stance on intentionalism. An intentionalist would be inclined to hold about (I) that the thought, idea, or meaning might nonetheless be relevant to interpretation of the work, while the thought, idea, or meaning in (II) should be eliminated; the anti-intentionalist would be inclined to endorse exactly the opposite.

However, if this does highlight one of the major sources of disagreement, then it serves conveniently to locate the issues in the broader context of critical practice. Now we see that (I) is just a particular instance of the wider debate about the relevance of biographical information among other kinds of "external evidence," while (II), not entirely unrelated, is an application of the debate about criteria for validity in interpretation.

Only by looking at critical practice itself can we see exactly what impact these debates have.

## Supplementary Readings

For a helpful survey of literary critical debates about the author, see Andrew Bennett, *The Author* (The New Critical Idiom, London: Routledge, 2005). On issues relating to biography and criticism, the seminal text is E. M. W. Tillyard and C. S. Lewis, *The Personal Heresy: A Controversy* (London: Oxford University Press, 1939). For philosophical discussion of ideas arising from T. S. Eliot's notion of the "impersonality" of literature and the role of "tradition," see Richard Shusterman, *T. S. Eliot and the Philosophy of Criticism* (London: Duckworth, 1988). On the idea of the "implied author," see Wayne Booth, *Rhetoric of Fiction* (Chicago: University of Chicago Press, rev. ed., 1983).

A valuable collection of papers on the "the death of the author," including the seminal articles by Roland Barthes and Michel Foucault, is: William Irwin, ed., *The Death and Resurrection of the Author* (Westport, CT: Greenwood Press, 2002). For discussion of the issue from a literary point of view, see Sean Burke, *The Death and Return of the Author* (New York: Columbia University Press, 2nd ed., 1998).

On the Intentional Fallacy, two collections of papers are of particular note: David Newton-de Molina, ed., *On Literary Intention* (Edinburgh: Edinburgh University Press, 1976), containing W. K. Wimsatt and M. C. Beardsley's original article "The Intentional Fallacy" and W. K. Wimsatt's "Genesis: A Fallacy Revisited"; and Gary Iseminger, ed., *Intention and Interpretation* (Philadelphia, PA: Temple University Press, 1992), containing papers by philosophers airing, among other things, the debate between "hypothetical" and "actual" intentionalism. The most influential book-length defense of intentionalism is E. D. Hirsch, Jr., *Validity in Interpretation* (New Haven, CT: Yale University Press, 1967). The anti-intentionalist case, addressing Hirsch, is succinctly put by Monroe C. Beardsley in *The Possibility of Criticism* (Detroit, MI: Wayne State University Press, 1970). Other treatments include: W. J. T. Mitchell, ed., *Against Theory: Literary Studies and the New Pragmatism* (Chicago: University of Chicago Press, 1985); Umberto Eco et al., *Interpretation and Overinterpretation*, ed. Stefan Collini (Cambridge: Cambridge University Press, 1992); William Irwin, *Intentionalist Interpretation: A Philosophical Explanation and Defense* (Westport, CT: Greenwood, 1999); Robert Stecker, *Artworks: Definition, Meaning, Value* (University Park, PA: Penn State University Press, 1997); Michael Krausz, ed., *Is There a Single Right Interpretation?* (University Park, PA: Penn State Press, 2002); Paisley Livingston, *Art and Intention: A Philosophical Study* (New York: Oxford University Press, 2005).

# Chapter Four
## Practice

We return to our central question: what is it to read a literary work *as a work of art*? Just as literary works themselves are distinctive among modes of discourse, so practices of reading are also distinctive. Reading is purposive, and readers come to texts with expectations of certain kinds of rewards. Reading a letter, a manual for dishwashers, a philosophical essay, or a police summons are quite different exercises; they satisfy different interests, and call for different modes of attention. What kind of attention does a literary work invite?

## Autonomy in the Practice of Reading

We examined in Chapter 3 attempts by the New Critics to establish the "autonomy" of the work. On strong versions of autonomy a literary work is conceived as a free-standing, self-sufficient "verbal icon," whose linguistic properties alone give it the interest and character that it possesses. But the limits of this view are apparent, for it tells us little about what kind of interest or character we should seek. If literary works are merely undifferentiated texts, or strings of sentences, or *écriture*, meaning all that the words in them could mean, it is impossible to see why they should have any special value.

Only by locating works in a wider "institutional" framework, as proposed in Chapter 2, can we see why literary works should engage readers and be sought after. So rather than stressing the autonomy of the individual work it seems more fruitful to emphasize the autonomy of the *practice* within which the works are read. What makes literary works distinctive is closely connected to what makes the reading practice distinctive when the works are read as literature. Exploring such a practice is the key to understanding what gives literary works the value and interest they have.

### The scope of "literary criticism"

An immediate objection to this way of proceeding is that there is no distinctive practice in reading literary works. People read in all kinds of ways, they bring all kinds of interests to bear on the works they read. To think otherwise is to endorse a totally unjustifiable essentialism in literary criticism. The objection is important but not insurmountable. In fact, if it cannot be met there are dire consequences for literary criticism itself. If there are not some distinctive and universally acknowledged features of a "literary" reading of a text, in contrast to other kinds of interests in the text, then there is no such thing as literary criticism and perhaps no such thing as "literature" either. There are, of course, those who take this extreme position but there is no empirical support for it in what critics actually do, nor does it have theoretical foundation.

The objection to "essentialism" about literary criticism has been pressed by Richard Rorty, who offers this account of how criticism has extended its bounds:

> It [i.e., literary criticism] originally meant comparison and evaluation of plays, poems, and novels — with perhaps an occasional glance at the visual arts. Then it got extended to cover past criticism (for example, Dryden's, Shelley's, Arnold's, and Eliot's prose, as well as their verse). Then, quite quickly, it got extended to the books which had supplied past critics with their critical vocabulary and were supplying present critics with theirs. This meant extending it to theology, philosophy, social theory, reformist political programs, and revolutionary manifestos. In short, it meant extending it to every book likely to provide candidates for a person's final vocabulary.[1]

But there is confusion here. Literary critics might well find themselves reading theology, philosophy, or revolutionary manifestos, but it does not mean that they regard these as works of *literary criticism*, far less that they are reading them as *literature* on a par with plays, poems, and novels. Also, literary critics can engage in other kinds of writing than literary criticism, as many of the most prominent critics did, from Dr. Johnson to T. S. Eliot. There is no reason to label all of their written work, any more than all of their reading, as literary criticism. As Stanley Fish puts it, defending the autonomy of critical practice: "Once you turn … from actually performing literary criticism to examining the 'network of forces and factors' that underlie the performance, literary criticism is no longer what you are performing."[2] Of course serious questions remain about the bounds of literary criticism but these cannot be determined solely by facts about what appears on reading lists.

[1]  Richard Rorty, *Contingency, Irony, and Solidarity* (Cambridge: Cambridge University Press, 1989), p. 81.
[2]  Stanley Fish, *There's No Such Thing as Free Speech, and It's a Good Thing Too* (New York: Oxford University Press, 1994), p. 240.

A related objection to an inquiry into the practice of criticism is based on the multiplicity of critical "approaches." How could there be core or essential features of critical practice when critics approach texts with such different critical presuppositions? We have listed before the usual stock of "approaches": Marxist, cultural materialist, structuralist, deconstructionist, psychoanalytic, feminist, New Critical. These differences are real and focus on different aspects of literary works and their contexts, but the philosopher of literature is concerned with underlying commonality. What makes these "approaches" all instances of "literary criticism"? It might be that in certain cases it is not beyond dispute that they are properly labeled as such or that the focus is sufficiently on the works *as literature* to merit the attention of the philosopher of literature. For example, the psychoanalytic critic whose sole focus is on what the work tells us about the author's unconscious or repressed desires might not be engaged in literary criticism properly so called.[3] It is important, though, not to beg the question.

It must be kept in mind what kind of inquiry we are engaged in. It is not an empirical survey of styles of literary criticism or an attempt to extract general principles from existing practice. It is rather to ask fundamental questions about what must be the case, minimally, for literature to be considered an art form. If literary works are works of art then it would be reasonable to expect them to invite a certain kind of attention not dissimilar from that associated with other forms of art. Of course if it turned out that practicing critics never do give works that kind of attention then the exercise is futile. Two possible conclusions would be drawn: either that critics simply do not treat literary works as works of art (they always have different interests in mind) or the projected conditions for doing so have been wrongly identified. Clearly there must be a constraint from actual practice, and it is important not to be too aprioristic in our procedure. But should it turn out that some of what critics do some of the time is not in line with treating works as works of art, that would not itself undermine the inquiry. This is not to be prescriptive about responses to literature, for there can be no objection to readers responding in any way they like. But it is to say that not any kind of response counts as a *literary* or *artistic* response, or a response to a work *as literature*.

A brief word should be interjected, before the inquiry starts, on the relation between "reader" and "literary critic." These terms have been used more or less interchangeably, yet it could be argued that while all literary critics are readers not all readers are literary critics. Is it the practice of professional

---

[3]　See Peter Lamarque, "On the Irrelevance of Psychoanalysis to Literary Criticism," in Peter Clark and Crispin Wright, eds., *Mind, Psychoanalysis and Science* (Oxford: Basil Blackwell, 1988), pp. 257–273.

criticism that is being explored or some wider practice of reading not directly linked to academic or scholarly activity? In fact the underlying assumption in the inquiry is that there is no sharp line between the practice of criticism, broadly conceived, and the responses of an educated reading public with an interest in art and literature. The kind of literary "appreciation" to be characterized is not unduly recondite or hard to achieve; it does not call on specialist or technical know-how or on theoretical frameworks essentially rooted in other areas of academic inquiry, such as psychoanalysis, Marxist theory, sociology, philosophy, or linguistics. Those modes of criticism that demand esoteric vocabulary or specialist theoretical knowledge cannot be seen as continuous with a tradition of reading that rests on pleasures of a more universal kind associated with literary art.[4]

This tradition ultimately draws on what Dr. Johnson calls the "common reader":

> I rejoice to concur with the common reader; for by the common sense of readers, uncorrupted by literary prejudices, after all the refinements of subtilty and the dogmatism of learning, must be finally decided all claim to poetical honours.[5]

Virginia Woolf expounds on this notion:

> The common reader, as Dr. Johnson implies, differs from the critic and the scholar. He is worse educated, and nature has not gifted him so generously. He reads for his own pleasure rather than to impart knowledge or correct the opinions of others. Above all, he is guided by an instinct to create for himself, out of whatever odds and ends he can come by, some kind of whole — a portrait of a man, a sketch of an age, a theory of the art of writing.[6]

The pleasures of literature are not restricted to a minority of specialists. But that is not to say that readers cannot get more or less out of their reading or that literary reading is not subject to improvement or training. The literary critic is simply a reader who has more experience and heightened perceptiveness than the "common reader"; the critic is further along the path toward David Hume's "true judges," who we shall discuss in Chapter 7. But if there were no common readers there would be no literary critics

---

[4] See Stein Haugom Olsen, "On Unilluminating Criticism," in *The End of Literary Theory* (Cambridge: Cambridge University Press, 1987).

[5] Samuel Johnson, "The Life of Gray," *Samuel Johnson: A Critical Edition of the Major Works*, ed. Donald Greene (Oxford: Oxford University Press, 1984), p. 768.

[6] Virginia Woolf, *The Common Reader*, First Series (1925) (London: The Hogarth Press, 1957), p. 11.

and ultimately no literary works. The institution of literature demands a community of readers with a shared interest in the values that literature can afford. It is unlikely the institution could be sustained only by a small clerisy of experts.

## The search for meaning

It is sometimes supposed that the search for *meaning* is the fundamental task of literary criticism and issues about where that meaning is located and how best to recover it are fundamental to any theorizing about literature. That is why the intention issue has been given such high priority. Under closer scrutiny, though, it becomes apparent that the picture is not quite so clear-cut, the pursuit of meaning not quite so central, or unequivocal, both for criticism and for theory, as it might at first seem. Questions about meaning are inextricably tied to wider aspects of the critical enterprise. Yet, on the face of it, it might seem strange that the overriding goal of criticism should be a grasp of what a work *means*. Normally we ask what something means not as an end in itself but with some further end in view: to guide action or facilitate response or simply to clear up misunderstanding. Admittedly meaning is a flexible and multivalent concept and there is a sense in which it connotes the "point" of something, what that thing seeks to achieve. Such a conception might well be central to critical practice. However, those who stress the pursuit of meaning in criticism, placing emphasis on semantic or pragmatic meaning, give the impression that literary works are puzzles to be solved more than experiences to be undergone. The focus is changed if we think of such works as works of art to be appreciated.

Part of what is involved in appreciating a work of art as a work of art is to appreciate it as an artifact designed for a purpose. If that sounds too intentionalistic then we should recall the notion of "categorial intentions" as opposed to meaning intentions. In making a work of art, an artist offers the work for artistic appreciation. That does not yet settle what constraints apply in interpretation, or at least it implies only that the constraints are those conventionally associated with artistic practice (what those constraints are might be debatable). In offering a work as literature an author invites attention to the work appropriate to that broad "category." We shall see what such attention is as we proceed.

Expanding on the two dimensions of literary art identified in Chapter 2 – the *imaginative–creative* dimension and the *content* dimension – it seems that the following, at least, are relevant to attending to literature as art, not all of which give focus to "meaning" in any narrowly linguistic sense:

- a heightened awareness of form and structure and the "design" of the whole;
- an expectation of coherence and inner connectedness;
- an expectation that the work presents a subject of some interest, either through narrative content, imagined emotion, or metaphoric illustration; and
- an expectation that the work exhibits and develops organizing principles or themes that provide unity and value in the work beyond the immediacy of the subject, inviting reflection on matters of more universal human concern.

## Exploring Form and Structure

Part of what it is to appreciate a work as literature is to appreciate it as an artifact, as a linguistic structure. This is comparable to appreciating the structure of a painting or a symphony. We ask: how does it *work*? How do the elements hang together to produce the desired effect? This is as true for narrative prose (the novel or short story) as for poetry or drama. All kinds of literary works are structured designs, and critics – whatever "approach" they adopt – will attend to structure and will adopt a *Principle of Functionality* that states that all aspects of the design can be presumed to fulfill a purpose. Again this need not be read intentionalistically, in the sense that the author must have envisaged (have in mind) a purpose for each element, but it means that readers should assume that there is no arbitrariness in the design. Even works that play on an apparently whimsical disorderliness – like *Tristram Shandy* or the novels of Alain Robbe-Grillet – should be read as structured wholes.

To ask about the structure of a work is not, in the first instance, to ask about meaning. Nor is it merely a matter of conjecture. Much structural analysis is purely descriptive. But a work's structure is only of interest to the extent that it contributes to a further achievement. Too much structural complexity can be a barrier to a work's success. Analysing a work's formal features is a stage toward a wider assessment of the work's interest and value.

### Formal analysis

Whether a work is a sonnet, of Italian (Petrachian) or English (Elizabethan), structure, whether lines are in iambic pentameters, whether a rhyme scheme is *abab* and the endings masculine or feminine, or whether a narrative is in the first or third person, are matters of fact rather than interpretation. They are not conjectured but discovered. Often formal features of this kind require little skill to identify, yet it can be important to take note of them as a first step to a fuller appreciation of the work. All texts have formal or rhetorical features but with literary works these are associated with some further end which makes them significant and invites attention to them.

Take as an example Edmund Spenser's poem *Epithalamion* (1595). In order to appreciate this work it is important to know certain facts about its form and the history of that form. In brief, the epithalamian genre was a highly conventionalized poetic form, popular in the Renaissance, written to celebrate weddings. The inspiration came from a Latin poem *Epithalamium* (ode no. 61) by the Roman poet Catullus (c. 84 – c. 54 BC). The conventions of the genre involve both content and poetic device. Spenser's poem follows convention in many respects. Conventional *topoi*, or familiar subjects, for example, are covered:

> the "maske" of Hymen; the attendance of the Graces upon the bride; the praise of the bride's beauty; the impatience with the tardy sun; the greeting of Hesperus; the bedding of the bridal couple, with the injunction to break off the revelry; the concluding invocations which replace the *allocutio sponsalis*.[7]

These are not work-specific but genre-specific features. What is of interest is not that they are present but how they are handled. However, it is important also to note that Spenser breaks with convention in several ways: he fuses the roles of bridegroom and poet-speaker, and he employs an unusual stanza form, derived from the Italian *canzone*. The final, shortest, stanza, "the concluding brief address to the poem, the envoy, was characteristic of the *canzone* and was called technically a *tornata* or *commiato*."[8]

In this description of the form and its conventions several technical terms are used. They belong in the literary critic's toolkit. In themselves they are not essential to appreciating the poem and might not be available to the "common reader." But for a full appreciation of the work's literary qualities the conventional aspects to which they refer are inescapable if the work is to be properly located, i.e., understood, in the right *category*. The terms provide a backdrop for more speculative – and more intriguing – reflections on the poem's form. For example, it has been suggested that the 24 stanzas – a higher number than usual in the *canzone* – represent hours in the day, and, no doubt more tendentiously, that

> the refrain, consistently positive for sixteen stanzas, is put negatively thereafter, an arrangement corresponding to the hours of light and darkness in southern

---

[7] Thomas M. Greene, "Spenser and the Epithalamic Convention," in *Edmund Spenser's Poetry*, sel. and ed. Hugh Maclean (New York: W. W. Norton, 1968), p. 645.

[8] Greene, "Spenser and the Epithalamic Convention," p. 646.

Ireland [where the poem is set and the wedding takes place] at the summer solstice; there are 365 "long lines" (lines of five feet or more) in the poem.[9]

Locating Spenser's *Epithalamion* in a conventionalized genre, and noting where it departs from certain of the conventions, aids appreciation of the poet's achievement. The formal features contribute to other poetic effects.

Formal features also appear at the level of thought and diction. To change the example, consider Shakespeare's Sonnet 4, which is not one of the better known:

> Unthrifty loveliness, why dost thou spend
> Upon thyself thy beauty's legacy?
> Nature's bequest gives nothing, but doth lend,
> And, being frank, she lends to those are free.
> Then, beauteous niggard, why dost thou abuse
> The bounteous largess given thee to give?
> Profitless usurer, why dost thou use
> So great a sum of sums, yet canst not live?
> For, having traffic with thyself alone,
> Thou of thyself thy sweet self dost deceive.
> Then how when nature calls thee to be gone?
> What acceptable audit canst thou leave?
>    Thy unus'd beauty must be tomb'd with thee,
>    Which, used, lives, th'executor to be.

Here is a critic's commentary on some of the formal structures in the poem:

> Firstly, the imagery of financial matters is sustained throughout. Secondly, there is within this integrated scheme a number of strongly marked subsidiary systems. The most immediately striking, which may therefore be cited first, is the ringing of the changes in lines 5–8 on "abuse"— "usurer"— "use," which is taken up in the couplet by "unus'd," "used." Another marked system is that of the reflexive constructions associated with "thee": "spend upon thyself"— "traffic with thyself"— "Thou of thyself thy sweet self dost deceive," taken up in the couplet by "thy … beauty … tomb'd with thee." That these are deliberate systems, not inept repetitions, is proved by the way they interlock in the couplet: "unus'd" is, in the first line of the couplet, linked with "thy beauty … tomb'd with thee," and this contrasts with the second line of the couplet, where there is a linking of "used," "executor," and "lives," to produce the complete formal balance in thought, diction and syntax, of:

> > Thy unus'd beauty must be tomb'd with thee,
> > Which, used, lives, th'executor to be.

[9] Editorial comment in *Edmund Spenser's Poetry*, sel. and ed. Maclean, p. 447.

This formal balance is of course closely related to the thought of the sonnet: Nature, which lends beauty in order that it may be given, is contrasted with the youth, whose self-regarding results in a usurious living on capital alone, which is a negation of Nature and of life; these paradoxes of the thought make possible the correspondences and contrasts of the verbal systems. ... We may note, then, that "Unthrifty loveliness," with which the sonnet opens, is, as it were, a first blending of those two distinct voices, "why dost thou spend upon thyself" and "Nature's bequest." The second quatrain blends them again in "beauteous niggard," which is itself an inversion, formally complete, of "unthrifty loveliness," and moreover an inversion which leads on to the extreme of "profitless usurer"; further, the movement toward the judgment represented by "profitless usurer" has all the while been less obtrusively going on in the verbs as well as in the vocatives ("spend" — "abuse" — "yet canst not live"). Then, with "yet canst not live," the sonnet brings out the second voice, that reflexive (and self-destructive) action announced in "spend upon thyself," but kept low in the first eight lines, maintaining itself there only by the formal parallels of "why dost thou spend" — "why dost thou abuse" — "why dost thou use." This voice now emerges predominant in "For, having traffic with thyself alone," and this voice in turn reaches its extreme of formal development in the line "Thou of thyself thy sweet self dost deceive."[10]

A number of points arise from this extended quotation (itself only part of a fuller analysis). The first is the distinctive and peculiar nature of this kind of analysis. Although it is familiar to trained readers of poetry it is not a mode of commentary much found in other contexts. Only on the assumption that the subject is a poem is such a minute concern with formal structure either desirable or fruitful. It would not be appropriate for a passage of philosophical or historical prose, unless, for whatever reason, a literary interest was taken in the passage.

Second, although the analysis is an integral part of literary criticism, when applied to poetry of this kind, it is not strictly interpretation or even a search for meaning. The formal organization of the poem is being identified, telling us something of how the poem works *as a poem*. While it might be possible to dispute some of the observations made, disagreements are likely to rest more on issues of *relevance* or *emphasis* than on objective existence or even authorial intention. It seems relatively unproblematic to say that the structures are discovered, not imposed, even if they exist as emergent properties, acquiring salience under a literary critical perspective.

Third, the analysis is not yet an end in itself. There is little intrinsic interest in identifying formal juxtapositions for its own sake. There needs to be a

---

[10]   Winifred M. T. Nowottny, "Formal Elements in Shakespeare's Sonnets: Sonnets I–IV," in William Shakespeare, *The Sonnets* (New York: Signet Classics, 1964), pp. 227–228. Originally published in *Essays in Criticism*, II ( January, 1952), pp. 76–84.

further point in doing so. This is where the question of relevance arises. What functions are the formal devices playing? What do they contribute to the work itself? One answer might be offered in simple aesthetic terms: "this sonnet, which in its absence of visual imagery has little attraction for the hasty reader, reveals itself to analysis as having an intricate beauty of form to which it would be hard to find a parallel in the work of any other poet."[11] The analysis also aids "a fuller understanding of Shakespeare's means of communication and a fuller possession of those poetic experiences with which the *Sonnets* deal."[12] The beauty and value of the poem are displayed in its intricate organization.

Fourth, although form is not in itself an aspect of meaning, there is a connection between form and meaning (or "thought"). Formal features in poetry nearly always, as in this case, play some role in the expression of thought. The critic notes how the syntactic and imagistic juxtapositions mirror the principal thematic balance between Nature and the poem's youthful protagonist: "Nature, which lends beauty in order that it may be given, is contrasted with the youth, whose self-regarding results in a usurious living on capital alone, which is a negation of Nature and of life." Again the relevance of the form is established by connecting it to one of the poem's broader themes.[13] This time the aim is not beauty but meaning.

## Explication

Beyond form, there is a level of critical commentary which is concerned directly with meaning. It is sometimes called "explication" and it focuses, as Monroe Beardsley puts it, on "relatively localized parts" of works.[14] Explication, in this sense, has two principal aims: identifying unusual, idiomatic, or problematic usages, and exploring ranges of connotations or symbolism, notably in poetry.

Consider again Spenser's *Epithalamion*, stanza 10:

> TELL me ye merchants daughters did ye see
> So fayre a creature in your towne before,
> So sweet, so lovely, and so mild as she,
> Adornd with beautyes grace and vertues store,          170

---

[11]   Ibid., p. 229.

[12]   Ibid., p. 231.

[13]   Arguably there are other, not least sexual, connotations and themes in the sonnet, which are unremarked in Nowottny's analysis. I owe the point to David Williams.

[14]   Monroe C. Beardsley, *Aesthetics: Problems in the Philosophy of Criticism*, 2nd ed. (Indianapolis, IN: Hackett, 1981), p. 130.

Her goodly eyes lyke Saphyres shining bright,
Her forehead yvory white,
Her cheekes lyke apples which the sun hath rudded,
Her lips lyke cherryes charming men to byte,
Her brest like to a bowle of creame uncrudded,
Her paps lyke lyllies budded,
Her snowie necke lyke to a marble towre,
And all her body like a pallace fayre,
Ascending uppe with many a stately stayre,
To honors seat and chastities sweet bowre.                      180
Why stand ye still ye virgins in amaze,
Upon her so to gaze,
Whiles ye forget your former lay to sing,
To which the woods did answer and your eccho ring?

For a modern reader help with sixteenth-century vocabulary is needed: "store" means "wealth," "rudded" means "reddened," "uncrudded" means "uncurdled." A good explicator will notice that line 177 is an allusion to Song of Solomon vii, 4: "Thy neck is as a tower of ivory." One textual commentator adds: "The scriptural allusion is appropriately placed, concluding the catalogue of physical attractions (for which Spenser draws on the conventions of classical and Renaissance precedents), and looking on to an account of beauty far more significantly powerful and directive."[15] Again, the highly conventionalized element in Spenser's description of female beauty must be noted. (We are reminded of the contextualist's insistence on the historical embeddedness of works – these lines can be understood properly only when grounded in the context of late-sixteenth-century poetry.) Line 180 refers to the head or seat of reason. What is notable overall is that the literal meaning of these lines is otherwise not difficult to discern. The explicator's task in this case is a kind of archaeology, recovering hidden or lost information.

Sometimes a critic will explicate a line by noticing an ambiguity or "richness" that might escape an inattentive reader. Speaking of the line in the final stanza of Keats's "Ode on a Grecian Urn," "When old age shall this generation waste," the critic Cleanth Brooks remarks: "The word 'generation' … is very rich. It means on one level 'that which is generated' — that which springs from human loins — Adam's breed; and yet, so intimately is death wedded to men, the word 'generation' itself has become, as here, a measure of time."[16]

Sometimes poetic meaning is much more elusive, as with these lines from Louis MacNeice:

---

[15]   *Edmund Spenser's Poetry*, sel. and ed. Maclean, p. 438.
[16]   Cleanth Brooks, *The Well Wrought Urn* (London: Methuen, 1960), pp. 133–134.

> One was found like Judas kissing flowers
> And one who sat between the clock and the sun
> Lies like a Saint Sebastian full of arrows
> Feathered from his own hobby, his pet hours.[17]

Here the critic has to rely on the poet's own explication:

> MacNeice tells us that his poem is in praise of those who live by routine. ...
> The image of the man kissing flowers is meant to depict a person who has
> neglected his routine duties for an alien preoccupation which may prove as
> fatal to him as kissing Christ proved to Judas. The clock and the sun are sym-
> bols of time and routine ...; the ticking of the clock has its equivalent in the
> dust-motes illuminated by the sun. MacNeice explains that, in certain moods,
> he finds both motes and ticking clocks hypnotic and sinister.[18]

Perhaps the line between explication, the investigation of verbal or sentential meaning, and interpretation, conceived as the attempt to assign significance or see the point of something, is not so clear in cases of this kind. But
the exercise still looks principally like an exploration of *meaning* in a familiar
sense. There is nothing particularly controversial in appealing to MacNeice's
own personal connotations to guide us at this level. But if, as seems likely, we
would struggle to make sense of the lines without the aid of the poet's gloss
it would be reasonable to take this as a weakness in the poem. Only "external
evidence" of meaning – beyond the shared cultural background about Judas
and Saint Sebastian – can provide the key to the personal connotations.

This leads to the first theoretical point about explication, namely that
*meaning* in this context does not take any essentially different form from that
found in other kinds of texts. All linguistic texts invite explication of meaning, and the procedures for recovering meaning will by and large be similar
across the board. Appeals to dictionaries, localized conventions, common
usages, even speaker's connotations, are legitimate resources for all explication, as the need arises. The attempt to identify something distinctive about
literary meaning in explication – as, for example, Beardsley's notion of
"semantical density" – founders because it applies only to a limited range of
works, notably certain styles of poetry. We would not expect sentences in a
novel, for example, to be "dense" with meaning in the manner of metaphoric
poetic imagery. This reinforces the claim that literature is not definable in

---

[17] Louis MacNiece, "Hidden Ice," from *Modern Poetry: A Personal Essay* (London: Oxford
University Press, 1938); quoted in John Press, *The Chequer'd Shade: Reflections on Obscurity in
Poetry* (Oxford: Oxford University Press, 1963), p. 158.

[18] Press, *The Chequer'd Shade*, p. 158.

linguistic terms alone. Those who seek to apply general theories of meaning to literature, drawn from philosophy of language, find in explication the most fruitful application. Sentential models of meaning, from "conversational meaning" to "utterance meaning" fit naturally in this context, even if there might be reasons for preferring some models over others.

A second theoretical point is that explication, however carried out, is not, in the literary case, an end in itself but a stage toward a fuller appreciation of a work as a whole. In this it is like the identification of formal structure. But the relation between the meaning of isolated phrases or sentences and a broad conception of a whole work is complicated by worries about the "hermeneutic circle." Segments of a work might not be explicable independently of an overall view of the work, yet the overall view might depend on meanings assigned to segments.

Something like the hermeneutic circle can be illustrated in the well-known crux about "buckle" at the start of the sestet of Gerard Manley Hopkins's sonnet "The Windhover":

> Brute beauty and valour and act, oh, air, pride, plume, here
> Buckle! AND the fire that breaks from thee then, a billion
> Times told lovelier, more dangerous, O my chevalier!

It is not clear to start with whether the first sentence is in imperative or indicative mood, a command or a statement. Also the word "buckle" can mean "join together" or "break under the strain" and the alternative, and contradictory, meanings could be associated with a hopeful, joyous vision in the poem as a whole or something darker and more ominous.[19] There is no clear-cut solution to this critical conundrum, no independent authority, even from the poet, for a preferred reading, and it seems that both senses, at a textual level, must be acknowledged. The explicator's task can go no further, in this instance, than pointing out the double meaning, for the verbal context alone cannot eliminate one meaning definitively. It is only at the level of interpretation (applied to the complete sonnet) that decisions about how to respond to the alternative readings must be taken: perhaps to highlight one meaning over the other, or perhaps to keep the tension alive and to emphasize the role of other tensions throughout the poem, as between Christ's humility and his soaring power. The thematic vision is left finely poised, in many ways troubling like the poem itself.

But the theoretical point stands, that explication is subordinate to work-encompassing interpretation. The ambiguity in "buckle" only matters because

---

[19]  For a useful survey of different meanings attributed to the line, see *The Poetical Works of Gerard Manley Hopkins*, ed. Norman H. Mackenzie (Oxford: Clarendon Press, 1990), pp. 382–383.

of its effect on the appreciation of the work as a whole. Interpretive decisions will rest on evaluative factors, weighing up what best supports whatever literary interest the poem holds, in concordance with the explicator's findings elsewhere. However, although interpretation, in a sense, selects meanings, the notion that a text, in Beardsley's phrase, "means all it *can* mean" is at best only a half truth.[20] Explication should explore *possible* meanings at a textual level, but the task of delimiting meaning is more important to the interpretive exercise than that of multiplying meaning. Too much meaning at the level of explication is more likely to hinder than aid literary appreciation. Explication in the style of William Empson or Roland Barthes, which merely catalogues what sentences or words could mean without showing the interpretive benefits, are at best incomplete and unsatisfactory.

## Exploring a Work's Subject

Before we turn to interpretation itself, we should consider another procedure in the critic's repertoire, which is the exploration of the immediate subject, or "world," of the work. This is related to what Monroe Beardsley has called "elucidation." In Beardsley's sense, elucidation is the quest for details about a narrative – what occurs in the world of the work – which are not made explicit in the narrative itself. Beardsley gives these examples: "What did Hamlet study at Wittenberg? What is the minister's secret sin in Hawthorne's short story, 'The Minister's Black Veil'? ... Who was Mrs Dalloway's great-grandfather?"[21] There are countless questions of this kind, arising in all narrative, and they come in different degrees of seriousness.

In his celebrated paper "How Many Children Had Lady Macbeth?" (1933), L. C. Knights warned against treating fictional characters, especially Shakespearean characters, as if they were real humans whose lives are open to gossip and speculation. In particular he had in mind the kind of criticism practiced by A. C. Bradley (1851–1935), for example, in *Shakespearean Tragedy* (1904), which focused heavily on the personal qualities of the characters. Questions about what might have happened to characters after the narrative closes or what they were like before it began or even what they are thinking on such and such an occasion are often of fascination to readers but they are now rarely thought to be integral to a literary critical approach. However, even accepting Knights's reservations, there remain serious and complex issues about how fictional narratives can be supplemented

20    Beardsley, *Aesthetics*, p. 144.
21    Ibid., p. 242.

constructively in the reading process through filling in implied but missing detail. The mechanics and presuppositions involved will be discussed in Chapter 5 on fiction.

For the time being we should note that while certain kinds of imaginative supplementation are often an important part of literary appreciation, they are not centrally concerned with *meaning*, in anything like the way meaning relates to explication. While elucidation aids our understanding of character and event it is not an exploration of verbal meaning as such. To the extent that interpretation is involved it is more like the interpretation of action than of sentences.

In this sense, critical elucidation can be both descriptive, expanding on narrative content, and explanatory, putting some construction on the content. Here is a critic's elucidation of a scene in *Epithalamion*.

> When Elizabeth [the poet's bride] blushes at the moment in the ceremony when the hands of the bride and groom are joined in a presaging of the sexual bond in marriage, the poet asks, "Why blush ye love to give to me your hand, | The pledge of all our band?" (13.238–239). That this moment is a highly charged and compelling one for Spenser is suggested by his slight reordering of the marriage ceremony. … Although the Book of Common Prayer stipulates that the priest's blessing follows the joining of the couple's hands, stanza 13 refers first to the priest's blessing and then to the joining of the hands. Like his sending forth of the masque of Hymen, Spenser's beginning with the priest's blessing emphasizes the spiritual dimension of the wedding. But it is also as if Spenser first passes over the moment (out of delicacy?) but then must return to it. Despite its compelling force, this first moment of physical contact between the bride and groom produces an unexpected reticence in the poet who, until this point, has displayed his bride openly, detailing her "beautyes grace" and "vertues store," and enjoining all to behold (10.170). While we can readily enough surmise, from the immediate context and from epithalamic convention, that this blush sustains a considerable erotic charge, Spenser does not articulate this conclusion.[22]

The passage illustrates one of the central tasks of critical practice, to characterize the *subject* of a work, its immediate content, through reflective redescription. This involves an exploration and reconstruction of the world of the work, what occurs in the narrative, what the characters are like. To say that the bride's "blush sustains a considerable erotic charge" is not to engage in the kind of character speculation that Knights warns against but instead to follow through, by appeal to "context" and "convention," what is already implicit in the explicated content.

---

[22]  Judith Owens, "The Poetics of Accommodation in Spenser's *Epithalamion*," *Studies in English Literature, 1500–1900,* vol. 40 (2000), pp. 48–49.

Implicit content, however, is often not quite so determinate. Redescription can merge into interpretation. Take the case of Ophelia's madness. Nothing in the narrative of *Hamlet* tells us precisely what the physical or psychological causes of her madness are. Elaine Showalter, in an illuminating essay, has tracked the different conceptions of Ophelia's madness from the Elizabethan period to our own times.[23] For the Elizabethans, Ophelia suffered from "female love-melancholy or erotomania" (Showalter's terms);[24] Ellen Terry, in the late Victorian era, "led the way in acting Ophelia in feminist terms as a consistent psychological study in sexual intimidation, a girl terrified of her father, of her lover, and of life itself";[25] for the early-twentieth-century Freudians Ophelia has "an unresolved oedipal attachment to her father … [and] has fantasies of a lover who will abduct her from and even kill her father, and when this actually happens, her reason is destroyed by guilt as well as by lingering incestuous feelings";[26] finally feminists in the 1970s viewed her madness as "protest and rebellion … [she is] the hysteric who refuses to speak the language of the patriarchal order."[27]

Perhaps some of these conceptions might be dismissed as fanciful but unlike more limited inquiries into narrative content, any final assessment of them must be informed by an overall view of the play and the contribution that Ophelia is seen to make. Like all characters Ophelia's properties are radically indeterminate. Interpretive reconstruction is called for, but where it matters it must again defer to a broader conception of the work. In the case of drama, different conceptions will be manifested in different productions.

Both explication and elucidation, in Beardsley's senses, can (but need not) involve interpretation, but the former is more closely linked with meaning as such. Neither is exclusive to literature in that all texts require explication to some degree, and elucidation is required for all, not just literary, narratives. However, the critic's task is distinctive because the procedures of formal analysis, explication, and elucidation are not carried out for their own sake as ends in themselves, nor even to enhance "understanding," but in pursuit of a distinctive kind of literary value. The ultimate aim is to reveal why the work is of interest, as literature.

---

[23]   Elaine Showalter, "Representing Ophelia: Women, Madness, and the Responsibilities of Feminist Criticism," in Patricia Parker and Geoffrey Hartman, eds., *Shakespeare and the Question of Theory* (London: Methuen, 1985).

[24]   Ibid., p. 81.

[25]   Ibid., p. 89.

[26]   Ibid., p. 90.

[27]   Ibid., p. 91.

# Interpretation

It is to literary interpretation that we look for a rounded view of a work, a view that will aid our appraisal of its worth and interest. Interpretation applied to literature is distinctive both in its aims and procedures. Nowhere is the relativity of interpretation to the object of interpretation more keenly felt.

## *Interpretive statements*

What kind of commentary do we mean in speaking of literary interpretation? Interpretation is called for wherever there is need to "make sense" of something that is initially puzzling or not open to any obvious construal.[28] In the literary case, interpretation might be needed at the level of individual words and sentences (e.g., complex metaphors) or with longer passages or at the level of the work itself. As the first two of the three possibilities will always ultimately be in the service of the third, it is the idea of giving a "reading" of a work as a whole, incorporating explication, elucidation, and micro-interpretation, that primarily occupies the philosopher of literature. What is it to interpret a work as a whole, to develop a comprehensive overview that reveals its unique literary interest?

Returning once more to the *Epithalamion* (to complete our progression through the stages of critical commentary), here are two rather different perspectives:

> in this poem, Spenser's expressly reformist designs, which largely depend on maintaining distance and distinction between English and Irish (and old Irish), repeatedly collapse or are qualified. Perhaps even more revealingly, the collapsing of distances and distinctions produces exuberance. The townspeople — the young women and, now, young men — retain a strong voice (in the stanzas and hours following the marriage ceremony) ... The connection of this celebration with St. Barnabas's day presents a particularly subtle and suggestive instance of Spenser's accommodation of Irish pressures.[29]

> The subtle time structure serves to reinforce the idea implicit throughout the poem that this marriage has reference to all marriages; it emphasises the endless cycle of time, measured by the passing of the hours and the years — as against which marriage, as a Christian sacrament, stands firm, "eterne in mutabilitie."[30]

---

[28]   The point that interpretation must involve what is non-obvious is stressed in Annette Barnes, *On Interpretation* (Oxford: Blackwell, 1988), chs. 2–3.

[29]   Owens, "The Poetics of Accommodation in Spenser's *Epithalamion*," pp. 54–55.

[30]   M. H. Abrams, E. T. Donaldson, et al., eds., *The Norton Anthology of English Literature*, 4th ed., vol. 1 (New York: W. W. Norton, 1979), p. 713.

The first is part of a reading of the poem as the "poetics of accommodation," focusing on Spenser's complex responses to the political situation in Ireland in the Elizabethan age and his "colonialist and reformist designs, not only for Ireland but also for his bride." The second highlights the theme of the "endless cycle of time" and the steadfastness of the sacrament of marriage.

These interpretations need not be in conflict; they are not incompatible. Conflict would arise only in claims of priority, that one theme is more central or important than the other. Strikingly, though, they do differ at the level of universality, and questions of value are soon evoked. If the central theme or principle of the poem resides in Elizabethan Irish politics then the poem's interest would seem more historical or parochial than if the more universal themes of time and marriage were paramount.

Here are some other examples of interpretation:

*Macbeth* is Shakespeare's most profound and mature vision of evil. ... This evil, being absolute and therefore alien to man, is in essence shown as inhuman and supernatural, and is most difficult of location within any philosophical scheme. *Macbeth* is fantastical and imaginative beyond other tragedies. Difficulty is increased by that implicit blurring of effects, that palling darkness, that overcasts plot, technique, style. The persons of the play are themselves groping. Yet we are left with an overpowering knowledge of suffocating, conquering evil, and fixed by the basilisk eye of a nameless terror.[31]

*King Lear* is, above all, a play about power, property and inheritance. ... [T]hroughout the play, we see the cherished norms of human kindness shown to have no "natural" sanction at all. A catastrophic redistribution of power and property ... disclose[s] the awful truth that these two things are somehow prior to the laws of human kindness rather than vice versa. Human values are not antecedent to these material realities but are, on the contrary, in-formed by them.[32]

*Othello* ... is about male attitudes towards women — and each other — and thus Desdemona must stand as a symbol of what men destroy. ... *Othello* is a profound examination of male modes of thought and behaviour, especially with regard to women and "feminine" qualities. Iago is honest; he speaks the ordinary wisdom of the male world. The consequences of the values he shares with the other males in the play destroy the "feminine" values held by Desdemona, above all, but also Othello, Emilia, Cassio, Roderigo.[33]

---

[31]    G. Wilson Knight, "*Macbeth* and the Metaphysic of Evil," in David Lodge, ed., *20th Century Literary Criticism* (London: Longman, 1972), p. 159. Originally published in *The Wheel of Fire: Interpretations of Shakespearean Tragedy* (London: Methuen, 1949).

[32]    J. Dollimore, "*King Lear* and Essentialist Humanism," in John Drakakis, ed., *Shakespearean Tragedy* (London: Longman, 1992), p. 201.

[33]    Marilyn French, "The Late Tragedies," in Drakakis, ed., *Shakespearean Tragedy*, p. 243. Originally published in *Shakespeare's Division of Experience* (London: Abacus, 1982), pp. 219–251.

These examples differ in certain regards, representing, respectively, a traditional "humanistic" approach, a "materialist" reading, and feminist criticism. But they have much in common. Each is a summary statement of a general theme identified in the works in question. These summaries are conclusions of arguments built on detailed textual citation. We can call them *interpretive statements*, noting, crucially, that the *interpretations* themselves are a far more extensive process. An interpretation that consists merely of a single interpretive statement without accompanying support is worthless. In each case an attempt is made to generalize across the work as a whole, to draw together aspects of the work under broad unifying concepts: concepts such as (of *Macbeth*) "evil," "inhuman and supernatural," "fantastical and imaginative," or (of *Lear*) "catastrophic redistribution of power and property," "laws of human kindness," or (of *Othello*) "male modes of thought and behavior," "'feminine' values."

### Aboutness: subject and theme

A feature of all the sample interpretive statements is that they make claims as to what the works are "about." In the literary context, "aboutness" has two applications: at a *subject* level and at a *thematic* level. Every literary work has an immediate subject. *Epithalamion* is about the poet's wedding to Elizabeth Boyle and the stages running up to it; *Macbeth* is about Macbeth's murder of King Duncan and its consequences; *Lear* is about King Lear's vexed relations with his three daughters, and *Othello* about the murderous jealousy of the Moor of Venice. To say what a work is about at subject level is in effect to retell the story or, in the case of non-narrative works, to redescribe the occasion or emotion presented. Explication and elucidation are primarily concerned with "aboutness" at this level.

Interpretation, in contrast, is concerned with aboutness at a thematic level. This, as illustrated in the examples, involves identifying a perspective or vision or general reflection that informs the subject matter and moves beyond the immediate events portrayed. With many narrative works of fiction – genre fiction – readers have little inclination to seek out underlying themes of this general nature. Such works seldom call for interpretation, although they might need subject elucidation. However, it is a peculiarity of *literary* works that they do invite this kind of interest. An informing vision or conception or organizing principle is expected. Indeed, it is a mark of what makes a work "literary" that it is of interest at a thematic as well as at a subject level; a reader who can do no more than rehearse the plot of a literary novel has, it is reasonable to suppose, missed something important about its literary qualities.

To speak of what a work is about, thematically, is to speak of a unifying thread that binds together incident and character in an illuminating way.

Of Jane Austen's *Emma*, a critic writes: "To believe that the novel is about marriage greed …, marriage snobbery, or even the marriage of true minds is to miss the point. It is really about marriage as an ordeal."[34] The statement (with its supporting citations) affords a prism through which to view the various couplings and uncouplings that make up the subject.

The subject/theme distinction has consequences too for originality. It is well known that Shakespeare took many of his plots from earlier sources. In that sense he didn't make up his subjects. The stories of Lear or Macbeth or Romeo and Juliet are borrowed. The genius of Shakespeare resides not in the invention of narrative subject but, vaguely put, in the "handling" of the subject. It is through the working out of character and action, the imposition of structure, and ultimately the shaping perspective of the whole that Shakespeare shows his originality. Many authors treat the same story. Aeschylus, Sophocles, and Euripides retell the story of Orestes; Christopher Marlowe, Goethe, and Thomas Mann offer versions of the Faust myth; Milton retold the story of the fall of Adam and Eve from the Book of Genesis. At the subject level in each case what the works are about is the same (even if the retellings show variations); at the thematic level, concerning a conception of the subject, they are different.

### Points of contention

Literary interpretation is a notoriously contentious issue. It is not that theorists are often in dispute about the kinds of commentary that count as interpretation. The examples above are not controversial *as examples*. But there is disagreement on many matters: what the aims of interpretation are; whether literary works are amenable to a single definitive interpretation or a plurality; what kinds of support are possible and desirable; whether interpretations can be true or merely plausible; what role should be given to authorial intention. In fact these questions are closely intertwined, and an answer to one is likely to have implications for the others. In the end the direction taken on these questions tends to reflect fundamental assumptions about what kinds of objects literary works are.

Before looking at the disagreements, though, we should highlight the broad agreements. Few critics, for example, would defend complete anarchy in interpretation, the idea that any interpretation is as good as any other and that any work could be about more or less anything, a view sometimes attributed, no doubt unfairly, to deconstructionism. (The anarchic conception

---

[34]   Ronald Blythe, "Introduction," Jane Austen, *Emma* (Harmondsworth: Penguin, 1972), p. 13.

could follow from an extreme application of the notion of an undifferentiated text.) There is general agreement too that some kind of distinction between description and interpretation is desirable. Simply describing, for example, the subject of a work (it is about the murder of a king, about a jealous husband) or the formal structures (it contains repetition, the images complement one another) is not interpreting.

As remarked earlier, what invites interpretation cannot be *obvious*. If it is obvious that Duncan is murdered, and I know that, then I do not interpret what happens to him as murder. Similarly, you don't need to *interpret* my greeting "Good morning" unless you think it is something other than a greeting. You grasp its meaning without further thought.

Finally, it is widely accepted that *theme* is important in literary interpretation, at least in the sense of "aboutness" just considered. Critics of different ideological persuasion, in pursuit of materialist, feminist, psychoanalytical, deconstructive, or other kinds of readings, are all likely to seek generalizations about a work beyond its immediate subject. They are, after all, encouraged to do so because literary works themselves often articulate thematic statements. It is common in sonnets, for example, to end with a generalizing reflection: as in Shakespeare's "And death once dead, there's no more dying then" (Sonnet 146).

Some disagreements, though, run deep. Two in particular are worth exploring: interpretation as recovery versus interpretation as construction and monism versus pluralism. These issues both connect in different ways with the intentionalist debate and the debate about evidence raised in Chapter 3.

### Recovery or imposition in interpretation

Do interpretive statements recover something that already exists in a work or do they impose a conception on the work? Our examples – "*Macbeth* is a profound and mature vision of evil"; "*King Lear* is about power, property and inheritance," "*Othello* is about male attitudes towards women" – suggest the former, for at one level each of these statements seems pretty incontrovertible. Macbeth's murder of a just and admired king is paradigmatic of evil; Lear loses power after a distribution of property; and Othello and Iago are men with distinct attitudes to women. The interpretations, though, are not just aboutness claims, they are also priority claims. These themes are said to capture something *significant* about the works. Is that not more like an imposition? Is it not a claim as much about value as of fact?

The distinction between what is "in" a work and what is "imposed on it" is not as clear-cut as it might seem. In simple cases we can get a reasonable grasp of what is "in" a work: the characters Othello and Iago are in *Othello*, as are the words "Put out the light, and then put out the light." But are the concepts of jealousy and innocence also "in" the work? It seems that any competent elucidation of the plot would deploy such concepts. It does not take interpretation to identify Othello's jealousy and Desdemona's innocence. In that sense they are "given." But when the psychoanalytic critic asserts

> As soon as Cassio's fall is encompassed, it revives in Othello an unconscious homosexual love, but since this love is unacceptable it can be expressed only through the debasement and defilement of Desdemona[35]

we are in the realms of interpretation – the outer reaches, some might say – and much less confident that this is a report of what is "in" the play rather than a speculation about the play.

Two of our earlier distinctions are important in this debate: text and work, and explication and interpretation.

To ask what is in a *text* is not the same as asking what is in a *work*. A text has lexicographical, syntactic, and semantic properties, identification of which determines the text's *content*. This is linguistic content, a product of linguistic convention, of syntactic and semantic rules that bear on the language in question. One problem we have noted for pure textual (or sentential) meaning – the meaning of an undifferentiated text – is that there is too much of it. A text that is not contextualized is not subject to constraints and can mean anything that the language permits. A work, in contrast, is contextualized; not only is it grounded in a time and culture but it also conforms to the conventions of an "institution." It is a text of a certain kind designed for a purpose. This is the intuition behind talk of "utterance meaning."

If we attend to a text in abstraction from a work and ask how it might be interpreted we would largely be at a loss how to proceed. Without some knowledge of the category to which the text belongs there could be nothing more to interpretation than an almost limitless kind of explication, listing all the possible meanings but with no further end in view. Interpretation only has purchase when applied to *works*. That is a reaffirmation of the thought that reading is purposive, that it involves expectations and conventions.

To illustrate how pure textual meaning is distinct from work meaning, recall Beardsley's example of the lines from Mark Akenside's poem *The Pleasures of Imagination* (1744), Bk. II, lines 311–313:

> Yet, by immense benignity inclin'd
> To spread about him that primeval joy
> Which fill'd himself, he rais'd his plastic arm.

---

[35]  André Green, "*Othello*: A Tragedy of Conversion: Black Magic and White Magic," in Drakakis, ed., *Shakespearean Tragedy*, p. 351.

The meaning of "plastic" as a synthetic substance is no doubt included in the semantic meaning of the *text* taken as a mere string of sentences. But it is also clear that this meaning should be *excluded* from any competent interpretation of the *work* (the synthetic substance is not "in" or relevant to the poem). Note that context is sufficient to determine this exclusion without reference to intention. The author would have been unable to form any intention about the synthetic substance.

Arguably, the distinction manifests itself in the opposite direction as well, where the content of a *work* extends beyond the content of its constituting *text*. An example might be this: the second occurrence of "put out the light" in *Othello*, V, ii ("Put out the light, and then put out the light") means, in the context of the work, "take away her life," but this is not part of the literal or textual meaning of the sentence itself. That Othello means first to refer to the light in the room ("Put out the light"), then, metaphorically, to Desdemona's life (he later repeats "put out thy light") is revealed through explication, without the need for further "interpretation." The context makes it all but explicit. Of the former, Othello says

> If I quench thee, thou flaming minister,
> I can again thy former light restore,
> Should I repent me

while of the latter:

> … but, once put out thy light,
> Thou cunning'st pattern of excelling Nature,
> I know not where is that Promethean heat
> That can thy light relume.

This explication of the metaphorical meaning of "put out the light" reveals meaning in the work beyond what is in the text per se. Again, though, intentions are only marginally relevant; rather than using Shakespeare's intention to infer the metaphorical meaning, we infer Shakespeare's intention (if that interests us) by first identifying the meaning.

But can interpretation, conceived as something more than explication of textual meaning, similarly reveal what is in a work?

Various theoretical efforts have been made to retain the idea of interpretation as a species of retrieval rather than imposition. The simplest line is to invoke the author who, it is supposed, has the power to put "into" the work just those kinds of general thematic conceptions that are at the heart of interpretation. If a work is seen as an "utterance" produced by an author and informed by a complex intention, and if the thematic as well as subject content is part of that intention, then interpretation can be viewed as an attempt at the recovery of authorial intention. This would be the view of the "actual intentionalist." On such a view the truth of our sample interpretive statements, about *Macbeth*, *King Lear*, and *Othello*, rests on whether they would be endorsed by Shakespeare: on strong versions, whether Shakespeare actually had such notions in mind.

A modification of intentionalism, which allows other constraining factors than just an author's own self-conscious thoughts, is offered by Richard Wollheim, for whom "criticism is *retrieval*." He goes on: "The task of criticism is the reconstruction of the creative process, where the creative process must in turn be thought of as something not stopping short of, but terminating on, the work of art itself."[36] Wollheim then argues that the "creative process," as he sees it, is broader than the artist's intentions and "includes the many background beliefs, conventions, and modes of artistic production against which the artist forms his intentions."[37] This allows for the consequence that a critic "is justified in using both theory and hindsight unavailable to the artist if thereby he can arrive at an account of what the artist was doing that is maximally explanatory."[38] The point is of significance in the debate about the "content" of a work as it allows for interpretations that might not be accessible to the author: an obvious example being an interpretation of *Hamlet* using the psychoanalytic terminology of the Oedipus complex. On Wollheim's view this could still be "retrieval."

But the idea that interpretation uncovers what is already present – but hidden – in a work is not restricted to versions of intentionalism. Anti-intentionalists, such as Beardsley, can defend interpretive meaning recovered rather than imposed. Thus Beardsley argues that "connotations and suggestions" are just as objectively part of a work's meaning ("public semantic facts") as are standard literal meanings and are not merely "psychological and personal."[39] So to find a "hint of pantheism" in the second stanza of Wordsworth's "A Slumber Did My Spirit Seal" is to recover connotations or suggestions that the text itself bears, regardless of authorial intention.[40] It might be difficult to sustain this view beyond fairly simple cases of interpretation – it depends how elastic the notions of "connotation" and "suggestion" are allowed to be – but that might be an argument for delimiting responsible interpretation to what

[36]   Richard Wollheim, "Criticism as Retrieval," Essay IV, in *Art and Its Objects*, 2nd ed. (Cambridge: Cambridge University Press, 1980), p. 185 [italics in original].

[37]   Ibid., p. 201.

[38]   Ibid.

[39]   Monroe C. Beardsley, *The Possibility of Criticism* (Detroit, MI: Wayne State University Press, 1970), pp. 48, 57.

[40]   Ibid., pp. 44–45.

has strong textual or linguistic support, as found in the "put out the light" case. In fact Beardsley distinguishes interpretation proper, which rests on "connotations and suggestions," and "superimposition":

> The story of "Jack and the Beanstalk," for example, can no doubt be taken as Freudian symbolism, as a Marxist fable, or as Christian allegory. I emphasise the phrase "can be taken as." It is true that "readings" such as these need not exclude each other. But the reason is surely that they do not bring out of the work something that lies momentarily hidden in it; they are rather ways of *using* the work to illustrate a pre-existent system of thought. Though they are sometimes called "interpretations" ... they merit a distinct label, like *superimpositions*.[41]

But it remains far from clear where imposition – or "superimposition" – starts and recovery ends. Or at least this is true for anti-intentionalists like Beardsley. Even if we focus – as we should – on the work as opposed to the mere text there is no clear limit on what a work "suggests." This might well, for example, depend on a "pre-existent system of thought" that a reader brings to the work. Wollheim's conception of "retrieval" allows for Freudian symbolism, which Beardsley sees as superimposition. The problem is a general one for interpretation, for when we reach for unifying thematic concepts – like those earlier listed – we are not drawing on semantic entailments of sentential content but on looser kinds of "implication." The aim is not to explicate literal meanings but to find what is *significant* or *interesting* or *rewarding* to thought and reflection in the work as a whole.

Arthur Danto has distinguished between "surface" and "deep" interpretation.[42] His position cuts across both Wollheim and Beardsley. Unlike Beardsley he is an intentionalist about surface interpretation: "we cannot be deeply wrong if we suppose that the correct interpretation of an object-as-artwork is the one which coincides most closely with the artist's own interpretation."[43] Surface interpretation must be accessible to the artist, who is the ultimate authority on it. Danto writes: "the artist is in some privileged position with regard to what his ... surface representations are."[44] This is not a requirement on Wollheim's criticism as retrieval.

Deep interpretation, in contrast, shares many of the features of Beardsley's "superimpositions" – Marxist and psychoanalytic readings are examples – yet

[41] Ibid., pp. 43–44.

[42] The use of "deep" is somewhat misleading as Danto explicitly states that he does not mean "profound": Arthur Danto, *The Philosophical Disenfranchisement of Art* (New York: Columbia University Press, 1986), p. 53.

[43] Ibid., p. 44.

[44] Ibid., p. 51.

they are characterized by a feature central to Wollheim's "retrieval": they have an explanatory role which might transcend the resources of the artist, who "has no privilege, hence no authority, for he must come to know them in ways no different from those imposed upon others."[45]

## Creative interpretation

There are those who promote a species of interpretation that has a much looser connection either to intention or to narrowly linguistic connotation and suggestion, acknowledging a degree of "imposition." They need not disregard justification and support, but they emphasize various kinds of "creativity" in the interpretive process. Here is Ronald Dworkin, who offers a "creative" view of interpretation both for the law and for art:

> Roughly, constructive interpretation is a matter of imposing purpose on an object or practice in order to make of it the best possible example of the form or genre to which it is taken to belong. It does not follow, even from that rough account, that an interpreter can make of a practice or work of art anything he would have wanted it to be …. For the history or shape of a practice or object constrains the available interpretations of it …. Creative interpretation, on the constructive view, is a matter of interaction between purpose and object.[46]

This might be thought of as a modest "impositional" view of interpretation, constrained by textual and historical factors but nevertheless seeking purpose or significance, not with the aim of retrieval but to find "the best possible example of the form."[47] The aim of interpretation, on this view, is to maximize interest in the work. Theatrical production exemplifies this well. Producers interpret plays, through staging and setting, to bring out features they find exciting or challenging. A production of *Julius Caesar* is performed in Nazi uniforms, *The Tempest* as a Japanese Noh play. Interpretations can also emerge without such overt changes. Arthur Miller describes in his autobiography how his play *The Crucible* was endlessly reinterpreted when performed across the world. In Poland in the 1970s the play became a lesson about Stalinism, in Shanghai in 1980 it "served as a metaphor for life under Mao and the Cultural Revolution."[48] Such interpretations are creative yet remain faithful to meanings at a textual level. The texts are not altered.

[45]  Ibid.

[46]  Ronald Dworkin, *Law's Empire* (London: Fontana Press, 1986), p. 52.

[47]  Stephen Davies calls this the "value-maximizing theory": "Authors' Intentions, Literary Interpretation, and Literary Value," *British Journal of Aesthetics*, vol. 46, no. 3 (2006), pp. 223–247.

[48]  Arthur Miller, *Timebends: A Life* (New York: Grove Press, 1987), p. 348.

## Constructivism

A more radical view of interpretation appears in "constructivist" theories. The idea common to such theories is that interpretations help to "construct" the very works themselves. The works are not autonomous independent entities waiting to be examined but essentially indeterminate objects that owe their character and ultimately their existence to the interpretive process.[49] A strong version claims that each interpretation creates its own distinct work, an "object-of-interpretation," so the psychoanalytic *Hamlet* is a different work from the Marxist *Hamlet*. A more moderate version holds that one and the same work can be subject to different interpretations, given sufficient properties held to be common across these interpretations.[50]

A feature of most versions of constructivism is that the constructed entities do not have a fixed nature but change over time. A work can mean one thing at one time, another at a later time. So *Hamlet* meant something different to Shakespeare's contemporaries than it does to us; that is not just because audiences have changed – their attitudes, tastes, beliefs – but because the work itself has changed. This view contrasts with *historicism* (in the sense coined by Anthony Savile[51]) which takes the opposite stance, holding that the work remains constant in its meaning, however other responses might fluctuate over time. A strict historicism maintains that a work retains its identity across time only in virtue of a "canonical interpretation," built from "the best available contemporary reading," that survives with the work – whether recognized or not – throughout its history.[52]

What constructivism shows, once again, is how close questions about interpretation are to questions about ontology (what kind of entities literary works are). Robert Stecker has identified a crucial dilemma for the constructivist:

> The problem is to understand how making a claim about an object, even an object-of-interpretation, can give it a property claimed for it. ... If the claim

---

[49]  See, for example, Joseph Margolis, *What, After All, Is a Work of Art?* (University Park, PA: Penn State University Press, 1999), ch. 3.

[50]  Michael Krausz: "When interpretations impute different properties, they must impute a sufficiently large number of properties in common to warrant the agreement that they are addressing a sufficiently common object-of-interpretation": *Rightness and Reasons: Interpretation in Cultural Practices* (Ithaca, NY: Cornell University Press, 1993), p. 121.

[51]  Anthony Savile, *The Test of Time* (Oxford: Oxford University Press, 1982), ch. 4: "the thesis of historicism is that a proper understanding and appreciation of a work of art at no matter what period must go through some canonical interpretation which does not change over time": p. 61.

[52]  Ibid., p. 64.

is true, the object already has the property. If it is false, the object does not have the property. If it is neither true nor false, then what difference can be made by saying that the object has the property, or even by telling a plausible story according to which the object has the property?[53]

One response might be that there is indeed something unusual about the kinds of "objects" that literary works are, and it is not always clear either what "properties" these objects have, or that literary critics are essentially in the business of identifying "properties." No doubt in their descriptive mode, undertaking formal analysis or certain kinds of explication or elucidation, this might be a reasonable way for critics to talk. But interpretation that seeks broader thematic connections in a work as a whole is often thought to leave room for "creativity," either in the sense of an imaginative search for possibilities or in the interests of "completing" an otherwise indeterminate object.

"Creative" interpretation, to which constructivism is committed, is constrained not by narrow predicative truth but by imaginativeness and possibility. The best creative interpretations are those that take the established aspects of works, those identified at the descriptive level, and find new saliences for them,[54] or new ways of thinking about the work's themes, motifs, or symbolic or figurative aspects. This is evident in the examples of theatrical interpretation; thinking of *Julius Caesar* as analogous to Nazism is "creative" (it could not have occurred to Shakespeare) yet it re-imagines themes more obviously "in" the play. Examples also arise where a critic gives prominence (or salience) to aspects sometimes regarded as merely part of the "background":

> I read Charlotte's [Charlotte Brontë's] novels as "myths" which work towards a balance or fusion of blunt bourgeois rationality and flamboyant Romanticism, brash initiative and genteel cultivation, passionate rebellion and cautious conformity; and those interchanges embody a complex structure of convergence and antagonism between the landed and industrial sectors of the contemporary ruling class.[55]

Perhaps we should simply recognize two distinct kinds of interpretation – as retrieval and as creation – without supposing that one has priority. Interpretation either *discovers* something about a work, through the intentions or creative processes behind it or through its implied meanings, or it *creates*

[53] Robert Stecker, "The Constructivist's Dilemma," *Journal of Aesthetics and Art Criticism*, vol. 55, no. 1 (1999), p. 50.

[54] The idea of interpretation as the assignment of saliences is developed by Michael Krausz in *Rightness and Reasons*.

[55] Terry Eagleton, *Myths of Power: A Marxist Study of the Brontës* (London: Macmillan, 1975), p. 4.

a new perspective on the work, a new way of making salient or reorganizing its elements. In fact when one looks at cases it might well turn out that there is not always a sharp line here. New perspectives can be discovered as well as created. But questions about truth and about the multiplicity of interpretations inevitably arise.

## Monism and pluralism

Is truth an issue for interpretation? Is it *true* that Charlotte Brontë's novels "work towards a balance or fusion of blunt bourgeois rationality and flamboyant Romanticism," or that "*King Lear* is about power, property and inheritance"? It looks as if this second question is about a matter of *fact*; no doubt on a strict "retrieval" conception that is how it is read. Intentionalists, for example, might well suppose it is a fact, or not, that some interpretive statement is true, i.e., true in reporting an intention. But more commonly questions about interpretive truth in practice focus on other things, and this is independent of the stand taken on intention. At least three levels of further inquiry can be discerned:

- Is this a perspective that *can* be taken on the work?
- Is this a perspective that it is *worthwhile* to take?
- Is this an *important* or central aspect of the work?

Arguably, to see our interpretive statements as *strong* claims (whether "truth" is at issue or not) there must be a positive answer to all three. Certainly the statements are *false* if there is a negative answer to all the questions, but the statements could be viewed as *weakly* true if a positive answer can be given to only the first one or two.

The strength (and truth) of any interpretive claim must be based on the evidence or support available. To ask if a perspective *can* be taken on a work is to ask whether it is supportable and plausible, not just whether someone or other has taken that perspective. The plausibility of an interpretation is always relative to textual support. Critics backing up their interpretive hypotheses cite textual passages and offer their own redescription of character and incident. To support the above claim about Charlotte Brontë's novels the critic must go into detail. Thus, about *Jane Eyre*:

> Rochester, an oppressed younger son of the gentry, has suffered at the hands of social convention and so like Jane has a history of deprivation; but unlike her he has achieved worldly success, cuts a glamorous figure in county society, and so blends social desirability with a spice of thwarted passion and an underdog past.[56]

---

[56]   Ibid., p. 20.

Redescription of this kind also needs to be appraised for its truth, but that derives directly from textual sources, resting on elucidation of the narrative "world," relying also on presuppositions about the subject matter (e.g., class structure). An accumulation of such redescription, in this case in terms of the social positions of the characters, gives substance to the suggested perspective ("bourgeois rationality" vs. "flamboyant Romanticism"). To show that the perspective not only *can* be taken but is *worthwhile* would call for further evidence of connectedness across the work. The more elements of the work that fit into this scheme of concepts the more worthwhile or fruitful the scheme will seem.

What is most difficult to establish is the third level, whether this is an *important* or central perspective on the work. That is essentially a value judgment and involves relating this perspective to others that have been proposed. But how can we say whether a Marxist or feminist or psychoanalytic interpretation is more "important" than the others? It is worries on this score that encourage critical pluralism. Pluralism is the view that there can be more than one acceptable interpretation of a work. But pluralism should allow for comparative judgments between interpretations even while acknowledging that different interpretations are tenable, plausible, and worthwhile.

There are many readings of *Jane Eyre* as well as the "Marxist" one just mentioned. Another critic writes:

> *Jane Eyre* … is largely a religious novel, concerned with the meaning of religion to man and its relevance to his behaviour. Jane discovers at Lowood that she can comprehend religion only when it has some relation to man, but at Thornfield she sees the opposite error, of man attempting to remake religion to his own convenience.[57]

A parallel with the Biblical Samson story is drawn when Rochester's house Thornfield is brought to ruin around him: "Like the Biblical hero, still more like the Miltonic Samson, he has been the creature of physical passion and he has sinned in attempting to substitute his own will for that of God." Rochester becomes "part of the great archetypal pattern of sin, suffering and redemption."[58]

Perhaps there is nothing to choose between these readings. But the theorist should have a conception of the considerations that could be brought to bear on the comparison. For the strong actual intentionalist the issue is

---

[57] Robert Bernard Martin, "Religious Discovery in *Jane Eyre*," in Charlotte Brontë, *Jane Eyre*, ed. Richard J. Dunn (New York: W. W. Norton, 1971). Originally published in *The Accents of Persuasion: Charlotte Brontë's Novels* (New York: W. W. Norton, 1966), p. 478.

[58] Martin, "Religious Discovery in *Jane Eyre*," p. 488.

simple (or relatively so): first, did Charlotte Brontë have in mind either the contrast between "bourgeois rationality" and "flamboyant Romanticism," or the connection between Rochester and Samson (and the religious theme generally), or both? We might need outside evidence to settle this, but if there is such evidence then the first stage is clear. Then the second intention-alist question arises, whether she gave priority to one over the other. Again, evidence would be sought wherever it could be found. A problem, though, immediately arises, namely whether we should only be satisfied if the evidence pointed to her thoughts in precisely these terms, including the Marxist vocabulary. On Wollheim's intentionalism, as we have seen, this is not necessary, and the issue could still be objectively decided. Intentionalism is not committed to monism but would hope to settle comparative judg-ments about competing interpretations.

The hypothetical intentionalist loosens the demands still further and asks whether it would be a reasonable hypothesis about Charlotte Brontë that she thought of her novel in these ways. The crucial question, though, is whether the reasonableness of the hypothesis is supported by internal or external evidence. In practice, when critics make interpretive claims of the kind under discussion they support them by internal or textual evidence. They cite passages which lend themselves to that particular interpretive redescrip-tion. A critic who simply went straight to "external" evidence and offered no textual support would have little credence.

To compare readings we inevitably ask which "gets the most out of" or does the "most justice to" the novel, which is the most satisfying or reward-ing, which offers the most comprehensive coverage. When we come to assess readings by different critics we examine the detailed support on offer and we ask which reading leaves the fewest elements in the work resistant to the interpretation. Are there scenes or characters or subplots not amenable to a plausible redescription or analysis with these concepts? How finely discrimi-nating are the concepts at a close textual level?

These criteria for testing the strength and support of an interpretation – plausibility, textual groundedness, coherence, comprehensiveness, discrimi-nation[59] – might seem to prejudge the meta-critical issue about pluralism and monism by presupposing that there will always be alternative (i.e., plural) ways of satisfying the criteria. Pluralism, we have seen, allows for distinct interpretations, equally acceptable, even true, while monism insists that ultimately there is only one correct interpretation. Certainly these large meta-critical categories cannot both be true, but in practice much interpretive activity is compatible with either stance. The criteria listed can

---

[59]  For a detailed examination and defense of such criteria, see Stein Haugom Olsen, *The Structure of Literary Understanding* (Cambridge: Cambridge University Press, 1978).

apply in both cases. The single correct interpretation, if there is such a thing, will reveal itself through its plausibility, textual groundedness, comprehensiveness, etc. Even those who are ardent supporters of monism do not suppose that the correct (comprehensive) interpretation will be easy to find. Nor do they suppose that such an interpretation must be simple rather than multifaceted.

The critic E. D. Hirsch, for example, one of the most influential defenders of monism in its strict intentionalist guise, holds that "no one can establish another's meaning with certainty." He goes on: "The interpreter's goal is simply this – to show that a given reading is more probable than others."[60] "The root problem of interpretation," he writes, "is always the same — to guess what the author meant."[61] He lists as criteria for establishing probability or aiding the guesswork: "legitimacy" ("the reading must be permissible within the public norms of … the text"), "correspondence" ("the reading must account for each linguistic component in the text"), "generic appropriateness" (bearing the text's genre in mind), and "plausibility or coherence."[62] It is only in testing for coherence that intentionalism has purchase: "verification by the criterion of coherence … implies a reconstruction of relevant aspects of the author's outlook."[63] There is little suggestion, though, that we should shortcut the process by resorting to extra-textual evidence.

For the monist who believes that there is "in principle one and only one correct interpretation of a work,"[64] whether or not that rests on the author's intentions, there are two ways of taking our alternative readings of *Jane Eyre*. Either they must be shown as two compatible aspects of a single wider interpretation, or at least one of them must be wrong. The first option puts the monist close to the pluralist. The monist is amenable to different perspectives on a work but always with the proviso that they must be "logically compatible" and "can be combined into one (comprehensive) interpretation."[65] The difficulty, though, with stressing such multifacetedness – *Jane Eyre* is thematically about both social class and religion and perhaps other things besides – is the issue of emphasis. Each of our critics is claiming that their reading both identifies an important or central aspect of the work and applies down to the level of significant detail. It cannot be a coherent reading to say that such different

[60]   E. D. Hirsch, Jr., *Validity in Interpretation* (New Haven, CT: Yale University Press, 1967), p. 236.

[61]   Ibid., p. 207.

[62]   Ibid., p. 236.

[63]   Ibid., p. 237.

[64]   P. D. Juhl, *Interpretation: An Essay in the Philosophy of Literary Criticism* (Princeton, NJ: Princeton University Press, 1980), p. 199.

[65]   Ibid., p. 199, n.11.

aspects can both be *central*. So Hirsch, the monist, insists: "whenever a reader confronts two interpretations which impose different emphases on similar meaning components, at least one of the interpretations must be wrong."[66] It is only here that the monist comes into conflict with the pluralist, for whom both interpretations, assuming they conform to the criteria, can stay in play.

Critical monism is often depicted as an ideal rather than as an actually achievable state.[67] Few critics attempt anything like a comprehensive interpretation of a work. In fact it is hard to conceive what this might be, even whether it is intelligible. Presumably it would have to give an account of every word in the work and its role in some total analysis (given the Principle of Functionality). But interpretation, we have seen, concerns not just what individual words mean but larger segments of text and their interconnectedness; yet what counts as a significant segment or a significant connection will itself depend on some overall interpretation. A comprehensive interpretation could only establish that its own segmentation is the uniquely correct one by showing that every other possible segmentation is incorrect.

It might be objected that if the decisive factor is the author's intention then no such process of elimination is needed. But here we get into fundamental questions about the scope of human intention, for it seems unlikely that an author could conceive a work through an interpretation so comprehensive that it accounted for every finest detail. Perhaps what should be concluded is that there could be no such thing as a comprehensive interpretation. That may be so, but then it becomes puzzling why some fine details of a work are accommodated but not others. And if the monist relies on a retrieval view of interpretation – that the correct interpretation is somehow there to be uncovered – then there shouldn't be unaccommodated details.

Just as retrieval views of interpretation are not restricted to intentionalism, so monism is also not logically tied to intentionalism. The single correct interpretation might be a function of linguistic meaning and cultural convention without relying solely, or at all, on authorial intention. Nor is monism incompatible with the very idea of a cultural or institutional object. It is sometimes supposed that cultural objects whose existence rests on "intentionality" – in other words, what they *are* is a function of how they are *thought to be* – must be indeterminate and yield to different interpretations.[68] But

---

[66]  Hirsch, *Validity in Interpretation*, p. 230.

[67]  Michael Krausz, *Limits of Rightness* (Lanham, MD: Rowman and Littlefield, 2000), p. 5.

[68]  Joseph Margolis, for example, holds that because of an irreducible *indeterminacy* in cultural objects and the fact that interpretations *impute* properties to their objects, there will always be different ways of interpreting those objects. See J. Margolis, "Reinterpreting Interpretation," in John W. Bender and H. Gene Blocker, eds., *Contemporary Philosophy of Art: Readings in Analytic Aesthetics* (Englewood Cliffs, NJ: Prentice Hall, 1993), pp. 454–470.

there are many cultural objects that are not multiply interpretable: a dollar bill, the bishop in chess. These have a single "meaning" given them by the "institutions" to which they belong.

It is nevertheless a deep and contentious matter whether there is anything in the nature of *literature* that encourages the monist ideal of a single correct interpretation. Those who stress the need for objectivity and determinacy in critical practice, or those who see literary works as extended kinds of communication between author and reader, or those who simply fear that pluralism leads to anarchy in interpretation will prefer the monist paradigm. They need not disparage the multiplicity of readings, but they insist that the proper aim of criticism is to "get it right."

Surprisingly the pluralist can endorse many of these considerations. Few pluralists promote an interpretive free-for-all, most are concerned with objectivity, even "getting it right," and they have no reason to discard some notion of literary communication, but they feel that different readings can be right in different ways. An analogy might be with musical or theatrical performance. It seems both unrealistic and excessively restrictive to suppose that there is one and only one correct way of performing, say, Mahler's Fifth Symphony or *King Lear*. There might be those who argue that Leonard Bernstein attains for Mahler or Paul Scofield for *Lear* a kind of "perfection" or "ideal" but this is always a judgment rather than a statement of fact and it would be absurd to propose that every interpreter subsequently should aim to imitate them. It is part of the very nature of music and drama to invite new styles of performance and new "insights" into the works.

For the critical pluralist the same applies to critical, as opposed to performance, interpretation. There is always scope for a new perspective to be taken, new saliences given to elements of a work. Indeed, a work that seems to yield some particular interpretation so comprehensively that it becomes pointless to pursue further interpretive possibilities would normally be deemed limited or uninteresting. Another analogy the pluralist might use could be the interpretation of metaphor. A good poetic metaphor is often thought to be almost limitless in its potential for "insight."[69] New resonances or new ways of thinking about it keep coming to light. There is resistance to the thought that a good metaphor can be paraphrased into a "single correct interpretation."

There is always a temptation for a monist to try to accommodate this acknowledged richness of interpretive possibilities by characterizing the multiplicity as different *aspects* of a work, all contributing toward a comprehensive understanding of the work. We have seen one problem with this

---

[69]  The point is emphasized by Donald Davidson in "What Metaphors Mean," in Sheldon Sacks, ed., *On Metaphor* (Chicago: University of Chicago Press, 1978).

approach, in the *Jane Eyre* example, where the claim is made that two independent readings capture something *central* about the work. But suppose the claim for centrality is dropped. The novel, it might be said, has a social and a religious aspect, both objectively supported, and both to be recognized in a final correct reading.

But there are problems with this idea of "aggregating" readings.[70] One is that it would entail dropping the performance analogy. Trying to incorporate aspects of Scofield's Lear, Orson Welles's Lear, Ian Holm's Lear, and so forth, into a composite performance would be a hopeless mess, not a move toward an ideal. Part of the reason is that each performance is itself comprehensive, informing every part of the play. The intonation of a sentence, the stagecraft, the emergent character traits, cannot take two different forms at the same time. So it is with at least large-scale critical interpretations. They are not combinable because each area of the work is already given distinctive significance, which excludes others. Another problem with the monist's "aggregation" is that it threatens the very idea of a work's yielding a coherent *experience* to the reader. Too many different aspects jostling for attention would not enhance but hinder an appreciation of a unified work.

### Incompatible interpretations

A third problem is perhaps the most pressing: that of incompatible interpretations. Much is made of this because if incompatible interpretations can be shown to be admissible (and well supported) then the monist ideal is threatened. (Interestingly, it does not in itself threaten intentionalism, for there seems no reason in principle why an author should not intend a work to be open to two logically opposed readings.) It also raises again the question of whether interpretations are *true*. Two incompatible sentences cannot be true together. Not all pluralists allow incompatible interpretations but, among those who do, some offer this as a reason for rejecting "bivalence" in interpretation, the view that any interpretation must be either true or false.[71]

Many examples have been offered of plausible, well-supported, but contradictory readings of literary works. One of the well-worn examples is Henry James's novella *The Turn of the Screw*, where the ghosts can be interpreted either as real or as mere figments of the governess's mind.[72] Although

---

[70]   The term comes from Michael Krausz, *Rightness and Reasons*, p. 58.

[71]   E.g., Joseph Margolis, *Art and Philosophy: Conceptual Issues in Aesthetics* (Atlantic Highlands, NJ: Humanities Press, 1980).

[72]   Robert Stecker discusses the example in *Artworks: Definition, Meaning, Value* (University Park, PA: Penn State University Press, 1997), p. 119.

this is more a matter of elucidation, uncovering "facts" about the "world" of the work, there are repercussions at the level of work interpretation: for example, whether it is a psychological tale or a fantasy.

But other examples perhaps go deeper. Take the case of *King Lear* again. Groups of critics take diametrically opposed views of the play. There are those who see the play as "a bleak exposition of meaningless suffering and a denial of providence and an afterlife," and those who maintain, in contrast, that "the suffering detailed by the play, though real and terrible, is not meaningless: it is allowed, or even ordained, by providence and prepares the good characters for the afterlife by subjecting them to a process of redemptive growth."[73] Arguably good internal evidence can be cited for each position, and the opposing sides have an account to give of the evidence each way:

> The "nihilists" could say that the features the "redemptivists" call attention to are indeed elements in the play but that they only serve to inflate our expectations of a happy ending; when those expectations are defeated, the effect is all the more shattering, and so is the blow to any conception of a metaphysically based world order. The redemptivists, conversely, may grant the validity of the observations made by the nihilists: the play recognizes the fact that there is, in this world, real suffering that may seem to dash all hopes and expectations and make a mockery of the whole idea of providence. But this, the redemptivists may argue, is part of the suffering necessary for purification and, furthermore, an example of the Christian conviction that God moves in mysterious ways: He may allow everything to look irremediably bleak but nevertheless presides over the events and holds out the possibility of salvation.[74]

If we think of literary works as "objects" which either do or do not possess a given "property," then it seems we must choose between one or other of these readings. No object can both possess and not possess a property (at the same time). *Lear*, on this view, could not both *be* and *not be* nihilistic. But if we reject talk of "properties" – at least in the context of interpretation – and think instead of "perspectives," then it seems altogether less worrying to countenance that both a nihilistic and a non-nihilistic ("redemptivist") perspective could be taken to the play, if not simultaneously at least without any further internal change.

We now ask: are these global perspectives rewarding, well-supported, coherent? Nor need we suppose that the perspectives are simply "imputed"

---

[73] The example, and this characterization, come from Torsten Pettersson, "The Literary Work as a Pliable Entity: Combining Realism and Pluralism," in Michael Krausz, ed., *Is There a Single Right Interpretation?* (University Park, PA: Penn State University Press, 2002), pp. 225, 226.

[74] Pettersson, "The Literary Work as a Pliable Entity," pp. 226–227.

or the product of "creative" thought. We can retain some analogue of property talk or even truth by thinking in terms of "truth-to-the-work."[75] The opposing perspectives could each be *true-to-the-work* because they are supported by textual properties and they do justice to major elements in the work. Not any perspective will be true-to-the-work in this way, and there will often be strong reasons for preferring one to another. It seems desirable, though, to leave room for finely balanced opposed perspectives, each having an equal call on our attention and each illuminating the work at hand. Such is the peculiar nature of the kinds of "objects" that are literary works. The monist forces us to choose but the pluralist allows for supportable multiplicity.

# Appreciation

We need to return once more, briefly, to some of the fundamental aims underlying the "practice" of reading literature. The principal thought in the foregoing discussion is that responses to literary works *as literary works* are at least partially determined by the kinds of objects we take such works to be. If we take them to be works of art, then, as with all works of art, our interest focuses on a consonance of means to ends, the ways the resources, linguistic resources in this case, are utilized toward some realized purpose or value.

## *Appreciation vs. understanding*

The thought that the overriding goal of critical reading is the pursuit of *meaning*, the enhancement of *understanding*, does not square comfortably with the familiar procedures outlined above: formal analysis, explication, the elaboration of subject, and thematic interpretation. Of these only explication is directly concerned with meaning in the standard semantic or pragmatic sense, and explicating the contextualized meanings of words and sentences is simply a stage in a wider process. What is of interest in reading literary works is not grasping sentential meaning (even "utterance meaning") but appreciating how a subject is structured so as to yield a satisfying and engaging perspective or vision. Any such unifying perspectives on the subject are elicited in interpretation through an effort to find connectedness and coherence across the constitutive elements of the work, from character and action to image and expression. It is not only formal analysis that focuses on structure for structure is also revealed in interpretation. Works are structured round their principal themes.

---

[75] See Stephen Davies, "Relativism and Interpretation," *Journal of Aesthetics and Art Criticism*, vol. 53, no. 1, Winter (1995), p. 10.

Although there are looser senses of "meaning" which extend beyond narrowly linguistic applications – senses associated with the point, purpose, or achievement of an activity – it can be misleading to identify interpretation, without qualification, with a search for the "meaning of the work" as this can distort both its procedures and its basic aims. For one thing, it is worth noting the oddity of speaking of the "meaning" of a whole work. It is not clear what sense can be made of the question "what does *King Lear* mean?" or indeed how the phrase "*Jane Eyre* means — " might be completed.[76] Philosophers do not ask about "the meaning of Hume's *Treatise*," as opposed to the meaning of particular passages or sentences in it. Yet there are those who adhere to the terminology of meaning in relation to literary works. Robert Stecker, for example, asserts: "the meaning of a work … is identical to its utterance meaning."[77] In answer to worries about the oddity of this, Stecker replies that "work meaning … is what the author does in the work in virtue of her intentions and historical contexts."[78] However, this gloss seems to slide from a notion of "utterance meaning" rooted in philosophy of language to a looser notion of "meaning" connected precisely to ideas like point, purpose, or achievement, as earlier mentioned. To inquire into "what the author does in the work" can look quite like inquiring into "what the work does," and that is indeed a proper focus for critical practice, particularly if it includes "*how* the work does what it does." But this rephrasing seems to move some way from an inquiry into what an utterance means, as that would normally be understood. If the disagreement is just about terminology then it is not of much significance. The proposed shift of emphasis, though, from *understanding* the *meaning* of an utterance to *appreciating* a *work of art* seems far from trivial.

Consider an example. On the face of it Daniel Defoe's novel *Moll Flanders* (1722) is not difficult to understand. It is a rollicking story full of incident and colorful characters. Even the title page tells us what to expect: it is about a woman "Who was born in Newgate, and during a Life of continu'd Variety for Threescore Years, besides her Childhood, was Twelve Year a *Whore*, five times a *Wife* (whereof once to her own Brother) Twelve Year a *Thief*, Eight Year a Transported *Felon* in *Virginia*, at last grew *Rich*, Liv'd *Honest*, and died a *Penitent*." For a modern readership a certain amount of explication might be necessary – eighteenth-century terminology, customs, places, laws, the sort of things a good critical edition would explain in footnotes – as a condition for a full understanding. But once the story is grasped and local explication completed, what more is there to *understand*?

[76] See the essays "Text and Meaning" and "The 'Meaning' of a Literary Work," in Olsen, *The End of Literary Theory*.
[77] Stecker, *Interpretation and Construction*, p. 59.
[78] Ibid., p. 62.

Yet nothing up to this point has touched on the *literary* properties of the work, why it should be deemed a literary classic, why it rewards attention. Only interpretation, focusing a particular kind of attention, will reveal the *interest* or *value* of the work from a literary point of view. Many novels from the eighteenth or nineteenth century, of a superficially similar nature, neither invite nor reward attention *as literature*; the effort would not be worthwhile. But a substantial critical literature has built up round *Moll Flanders* and, in spite of the famous denunciation of Defoe by F. R. Leavis in *The Great Tradition* and the equivocal judgment of this novel by Ian Watt in *The Rise of the Novel*, positive statements of the novel's achievement, encouraged by plaudits from James Joyce, Virginia Woolf, and E. M. Forster, are now numerous. What has happened is that new perspectives on the novel have been opened up which deepen, not so much *understanding*, but *appreciation*.

Terence Martin, for example, invites us to see unity in the novel through "the significance of the pattern of theft":

> if we examine the details of theft, we find ... that the second large part of the novel operates as an attempt to win back the relative security of the first part: Moll's desire for economic security manifests itself in a series of adventures which testify to the quality of this desire by falling into a significant episodic pattern.[79]

Arnold Kettle, in a defense of *Moll Flanders* against the criticisms of Ian Watt, suggests: "The whole nature of Defoe's book – its construction, its texture, its detail, its vitality, its power to move us – is determined by his awareness of the contradiction between Moll's human aspiration and the facts of the human world she lives in." He describes in detail how much of the attempted resolution of this "insoluble" contradiction "takes the form of ambiguous or ironical statement."[80]

Robert Alan Donovan sees different modes of irony unifying the novel:

> There is, for example, the irony implicit in Moll's assumption that the guilt of her life is her own rather than that of the heartless and venal society that has produced her. There is also an irony of a particularly devastating kind in Moll's innocent acknowledgment ... that an immoral act is nullified if the perpetrator

---

[79] Terence Martin, "The Unity of *Moll Flanders*," in *Moll Flanders*, Norton Critical Edition, ed. Edward Kelly (New York: W. W. Norton, 1973), p. 363. Originally published in *Modern Language Quarterly* XXII (1961), pp. 115–124.

[80] Arnold Kettle, "In Defence of *Moll Flanders*," in *Moll Flanders*, Norton Critical Edition, p. 395. Originally published in *Of Books and Humankind*, ed. John Butt (London: Routledge, 1964), pp. 55–67.

is ignorant of its moral bearings. The agent's ignorance, in other words, not only excuses him, it changes the nature of his act. ... But the fundamental, shaping irony of *Moll Flanders* is the double vision of the heroine.[81]

Such remarks are typical of the literary treatment of a novel. We *could* say, following philosophers like Stecker, that the comments involve "work meaning" and help increase "understanding." But we are not *forced* to use this idiom. Also, as earlier suggested, to emphasize meaning, especially "utterance meaning," in the context of works, can be misleading. What we are brought to understand is not the work's *meaning*, except in some loose sense of its achievement, but its interest or value. With the help of the critics we come to understand *why it is worth reflecting further on the novel*. The interpretive comments enhance appreciation of the novel's literary or aesthetic features. These features might be entirely missed by someone who follows the story in all its details and is fully apprised of all the sentence meanings in the work. Yet they are the features – and others besides – that give the work its literary interest and in virtue of which the work can be called "literary," rather than merely "fictional." These features, the "pattern of theft," the "contradictions," the "double vision" of the heroine, are not properties inherent in the language of the text. They "emerge" only under imaginative reconstruction. This is precisely why the perennial question whether thematic features are "in" a text or "imputed to" it is again misleading. They are not *in the text* in the way that semantic meanings might be, yet they can come to be seen as *in the work* once the work has been identified as an appropriate object of (literary) interpretation.

The terminological point about "work meaning" disguises a deeper point about the purpose of interpretation: its connection with value. What an illuminating interpretation reveals are the features which help to qualify the work as a work of art, its artistic features. It is for this reason that the refocusing of critical practice from *meaning* to *appreciation* can be helpful. This is not a prescription for critical practice, a change of direction, merely a redescription of the fundamental aims. Nor does it sideline the obvious roles for meaning. If reading a work *as a literary work* or *as a work of art* is seen to aim at enhancing appreciation rather than exploring meaning, then much more unity can be discerned in the different aspects of the practice. The aim of discovering why a work rewards continued attention – close reading, repeated reading – brings together the analysis of structure with the eliciting of themes and the elaboration of subject with the explication of contextualized meaning. Too much

[81] Robert Alan Donovan, "The Two Heroines of *Moll Flanders*," in *Moll Flanders*, Norton Critical Edition, p. 403. Originally published in *The Shaping Vision: Imagination in the English Novel from Defoe to Dickens* (Ithaca: NY: Cornell University Press, 1966).

emphasis on meaning tends to enforce an artificial divide between "form" and "content" and to view thematic interpretation as just an instance of explication. Such an emphasis leaves the value of reading unexplained.

### Appreciation and pleasure

The term "appreciation" is used in different, often ill-defined, ways applied to the arts and to literature. It has connotations of both pleasure and perception. When applied to literature both connotations are in place, although without demanding an overly experiential or phenomenological sense of "perception." Readers need not have determinate *feelings* when appreciating literature so much as a determinate focus of attention. Our account of the practice has sought to capture just such a focus.

There are accounts of literary appreciation that give more emphasis to affective response and emotion: Susan Feagin describes it as "reading with feeling."[82] Feagin recognizes, though, that full literary appreciation has theoretical and reflective components, involving interpretation and, as she sees it, a kind of meta-reflection on the appropriateness of the first-order responses. She also acknowledges that a desire to appreciate a work is a desire to "get the good out of the work," to make it "work," not merely to accumulate facts about it.

As with appreciation in other contexts, literary appreciation is a trained response, calling for skills of discernment. The appreciation of wine, jewelery, or paintings is not merely a spontaneous pleasure but can grow with experience and knowledge. The pleasures of appreciating literature are likewise acquired rather than "natural." We appreciate Spenser's *Epithalamion* more as we learn about the tradition to which it belongs and the subtleties of its form and thematic development. The perception of literary qualities involves both imagination and reflection.

It follows from this that the pleasures associated with literary appreciation are not of a purely hedonic kind. As mentioned at the end of Chapter 1, there have been attempts to explain the pleasures of reading in "sensory" terms, or as "erotic," as with Roland Barthes's distinction between *plaisir* and *jouissance*[83] or Susan Sontag's conception of "an erotics of art."[84] But these are more playful than serious attempts to come to grips with the practice. Similarly, there is nothing in the account we have offered that gives comfort to overly *formalistic*

---

[82]   Susan L. Feagin, *Reading with Feeling: The Aesthetics of Appreciation* (Ithaca, NY: Cornell University Press, 1996).

[83]   Roland Barthes, *The Pleasure of the Text* (*Le Plaisir du Texte* [Paris: Seuil, 1975]), trans. R. Miller (London: Cape, 1976).

[84]   Susan Sontag, "Against Interpretation," in *Against Interpretation* (New York: Farrar, Straus, and Giroux, 1961), p. 23.

or *reductive* instincts in characterizing the "love of poetry." The familiar procedures of the critic that we have outlined – without giving priority to any particular "approach" – show a multiplicity in the pleasures of reading, from form through to theme, reflecting multiplicity in the work itself.

Nevertheless, even if we accept that the practice of reading involves more than the pursuit of meaning, and resides in a distinctive mode of appreciation, there remain deep questions about other kinds of interests in literature: an interest in fiction, for example, and an interest in truth. It is to these that we now turn.

## Supplementary Readings

The idea of literature as a "practice" or "institution" with its own conventions and concepts is developed by Stein Haugom Olsen in *The Structure of Literary Understanding* (Cambridge: Cambridge University Press, 1978) and Peter Lamarque and Stein Haugom Olsen, *Truth, Fiction, and Literature: A Philosophical Perspective* (Oxford: Clarendon Press, 1994). These in turn draw on ideas from Ludwig Wittgenstein's *Philosophical Investigations* (Oxford: Blackwell, 1968) and the work of John R. Searle: J. R. Searle, *Speech Acts: An Essay in the Philosophy of Language* (Cambridge: Cambridge University Press, 1969) and J. R. Searle, *The Construction of Social Reality* (London: Allen Lane, 1995). Institutional accounts of a different kind can be found in Jonathan Culler, *Structuralist Poetics: Structuralism, Linguistics and the Study of Literature* (London: Routledge, 2nd ed. 2002; first published in 1975) and Stanley Fish, *Is There a Text in This Class? The Authority of Interpretive Communities* (Cambridge, MA: Harvard University Press, 1980).

Philosophical treatments of interpretation in the arts, in the analytic tradition, include Joseph Margolis, *Art and Philosophy: Conceptual Issues in Aesthetics* (Atlantic Highlands, NJ: Humanities Press, 1980); P. D. Juhl, *Interpretation: An Essay in the Philosophy of Literary Criticism* (Princeton, NJ: Princeton University Press, 1980); Annette Barnes, *On Interpretation* (Oxford: Blackwell, 1988); Michael Krausz, *Rightness and Reasons: Interpretation in Cultural Practices* (Ithaca, NY: Cornell University Press, 1993); Joseph Margolis and Tom Rockmore, eds., *The Philosophy of Interpretation* (Oxford: Blackwell, 2000); Paul Thom, *Making Sense: A Theory of Interpretation* (Lanham, MD: Rowman and Littlefield, 2000); Michael Krausz, ed., *Is There a Single Right Interpretation?* (University Park, PA: Penn State Press, 2002); and Robert Stecker, *Interpretation and Construction: Art, Speech, and the Law* (Oxford: Blackwell, 2003). For sophisticated philosophical readings of literary works (*Middlemarch, Anna Karenina, The Brothers Karamazov, À la recherche du temps perdu*), see Peter Jones, *Philosophy and the Novel* (Oxford: Oxford University Press, 1975).

# Chapter Five

# Fiction

Philosophers have an interest in fictionality that extends beyond any interest they have in literature. Explaining the nature and status of "fictitious" or "non-existent" entities has occupied a central role in logic and metaphysics at least since the early days of analytic philosophy at the beginning of the twentieth century. The fact that ordinary language appears to contain names of entities that do not exist – "Pegasus," "Pickwick," "phlogiston," "the highest prime," "the present King of France" – poses a serious problem for philosophers who seek to explain meaning in terms of semantic "relations" between word and object. The problem, in brief, is that ordinary language condones meaning without denotation, so either ordinary language is deceptive and requires "regimentation," or some deep preconceptions about meaning need re-examining. Philosophy of literature intersects with debates in logic and metaphysics round its own concerns with existence, reference, truth, and reality.

Care, however, must be taken in applying the work done by philosophers on the semantics or ontology of fiction to issues relevant to literary criticism. It can often seem as if the concerns of logicians and critics are at odds with each other, even incommensurable. Logical inquiry is indifferent to literary value, and the simple examples used by logicians – Pickwick, Sherlock Holmes, Pegasus – are seldom related back to their originating texts. When literary critics give attention to fictionality they are likely to focus on narrative devices or character development or distinctive "worlds" created by authors. The logic of "fictional reference" or even the ontology of fictional objects seldom detains them. The philosopher of literature should take care to match the two sets of interests or give an account of the reasons why they do not match.

Fictionality is a characteristic feature of literary works, so inevitably certain fundamental questions that tie the two together need to be addressed:

- What is fictionality? In virtue of what is a work "fictional"?
- What are fictional characters? How, if at all, are they created?

- How is it possible to discover truths about fictional characters?
- Can the two aspects of characters, as imaginary human beings and as literary artifacts, be reconciled?
- How can readers respond emotionally to fictional characters, knowing them to be fiction?

## Fiction and Literature

As observed briefly in Chapter 2, the concepts of fiction and literature are not the same. The terms "fiction" and "literature" have different extensions and different meanings. Not all fictions are "literary" – most genre fiction, whodunit, spy, horror, romance, sci fi, is not deemed to be literature – nor are all literary works fictional, e.g., belles lettres writing of biography or history; also, arguably, some lyric poetry. The meanings of the terms differ not least because "literature" has an evaluative element lacking in "fiction." John Searle captures one difference nicely, if not entirely uncontroversially: "Whether or not a work is literature is for readers to decide, whether or not it is fictional is for the author to decide."[1] Of course many of the great works of literature, including novels, narrative poetry, and drama, are fictional, so an analysis of fiction will shed light on one important aspect of them. But it should not be supposed that an analysis of fiction is thereby an analysis of literature, nor that such an analysis will encompass distinctively literary qualities.

## Object and Description

The term "fiction" applies to *objects* of a certain kind as well as *descriptions* of a certain kind.[2] Fictional objects include imaginary characters, places, and events as characterized in works of fiction, while fictional descriptions include those statements or whole works which have this characterizing function. To say of an object that it is fictional normally implies that it is not *real*; fictional objects are "made up," "invented," "products of the imagination." To say of a description that it is fictional normally implies that it is not *true*; fictional descriptions are "false," "made up," "pretended."

---

[1] John R. Searle, "The Logical Status of Fictional Discourse," in *Expression and Meaning: Studies in the Theory of Speech Acts* (Cambridge: Cambridge University Press, 1979), p. 59.

[2] Peter Lamarque and Stein Haugom Olsen, *Truth, Fiction, and Literature: A Philosophical Perspective* (Oxford: Clarendon Press, 1994), pp. 16 ff.

Initial attention thus falls on the notions of reality and truth, but it is debatable whether these can provide a comprehensive explanation of fictionality, or even whether the normal implications hold without exception. Not everything unreal is a fictional object or everything false a fictional description and it can be argued that a certain kind of reality pertains to fictional objects and a certain kind of truth to fictional descriptions.

Philosophical questions arise about fictional entities as "objects" – their status, their relation to other kinds of objects, their place in a broader ontology. There are also questions about fictional sentences or descriptions. For example, it is helpful to distinguish between *discourse about fiction* and *fictional discourse*.[3] The former (by readers or critics) reports the content of works of fiction and can be judged for its accuracy and inaccuracy or its truth or falsity. The latter involves story-telling itself, which is not so obviously amenable to truth-assessment.

It should be noted that the difference between these modes of discourse – story-commentary and story-telling – cannot be identified through surface features of sentences alone. One and the same sentence-type can appear now in a story, now in a report about a story. The sentence "Gregor Samsa awoke one morning … transformed into a gigantic insect," when uttered by Kafka telling the story (*Metamorphosis*), proposes something imaginary and mysterious, but when uttered by a reader recounting the story, says something true (about "what happened"). Contextual factors will determine which usage applies and thus the appropriate mode of evaluation. Furthermore, not all fictional discourse is creative. Sometimes story-telling coincides with making up a story, where the story is told for the first time, sometimes the telling is a retelling. But retelling a story is still a mode of fictional discourse, distinct from discourse about fiction.

## Fictional Discourse: Telling a Story

### *Reference and truth*

What is it to tell a story, to write fiction? How can fictional story-telling be distinguished from the non-fictional kind? It is sometimes said that the line between fact and fiction is thin or non-existent and there do seem to be people who take pleasure in blurring the two, not least with popular entertainment: "reality TV" can seem like soap opera and characters in

---

[3]  The distinction appears in Peter van Inwagen, "Creatures of Fiction," *American Philosophical Quarterly*, 14 (1977), pp. 299–308.

soap operas like real people. There can be made-up stories based on fact, factual stories told like fiction, and stories where no one is quite clear what is made up and what is fact. Is there a genuine line between fiction and non-fiction?

At the theoretical level, the problem arises because there seem to be no surface features of language – syntactical or rhetorical – that decisively mark the fictive from the non-fictive, a point exploited by novelists and dramatists seeking realism. Here is the opening sentence of Graham Greene's novel *The Quiet American*:

> After dinner I sat and waited for Pyle in my room over the rue Catinat; he had said 'I'll be with you at latest by ten,' and when midnight struck I couldn't stay quiet any longer and went down into the street.

Nothing about the sentence itself points to its being fiction. Only later (assuming we do not know in advance that the sentence is from a novel) do we discover that the "I" refers not to the author Graham Greene but to the narrator, Thomas Fowler, a foreign correspondent, and that "Pyle" is the name of the "quiet American." Both these characters are "made up." Is reference, then, the decisive measure? But using fictional names is not a necessary or inevitable part of fictional story-telling. Historical fictions might employ only the names of real people. Nor, arguably, is the presence of non-denoting names *sufficient* for fiction. Some non-denoting names originate not in acts of story-telling but in genuine beliefs: the Garden of Eden, Atlantis, Eldorado, Vulcan the intra-Mercurial planet, might be examples. Although we might now call these the names of "fictitious" objects, they were not "made up" in the way that the characters Fowler or Pyle were in Greene's novel. If this is right then failure of reference is neither necessary nor sufficient for fictional story-telling.

Is falsehood, then, the mark of the fictional? Some theorists have thought so. Nelson Goodman states that "[a]ll fiction is literal, literary falsehood."[4] He includes "literal" because he holds that some fiction can be metaphorically true and "literary," because being false is not sufficient for fictionality. For Goodman, works of fiction commonly contain a mixture of truths and falsehoods, so "pure fiction" is rare. He thinks that the distinction between fiction and non-fiction is in practice a matter of degree, determined by percentages of truths and falsehoods.[5]

---

[4] Nelson Goodman, *Of Mind and Other Matters* (Cambridge, MA: Harvard University Press, 1984), p. 124; also "Fiction for Five Fingers," *Philosophy and Literature*, vol. 6, nos. 1/2 (1982), p. 162.

[5] Goodman, *Of Mind and Other Matters*, p. 126; "Fiction for Five Fingers," p. 164.

The falsity view of fiction has some plausibility, partly because the expression "pure fiction" is often colloquially used to mean "completely false" and partly because what is invented is unlikely to be true. Yet it seems curious to say that we do not know whether a work is fiction until we have calculated the percentage of falsehoods it contains. As Kendall Walton notes, "[w]e did not have to compare George Orwell's *1984* with the events of that year to decide whether it is fiction or non-fiction."[6] Also a work of fiction might, in principle, consist entirely of non-declarative sentences – interrogatives, imperatives, exclamations – which do not admit of truth assessment, so falsehood could not strictly be a condition of fictionality.

Finally, telling a story, in the sense relevant to novels and narrative poems, must be kept distinct from lying and from making a mistake. To explain that difference it is necessary to look beyond the truth or falsity of sentences themselves and toward the "acts" or "utterances" made. The fact that the story-teller is not trying to deceive and is not "getting it wrong" suggests the underlying purposes of story-telling are more fundamental to fiction than truth-value alone.

## Affirming nothing

What are the purposes that underlie story-telling? Here we are not concerned with "literary" purposes, such as, following Horace, to "please" and "instruct," nor are we concerned with incidental purposes of particular writers – to provoke controversy, to satirize convention, to write a comic epic in prose – but rather with the defining purposes behind any kind of narrative fiction. Are there core or constitutive intentions of the story-teller? Different views have been advanced.

One of the simplest views rests on the contrast between telling a story and making an assertion. Story-telling, on this view, is just speaking (or writing) without commitment to the truth of what is said. Fiction, then, stands to assertion rather as imagination stands to belief. A story-teller does not endorse the propositions put forward. Sir Philip Sidney in his *Defence of Poesie* (1595) was one of the first to present this view:

> Now for the Poet, he nothing affirmeth, and therefore never lieth: for as I take it, to lie, is to affirm that to be true, which is false. So as the other Artists, and especially the Historian, affirming many things, can in the cloudy knowledge of man, hardly escape from many lies. But the Poet as I said before, never affirmeth, the Poet never maketh any Circles about your imagination,

---

[6] Kendall Walton, *Mimesis as Make-Believe* (Cambridge MA: Harvard University Press, 1990), p. 74.

to conjure you to believe for true, what he writeth: he citeth not authorities of other histories, even for his entry, calleth the sweet Muses to inspire unto him a good invention. In truth, not laboring to tell you what is, or is not, but what should, or should not be. And therefore though he recount things not true, yet because he telleth them not for true, he lieth not.[7]

Twentieth-century philosophers have developed their own versions. Monroe Beardsley writes: "a fiction, in the literary sense, is a discourse in which the Report-sentences are not asserted."[8] J. O. Urmson offers a similar account, with a conclusion about the truth-value of fictive sentences: "I assert nothing when I make up a story as fiction, so *a fortiori* I do not assert something that is true or false, even by coincidence."[9]

However, to say merely negatively that the story-teller does not make assertions seems only a small advance. Furthermore, it is questionable as a necessary condition. Perhaps on occasion a story-teller does aim to make an assertion. Kendall Walton thinks so:

> There is no reason why, in appropriate circumstances, one should not be able to make an assertion by writing fiction. Indeed, there is a long tradition of doing just that. There is what we call *didactic* fiction — fiction used for instruction, advertising, propaganda, and so on. There is also the not uncommon practice, even in ordinary conversation, of making a point by telling a story, of speaking in parables.[10]

In defense of the no-assertion view, we need to distinguish between the status of the immediate fictive "report," as in the example from Graham Greene, which is clearly not asserted, and some further assertive purpose of the story-teller by way of "making a point." Descriptions at subject level – the level of the story itself – are distinct from wider reflections and purposes at a thematic level. Sidney acknowledges that there can be a moral purpose in poetry. Nicholas Wolterstorff puts the no-assertion theory in more positive terms: the defining "stance" of the story-teller "consists of *presenting*, of *offering for consideration*, certain states of affairs – for us to reflect on, to ponder

---

[7]    Philip Sidney's *Defence of Poesie*, from the Scolar Press facsimile of the British Museum's copy (Shelf-mark: C.57.b.38) of the Ponsonby edition (1595) [modern spelling has been substituted].

[8]    Monroe C. Beardsley, *Aesthetics: Problems in the Philosophy of Criticism* (Detroit, MI: Wayne State University Press, 1970), p. 420.

[9]    J. O. Urmson, "Fiction," *American Philosophical Quarterly*, 13 (1976), p. 155.

[10]   Walton, *Mimesis as Make-Believe*, p. 78; see also "Fiction, Fiction-Making, and Styles of Fictionality," *Philosophy and Literature*, vol. 7, no. 1 (1983), pp. 78–88.

over, to explore the implications of, to conduct strandwise extrapolation on."[11] That is plausible as far as it goes but it still seems insufficient, failing to capture something unique to fiction. Presenting a thought without asserting it is not peculiar to story-telling, and it says little about why stories are told and enjoyed.

### Fiction and pretense

More promising are attempts to explain the core of fiction in terms of pretense, an approach supported by the etymology of "fiction" from *fingere*, meaning, among other things, to "feign." The problem is to say what exactly is pretended. John Searle has proposed a well-known version of the pretense theory, in terms of speech acts. "The author of a work of fiction," he writes, "pretends to perform a series of illocutionary acts, normally of the assertive type," namely "statements, assertions, descriptions, characterizations, identifications, explanations, and numerous others," although without any intended deception.[12] The pretending is a "nondeceptive pseudoperformance"; for Searle it is a matter of indifference whether we describe it as "pretending" or "acting as if," or "going through the motions," or "imitating."[13]

Related theses help to clarify Searle's theory:

> [T]he pretended illocutions which constitute a work of fiction are made possible by the existence of a set of conventions which suspend the normal operation of the rules relating illocutionary acts and the world.[14]

> [T]he pretended performances of illocutionary acts which constitute the writing of a work of fiction consist in actually performing utterance acts with the intention of invoking the horizontal conventions that suspend the normal illocutionary commitments of the utterances.[15]

So, on this account, Graham Greene is *pretending* to make an assertion (about matters of fact) while doing so such thing. Readers in this case have no difficulty recognizing the pretense, although there might be cases where the pretense is not recognized. Searle's theory rightly emphasizes the *conventional* nature of story-telling. Without conventions about what is intended by story-tellers and what is expected of story-audiences there would be no possibility of such a "nondeceptive pseudoperformance." There must be background

---

[11]  Nicholas Wolterstorff, *Works and Worlds of Art* (Oxford: Clarendon Press, 1980), p. 233.

[12]  Searle, "The Logical Status of Fictional Discourse," p. 65.

[13]  Ibid., p. 65.

[14]  Ibid., p. 67.

[15]  Ibid., p. 68.

assumptions in place that allow for superficially similar kinds of utterance to be treated in such markedly different ways. What is notable, though, is how easily the conventions are learned and at how early an age. Very young children grasp the "point" of story-telling without any conventions being spelt out, although it seems likely that strong contextual cues (how the stories are told, tone of voice, etc.) have a significant role to play. Part of what Searle means by "suspend[ing] ... the rules relating illocutionary acts and the world" is the suspending of kinds of "uptake," either belief or action. The child who believes a story or who acts as if the story were true has either not grasped the convention or has not recognized its operation at the time.

The second thesis emphasizes that not all the author does is pretended: only the "illocutionary acts," not the "utterance acts." An utterance act is the act of "uttering words (morphemes, sentences)," something one can do "without performing a propositional or illocutionary act at all."[16] The question of how much more an author does than just uttering sentences, short of performing full-blown illocutionary acts, takes us back to the issues about texts and authorial intention, raised in Chapter 3. Unless one takes the extreme view of Roland Barthes, that in being uttered (or written) sentences become undifferentiated *écriture*, it seems that the utterances must have more or less determinate propositional content. Searle's view is that it is not meaning that is affected by fictive utterance but "force." What is important is that the "normal illocutionary commitments" are "suspended." In this, Searle's theory has something in common with the no-assertion view.

Searle offers two qualifications to the idea that pretending to perform illocutionary acts constitutes the writing of fiction. First, he allows that "serious (i.e., non-fictional) speech acts can be conveyed by fictional texts, even though the conveyed speech act is not represented in the text."[17] In other words it is possible, according to Searle, to perform non-pretended illocutionary acts through fictive utterance, even though this is done indirectly. The idea is that a work of fiction might "make a statement" or perhaps "raise a question" as part of its overall purpose. The point is similar to that made by Walton.

It is not only indirect assertions that can be made through fictive stories. It is often important to recognize other kinds of illocutionary intentions in a narrative: a writer might be *parodying* a sentimental style, *rejecting* liberal values, *pleading* for more tolerance in the world, *inviting* readers to take a certain view, as well as warning, cajoling, advising, entreating, requesting,

[16]  J. R. Searle, *Speech Acts: An Essay in the Philosophy of Language* (Cambridge: Cambridge University Press, 1969), p. 24.

[17]  Searle, "The Logical Status of Fictional Discourse," p. 74.

or admonishing.[18] These are supplementary purposes behind the more basic purpose of telling a story; they are not in competition with, nor entail any weakening of, the primary fictive intent.

Searle's second qualification potentially raises further problems for the "pretended speech acts" view of fiction. For he also allows that in works of fiction there can be genuine illocutionary acts not merely indirectly performed, as in the cases just given, but directly so. He gives the example of the opening sentence of *Anna Karenina* – "Happy families are all happy in the same way, unhappy families unhappy in their separate different ways" – which he describes as a "genuine assertion." This leads him to distinguish between a "work of fiction" and "fictional discourse," only the latter consisting of pretended (direct) illocutionary acts.

It is a matter of debate what status to give to sentences of the *Anna Karenina* kind, and perhaps different instances should be treated in different ways. But Searle is surely not right to *take it for granted* that the sentence in question is a genuine assertion. The sentiment expressed might well be something the author, Tolstoy, wishes to endorse but the appearance of the sentence in a *novel* signals caution. After all, few readers would suppose that the equally famous first sentence of *Pride and Prejudice* had the unequivocal endorsement of Jane Austen: "It is a truth universally acknowledged, that a single man in possession of a good fortune, must be in want of a wife." The cautious and proper first step in both cases is to assume a distance between author and statement, for example by attributing the content to an implied speaker, or noticing an ironic tone, or identifying the sentence as *thematic*, pointing to motifs in the work to come.

David Lewis offers a slightly different version of the pretense theory:

> Storytelling is pretence. The storyteller purports to be telling the truth about matters whereof he has knowledge. He purports to be talking about characters who are known to him, and whom he refers to, typically, by means of their ordinary proper names. But if his story is fiction, he is not really doing these things.[19]

In first-person narratives, like *The Quiet American*, the author pretends to be the narrator: Greene pretends to be Fowler. In third-person narratives,

---

[18]   For further arguments on the relevance of such authorial illocutionary intentions: see, e.g., Quentin Skinner, "Motives, Intentions and the Interpretations of Texts," *New Literary History*, 3 (1972) and A. J. Close, "*Don Quixote* and the 'Intentionalist Fallacy,'" *British Journal of Aesthetics*, vol. 12, no. 1 (1972), pp. 13–39.

[19]   David Lewis, "Truth in Fiction," *American Philosophical Quarterly*, vol. 15, no. 1 (1978), pp. 37–46 at p. 40.

like *Pride and Prejudice*, the author pretends to have knowledge of the events described and pretends to be telling the truth about them. Lewis's prime concern is to account for our reasoning about what is "true" in fictional worlds. We will return to that. Is he right about an author's pretending to be someone? Arguably, the crucial aspect of Lewis's account is not the pretense but the recognition of a narrator distinct from the author in both first- and third-person cases. Whether we say that the real author *pretends* to be that narrator or simply postulates the narrator does not seem of great significance.

A third kind of pretense theory involves neither pretending to perform illocutionary acts nor pretending to be a character (narrator) in a fictional world. It rests on the idea of a story-teller's pretending *that* such-and-such is the case. Thus, for example, Gilbert Ryle writes: "what Dickens did [in creating Mr. Pickwick] was to compound a highly complex predicate and pretend that someone had the characters so signified."[20] Ryle takes pretense to be interchangeable with imagining: "Dickens invented a composite description … [and] simply imagined or pretended or 'said' that it was true of someone."[21] By insisting on the propositional nature of imagining – "[i]magining is always imagining that something is the case"[22] – Ryle seeks to remove any possible ontological confusion about "imaginary objects": "[w]here we seem to be imaginatively creating a thing or person, we are in fact imagining that someone or something has a complex of characters."[23] So pretense in fiction is strictly pretense concerning existence or instantiation.

A consequence of Ryle's view is that if by coincidence something (real) does happen to instantiate the predicates in a story, then the story ceases to be fiction and becomes history or biography. So if the descriptions in *Pickwick Papers* should turn out to be true of some actual person, then "we should say that while previously we had thought *Pickwick Papers* was only a *pretense* biography, we now find that, by coincidence, it is a real one."[24] That conclusion is counterintuitive precisely because it seems so natural to assume that what makes a work fiction is the intent behind its creation more than the truth or otherwise of its sentences. Another objection is that the *particularity* of fictional creations is lost in an account which emphasizes only the generality of descriptions waiting for instantiation.

---

[20] Gilbert Ryle, "Imaginary Objects," *Proceedings of the Aristotelian Society*, suppl. vol. 12 (1933), reprinted in Gilbert Ryle, *Collected Papers, Vol. II: Collected Essays 1929–1968* (London: Hutchinson, 1971), p. 78.

[21] Ibid., p. 79.

[22] Ibid., p. 81.

[23] Ibid.

[24] Ibid., p. 79.

The association of fiction with pretense in some form or other seems fairly innocuous. But to *identify* story-telling with pretending might still seem too limited or negative. On the face of it, it emphasizes only what story-tellers are *not* doing, i.e., what they are merely *pretending* to do, rather than in a more positive way characterizing what they *are* doing, and aiming to achieve. If the novelist is merely pretending to do what the historian or biographer is actually doing it makes writing novels seem like a secondary or derived activity.

## Fictive utterance

In seeking a more positive account, still based on a writer's intentions, other theorists have preferred to locate pretense not in what the story-teller does but in what the story-*audience* does. On this view the story-teller's primary intention is not to pretend anything himself but to get an *audience* to pretend or make-believe or imagine something (without intended deception). Gregory Currie has developed a view of this kind, although he prefers *make-believe* to *pretense*.[25] Currie emphasizes the role of *fictive utterance* and *fictive intention* in a theory of fiction, the latter being an intention of the fiction-maker that an audience make-believe a proposition. This intention is "Gricean," in the sense that a fiction-maker intends an audience to undertake the requisite make-believe as a result of recognizing that very intention.[26] Informally, and subject to further refinements, Currie presents his account of fictive utterance as follows:

> I want you to make believe some proposition *P*; I utter a sentence that means *P*, intending that you shall recognize that this is what the sentence means, and to recognize that I intend to produce a sentence that means *P*; and I intend you to infer from this that I intend you to make believe that *P*, and, finally, I intend that you shall, partly as a result of this intention, come to make believe that *P*.[27]

A feature of all such intention-based views is that they focus on the origins of fictions in utterances of a certain kind, "fictive utterances," rather than in

[25]   Gregory Currie, *The Nature of Fiction* (Cambridge: Cambridge University Press, 1990), pp. 50–51.

[26]   See H. P. Grice, "Meaning," *Philosophical Review*, vol. 66, no. 3 (1957), pp. 377–388, reprinted in *Studies in the Ways of Words* (Cambridge, MA: Harvard University Press, 1989), pp. 213–224, and "Utterer's Meaning and Intentions," *Philosophical Review*, 78 (1969), pp. 147–177, reprinted in *Studies in the Ways of Words*, pp. 86–117. For a systematic application to fiction, see Gregory Currie, "What is Fiction?" *Journal of Aesthetics and Art Criticism*, 43 (1985), pp. 385–392 and *The Nature of Fiction*.

[27]   Currie, *Nature of Fiction*, p. 31.

relations between fiction and fact.[28] To make up a fiction in story-telling is to make utterances with these intentions and expectations. The stories will characteristically include names and descriptions of people and places that are pure invention and sentences that are literally false. But it is not the references or the falsity that determine fictionality.

A serious question, however, for all such accounts is whether an utterer's intention is sufficient to explain fiction. Surely the *content* of what is uttered is as important in determining fictionality as intended mode of utterance? Currie, like other theorists of this kind, wants to allow (in admittedly extreme and unusual cases) that a fiction could consist entirely of true sentences and ordinarily denoting names. *Pickwick Papers* would remain a fiction even if, by massive coincidence, all its sentences turned out to be true. Currie aims to meet the objection that fictive utterance is not sufficient to underwrite such cases by proposing the further condition that the content be "at most accidentally true." The trouble is the proposal looks ad hoc. How can intentions alone turn a resolutely non-fictional content into fiction? What is fictional is what is *made up*, which has to do with both origin and content.

One answer to the conundrum is this. The origin can be explained, as Currie rightly shows, in terms of an act with a certain kind of intention. But then the requisite content can be defined in terms of that origin, without the need for any condition about "accidental truth." The principle is simple: how things are *described* in a fictive utterance determines how things *are* in the fictional world. This is the connection between fictional content and fictive utterance. It marks a sharp contrast with non-fiction or truth, for *how things are (in the world)* is not determined by any kind of utterance.[29] This deep dependence of the fictional on modes of presentation is at the heart of the distinction between fiction and non-fiction.

Not all theorists, though, accept a central place for intention. It is not that this runs up against the Intentional Fallacy, for fictive intention does not determine *meaning* and it can fall under Levinson's conception of "categorial intention." But Kendall Walton has denied that fiction-making – or any intentional act – is at the heart of the practice of fiction. For him it is objects, namely those "whose function is to serve as props in games of make-believe," not acts, which are definitive of fiction:

> [t]he institution of fiction centers not on the activity of fiction makers but on
> objects — works of fiction or natural objects — and their role in appreciators'

---

[28]   A similar account is presented in Lamarque and Olsen, *Truth, Fiction, and Literature*, who hold that in fictive utterance an author invites an audience to make-believe that standard speech acts are being performed even while knowing that they are not.

[29]   See Lamarque and Olsen, *Truth, Fiction, and Literature*, p. 51.

activities, objects whose function is to serve as props in games of make-believe. Fiction making is merely the activity of constructing such props.[30]

Walton emphasizes the variety of fictions, which are not restricted to narratives – a reason in itself to reject speech act accounts of fiction – even including dolls, children's mud pies, family portraits, indeed all representations, in the class of fictions. In the literary case the props would be sentences. Whatever one thinks of this permissive broadening of the extension, which rests more on theoretical stipulation than on ordinary usage, it seems implausible to remove intention altogether from an account of fiction. Even the faces we see in the clouds or the freak writing on seaside rocks (Walton's examples) only become representations, contra Walton, by being purposively assimilated into human activities or imaginings.[31]

## Fictional Characters

In the literary context, to think about fictional characters is naturally to think of the great iconic characters from Shakespeare or the nineteenth-century novel: Othello, Falstaff, Shylock, Nicholas Nickleby, Emma Bovary, Anna Karenina, Jane Eyre, Raskolnikov. Such characters seem "rounded," full of psychological depth, recognizable as human beings, but also fully fictional in the sense of being creatures of the imagination. The list might not so readily include Richard III or Antony and Cleopatra, even though these appear in fictionalized dramas. Being "based on" real historical figures they seem somewhat less than purely fictional, if fictional at all. Other characters for other reasons seem remote from the paradigm. The character of Everyman, from the sixteenth-century morality play, is certainly not "round," any more than are his companions Fellowship, Kindred, Cousin, and Good Deeds. Minor characters lack not just depth but detail: in *As You Like It* (V iii) two pages enter, exchange a few words, sing the song "It was a lover and his lass | With a hey, and a ho, and a hey nonino" and depart, never to return. What these pages look like or think, even what their names are, is not specified. A different kind of indeterminacy is manifested in the fragmentary characters of postmodernist writing: Samuel Beckett's play *Not I* presents only a speaking mouth with barely any discernible personality. In the Japanese Noh theater,

---

[30] Walton, *Mimesis as Make-Believe*, p. 88.

[31] Jerrold Levinson, *The Pleasures of Aesthetics: Philosophical Essays* (Ithaca, NY: Cornell University Press, 1996), p. 296; Lamarque and Olsen, *Truth, Fiction, and Literature*, pp. 47–49.

characters are deliberately stylized to dissolve personality.[32] In the light of such diversity it is reasonable to ask whether there is anything substantial to be said about fictional characters from a theoretical point of view.

In literary studies there has been deep skepticism about character-centered criticism for over fifty years. This partly stems from a critical shift toward formalism, partly also from a shift within literary theory away from "liberal humanism" with its emphasis on self, subject, human nature, and personality. In postmodernist thought, a curious reversal has taken place, whereby rather than seeing fictional characters as human beings, theorists have come to see human beings as more like fictional characters: uncentered, diffuse, lacking unity, mere constructs of discourses.

For the philosopher of literature, though, fundamental questions remain about the nature and status of characters, bearing in mind precisely the kind of diversity just noted, yet without needing to engage further issues about the postmodernist self. Can fictional characters be said to have any kind of reality *as characters?* We certainly speak as if they do, because however much critics might disdain character-based criticism, there is a wealth of ordinary discourse "about characters" which calls for explanation. But the critics' warnings against treating characters just as if they were real people who we get to know – and enjoy speculating about – should be heeded not just as a constraint on serious critical practice but in philosophical theorizing.

Philosophers have taken radically different positions on ordinary talk "about characters," some taking it at face value, others insisting that any apparent reference to a realm of fictitious objects is pure linguistic illusion. The differences of approach often reflect deep disagreements within both semantics and metaphysics. In the early years of analytic philosophy these differences came to light when basic questions about truth and meaning were first raised as central to philosophy. *If names fail to denote anything real – as is the case with paradigmatic fictional names – then how could sentences in which they appear have meaning?*

Two prominent lines of thought were proposed. The first, taken by Bertrand Russell, in the early years of the twentieth century, is to deny that these apparent names – "Othello," "Falstaff," "Shylock," and the rest – are really names at all, in a strict sense.[33] Russell wrote:

> To maintain that Hamlet, for example, exists in his own world, namely, in the world of Shakespeare's imagination, just as truly as (say) Napoleon existed

[32] See Peter Lamarque, "Expression and the Mask" in *Fictional Points of View* (Ithaca, NY: Cornell University Press, 1996).

[33] Bertrand Russell, *Logic and Knowledge*, ed. R. C. Marsh (London: George Allen and Unwin, 1956): notably in "On Denoting" and "The Philosophy of Logical Atomism."

in the ordinary world, is to say something deliberately confusing, or else confused to a degree which is scarcely credible. There is only one world, the 'real' world: Shakespeare's imagination is part of it, and the thoughts that he had in writing Hamlet are real. So are the thoughts that we have in reading the play. But it is of the very essence of fiction that only the thoughts, feelings, etc., in Shakespeare and his readers are real, and that there is not, in addition to them, an objective Hamlet.[34]

Logical analysis, notably Russell's Theory of Descriptions and the theory that ordinary names are disguised descriptions, can show, according to Russell, that what look like genuine denoting terms might be no such thing, and that the appearance of denotation can be entirely removed through logical paraphrase, leaving nothing more puzzling than general terms and quantifiers.

The second line, taken by Alexius Meinong, at roughly the same period, is to insist that all such names, including the most obviously fictional, are in fact denoting terms, but that what they denote are objects with different kinds of being, full-blown existence being only one such kind.[35] Othello can *be* without *existing*. Thus while Russell sought to eliminate fictional entities as denotata of fictional names, Meinong sought to accommodate them within a general "theory of objects." Descendants of these two strategies, which can be labeled *eliminativism* and *accommodationism*, are still in evidence.

### Eliminativism: paraphrasing talk "about characters"

One aim of logical analysis is to remove unwanted "ontological commitments."[36] Fiction provides an obvious case of problematic commitments because sentences in works of fiction seem to make reference to entities that have no existence in reality. Yet the application of logical analysis affords somewhat mixed results. Take the simplest kind of example, typical of the logician:

(1) Sherlock Holmes is a detective.

What is striking about the sentence is that it seems obviously *true*, yet there is no such person as Sherlock Holmes. On the analysis promoted by Russell and Quine (and reminiscent of Ryle), the apparent commitment to a

---

[34] Bertrand Russell, *Introduction to Mathematical Philosophy* (London: Routledge, 1993), p. 169.

[35] A. Meinong, "Theory of Objects," in R. M. Chisholm, ed., *Realism and the Background of Phenomenology* (Glencoe, IL: Free Press, 1960).

[36] E.g., W. V. O. Quine, "On What There Is," in *From a Logical Point of View* (Cambridge, MA: Harvard University Press, 1953).

fictitious entity *Holmes* is removed by paraphrasing away the name in favor of a quantifier and a complex predicate, yielding something like this:

> (2) There is some unique thing that satisfies the Holmes-description and is a detective.

This latter sentence is meaningful, can be assessed for truth or falsity, and makes no commitment to a realm of fictitious entities.

However, the analysis seems deficient in a number of respects. First, it loses the truth of (1) because (2), which makes an existence claim, is false. By making all sentences "about" fictional characters turn out false, the analysis fails to capture a distinction between those, like (1), which seem to have an element of truth, and those, like "Holmes is unintelligent," that seem manifestly false. Second, it treats (1) as if it were an assertion about the real world, rather than about a fictional world. Third, related to this, it makes the truth-value of (1) contingent not on how things are in a fictional world but how things are in reality, with the result that the sentence could turn out to be true if, by coincidence, the predicates in (2) were satisfied. Yet, as we saw in responding to Ryle's account of *Pickwick Papers*, the truth-value of "Holmes is a detective" should not depend on whether any actual person happens to instantiate the Holmes-properties. Finally, it fails to distinguish fictional discourse from discourse about fiction, for it deals only with the latter and gives the wrong result. But arguably it gives the wrong result too as an analysis of the former, for to claim that all sentences in Conan Doyle's novels are false seems unhelpful, since it fails to acknowledge the author's aim of making up a story rather than reporting facts about the world.

Admittedly, elimination by logical paraphrase can take different forms. Another influential proposal is offered by Nelson Goodman, who focuses on pictorial representation, although the theory offered can be applied readily to linguistic fictions. Goodman suggests that we analyse "X is a picture of a unicorn," not as a relation between a picture and a fictitious entity but as a one-place predication captured as "X is a unicorn-picture."[37] The predicate "is a unicorn-picture" serves only to classify picture types, and thus bears no referential commitments. Goodman has shown in general how apparent commitments in talking *about Holmes* can be avoided by using the non-referential locution "Holmes-about"; so sentence (1) is not *about Holmes* in a relational sense, but *Holmes-about* in a predicative, non-relational, sense.[38]

Goodman's strategy is effective up to a point, but like all such paraphrasing strategies its scope is limited. Supposed references to fictitious entities crop

[37]  Nelson Goodman, *The Languages of Art* (New York: Bobbs-Merrill, 1968), pp. 21–26.
[38]  Nelson Goodman, "About," *Mind*, 70 (1961), pp. 1–24.

up in contexts where Russellian or Goodmanian paraphrases seem problematic. In addition to simple descriptive sentences like (1), there are also sentences like the following, which an adequate theory should accommodate:

(3) Holmes was created by Conan Doyle.
(4) Holmes is a fictional character.
(5) Holmes doesn't really exist.
(6) Holmes is smarter than Poirot.
(7) Holmes is an emblematic character of modern fiction.

Eliminativists often struggle to find paraphrases for such usages, and how they tackle these different contexts is sometimes thought to be an appropriate test for eliminativist programmes.[39] For example, the expedient of placing the prefix "In the fiction" before sentences like (1), to signal their fictive status,[40] is not available for (3)–(7) because it is not true *in the world of the Holmes stories* that Holmes is an emblematic fictional character created by Conan Doyle. In his own world he is a detective! Also, the use of quantifiers and functions, as in (2), threatens to yield quite the wrong truth-values in at least (3), (4), and (7). Accommodationists often base their own acceptance of fictional entities on what they take to be the literal truth of sentences like (4), and it is just such sentences that pose the biggest problem for the eliminativist.

Kendall Walton's eliminativist strategy appeals not to logical analysis of the Russellian kind but to the idea of "make-believe." For Walton, as we have seen, to be fictional is to be a "prop in a game of make-believe." Games and their associated props are real enough, but there is no further reality to Holmes or Poirot. Indeed, because "Holmes" has no denotation there are, according to Walton, strictly no propositions about Holmes, and thus sentence (1), taken literally, expresses no proposition. This is a strong claim, for it implies that attempts to capture the meaning of (1) through paraphrase are futile, since it has no meaning.[41] Instead, on Walton's account, we pretend that (1) has a meaning, and we pretend that in using it we are stating something true. Walton explains his example "Tom Sawyer attended his own funeral" as follows: "*The Adventures of Tom Sawyer* is such that one who engages in pretense of kind K in a game authorized for it makes it fictional of himself

[39]    R. Howell, "Fictional Objects: How They Are and How They Aren't," *Poetics*, 8 (1979), pp. 129–177; Lamarque, *Fictional Points of View*; A. L. Thomasson, *Fiction and Metaphysics* (Cambridge: Cambridge University Press, 1999).

[40]    As recommended by Lewis, "Truth in Fiction."

[41]    For objections, see E. Zemach, "Tom Sawyer and the Beige Unicorn," *British Journal of Aesthetics*, vol. 38, no. 2 (1998), pp. 167–179.

in that game that he speaks truly."[42] We learn what kind K is ostensively by confronting appropriate acts of game playing.

Walton's eliminivatism is subtle, with applications to all the problem cases, and is well motivated within his broader theory of representation. However, arguably, the theory extends pretense too widely and postulates games of make-believe, for example, in cases like (3), (4), and (7), where literal construal seems more intuitive.[43]

### Accommodationism: finding some reality in fictional characters

Attempts to accommodate fictional entities take even more varied forms than attempts to eliminate them. A good starting point is Meinong, who proposed that there are nonexistent as well as existent objects. Anything that can be talked about, as the referent of a singular term, has, according to Meinong, some kind of *being*, including even contradictory entities like round squares. So Holmes is an object, possessing all the Holmes properties, but lacking the property of existence. Sentences like (1) are thus construed literally as subject/object predications.

Refinements of Meinong's theory have been developed by, among others, Terence Parsons, who holds that there is at least one object correlated with every combination of "nuclear" properties; these are properties such as *being a detective, smoking a pipe, having the name "Holmes,"* etc.[44] Many such objects do not exist; fictional characters, like Holmes, differ from ordinary humans not only in lacking existence but in being "incomplete," in the sense that for any given property it is not always determinate whether the character possesses that property or not. There is no answer to the question whether Holmes has a mole on his back (assuming this is unspecified in the stories) so, on Parsons's view, Holmes is "incomplete" in this respect. Parsons distinguishes a nonexistent object's "nuclear" properties, as in (1), from its "extra-nuclear" properties, as in (3), (4), and (7).[45]

Similar but not identical views are held by other accommodationists.[46] Charles Crittenden might be classed among the Meinongians, in giving a literal construal of talk about fiction, but his version is anti-metaphysical, influenced by Wittgenstein's notion of language-games. Fictional objects,

[42]   Walton, *Mimesis as Make-Believe*, p. 400.

[43]   F. Kroon, "Make-Believe and Fictional Reference," *Journal of Aesthetics and Art Criticism*, vol. 52, no. 2 (1994), pp. 207–214; Thomasson, *Fiction and Metaphysics*.

[44]   Terence Parsons, *Nonexistent Objects* (New Haven, CT: Yale University Press, 1980).

[45]   For a discussion and appraisal of Parsons' theory, see J. Levinson, Review of Terence Parsons, *Nonexistent Objects*, *Journal of Aesthetics and Art Criticism*, 40 (1981), pp. 96–99.

[46]   E.g., Edward Zalta, *Abstract Objects* (Dordrecht: Reidel, 1983).

Crittenden believes, are "grammatical objects" arising within a "practice."[47] Richard Rorty likewise rejects metaphysics and ontology but thinks it is pointless to try to "eliminate" fictional entities, because he sees the "problem about fictional discourse" as a pseudo-problem arising from two misguided conceptions: truth as "correspondence" with the facts, and language as a "picture" of the world.[48]

Other theorists take fictional objects to be not *nonexistent* objects but instead a species of *abstract* objects. For example, Peter van Inwagen describes fictional characters as "theoretical entities of literary criticism,"[49] Nicholas Wolterstorff sees them as "person-kinds," in contrast to "kinds of persons."[50]

## Creating fictional characters

A problem confronts certain theories that attribute the status of abstract existence to fictional objects (a problem also acknowledged by Parsons for his theory of "nonexistent objects"), namely that fictional characters so conceived cannot, it has been argued, be *created*, given the timeless nature of abstract entities. Numbers, for example, which are often taken to be typical examples of abstract entities, are not created as such, although of course *numerals*, used to denote numbers, are human inventions. We speak of mathematicians discovering, not inventing, mathematical theorems. But can it be true that characters are not created but discovered? Did Conan Doyle discover not create Sherlock Holmes? The idea seems implausible. But some theorists are prepared to accept the consequences. Wolterstorff, for example, who holds that characters are "person-kinds," argues that while authors might be *creative* in delineating a character, they are not literally *creators*:

> to be thus creative is not to bring the character into existence. It is not to create it. ... From the infinitude of person-kinds the author selects one. His creativity lies in the freshness, the imaginativeness, the originality, of his selection, rather than his bringing into existence what did not before exist.[51]

[47]   C. Crittenden, *Unreality: The Metaphysics of Fictional Objects* (Ithaca, NY: Cornell University Press, 1991).

[48]   R. Rorty, "Is There a Problem about Fictional Discourse?" in *Consequences of Pragmatism* (Brighton: Harvester Press, 1982). C. G. Prado, *Making Believe: Philosophical Reflections on Fiction* (Westport, CT: Greenwood, 1984) further develops this approach.

[49]   P. van Inwagen, "Creatures of Fiction," *American Philosophical Quarterly*, vol. 14, no. 4 (1977), pp. 299–308.

[50]   N. Wolterstorff, *Works and Worlds of Art* (Oxford: Clarendon Press, 1980).

[51]   E.g., ibid., p. 145.

The idea is similar to that discussed in Chapter 2 about the ontology of music. Platonists about music – those who hold that musical works are timeless abstract structures – also hold that composers select but do not create their works.

It would be wrong, however, to think, given how counterintuitive this seems, that eliminativists gain the upper hand, for they too find the creation of characters problematic. In denying any reality to characters they are not in a position to say that authors create characters, in the sense of bringing characters into existence. Again, they need to paraphrase sentences like (3). Authors might create things like sentences, descriptions, stories, Pickwick-pictures, or props in games of make-believe, depending on the theory at hand, but it could not be admitted that they create fictional characters, because, on these accounts, there are no such things.

There is a kind of accommodationism, though, that takes fictional characters to be both abstract entities and created artifacts.[52] Amie Thomasson has developed such a conception in detail, based on a theory of dependence, whereby fictional characters have a necessary dependence both on the linguistic acts which bring them into existence and on the continued existence of the works (as distinct from individual texts) which sustain them in existence. On this view, fictional objects are historical not timeless entities, their historical origins being essential to them, and they can cease to exist as well as come into existence. They have a similar status to laws, theories, governments, and indeed literary works. The attraction of this kind of accommodationism, setting aside worries about the ontological category of "abstract artifact," is that it acknowledges some kind of reality for fictional characters, allowing that there can be literal truths about them, without postulating anomalous "nonexistent objects."

But even if we allow for the literal creation of characters there are other problems beyond those of ontology. One is the problem of "borrowing." Few fictional characters are entirely original. If I create a fictional character and it turns out – as it inevitably will – to have features in common with other fictional characters, just how creative have I been? Have I produced something new or just a variant on something old? Did Shakespeare *create* his central characters or just rework those of his sources? How similar can characters become yet remain distinct? Indeed, how different can they be (e.g., in different versions) yet remain the same?

---

[52] Nathan Salmon, "Nonexistence," *Nous*, 32 (1998), pp. 277–319; Thomasson, *Fiction and Metaphysics*; J. Emt, "On the Nature of Fictional Entities," in J. Emt and G. Hermerén, eds., *Understanding the Arts: Contemporary Scandinavian Aesthetics* (Lund: Lund University Press, 1992).

The question about creativity shades into questions about character identity. Shakespeare's *Romeo and Juliet* (1593/4) has as its source Arthur Brooke's rhymed novella *The Tragicall Historye of Romeus and Juliet* (1562); in fact the story was not new to Brooke and was familiar at the time, perhaps originating in Italy.[53] Beyond the bare outline of the story, there is not much in common between the two works, and it is not difficult to acknowledge Shakespeare's play as original and creative. But are his characters the *same* as Brooke's? Is Shakespeare's Juliet the very same character as Brooke's Juliet? They speak different lines, they are described differently, even the attitude of the authors to them is different. It is tempting to say that *in some respects* they are the same, in other respects different. Yet identity seems not to be a matter of degree. Jones might have much in common with Smith, sharing many qualities, but we would not say that Jones is the *same person* as Smith unless a true ("numerical") identity holds, as when we say that George Orwell and Eric Blair are one and the same.

Sameness of character is problematic because judgments of identity, in this case, seem to be relative to interests. If we are interested in Romeo and Juliet as prototypical lovers, iconic figures alongside Paris and Helen, Odysseus and Penelope, Tristan and Isolde, then it would be important to affirm that Brooke and Shakespeare were offering versions of one and same character. But if we are concerned with the fine specification of the characters in the two works, we would most likely insist that they were essentially different, differently conceived. In the better known case of the Faust renditions we might readily affirm, from the perspective of literary history, that Marlowe, Goethe, and Mann depicted the same character, but that, from the point of view of critical analysis, three importantly different characters are presented in the three works. It is not just that different descriptions are applied to them, different emphases laid, for that is true of characters that appear in sequences of works, such as the Palliser novels or indeed the Bertie Wooster or Sherlock Holmes stories. There is no doubt that it is the very same Holmes in *A Study in Scarlet* and *The Hound of the Baskervilles* even though quite different events are portrayed, and all that is in common in the characterization is just that kind of shared core found between the two Juliets or the multiple Fausts. Nor do these cases rest on the continuity of the same author, for sequences by different authors might indisputably portray the same character: Jean Rhys's novel *Wide Sargasso Sea* (1966) fills in, creatively and imaginatively, the life of the under-specified mad first wife of Mr. Rochester in *Jane Eyre* (1847); the interest and point of the story rest on the identity of the characters.

---

[53] An earlier Italian source seems to be Luigi da Porto's *Historia novellamente ritrovata di due nobili amanti* (c. 1530).

It seems, then, as if character identity is quite unlike personal identity in exhibiting what can be called interest-relativity.[54] Two characters might be identical relative to one set of interests, but different relative to another. This connects to the ontological thesis that characters are abstract types. The broadly specified Faust-character possesses the essential property of making a pact with the devil; the more finely specified characters appearing in the three works have further essential, and different, properties. In another example, there is a single generic character-type the *inspired amateur detective*, exemplified by Sherlock Holmes, Hercule Poirot, Miss Marple, and Lord Peter Wimsey. Are these the same character? Relative to some interests, yes, relative to most, no, because the set of essential characteristics that matter are fuller than just the single trope. The same goes for the character-type *unhappily-married-adulterous-and-doomed-woman*: Emma Bovary, Thérèse Raquin, and Anna Karenina are the same type (thus the same character) under a broad cultural perspective, yet differ radically under other, more refined, perspectives.

It is not enough, though, to identify characters with types, for then we are open to the problem facing Russell and Ryle, that if a real person were to instantiate the type, then in effect the character becomes that person. There is also the problem that general types are not created. The properties – or types – *star-crossed lover, maker of a pact with the devil, amateur detective, unhappily-married-adulterous-and-doomed-woman*, are not in themselves created. These are character-types that are discovered, borrowed, or "selected" rather than made; such is the idea behind the accommodationist theories of Parsons and Wolterstorff. However, when authors co-opt these types for their own narratives they do, arguably, create something. In Shakespeare's terms, "the poet's pen | Turns them to shapes, and gives to airy nothing | A local habitation and a name."[55] Fictional characters gain their individuality by being "indicated" in a particular narrative.[56] Even the most minimally specified characters, like the anonymous singing pages in *As You Like It*, attain a kind of individuality arising out of the context of their presentation. Shakespeare did not create the character *singing page* but he did create the two singing pages in that scene. What the grounding narrative affords is something akin to *indexicality*, allowing us to distinguish *that* page from *that* page in this brief scene. After all, the characters speak different lines and have different individuating qualities. Also they are essentially fictive. Even if Shakespeare

[54] See Peter Lamarque, "How to Create a Fictional Character," in Berys Gaut and Paisley Livingston, eds., *The Creation of Art* (Cambridge University Press, 2003), pp. 33–52.

[55] *A Midsummer Night's Dream* (V i 10–12).

[56] The idea of an "indicated type" is developed by Jerrold Levinson in "What a Musical Work Is," and "What a Musical Work Is, Again," in *Music, Art, & Metaphysics* (Ithaca, NY: Cornell University Press, 1990).

based his portrayal on real-world pages who did indeed speak just those words and sing just that song, it would still be wrong to identify the fictional pages with any real person.

Even a minimally specified character is created by an author to the extent that the author creates a narrative in which the character is individuated. According to Searle, all that is needed to create a fictional character is to "pretend to refer to a person."[57] But if a narrative simply states "Three soldiers were killed" without further detail, has the author pretended to refer to three persons? Even if so, the author cannot be said to have created three characters. The reason is that conditions for individuation have not been provided. A minimal requirement for character creation is that means are available for distinguishing one character from another, a condition that does not obtain for the three soldiers.

Are fictional characters essentially tied to their originating narratives? Could Emma Bovary have originated in a different novel? Even a novel by a different author? By Zola, perhaps, or Baudelaire, or Proust? There is no determinate answer because there are no determinate, non-relative criteria for the identity of the Emma-Bovary-character. To the extent that we want to talk about *that* Emma Bovary, indicating Flaubert's novel, then that particular character probably could not have originated elsewhere, although the character could reappear in sequels either by Flaubert or someone else (given a causal link to the originating novel). But to the extent that we are interested only in the general type sharing the core properties of the Bovary-character, then there is no difficulty supposing different origins. Similarly, we can allow that Shakespeare's Juliet is the same core character as Brooke's Juliet while also insisting that Shakespeare's own finely drawn character is unique to *Romeo and Juliet*. The anonymous pages so fleetingly "indicated" in *As You Like It* could be reincarnated in another work – just as Rosancrantz and Guildenstern reappear in *Rosencrantz and Guildenstern Are Dead*, or the first Mrs. Rochester reappears in *Wide Sargasso Sea* – but they could not be identified, except in generic terms, with similarly anonymous pages in previous plays.

## Discourse about Fiction

Many of the theoretical problems that arise in discussions of the status of fictional characters come from an irreducible duality in their nature reflected in discourse about them. On the one hand, characters – at least those in realist narratives – are spoken of as *human beings*, with human qualities naturally attributed to them. On the other, they are spoken of as *constructs*,

---

[57] Searle, *Expression and Meaning*, pp. 71–72.

artifacts or devices in narrative. Characters invite these two radically different perspectives, sometimes called "internal" and "external,"[58] the perspective from within a *fictional* world, where they act as ordinary human agents, and the perspective of the *real* world, where they are bound up with linguistic forms and artifice. This duality reflects a broader bifurcation in criticism itself between an interest in the human worlds depicted and an interest in the rhetorical means of that depiction.

### Fictional worlds

Characters are presented in narratives, and only by engaging with narrative content can readers have access to them. One kind of engagement, imaginatively exploring the internal "world" of the work, relates to what was called, in Chapter 4, the "elucidation" of the subject. We saw there that it is an integral part of critical practice to examine, enlarge on, and clarify the immediate content presented in a work, either that of narrative and character or, in the case of some lyric poetry, the emotion or experience expressed. One concern that has interested philosophers of literature is what principles underlie this exploration of fictional worlds, in particular what inferential principles can licence the move from explicit narrative description to wider non-explicit "truths" about the world portrayed.

First, though, what is meant by "fictional world"? Sometimes we speak of the distinctive worlds of particularly novelists: Dickens's world or Kafka's or Iris Murdoch's or Anita Brookner's. What is meant is that there are distinctive and recurring characteristics associated with these authors – an atmosphere, kinds of people, settings, or plots. But every narrative fiction presents a "world" which might or might not be distinctive to the author and, depending on the genre, will be more or less like the real world. It might be a futuristic world of science fiction, or a fantasy world of magic and mystery, or a "noir" world of gangsters and murder. In each case the world encompasses the actions, events, and characters depicted. But there is always more to a world than what is immediately described in the narrative.

Reading fiction is an exercise in supplementing what is explicitly "given." There are connections, clearly, with both explication and interpretation, for they too are concerned with drawing out what is implicit. But the supplementation of worlds is not a search for meaning – although it presupposes descriptive meaning in narrative – nor is it a search for a work's value as literature. All fictional narrative, whether literature or not, invites supplementation; again it is common to find philosophers dwelling on the simplest cases, like the putative mole on Holmes's back or the numbers of hairs on his head.

---

[58] See Lamarque, *Fictional Points of View*, ch. 2.

Readers will often "fill in" the setting for a narrative in idiosyncratic ways. Their reflections on characters could draw on their own personal experiences, and they might attribute motive and purpose from the limited perspective of that experience largely independent of what is suggested in the narrative itself. It is helpful to distinguish between a supplementation that is purely whimsical or personal and one that is responsive to the work itself. Kendall Walton, using his own idiom, introduces the idea of an *authorized game of make-believe* to capture something like the latter notion.[59] It might not always be clear what is "authorized" by a work, but using the work as merely a prompt for private imaginings is not the way to try to comprehend the "world" being presented.

### The Reality Principle and the Mutual Belief Principle

Walton identifies two competing principles for drawing inferences about what is "true" in fictional worlds – the Reality Principle and the Mutual Belief Principle – although his considered view is that neither principle comprehends all the intuitively correct inferences, and that the "mechanics of generation" are fundamentally "disorderly."[60]

According to the Reality Principle, readers assume the fictional world to be as like the real world as is compatible with what is explicitly stated, and they make inferences about the fictional world accordingly. Missing fictional details are filled in against a background of fact. In realist fiction from Jane Austen to Trollope to Anthony Powell, a wide background of familiar fact is kept constant across the fictional imaginings; these might be facts about English social and cultural life of the period, but they are also more basic facts about human beings, geography, and physics, all of which make up a "setting" taken for granted. In Austen's novels people move from place to place by walking or by carriage, not by teleportation or even motor car; when they converse they do not use telepathy or even telephones; in her world, like ours, wheels go round, horses trot, humans are mortal and the seasons come and go. In *Lord of the Rings* massive adjustments are needed in enlargement of the story, but if the Reality Principle is operative we still assume basic facts which are not explicitly contradicted in the narrative. We allow for magic and wizards and "orcs," but clothes are still for wearing, conversations still for communicating, and the sky is above and the earth below. Without

---

[59] Walton, *Mimesis as Make-Believe*, p. 51, pp. 397f. See also Kendall Walton, "Do We Need Fictional Entities? Notes towards a Theory," in *Aesthetics: Proceedings of the Eighth International Wittgenstein Symposium* (Vienna, 1984), pp. 180–181.

[60] Walton, *Mimesis as Make-Believe*, p. 184.

retaining some familiar assumptions about reality we would not have any way of grasping the content of fantasy, science fiction, or horror stories.

According to the second, Mutual Belief Principle, it is not reality or fact that constrains our inferences but common shared beliefs at the time the narrative was written. We know that the heart pumps blood, that the theory of evolution explains the diversity of species, and that bubonic plague is spread by fleas on rats, but can these count as background "truths" in Chaucer's *Canterbury Tales*? Much of the symbolism in Ibsen's *Ghosts* rests on the moral stigma of syphilis and its being passed from Captain Alving to his son Osvald. But Ibsen and his contemporaries had a quite different conception of syphilis from our own: they were wrong about the heritability of the disease (it passes not from father to son but through an infected mother); today the disease is easily treated; and, arguably, in more sexually emancipated times, it carries little moral stigma.[61] Yet to incorporate known facts about syphilis into the world of *Ghosts* would completely undermine the symbolic force the disease carries in the play, indeed would make the play virtually unintelligible.

A common objection, then, to the Reality Principle is that it licences seemingly inappropriate or anachronistic inferences.[62] Modern theories of astronomy or nuclear physics or human psychology would generate fictional truths in the worlds of Sophocles or Chaucer totally at odds with the implied contemporary background. Not only are the truths anachronistic, but arguably there are too many of them, in too great detail.[63] Do abstruse facts about quarks or quasars belong in the world of *Oedipus Rex*? Of course the idea of a "fictional world" is itself unclear, so how determinate or wide in scope the "contents" of such a world might be is debatable.

Rather more problematic from the point of view of the literary critic are inferences drawn about characters based on theories or perspectives that were not current at the time of a work's inception, or were not readily attributable to the author. The obvious case might be the imputation of an Oedipus complex to Hamlet, by supporters of Freudian theory, on the grounds that *anyone in the real world who behaves as Hamlet behaves is exhibiting classic signs of an Oedipus complex*. Here facts – putative facts – about the real world are used to draw inferences about the fictional world. Another similar, if even more contentious, application of such a principle is the imputation of a homosexual relationship between Huck and Jim in Mark Twain's

---

[61]    The example comes from Olsen, *The End of Literary Theory*, p. 65.

[62]    The point is made in Walton, *Mimesis as Make-Believe*; Lewis, "Truth in Fiction"; and Currie, *The Nature of Fiction*.

[63]    See Parsons, *Nonexistent Objects*; Wolterstorff, *Works and Worlds of Art*.

*The Adventures of Huckleberry Finn.*[64] The objection to such an inference is that although the novel does not explicitly rule it out, there is no indication that the hypothesis is even implicit in the story or something a reader is invited to consider.

One advantage of the Mutual Belief Principle is that, as Walton says, it "gives the artist better control over what is fictional."[65] If a writer and his community believe that the earth is flat or is stationary, then those become fictional truths in his stories, assuming no indications to the contrary. However, it is not always clear what are the mutual beliefs in a community, and if a writer is at odds with such beliefs then distorted inferences, particularly about psychological or moral matters, might result from too rigid an appeal to contemporary attitudes. For example, several of Thomas Hardy's heroines, such as Sue Bridehead (in *Jude the Obscure*) or Tess of the d'Urbervilles, act in ways that would be strongly condemned by prevailing moral beliefs in Hardy's Britain, but it would be absurd to infer that the characters are selfish and immoral (where it is not explicitly stated otherwise) simply on that basis, regardless of the implied authorial attitude throughout.

Gregory Currie has offered a version of the Mutual Belief Principle according to which what is true in fiction is what it is reasonable for an informed reader to infer that the "fictional author" believes.[66] What such an author believes will be a construction from common beliefs of the time, but also constrained by the tone and implications of the actual narrative. For Currie, "the fictional author … is that fictional character constructed within our make-believe whom we take to be telling us the story as known fact."[67] Such an author will not be either the real author or any explicit narrator indicated by "I." But it is a person within the world of the story. Stories that purport to describe a world in which there is no intelligent life – thus no one who could recount the story – must, according to Currie, involve a contradiction, even if an inconsequential one.[68]

### Possible worlds and truth in fiction

The idea of a world where the story is told as known fact is associated with an acclaimed paper by David Lewis, who has offered versions of both principles in

[64]   The idea is advanced in the famous essay by Leslie Fielder, "'Come Back to the Raft Ag'in, Huck, Honey,'" in *An Age of Innocence* (Boston, MA: Beacon Press, 1966). The example is discussed in this context by Wolterstorff in *Works and Worlds of Art*, p. 120.

[65]   Walton, *Mimesis as Make-Believe*, p. 153.

[66]   Currie, *Nature of Fiction*, ch. 2.6.

[67]   Ibid., p. 76.

[68]   Ibid., pp. 125–126.

terms of possible worlds.[69] Lewis compares reasoning about what is true in fiction to counterfactual reasoning (what would be the case if …). To discover what is true in the world of a story we need to compare the worlds where the story is told as known fact with, following the Reality Principle, the real world or, following the Mutual Belief Principle, the "collective belief worlds of the community of origin," and in both cases then determine the closest fit. Lewis holds that there is not just a single possible world associated with each work of fiction but rather a set of such. He makes this suggestion in order to accommodate indeterminacies in fictions. Assuming there is no indication what day of the week, say, Holmes was born on, there will be a possible world (in which the story is told as known fact) where he was born on Monday, a possible world where he was born on Tuesday, and so forth. The set of such worlds will be the worlds of the Holmes stories.

Objections have been made, though, to this possible-world analysis. Although possible worlds have proved a powerful theoretical tool in the semantics of modal concepts (necessity, possibility) or in analytical meta-physics, and although at first sight they seem to have a natural connection to fiction, they nevertheless have features that do not fit well with concep-tions of "worlds" linked to fiction.[70] First, possible worlds are unlike fic-tional worlds in being determinate in every detail; roughly speaking, for any proposition that proposition must be either true or false in a possible world, yet we have seen that there are many propositions that are neither true nor false in fictional worlds (the details are not specified or implied). Also pos-sible worlds must be self-consistent; they cannot be *impossible*. Yet the worlds of fantasy or sci fi are not always logically possible.

A deeper problem faces not only Lewis's possible-world analysis but also analyses such as Currie's, which appear to make the inquiry into truth in fiction something like a quasi-factual inquiry. In simple cases there do seem to be plain matters of fact associated with fictional worlds: it is *fact* that in the Holmes stories Holmes is a detective, a human being (not a robot), a creature with lungs and a heart, who never traveled in a rocket. These can be inferred by quasi-factual investigations into what has to be the case in worlds where the story is told as known fact. Literary critics have an inter-est in such facts as they build up a picture of narrative content: plot, story, and character. But this inquiry, which connects to critical elucidation of a work's subject, is principally an inquiry into the "internal" perspective on content, namely the perspective in which characters are viewed as ordinary human agents in a world. Critics, though, also have a crucial interest in the "external" perspective, where characters are seen as constructs and works

---

[69]  Lewis, "Truth in Fiction," pp. 37–46.
[70]  The point is made in Currie, *Nature of Fiction*, pp. 54–55.

as artifacts. Under this perspective the quasi-factual inquiry comes to seem inadequate to the critic's demands, and its scope more and more limited.

## Characters as Literary Artifacts

Adopting the external perspective, a critic is interested in how the imaginative engagement of the internal perspective is mediated by language. A number of principles are involved, and these can show not only how the external perspective interacts with the internal but also how remote from real people fictional characters can come to seem.

### The Character Identity Principle

The first principle reinforces the closeness of fictional characters to the modes of their presentation in narratives. Let us call this the Character Identity Principle:

> *In literary works character identity is indissolubly linked to character description.*

Part of what this means – as we have seen – is that individuated characters, as opposed to general character-types, come into being only through being "characterized" and identified in narratives. What it also means is that the manner of character description determines the very nature of the character described. This applies to fine-grained identity conditions under which we say that Shakespeare's Juliet is different from Brooke's Juliet. Characters under these fine-grained conditions are in a special sense perspectival entities.[71] This implies not just that the precise nature of the characters rests on the precision of their identifying descriptions but also that the descriptions embody points of view on them, both physical and evaluative.

Take an example from Dickens's *Our Mutual Friend*. When Dickens first introduces the despicable Veneerings, he does so with a well-known flourish both comic and contemptuous:

> Mr and Mrs Veneering were bran-new [sic] people in a bran-new house in a bran-new quarter of London. Everything about the Veneerings was spick-and-span new. All their furniture was new, all their friends were new, all their servants were new, their plate was new, their carriage was new, their harness was new, their horses were new, their pictures were new, they themselves

---

[71]  See Lamarque and Olsen, *Truth, Fiction, and Literature*, ch. 6.

were new … [A]ll things were in a state of high varnish and polish. And what was observable in the furniture, was observable in the Veneerings — the surface smelt a little too much of the workshop and was a trifle sticky.[72]

The superficiality, the worship of possessions and ostentatious wealth, the shallowness connoted in the very name "Veneering," are all intrinsic qualities of the characters themselves. Dickens's judgment of the Veneerings, which he invites us to share, indeed which we *must* share if we are to grasp the role of the characters in the novel, is part of the very identity of the characters. It is not as if there is some other perspective on the Veneerings which depicts them as decent, honest, kindly, altruistic folk who have somehow been falsely captured by the mocking tone of the narrator. The mocking tone, as it were, makes them the characters they are.

If characters are perspectival in this way, then the Character Identity Principle reveals a further important fact about characters which points to something fundamental about literary appreciation. The character descriptions, indissolubly tied to character identity, are seen to have a dual function: a characterizing function and a connective or thematic function. Again this reflects the internal and external. The characterizing function provides us with quasi-factual information about the characters: we take it to be true of the Veneerings that everything they own is new. This guides our internal imaginative perspective on them and guides inferences of the kind we have been examining. When we picture the Veneerings we picture them as surrounded by new objects shiningly clean. But the mocking tone that informs the description has a wider function in the novel as a whole. It serves to locate the Veneerings in the social scheme of things, to situate them among a cluster of characters, like the Lammles and the Podsnaps, who see no value beyond monetary value. It also sets up a thematic contrast with characters like John Harmon, Eugene Wrayburn, and Lizzie Hexam who reject these false values and the social attitudes they engender. The Veneerings are not just people in a world but elements in an artistic design.

### The Opacity Principle

In addition to the Character Identity Principle is a second, related, principle which I shall call Opacity. According to the Opacity Principle,

*In literary works not only are characters and incidents presented to us but attention is conventionally drawn to the modes of presentation themselves.*

---

[72]  Charles Dickens, *Our Mutual Friend* (New York: Signet, 1964), p. 20.

This principle is familiar to literary critics and informs critical practice. It acknowledges the fact that linguistic resources are not merely contingent elements in literary artifice – the thought that somehow the very same content might have been presented in other ways – but also what Roman Jakobson called the "palpability of signs" and other structuralists called "foregrounding."[73]

It is a peculiarity of literary fiction that attention is drawn to the connective and thematic functions of character descriptions. Rather than being merely transparent vehicles for identifying fictitious objects and prompting imaginings, the descriptions provide a more opaque kind of perspective for observing and making sense of a fictional world. Although make-believe is prompted by literary works and we are often able to imagine the goings on as if they were real events, we find in the literary case that there is a nice interplay between what we imagine and what we notice of the literary artifice that does the prompting. At the same time as we picture the Veneerings we notice the modes in which they are presented to us, in particular the attitudes we are invited to take, and the significance of those attitudes against the wider canvas of the novel.

### The Functionality Principle

A third principle of literary criticism, which was touched on in the previous chapter, also encourages the thought that there is more to literary description, be it of character or incident, than the conveying of fictional facts. This concerns the curious role of descriptive detail. We have already seen in the Character Identity and Opacity Principles how detail determines identity. But detail also is assigned significance. What operates is a Principle of Functionality, as follows:

> It is always reasonable to ask of any detail in a literary work what literary or aesthetic function that detail is performing.

The principle applies across all the arts. As Roger Scruton has written: "Art provides a medium transparent to human intention, a medium for which the question, Why? can be asked of every observable feature, even if it may sometimes prove impossible to answer."[74]

---

[73] See Victor Erlich, *Russian Formalism: History-Doctrine* (The Hague: Mouton, rev. ed., 1965), p. 183.

[74] Roger Scruton, "Photography and Representation," in Peter Lamarque and Stein Haugom Olsen, eds., *Aesthetics and the Philosophy of Art: The Analytic Tradition: An Anthology* (Oxford: Blackwell, 2003), p. 368.

Take the brief but poignant scene near the beginning of *Tess of the d'Urbervilles* when Tess's father's horse Prince is killed in an accident on the road. Tess had fallen asleep when driving her carriage and the mail-cart had rammed into her, piercing the horse's heart. This is how the critic Dorothy Van Ghent describes the passage:

> With this accident are concatenated in fatal union Tess's going to "claim kin" of the d'Urbervilles and all the other links in her tragedy down to the murder of Alec. The symbolism of the detail is naïve and forthright to the point of temerity: the accident occurs in darkness and Tess has fallen asleep — just as the whole system of mischances and cross-purposes in the novel is a function of psychic and cosmic blindness; she "has put her hand upon the hole" — and the gesture is as absurdly ineffectual as all her effort will be; the only result is that she becomes splashed with blood — as she will be at the end; the shaft pierces Prince's breast "like a sword" — Alec is stabbed in the heart with a knife; with the arousal and twittering of the birds we are aware of the oblivious manifold of nature stretching infinite and detached beyond the isolated human figure; the iridescence of the coagulating blood is, in its incongruity with the dark human trouble, a note of the same indifferent cosmic chemistry that has brought about the accident; and the smallness of the hole in Prince's chest, that looked "scarcely large enough to have let out all that had animated him," is the minor remark of that irony by which Tess's great cruel trial appears as a vanishing incidental in the blind waste of time and space and biological repetition.

Significantly, Van Ghent completes the paragraph by observing the otherwise naturalness of the scene and its description:

> Nevertheless, there is nothing in this event that has not the natural "grain" of concrete fact; and what it signifies — of the complicity of doom with the most random occurrence, of the cross-purposing of purpose in a multiple world, of cosmic indifference and of moral desolation — is a local truth of a particular experience and irrefutable as the experience itself.[75]

Again the internal and external perspectives interact. In the imaginative world of the novel the scene of the accident is pictured to be just what it seems, a terrible accident. From the external critical perspective it serves a narrative function as well, anticipating, with awful foreboding, all the main events to come and assigns weight and significance to them.

Symbolism is a common literary device. The mud and fog at the beginning of *Bleak House*, as every trained reader easily recognizes (Dickens himself

[75] Dorothy Van Ghent, "On *Tess of the d'Urbervilles*," in Thomas Hardy, *Tess of the d'Urbervilles*, ed. Scott Elledge (New York: W. W. Norton, 1979), pp. 429–430.

rather heavy-handedly spells out the connection with the High Court of Chancery), are more than just passing descriptive detail. Here is how one critic interprets the symbolism:

> The mud and fog of the opening paragraph of the novel are not, we can now see, the primeval stuff out of which all highly developed forms evolve. They are the symptoms of a general return to the primal slime, a return to chaos which is going on everywhere in the novel and is already nearing its final end when the novel begins.
>
> The human condition of the characters of *Bleak House* is, then, to be thrown into a world which is neither fresh and new nor already highly organised, but is a world which has already gone bad.[76]

The Functionality Principle, though, does not relate exclusively to literary symbolism, in the narrow sense of the term. Having symbolic significance is only one kind of function, indeed one kind of significance. Drawing connections across a work is another function of literary detail. The opening scene of *Macbeth* with the contradictions and confusions of the witches ("Fair is foul and foul is fair") connects with multiple elements throughout the play, developing what L. C. Knights calls "the themes of the reversal of values and of unnatural disorder."[77]

Another function of narrative detail is identified by Roland Barthes in what he calls the "reality effect." Barthes is intrigued by the way that realist novelists, like Flaubert or Balzac, pile up apparently random descriptive detail. In a somewhat laboured manner, he describes it as follows:

> The truth of this illusion is this: eliminated from the realist speech act as a signified of denotation, the "real" returns to it as a signified of connotation; for just when these details are reputed to *denote* the real directly, all that they do — without saying so — is *signify* it; Flaubert's barometer, Michelet's little door finally say nothing but this: *we are the real*; it is the category of "the real" ... which is then signified; in other words, the very absence of the signified, to the advantage of the referent alone, becomes the very signifier of realism ...[78]

The idea, more plainly put, is that the accumulation of seemingly trivial detail in a literary narrative, serves to *signify* (or connote) reality, while failing to

[76]   J. Hillis Miller, "The World of *Bleak House*," in Charles Dickens, *Bleak House*, Norton Critical Edition, ed. G. Ford and S. Monod (New York: W. W. Norton, 1977), pp. 951–952.

[77]   L. C. Knights, "How Many Children Had Lady Macbeth?" in *Explorations* (Harmondsworth: Penguin, 1964), p. 29.

[78]   Roland Barthes, "The Reality Effect," in *The Rustle of Language*, trans. Richard Howard (Oxford: Blackwell, 1986), p. 148.

denote it. This provides a striking contrast between the use of trivial detail in non-fictional narratives. Where the details actually *do* describe the real, where there is no "absence of the signifier" or no "referential illusion," there can be no "reality effect." What Barthes sees as definitive of literary realism is, curiously, missing – and impossible – in the case where facts alone are described. The piling up of detail might have the same impact in the two cases – enriching the atmosphere – but they operate, if Barthes is right, under almost exactly opposite narrative constraints.

### The Teleology Principle

A fourth principle concerns the kinds of explanation available to incident and action in a literary work. In the real world of fact and action, explanation is causal or rational. To explain why something happened we offer causes or an agent's reasons. To the extent that we imagine, from the internal point of view, the events in a literary work these are the explanations we reach for. What caused Tess's accident? The answer, within the fictional world, is that she fell asleep and was run into by the mail-cart. Why did Tess kill Alec d'Urberville? The answer, as one critic writes, is that it was "an act of desperate assertion which places Tess in the line of folk heroines who kill because they can no longer bear outrage."[79] But there is a literary mode of explanation quite different from the causal and the rational. As the critic just cited goes on to say of the killing: "it signifies an end to Tess's journey," it is "traditional, part of the accepted heritage that has come down to us through popular and literary channels." In other words the killing has a conventional function in the structure of the plot. It happens, we might say, because it has to happen in a story of this kind. That explanation is of a radically different kind from an explanation in terms of agents' reasons.

The principle operating here can be labeled the Teleology Principle, as follows:

> In literary works the explanation of why an episode occurs as it does and where it does often centers on the contribution the episode makes to the completed artistic structure.

Thus in the reverse order of normal causal explanation a prior event might be explained in terms of a later event. Oedipus's fateful remark early on in Sophocles's play that those who have brought disaster on Thebes will suffer a terrible fate acquires its literary significance and function from the

---

[79]    Irving Howe, "The Center of Hardy's Achievement," in Thomas Hardy, *Tess of the d'Urbervilles*, ed. Scott Elledge (New York: W. W. Norton, 1979), p. 451.

revelations at the end of the play. In a different example, consider how the word "explains" is used by this critic, speaking of the character Frank Churchill in Jane Austen's *Emma*:

> *Frank is important because he explains Emma herself*. He embodies the vital differ-
> ence between the artistic principles governing Emma — foolish conduct
> resulting from faulty judgement, but from motives fundamentally irreproach-
> able, invariably honest and as frank as possible — and his own downright
> wrong actions causing deliberate and consistent deceit, which produce some
> of the same effects as Emma's own.[80]

Again, just like the Veneerings in the earlier example, Frank Churchill is not just a person in an imaginary world, he is also an element in a structured plot. His actions and failings gain their significance in contrast to superficially similar failings in Emma herself – tactlessness and lack of self-awareness – though the implied judgments are different. It is characteristic of literary criticism to explain the artistic role of such elements: the explanation is a kind of teleology. Another critic notes the role played by the married pairs at the end of the novel:

> The young generation poses a challenge to the moral order of Highbury, and
> the book ends when the challenge is fought off, when the young are married
> and have been assimilated by the mature generation. The story, of course, is
> first and foremost Emma's story, but she is flanked by important characters.
> Frank Churchill and Jane Fairfax, Mr Elton and Augusta Hawkins, Harriet
> Smith and Robert Martin, all these couples form important variations on the
> theme of assimilation.[81]

### The Thematic Principle

The reference to variations on a theme brings us to the final, again familiar, principle, in literary appreciation, which we can formulate as a Thematic Principle:

> *Narrative content of a literary work not only presents a world but invites thematic
> interpretation under which the content acquires broader significance.*

Literary themes, as discussed in Chapter 4, are conceptions that bind elements in a work together, encapsulating the work's significance and "moral

---

[80]  W. A. Craik, "Emma," in Jane Austen, *Emma*, ed. Stephen M. Parrish (New York: W. W. Norton, 1972), p. 445 (italics added).

[81]  Stein Haugom Olsen, "Do You Like Emma Woodhouse?" *Critical Quarterly*, vol. 19, no. 4 (1977), pp. 3–19 at p. 13.

seriousness." The descriptions under which they are identified are either given in the work itself or brought to the work in the pursuit of wider significance. They take different forms, sometimes stand-alone predicates like "love" or "despair," sometimes noun phrases like "the conflict between private and social duty" or whole sentences like "human freedom is an illusion." However, from our earlier detailed discussion of how themes are elicited it seems clear that the process is a quite different kind of activity from that of finding quasi-factual truths in fiction.

## Fiction and Emotion

A final topic that has attracted a great deal of philosophical attention concerns the very possibility of emotional responses to fiction. To some extent the problem, sometimes called the "paradox of fiction," is a technical one, arising out of conflicting views on the nature of emotion. But underlying the paradox are deep issues, of interest to literary critics, about, as it were, our "state of mind" in engaging with fictional works.

### Tragedy and emotion

The idea that emotions are integrally part of a proper response to literature goes back to Aristotle, who defined tragedy, partially, in terms of the emotions it arouses:

> A tragedy, then, is the imitation of an action that is serious and also, as having magnitude, complete in itself; in language with pleasurable accessories, each kind brought in separately in the parts of the work; in a dramatic, not in a narrative form; with incidents arousing pity and fear, wherewith to accomplish its catharsis of such emotions.[82]

For Aristotle an audience should be brought to experience pity and fear at the fate of the tragic hero not through flashy stage effects but through reflection on the events portrayed:

> The tragic fear and pity may be aroused by the Spectacle; but they may also be aroused by the very structure and incidents of the play — which is the better way and shows the better poet.[83]

---

[82] Aristotle, *Poetics*, in *The Complete Works of Aristotle: The Revised Oxford Translation*, ed. Jonathan Barnes, vol. 2 (Princeton, NJ: Princeton University Press, 1984), p. 2,320.

[83] Ibid., p. 2,326.

When we reflect on the downfall of a decent person through *hamartia*, or "error," a downfall necessitated in the very fabric of the plot, we pity the protagonist and fear for ourselves lest a similar fate await us. Hume famously wonders at the "unaccountable pleasure which the spectators of a well-written tragedy receive from sorrow, terror, anxiety, and other passions, that are in themselves disagreeable and uneasy."[84] He goes on:

> The whole art of the poet is employed in rousing and supporting the compassion and indignation, the anxiety and resentment of his audience. They are pleased in proportion as they are afflicted, and never are so happy as when they employ tears, sobs, and cries to give vent to their sorrow, and relieve their heart, swollen with the tenderest sympathy and compassion.

This "unaccountable pleasure" is explained by Hume in terms of the "overpowering" of the pain of the represented scenes by the pleasure of artifice and eloquence:

> This extraordinary effect proceeds from that very eloquence, with which the melancholy scene is represented. The genius required to paint objects in a lively manner, the art employed in collecting all the pathetic circumstances, the judgment displayed in disposing them: the exercise, I say, of these noble talents, together with the force of expression, and beauty of oratorial numbers, diffuse the highest satisfaction on the audience, and excite the most delightful movements. By this means, the uneasiness of the melancholy passions is not only overpowered and effaced by something stronger of an opposite kind; but the whole impulse of those passions is converted into pleasure, and swells the delight which the eloquence raises in us.[85]

Hume's solution to the paradox of tragedy is a nice application of the distinction between the internal and external points of view. Narrative, as we have shown, can be both a pleasing artifact as well as a (painful) world revealed.

There is, though, a related philosophical issue, which neither Hume nor Aristotle address, namely what makes an audience have such strong emotional reactions in the face of what they know to be a mere presentation on stage by actors: in other words, a fiction. If Hume and Aristotle are right that tragedy would not be tragedy, and would have no artistic value, if it failed to rouse these feelings, then an account is needed of the source of those feelings.

This is a question Dr. Johnson raised in a discussion of the "unities" in drama, whether Shakespeare should be criticized for not maintaining the

---

[84]   David Hume, "Of Tragedy," in *The Philosophical Works of David Hume*, ed. T. H. Green and T. H. Grose (London: Longman, Green, 1874–1875), vol. 3, p. 258.

[85]   Hume, "Of Tragedy," p. 261.

Aristotelian unities (of time and place) in his tragedies. Johnson argued that the unities were only needed to make the drama "credible," but that those who "credit" drama (i.e., believe in its veracity) are merely deluded; so the unities are pointless. Here is what he says on the question about emotion:

> It will be asked how the drama moves [i.e., rouses emotion], if it is not credited [i.e., believed]. It is credited with all the credit due to a drama. It is credited, whenever it moves, as a just picture of a real original; as representing to the auditor what he would himself feel, if he were to do or suffer what is there feigned to be suffered or to be done. The reflection that strikes the heart is not that the evils before us are real evils, but that they are evils to which we ourselves may be exposed. If there is any fallacy, it is not that we fancy [i.e., make-believe] the players but that we fancy ourselves unhappy for a moment; but we rather lament the possibility than suppose the presence of misery, as a mother weeps over her babe when she remembers that death may take it from her. The delight of tragedy proceeds from our consciousness of fiction; if we thought murders and treasons real they would please no more.
>
> Imitations produce pain or pleasure not because they are mistaken for realities but because they bring realities to mind.[86]

For Johnson the "delight" of tragedy stems from our awareness of its fictionality, while the emotions (such as pity and fear) arise from thinking of ourselves in a similar situation. Johnson, the rationalist, is suspicious of being "swept up" in fictive imaginings; he holds the classical mimetic theory of art, that good art must "imitate" or picture reality. If the imitation strikes us as "just" or convincing, then reflecting on the "possibility" it presents is enough to move us.

Johnson's contemporary, William Kenrick, takes issue with this and suggests that audiences are much more involved imaginatively than Johnson's somewhat cerebral account implies:

> We do not pretend to say that the spectators are not always in their senses; or that they do not know (if the question were put to them) that the stage is only a stage, and the players only players. But we will venture to say that they are often so intent on the scene as to be absent with regard to every thing else. A spectator properly affected by a dramatic representation makes no reflections about the fiction or the reality of it.[87]

Kenrick even supposes that there is a kind of "deception": "The spectator is unquestionably deceived, but the deception goes no further than the passions,

[86]    Samuel Johnson, "Prefaces to Shakespeare's Plays," in *Shakespeare: The Critical Heritage*, vol. 5, 1765–1774, ed. Brian Vickers (London: Routledge, 1974), pp. 70–71.

[87]    William Kenrick, in *Shakespeare: The Critical Heritage*, vol. 5, 1765–1774, p. 189.

it affects our sensibility but not our understanding; and is by no means so powerful a delusion as to affect our *belief*." The terrors before us bypass belief altogether and strike directly at the emotions:

> The audience are moved by mere mechanical motives; they laugh and cry from mere sympathy at what a moment's reflection would very often prevent them from laughing or crying at all. ... [W]e are in this case merely passive, our organs are in unison with those of the players on the stage, and the convulsions of grief or laughter are purely involuntary.[88]

## Paradox of fiction

Worries whether emotions can indeed be cut off from beliefs underlie the current philosophical debate over the "paradox of fiction." What concerns philosophers is how an audience could know that the events before them are fictional yet still evince emotional responses that seem explicable only on the assumption that they believe the events are not fictional. The paradox is sometimes expressed by highlighting three mutually inconsistent but intuitively plausible propositions along the following lines:

(A) Readers or audiences often experience emotions such as pity and fear toward objects they know to be fictional, e.g., fictional characters;

(B) A necessary condition for experiencing emotions such as pity and fear is that those experiencing them believe the objects of their emotions to exist;

(C) Readers or audiences who know that the objects are fictional do not believe that these objects exist.[89]

In a helpful survey of the literature, Jerrold Levinson has discerned no fewer than seven distinct classes of solutions, some with multiple sub-variants, covering seemingly every possible route out of the paradox.[90] Some purported solutions have had less support than others. For example, the idea that we should reject (C) has few modern adherents.

The assumption in the debate is that reasonably sophisticated adults, not gullible children or simpletons, are involved. Such people, it seems, do not

---

[88] Ibid., pp. 189–191.

[89] Something similar is found in J. Levinson, "Emotion in Response to Art: A Survey of the Terrain," in M. Hjort and S. Laver, eds., *Emotion and the Arts* (Oxford: Oxford University Press, 1997); R.J. Yanal, *Paradoxes of Emotion and Fiction* (University Park, PA: Penn State University Press, 1999); R. Joyce, "Rational Fear of Monsters," *British Journal of Aesthetics*, vol. 40, no. 2 (2000), pp. 209–224.

[90] Levinson, "Emotion in Response to Art: A Survey of the Terrain."

forget that what they are watching/reading is fictional. Most agree with Kenrick that "we do not pretend to say that the spectators are not always in their senses; or that they do not know (if the question were put to them) that the stage is only a stage."

## Suspension of disbelief

One thought, however, might be to develop Samuel Taylor Coleridge's suggestion that audiences engage in a "willing suspension of disbelief."[91] In other words they do "disbelieve" what they see, i.e., they know it is mere fiction, but they "suspend" that disbelief (or knowledge) for the sake of the theatrical or literary experience. But what is involved in "suspending disbelief"? It is open to different interpretations:

- setting aside disbelief and actually coming to *believe* that the scenes are real; this seems to describe the child or simpleton;
- setting aside disbelief and coming to believe only *at some level* (perhaps "half believe" or believe at a "visceral" level); but if "half believing" means retaining a suspicion that the scenes might be real then that seems too strong, and "visceral" belief is just unclear;
- not letting disbelief disturb our natural emotional responses; but what is at issue is how emotions relate to belief, and Kenrick's notion, for example, that we are "moved by mere mechanical motives" calls for further explanation;
- setting aside both belief and disbelief: as Kenrick says, "a spectator properly affected by a dramatic representation makes no reflections about the fiction or the reality of it"; this idea seems promising but if beliefs get set aside an account is needed of how that occurs and precisely what cognitive state a spectator is in. Perhaps Thought Theory, below, can help.

In fact, the truth of (C), as noted, is not widely contested, and any benefits from the "suspension of disbelief" conception will need to confront (A) and (B), which remain the key suspects in the paradox.

## Make-believe fear and pity

One of the most influential theories, advanced by Kendall Walton, favors the rejection of (A). According to Walton it is only make-believe, not literally true,

---

[91]  Samuel Taylor Coleridge: "my endeavours should be directed to persons and characters supernatural, or at least romantic, yet so as to transfer from our inward nature a human interest and a semblance of truth sufficient to procure for these shadows of imagination that

that we fear or pity or admire fictional characters, even though the emotions we do experience toward them have certain phenomenological similarities to fear, pity, or admiration. Walton labels the feelings actually experienced (as well as any physiological manifestations) "quasi-fear," "quasi-pity," and so on, emphasizing that although these responses are not the same as real fear, real pity, etc., they may nonetheless be "highly charged emotionally."[92]

Walton develops his theory through a now famous example of a viewer Charles watching a horror movie in which a monstrous green slime oozes forward as if to devour him. Charles shows all the signs of being terrified – "his muscles are tensed, he clutches his chair, his pulse quickens, his adrenaline flows" – but this indicates only his "physiological-psychological state" of *quasi-fear*. In fact, Walton proposes, Charles, knowing that it is just a fiction, is *playing a game of make-believe*. "He [Charles] experiences quasi fear as a result of realising that fictionally the slime threatens him. This makes it fictional that his quasi fear is caused by a belief that the slime poses a threat, and hence that he fears the slime."[93] Walton compares Charles to a child playing a game:

> In many ways Charles is like a child, Timmy, playing a game of make-believe with his father. The father pretends to be a ferocious monster who cunningly stalks him and, at a crucial moment, lunges "viciously" at him. Timmy flees screaming to the next room. The scream is more or less involuntary, and so is the flight. But Timmy has a delighted grin on his face even as he runs, and he unhesitatingly comes back for more. He is perfectly aware that his father is only playing, that the whole thing is just a game, and that only fictionally is there a vicious monster after him. He is not really afraid. But it is fictional that he is afraid. Fictionally the monster attacks; fictionally Timmy is in mortal danger and knows that he is; and when he screams and runs, it is fictional that he is terrified. Likewise, when the slime raises its head, spies the camera, and begins oozing toward it, it is fictional in Charles's game that he is threatened. And when as a result Charles gasps and grips his chair, fictionally he is afraid.[94]

Rejecting (A), the idea that we do commonly experience real fear and real pity and other such emotions in response to fiction, a view taken for granted by the likes of Aristotle, Hume, and Dr. Johnson, is a bold move, to say the least. But it fits neatly into Walton's more general theory of fictions and squares with his uncompromising eliminativist ontology. A main plank of

---

willing suspension of disbelief for the moment, which constitutes poetic faith." *Biographia Literaria* (1817), ch. XIV.

[92] Kendall L. Walton, "Spelunking, Simulation, and Slime: On Being Moved by Fiction," in M. Hjort and S. Laver, *Emotion and the Arts*, p. 38.

[93] Walton, *Mimesis as Make-Believe*, p. 245.

[94] Ibid., p. 241.

Walton's argument is a defense of (B), the proposition that fear is essentially bound to beliefs of a certain kind. The fact that Charles does not *believe* he is in danger, nor believes the slime is real, nor shows any disposition to take evasive action or warn his friends, etc., is sufficient for Walton to conclude that Charles cannot be genuinely afraid.[95]

In support of (B) it is important to distinguish emotions with a putative "cognitive" element – which might include fear, pity, love, admiration, or desire – and those that do not, such as shock, revulsion, sexual attraction, anxiety, being startled or amused. It is commonly claimed of the latter group that they do not involve *intentional* states, e.g., thoughts about their objects. They are identified through physiological states and causes alone. There is no paradox of fiction associated with these emotions, for whether or not an object is fictional or real (or believed to be so) does not affect the response itself. We can be startled or shocked by an actual object, an image, something we know to be unreal, or something we know nothing about at all.

The other set of emotions is more complicated. There seem to be several conditions connected to "X is afraid of Y," such as: (a) X believes that Y presents a danger, (b) X desires to avoid the danger presented by Y, (c) X has a disposition to take evasive action, (d) X believes that Y is real (exists), (e) X exhibits some physiological symptoms of fear. These conditions are not uncontested. Perhaps not all are necessary. Maybe (e) is not, or even (b) in cases where people seek out fear. More controversially, is (a) necessary, as Walton believes? Could, for example, X's *imagining* that X is in danger be substituted for X's *believing* this? Could we not fear without having any real sense of *what* we fear? Could there be objectless fears? General anxieties? Some fears – like phobias, or irrational fears – seem to arise even when there is no belief about danger. But can we rescue (A) by abandoning (B)?

Versions of Walton's make-believe account have been advanced by Gregory Currie, who incorporates "simulation theory," and by Jerrold Levinson.[96] However, for many it is just too counterintuitive to deny that audiences experience real fear or pity or desire or admiration toward fictional characters in standard cases, not just in exceptional ones.[97] How could people be

---

[95]   Walton allows that a spectator *might* experience genuine fear in a horror movie – fear of having a heart attack, fear of real sharks in watching *Jaws*, etc. – but these, he thinks, are not standard cases.

[96]   Currie, *Nature of Fiction*; Levinson, *The Pleasures of Aesthetics*; Levinson, "Emotion in Response to Art: A Survey of the Terrain."

[97]   Peter Lamarque, "How Can We Fear and Pity Fictions?" *British Journal of Aesthetics*, vol. 21, no. 4 (1981), pp. 291–304, reprinted in *Fictional Points of View*; A. Neill, "Fear, Fiction and Make-Believe," *Journal of Aesthetics and Art Criticism*, vol. 49, no. 1 (1991), pp. 47–56; A. Neill, "Fiction and the Emotions," *American Philosophical Quarterly*, vol. 30, no. 1 (1993), pp. 1–13;

so systematically mistaken about their emotional states? How could they be playing a game when they don't realize this is what they are doing? Why should imagining horrific scenes lead only to imagining being afraid?

### Thought Theory

Some alternative solutions choose to reject (B). Perhaps the belief condition for emotions like fear, pity, and admiration can be relaxed.[98] After all, there are kinds of fears, phobic fears, where the fearer apparently does not believe he is in danger. However, it does not seem right to assimilate fear in the fictional cases with phobia.[99] Also, as Levinson points out, the belief that an object *exists* could be a requirement for fear even if belief that the object is *dangerous* is not. But is existential belief in fact required? Arguably not.

At the heart of one prominent alternative to the make-believe theory, so-called Thought Theory, is the claim that vivid imagining can be a substitute for belief.[100] By bringing to mind fictional events and characters, an audience can, according to this view, be genuinely frightened, or moved to pity, or struck by desire or admiration. The mechanism is causal: the fear or the pity is caused *by* the thought. But the fear is not *of* the thought. The "of" locution ("fear of the slime") captures the *content* of the emotion, providing a non-relational way of characterizing the emotion ("slime-fear," as opposed to, say, "vampire-fear"). That thoughts can have physiological effects is well recognized in the case of revulsion, embarrassment, or sexual arousal. An analogue of the behavioral disposition condition is also met in Thought Theory, for the disposition to block out a thought takes the place of a disposition to flee from a danger.

Opponents of Thought Theory, apart from objecting to the weakening of (B), worry that there is, on this account, no *object* of the emotion.[101] If Charles

R. Moran, "The Expression of Feeling in Imagination," *Philosophical Review*, vol. 103, no. 1 (1994), pp. 75–106; E. M. Dadlez, *What's Hecuba to Him? Fictional Events and Actual Emotions* (Philadelphia, PA: Penn State University Press, 1997); Yanal, *Paradoxes of Emotion and Fiction*.

[98]   J. Morreall, "Fear without Belief," *Journal of Philosophy*, vol. 90, no. 7 (1993), pp. 359–366.

[99]   A. Neill, "Fear and Belief," *Philosophy and Literature*, vol. 19, no. 1 (1995), pp. 94–101; Joyce, "Rational Fear of Monsters."

[100]   Thought Theory originated in Lamarque, "How Can We Fear and Pity Fictions?" (1981); it acquired the name "Thought Theory" in Noël Carroll, *The Philosophy of Horror, or Paradoxes of the Heart* (New York: Routledge, Chapman, and Hall, 1990) and versions have been defended in Feagin, *Reading with Feeling*; E. Gron, "Defending Thought Theory from a Make-Believe Threat," *British Journal of Aesthetics*, vol. 36, no. 3 (1996), pp. 311–312; Dadlez, *What's Hecuba to Him?*; Yanal, *Paradoxes of Emotion and Fiction*.

[101]   Walton, *Mimesis as Make-Believe*; Levinson, *The Pleasures of Aesthetics*.

is genuinely afraid, they insist, then what is he afraid *of*? One response is to say that there is only an *imagined* object of the fear – the imagined slime – and to repeat again that to speak of the object of the fear is to speak of the intentional characterization of the fear.[102] Another, related, response is to concede that strictly speaking (*de re*) there is nothing that Charles is afraid of, just as, strictly speaking, although it is true that the Egyptians worshipped Osiris, there is no *thing* that could be pointed to as the object of their worship.[103] It was never part of Thought Theory to suppose that the slime in the movie, the natural candidate for the object of fear, had any kind of reality – in contrast to the reality of *images* of the slime and *thoughts* about it – nor to suppose that Charles is frightened of (in contrast to *by*) a thought. Even on make-believe theories it is only *make-believe* that there is an object of fear, and "quasi-fear" itself has no object. While we might loosely speak of Charles being "afraid of the slime", what that strictly means is (a) Charles is frightened by the thought of the slime, and (b) "slime" characterizes the kind of fear he experiences. Perhaps there is a parallel with Nelson Goodman's claim that "X is a picture of a unicorn" means, under analysis, "X is a unicorn-picture."

Real-life counterparts are sometimes proposed for the role of objects of fictionally generated emotions. When we grieve for Anna Karenina, it is argued, we are in fact grieving for actual women who themselves suffer similar fates,[104] when we fear the movie slime we are fearing actual slimy things. William Charlton holds such a view, linking emotion to a disposition to act in the real world.[105] But this solution arguably misses the particularity of response to fiction: we pity Anna Karenina herself, not just *women-in-Anna-Karenina's-predicament*.[106] Stressing the former of course simply returns us to the paradox.

Levinson, although supporting a broadly Waltonian line, has suggested, plausibly, that elements of truth from different theories should be encompassed in any general solution.[107] Perhaps each of the propositions in the original paradox needs some refinement. Colin Radford has proposed in effect that the paradox represents a deep irrationality in human behavior with

[102] Peter Lamarque, Essay Review of Kendall Walton *Mimesis as Make-Believe*, *Journal of Aesthetics and Art Criticism*, vol. 49, no. 2 (1991), pp. 161–166.

[103] Gron, "Defending Thought Theory from a Make-Believe Threat."

[104] B. Paskins, "On Being Moved by Anna Karenina and *Anna Karenina*," *Philosophy*, vol. 52, no. 201 (1977), pp. 344–347.

[105] W. Charlton, "Feeling for the Fictitious," *British Journal of Aesthetics*, vol. 24, no. 3 (1984), pp. 206–216.

[106] B. Boruah, *Fiction and Emotion: A Study in Aesthetics and the Philosophy of Mind* (Oxford: Clarendon Press, 1988).

[107] Levinson, *The Pleasures of Aesthetics*, p. 303.

regard to fiction.[108] We do, he believes, feel genuine pity (admiration, etc.) for fictional characters but in knowing at the same time that there is nothing real to feel pity toward, our behavior (though "natural") is irrational and involves "inconsistency and incoherence." Few have accepted this line, although it has generated a huge amount of debate.[109] A common rejoinder is that it probably seems irrational *not* to feel some emotions toward fictional characters. A viewer or reader who remained entirely unmoved by a tragic drama is not acting appropriately but *inappropriately*. Even the arch-rationalist Dr. Johnson recognized that emotional uptake was a proper response to tragedy.

What the discussion of fiction and emotion serves to emphasize is the importance that human beings attach to engaging imaginatively with fictional characters and situations. Any account of the value of fiction in human lives should probably begin with that fact. Of course it remains a further question what values are to be sought in fictional works. One prominent suggestion is that a principal value is that of *learning*. Is fiction a vehicle for truth? That is the question that must now be addressed.

## Supplementary Readings

Questions about "fictitious entities," reference and non-existence, as they arise in analytic philosophy, are best illustrated in Bertrand Russell, *Logic and Knowledge*, ed. R. C. Marsh (London: George Allen and Unwin, 1956); W. V. O. Quine, *From a Logical Point of View* (Cambridge, MA: Harvard University Press, 1953); Alexius Meinong, "Theory of Objects," in R. M. Chisholm, ed., *Realism and the Background of Phenomenology* (Glencoe, IL: Free Press, 1960); John Woods, *The Logic of Fiction: A Philosophical Sounding of Deviant Logic* (The Hague: Mouton, 1974); Terence Parsons, *Nonexistent Objects* (New Haven, CT: Yale University Press, 1980); Edward Zalta, *Abstract Objects* (Dordrecht: Reidel, 1983); Kit Fine, *Reasoning with Arbitrary Objects* (Oxford: Blackwell, 1985); Anthony Everett and Thomas Hofweber, eds., *Empty Names, Fiction and the Puzzles of Non-Existence* (Stanford, CA: Center for the Study of Language and Information, 2000); Tamar Szabo Gendler and John Hawthorne, eds., *Conceivability and Possibility* (New York: Oxford University Press, 2002).

Issues about the nature of fiction and the connections between fiction and art can be found in Nelson Goodman, *The Languages of Art* (New York: Bobbs-Merrill, 1968); Nicholas Wolterstorff, *Works and Worlds of Art*

---

[108] C. Radford, "How Can We Be Moved by the Fate of Anna Karenina?" *Proceedings of the Aristotelian Society*, suppl. vol. 49 (1975), pp. 67–80.

[109] For extended commentary, see Boruah, *Fiction and Emotion*; Dadlez, *What's Hecuba to Him?*; Yanal, *Paradoxes of Emotion and Fiction*; Joyce, "Rational Fear of Monsters."

(Oxford: Clarendon Press, 1980); Thomas Pavel, *Fictional Worlds* (Cambridge, MA: Harvard University Press, 1986); Gregory Currie, *The Nature of Fiction* (Cambridge: Cambridge University Press, 1990); Kendall Walton, *Mimesis as Make-Believe* (Cambridge, MA: Harvard University Press, 1990); Charles Crittenden, *Unreality: The Metaphysics of Fictional Objects* (Ithaca, NY: Cornell University Press, 1991); Peter Lamarque and Stein Haugom Olsen, *Truth, Fiction, and Literature: A Philosophical Perspective* (Oxford: Clarendon Press, 1994); Amie Thomasson, *Fiction and Metaphysics* (Cambridge: Cambridge University Press, 1999); and Matthew Kieran and Dominic McIver Lopes, eds., *Imagination, Philosophy and the Arts* (London: Routledge, 2003).

There are numerous journal articles discussing the "paradox of fiction" about fiction and emotion, some of which are mentioned in the text. There are also book-length treatments, among which the following are noteworthy: Bijoy Boruah, *Fiction and Emotion: A Study in Aesthetics and the Philosophy of Mind* (Oxford: Clarendon Press, 1988); E. M. Dadlez, *What's Hecuba to Him? Fictional Events and Actual Emotion* (University Park, PA: Penn State University Press, 1997); Mette Hjort and Sue Laver, eds., *Emotion and the Arts* (Oxford: Oxford University Press, 1997); and R. J. Yanal, *Paradoxes of Emotion and Fiction* (University Park, PA: Penn State University Press, 1999). Dadlez and Yanal develop versions of "thought theory," which is also represented in: Noël Carroll, *The Philosophy of Horror, or Paradoxes of the Heart* (New York: Routledge, Chapman, and Hall, 1990); Peter Lamarque, *Fictional Points of View* (Ithaca, NY: Cornell University Press, 1996); and Susan L. Feagin, *Reading with Feeling: The Aesthetics of Appreciation* (Ithaca, NY: Cornell University Press, 1996).

For more general philosophical discussion of literature and emotion, see Derek Matravers, *Art and Emotion* (Oxford: Clarendon Press, 2001); Jenefer Robinson, *Deeper than Reason: Emotion and Its Role in Literature, Music, and Art* (Oxford: Oxford University Press, 2005); and Berys Gaut, *Art, Emotion, and Ethics* (Oxford: Clarendon Press, 2007).

# Chapter Six

# Truth

There are all kinds of connections between literature and truth. Sorting them out and assessing them is a major task of the philosopher of literature. The key question, though, at the heart of an age-old debate is whether truth is a criterion of literary value. Is great literature "great" in virtue of, even partly in virtue of, its truth? For all the simplicity of its formulation, the question conceals deep and contentious issues about the nature of literature and its status among other kinds of discourse.

The time-honored formula that poetry aims to "instruct" as well as give "pleasure" might initially encourage a positive answer. Yet further reflection shows that not all instruction involves the imparting of truths or the acquisition of beliefs. Instruction can be in skills or know-how, how to look or how to respond. Poetry can be "instructive" by opening the mind to new possibilities, by developing novel perspectives on its subject matter, by "defamiliarizing" the everyday, by training the emotions, or even just by having a serious content, worthy of serious thought. Exercising the imagination can come to seem a higher poetic achievement than the more worldly-rooted transmission of fact. Even those who promote a mimetic conception of literature – "holding a mirror to the world" – might admit fundamental differences between the literary and the philosophic pursuit of truth.

## The Scope of the Truth Issue

Traditionally the debate has been about "poetry" or "poetic truth," which has the merit of narrowing down the topic, although arguably it narrows it too much, as we want to include prose fiction of a kind rarely described as poetry. The trouble, as we saw in Chapter 2, is that there is a broader, generic sense of "literature" beyond poetry and fiction, which includes works such as Gibbon's *Decline and Fall of the Roman Empire*, Hume's *Dialogues on Natural Religion*, perhaps Lincoln's Gettysburg Address. If history, philosophy, and political speeches are let in then it does look as if some literary works, those falling under this generic sense, are unproblematically valued for their truth and have truth as one of their aims. It would hopelessly beg the question to pursue the debate simply by agreeing to set aside this class of truth-aspiring works.

In fact we need not do this. The position is more complicated, for we should recall the reason such works are called literature in the first place, namely their being "belles lettres" or examples of "fine writing." If we ask whether truth is a criterion of *fine writing* the answer seems to be unproblematically *no*. Why should truth or falsity have anything to do with whether something is well or badly written? The "literary" aspects of history or philosophy would seem to be aspects that have nothing to do with truth. Assessing the *literary* merits of *Decline and Fall of the Roman Empire* or *Dialogues on Natural Religion* involves setting aside concern with historical accuracy or philosophical acumen. So the very cases that seem to establish an irrefutable connection between literature and truth turn out to do no such thing.

But this might seem to establish too much, too early on, namely that no literary works could be valued for their truth. So we come back to the paradigms of literature that concern us: poetry, drama, and prose fiction. These are often thought to make a special claim to truth and to be valued for that. The reason we should not dismiss this claim so quickly is that there is more to literature in this sense than fine writing. If all that made poetry and the novel into "literature" were their belles-lettrist qualities then we would not have a problem with truth. But imaginative literature, as we have seen, is not to be defined as fine writing, so the problem remains.

It might be thought that the prominence of *fiction* in imaginative literature makes the truth issue easy to solve, for how could something fictional or made up aspire to truth? But our discussion of fiction in the last chapter showed that fictional discourse is not incompatible with truth. Fiction has all kinds of connections with fact. Works of fiction can make reference to people and objects in the real world; they often have a real-world setting (place and historical period); in realist genres they are constrained by principles of verisimilitude, portraying characters as having habits, modes of speech, appearance, motivation, desires, and human competences familiar in actual people; readers make inferences about characters on the strength of their knowledge of the real world, and to be understood and appreciated fiction requires such worldly knowledge; works of fiction can offer generalizations about human nature.

No one could dispute that readers can learn about the real world from fiction: they pick up facts about history, geography, points of etiquette, clothing and fashions, idiomatic usage, as well as how to perform practical tasks, how people behave in certain situations, what it is like to be in an earthquake, a storm at sea, or a blazing house. Fiction is often a vehicle for teaching even outside the normal literary context. Parables, moral tales told to children, philosophers' thought-experiments, sermons, and police profiles, all employ fiction (i.e., imaginary examples) to convey ideas or lessons. The question is not whether we can learn truths from fiction – that is an inescapable fact – but what value to attach to this learning.

## The Historical Context

The historical debate about poetry and truth traditionally begins with Plato, even though he himself famously referred to the "quarrel" between poetry and philosophy as "ancient."

### Plato on the deceptions of poetry

For Plato, poetry, like painting and sculpture, is a form of mimesis or "imitation"; in all cases what the artist imitates are imperfect and deceptive appearances in the world. Although poets purport to speak about the world, their representations are not to be trusted as they are not grounded in rational methods. Plato lays serious charges against poetry. Poets, he thinks, are:

- ignorant (they merely mimic the talk of experts, without knowledge themselves)
- beguiling (they put pleasure – enhanced by the devices of poetry – before truth); and
- deceitful (they imitate appearance not reality).

Here is a passage from Plato:

> he [the poet] uses words and phrases to block in some of the colours of each area of expertise, although all he understands is how to represent things in a way which makes other superficial people, who base their conclusions on the words they can hear, think that he's written a really good poem about shoe-making or military command or whatever else it is he's set to metre, rhythm, and music. It only takes these features to cast this powerful a spell: that's what they're for. But when the poets' work is stripped of its musical hues and expressed in plain words, I think you've seen what kind of impression it gives ... An image-maker, a representer, understands only appearance, while reality is beyond him.[1]

---

[1]  Plato, *The Republic*, trans. Robin Waterfield (Oxford: Oxford University Press, 1994), p. 352.

Plato recognized the seductive power of poetry and had much to say in its favor, but on balance he tended to stress its dangers over its benefits. He was concerned about the potentially harmful effects in schools and suggested censorship of selected passages, notably depictions of unsavory behavior by the gods in Homer, and any poetry deemed to be immoral.[2] Yet it is often remarked that in writing dialogues Plato himself was using a literary or poetic form. And he does offer an olive branch to the poets, saying that if they can offer a "poetic rebuttal [to his views] in lyric verse" or if lovers of poetry, who are not poets themselves, could "prove that there is more to poetry than mere pleasure – that it also has a beneficial effect on society and human life in general" then they might be readmitted to his republic.[3]

Plato's strictures about poetry resonate through history. Attempts to suppress poetry (including drama and story-telling) for its immorality and seductiveness are recurrent wherever puritanical thinking prevails. Similarly, "defenses" of poetry are equally common, addressed, as most are, more or less overtly to the charges laid by Plato. Arguably, Plato's invitation to defend poetry in terms of its "beneficial effect on society" has itself had a deleterious effect on the debate about literary value because the effect sought (coupled with the commitment to mimesis) has almost always been connected to moral or other kinds of truth. This has meant that poetry, rather than being considered in its own terms, has been constantly compared with philosophy.

### Aristotle and universal truths

In fact Plato's invitation for a defense of poetry was soon answered by his own pupil, Aristotle. Aristotle does not dispute Plato's premise that poetry is mimesis or, indeed, that any willful distortion of reality would be morally objectionable. But he promotes a more flexible view about what poetry might "imitate": the poet "must necessarily in all instances represent things in one or other of three aspects, ... either as they were or are, or as they are said or thought to be or to have been, or as they ought to be."[4] He rejects Plato's theory of forms (universals), so he allows that poetry might imitate reality not merely "appearance." He also locates the great tragedies – the paradigms of poetic achievement – between history and philosophy:

> The distinction between historian and poet is not in the one writing prose and the other verse — you might put the work of Herodotus into verse, and

---

[2]  *The Republic*, pp. 72–73; Plato, *The Laws*, trans. Trevor J. Saunders (Harmondsworth: Penguin, 1976), Bk. 7, 801, pp. 288–289.

[3]  *The Republic*, pp. 361–362.

[4]  Aristotle, *Poetics*, 1460b, p. 2,337.

it would still be a species of history; it consists really in this, that the one describes the thing that has been, and the other a kind of thing that might be. Hence poetry is something more philosophic and of graver import than history, since its statements are of the nature rather of universals, whereas those of history are singulars. By a universal statement I mean one as to what such or such a kind of man will probably or necessarily say or do — which is the aim of poetry, though it affixes proper names to the characters; by a singular statement, one as to what, say, Alcibiades did or had done to him.[5]

In tragedy, the principal object of imitation is human action (not character), and the way the plot is structured is of paramount importance in yielding the desired effects, both pleasure and catharsis of the emotions. The plot has a beginning, middle, and end, it must be "of a certain magnitude," though possessing "unity," and it will have characteristic features like "change of fortune" (*catastrophe*), "reversal" (*peripeteia*), and "recognition" (*anagnorisis*). The poet's use of artifice is not, as with Plato, seen as serving mere trickery or beguiling illusion but as part of the craft of constructing a convincing plot from which controlled effects and universal truths can emerge.

There has been much debate about exactly what Aristotle meant by "universal statements." His own suggestion that what we can learn from poetry is "what such or such a kind of man will probably or necessarily say or do" might seem unambitious in the context of grander claims for poetry's cognitive achievement. It might be thought, too, that his view of history, as merely describing particularities, does not do justice to the ambitions of historians to extract something universal from their own case studies.

Nevertheless the idea that poetry aspires to say something "universal" through its plots and characters is one that has motivated much of the quest for a truth-seeking value in literature. It is manifested in the neoclassical "mimetic" theories of the eighteenth century, exemplified in Dr. Johnson's remark: "The business of a poet ... is to examine, not the individual, but the species; to remark general properties and large appearances."[6] A similar sentiment appears in the Romantics, when Wordsworth says of poetry: "Its object is truth, not individual and local, but general and operative."[7] Perhaps some such view is evident in Byron's denial, quoted in Chapter 3, that he is to be identified with his creation Childe Harold: "I have made my hero for all the world," i.e., Childe Harold is not just tied to the particularities of Byron's

[5]   Aristotle, *Poetics*, 1451b, 2–10, p. 2,323.

[6]   Samuel Johnson, *Rasselas* (1759), in *Rasselas and Other Tales*, ed. Gwin J. Kolb, vol. XVI, The Yale Edition of the Works of Samuel Johnson (New Haven, CT: Yale University Press, 1990), ch. 10, p. 43.

[7]   William Wordsworth, "1802 Preface to the *Lyrical Ballads*," in *Romanticism*, ed. Duncan Wu (Oxford: Blackwell, 1994), p. 258.

own life. But it also shows up in twentieth-century Marxist theories of "realism" which demand that the writer, in the words of György Lukács, "discover the underlying essence, i.e., the real factors that relate their experiences to the hidden social forces that produce them."[8]

## Conceptions of Literary Truth

Those who maintain that truth is one of the values of literature do not always agree on what is meant by "truth." Even among philosophers of literature it is possible to discern two broad camps: those, on the one hand, who hold that some special sense of "truth" is needed to capture the peculiarity of literary truth; and those, on the other, who hold that if truth is at issue in this context then it had better be a conception familiar to philosophy and science.

### Sui generis *conceptions*

Those in the former camp have gone to great lengths to characterize a *sui generis* conception of truth that captures the special contribution of literature to cognition. The critic I. A. Richards, for example, while denying that the "scientific sense" of "truth" is relevant to the arts, suggests that within criticism "truth" most often means "acceptability" and "sincerity."[9] A related conception is that of "authenticity."[10] Here truth is connected to truthfulness, honesty, or lack of sentimentality. A work is "true" if it doesn't attempt to deceive or flatter or charm or soften the edges. John Hospers promotes the idea that literature is "true to life" or "true to human nature," by which he means that "the characters described by the novelist behave, feel, and are motivated the way people in real life behave, feel, and are motivated."[11] The notion of "true to" is similar to that of "verisimilitude," a conception of truth implying resemblance to fact, or "realistic" description. Plots that involve fantastic improbabilities, unbelievable coincidences, or unconvincingly timely intervention from a *deus ex machina* will not "ring true"; they will seem false or contrived. Note, though, that genre conventions are relevant

[8]   György Lukács, "Realism in the Balance" (1938), in *The Norton Anthology of Theory and Criticism*, ed. Vincent B. Leitch (New York: Norton, 2001) pp 1,033–1,058.

[9]   I. A. Richards, *Principles of Literary Criticism*, 2nd ed. (London: Routledge and Kegan Paul, 1926), pp. 212–213.

[10]   Dorothy Walsh, *Literature and Knowledge* (Middletown, CT: Wesleyan University Press, 1969).

[11]   John Hospers, "Literature and Human Nature," *Journal of Aesthetics and Art Criticism*, vol. 17, no. 1. (1958), pp. 45–57 at p. 46.

to such judgments. In fantasies, slapstick comedies, or pantomime, for example, "verisimilitude" is not a value, nor indeed is truthfulness or honesty. Other *sui generis* conceptions include "ideal possibility,"[12] the "concrete universal,"[13] or "depth meaning."[14]

The novelist and philosopher Iris Murdoch has developed a sophisticated truth theory, which incorporates some of the elements just mentioned:

> 'Truth' is something we recognize in good art when we are led to a juster, clearer, more detailed, more refined understanding. Good art 'explains' truth itself, by *manifesting* deep conceptual connections. Truth is clarification, justice, compassion.

She also writes:

> Truth is not a simple or easy concept. Critical terminology imputes falsehood to an artist by using terms such as fantastic, sentimental, self-indulgent, banal, grotesque, tendentious, unclarified, wilfully obscure and so on. The positive aspect of the avoidance of these faults is a kind of transcendence: the ability to see other non-self things clearly and to criticise and celebrate them freely and justly.[15]

Even here, though, literary truth takes different forms: clarification, justice, compassion, a kind of transcendence. It is not obvious that any unified concept underlies them all, any more than that they are simply further aspects of those conceptions noted from the other theorists. Perhaps there is no unified conception of a *sui generis* truth for literature. However, rather than heightening the controversy over literary truth, it could be argued that these nonstandard conceptions make the debate easier to resolve. Those who think that "truth" is not an appropriate mode of valuation for literature – inviting misleading comparisons with science and philosophy – might well be happy to concede that there is a place for sincerity or authenticity or verisimilitude or clarification or even "a kind of transcendence" among the values of literature. Their skepticism is only whether the term "truth" is apt. If that is right, then the debate can begin to look merely terminological. Let us agree, they might say, that in certain kinds of literature sincerity is a value, but let us reserve judgment on whether to call it "truth."

[12]  Dorothy Walsh, "The Cognitive Content of Art," *Philosophical Review*, vol. 52, no. 5 (1943), pp. 433–451.

[13]  W. K. Wimsatt, *The Verbal Icon: Studies in the Meaning of Poetry* (Lexington: University of Kentucky Press, 1954).

[14]  Morris Weitz, "Truth in Literature," *Revue Internationale de Philosophie*, IX (1955), pp. 1–14.

[15]  Both quotations are from Iris Murdoch, *Metaphysics as a Guide to Morals* (Harmondsworth: Penguin, 1992), pp. 321, 86.

## *A philosopher's paradigm*

For analytic philosophers the paradigm of truth is the true proposition, a proposition subject to determinate truth conditions. Thus the sentence "Socrates is wise" is true just in case the name "Socrates" picks out an object of reference and the predicate "is wise" correctly characterizes that object. The simplicity of this notion of truth is captured nicely by Aristotle's dictum: "to say of what is that it is, and of what is not that it is not, is true."[16] Simple though it is, this formula is not without substance. It rules out, for example, the attribution of truth to mere ideas or concepts. To say that a work is about love or pride and prejudice or the conflict of duty and desire is not yet to ascribe truth, for there is not yet a proposition to be assessed for truth. Mere "aboutness" is not the same as truth.

It would be equally wrong to suppose that by delimiting the debate to simple propositional truth, the issue of literary truth – particularly associated with works of fiction – is foreclosed. On inspection there turn out to be plenty of propositions in the offing that are candidates for truth. In fiction and in poetry it is not uncommon to find both factual descriptions *and* explicit generalizations about human nature or psychology. Also, when readers reflect on the content of such works they often seek to derive their own generalizations, summarizing or extending what is explicitly given. It is worth attending to such cases and asking how far truth matters.

## Factual Description

To the extent that poems, plays, and novels are set in the real world, authors frequently spell out relevant facts about that world. In David Lodge's novel *Therapy* (1995) the final chapter describes a pilgrimage to Santiago de Compostela taken by two characters. The narrator offers an extended factual description about the real-world pilgrimage: e.g., "Tens of thousands hit the road every summer, following the blue and yellow *coquille* signs erected by the Council of Europe."[17] Wearing his literary critical rather than novelistic hat, Lodge has written in another place that "novels burn facts as engines burn fuel, and the facts can come only from the novelist's own experience or acquired knowledge."[18]

---

[16]    Aristotle, *Metaphysics*, 1011b, 25–28, *The Complete Works of Aristotle: The Revised Oxford Translation*, ed. Jonathan Barnes (Princeton, NJ: Princeton University Press, 1984), vol. 2, p. 1,597.

[17]    David Lodge, *Therapy* (Harmondsworth: Penguin, 1995), p. 287.

[18]    David Lodge, "Fact and Fiction in the Novel," in *The Practice of Writing* (Harmondsworth: Penguin, 1997), p. 27.

*Facts in fiction*

In the carefully crafted Author's Note to his novel *Small World* (1984), Lodge describes the complex interaction of fact and fiction in that novel:

> *Small World* resembles what is sometimes called the real world, without corresponding exactly to it, and is peopled by figments of the imagination. Rummidge is not Birmingham, though it owes something to popular prejudices about that city. There really is an underground chapel at Heathrow and a James Joyce pub in Zurich.... The MLA convention of 1979 did not take place in New York, though I have drawn on the programme for the 1978 one, which did. And so on.

Elsewhere, in commenting on this Author's Note, he explains:

> I wanted my readers to know, for instance, that the panel discussions at the MLA Convention in Part V [of *Small World*], on "Lesbian-feminist Teaching and Learning" and "Problems of Cultural Distinction in Translating Expletives in the Work of Cortazar, Sender, Baudelaire and Flaubert," were not parodies but the real thing. I wanted them to know that the Dublin pub painstakingly dismantled and re-erected in Zurich in memory of James Joyce, who wrote most of *Ulysses* in that city, was not some strained conceit of mine but a fact: a fact that says much about the curious intertwining of high culture and popular culture in our epoch, about the reification of literary reputations and the deification of dead writers, a process in which the academic literary profession is deeply implicated.[19]

Lodge writes of what he "wanted [his] readers to know," indicating that it can be important for novelists to incorporate facts and for readers to recognize that. In this case his reason for insisting on the presence of fact is that he didn't want his readers to think he was exaggerating certain descriptions – e.g., the programme of the Convention and the re-erected Joyce pub. He even tells us why the latter fact is significant: it illustrates "the curious intertwining of high culture and popular culture in our epoch." But the example also shows how facts seem not always to matter: without explanation Lodge changes the date and place of the MLA convention.

   That factual propositions can be integral to works of imaginative literature is not in dispute. Dickens famously asserted in his Preface to *Bleak House* that "everything set forth in these pages concerning the Court of Chancery is substantially true, and within the truth." It is more difficult, though, to pin

---

[19]   Ibid., pp. 28–29.

down the importance attached to getting the facts right. M. W. Rowe has insisted in this context that "truth is always a virtue and falsehood always a vice."[20] However, immediately preceding that, he remarks: "In fiction, truth is neither necessary nor sufficient for literary merit, since our interest can always be sustained by a work's wit, energy, epic sweep, pathos or humour." The latter seems right but Rowe offers examples in support of the former, the idea that "falsehood [is] always a vice."

One such is Philip Larkin's poem "Absences," which starts as follows:

> Rain patters on a sea that tilts and sighs.
> Fast running floors collapsing into hollows,
> Tower suddenly, spray-aired. Contrariwise,
> A wave drops like a wall: another follows,
> Wilting and scrambling, tirelessly at play
> Where there are no ships and no shallows.[21]

Rowe quotes a letter to Larkin from an oceanographer, Frank Evans:

> When I first read the poem … I thought: he's got his images wrong. Like so many people who walk along the shore and watch the breakers rolling in he thinks that waves in the ocean do the same. But it is only waves coming into the beach that roll over and drop like a wall; offshore, no matter how big the waves are, when they break the water just spills down the front. It is the size not the shape of the deep water waves that changes with the wind strength. Whether in storms or summer breezes make no difference to the profile of the breaking waves.[22]

Larkin admitted the mistake and replied: "I hope not many of my readers are oceanographers"; in a later American edition he added a note, saying that the mistake "seriously damaged the poem from a technical viewpoint … but I do not see how to amend it now." The example is instructive. The facts concerned are recondite, non-oceanographically trained readers will not notice the error, and the image will work effectively. But once pointed out the error does irreparable damage. There is no artistic intention behind the distortion of fact so no explanation is forthcoming in terms of "artistic licence." Here a factual mistake does lead to a literary weakness. It is a failure of mimesis or verisimilitude.

---

[20]  M. W. Rowe, "Lamarque and Olsen on Literature and Truth," *Philosophical Quarterly*, vol. 47, no. 188 (1997), pp. 322–341 at p. 335.

[21]  Philip Larkin, "Absences," in *Collected Poems* (London: Faber and Faber, 1988), p. 49.

[22]  Philip Larkin, *Selected Letters of Philip Larkin*, ed. Anthony Thwaite (London: Faber and Faber, 1992), p. 332.

Christopher Ricks presents an array of similar cases.[23] He argues that the mistakes are worse, from a literary point of view, than merely being (for the author) irritating slip-ups. One example is in William Golding's novel *Lord of the Flies*, where Piggy's glasses are used to light a fire at a crucial stage in the plot. But Piggy is shortsighted so his glasses would contain diverging or concave lenses, which would diffuse not concentrate the sun's rays. They could not be used to light a fire. It is hard to see how the mistake could be remedied without subtle changes in the dynamics of the story, e.g., being longsighted would not have been an obvious disadvantage to Piggy. Ricks comments: "not only does he die because he is shortsighted, but the moral and spiritual impulse of the book is behind the irony that, of all the boys, he is the one who is *least* shortsighted – except physically." Also the "Promethean" theme – "Piggy the fire-bringer is hideously sacrificed" – is compromised.

Another example is from Dickens's *Great Expectations*:

> Magwitch, the convict who comes back from Australia and risks his life to repay Pip, would *not* have been liable to the death penalty at that date for doing so. Yet it is essential to the novel that he should be deemed liable to the death penalty. Not only does his act thereby incarnate a supremely loving danger, but it is his being liable to the death penalty which underwrites, first, his destroying the evil Compeyson, and, second, his dying a natural death — eluding the penalty of his return — as a consequence of that violent river-struggle with his antagonist. ... What might have seemed to be only a legal detail radiates into the central life of the book.[24]

Factual mistakes of this kind, when brought to the surface, do have an adverse affect. Yet such cases seem curiously peripheral to the formula of "instruct" and "please." The Larkin poem and the two novels still give pleasure and retain their essential literary interest. It would be perverse to suppose that among the aims of these works was to instruct readers on wave movement, lenses, or death penalties. These components are part of the subject and imagery of the works but not part of any significant "truth" the works impart.

### Accuracy and genre conventions

What the examples do not establish is Rowe's strong claim that "falsehood [is] always a vice" in literature. The case of historical fiction well illustrates

---

[23] Christopher Ricks, "Literature and the Matter of Fact," in *Essays in Appreciation* (Oxford: Clarendon Press, 1996).

[24] Ibid., pp. 305–306.

the constraints on truth-telling and the role of falsehood. The modern genre of the historical novel probably began with Walter Scott's *Waverley* (1814), but the genre's diversity is shown if we include Leo Tolstoy's *War and Peace*, Georgette Heyer's Regency romances, Gore Vidal's *Burr*, and Alexander Solzhenitsyn's *August 1914*. The genre can be mixed with other genres, such as the acclaimed murder mystery, *An Instance of the Fingerpost* (1998) by Iain Pears, set in seventeenth-century England against a finely researched background in seventeenth-century science and the English Civil War. The basic genre convention of all historical fiction is that historical detail should be adhered to as closely as possible while allowing an imaginative element in made-up dialogue and the introduction of non-historical characters. This imaginative element strictly involves "falsehood" but is surely no "vice." Literary vice occurs only where genre conventions are breached, which in historical fiction might involve flagrant, unmotivated – usually accidental – departure from fact, e.g., mistakes about dress, manners, speech, geography, chronology, common knowledge, etc.

But now we can see that the source of literary flaws in such cases is not so much falsehood per se but the flouting of genre convention. Such conventions raise expectations in readers, and where these are let down, unintentionally and to no literary purpose, then a work is weakened from a literary perspective. Aristotle's account of tragedy in effect outlines the conventions of the genre. These are not just formal conventions – the "unities" of the plot – but conventions about the appropriateness of kinds of characters and kinds of actions. To depict the tragic fall of too noble or perfect a character might be described as "falsehood" or lack of verisimilitude (this wouldn't or shouldn't happen), although at root the failure is a breach not of truth-telling but of literary convention. David Lodge's satires on university life are effective, as with all satires, precisely because of the balance they strike between exaggeration and recognized fact. If the exaggeration becomes too extreme and implausible – flouting a convention of satire – then the works would lose their appeal. In his comments on these novels Lodge is concerned to show just how close to the facts he has stayed.

## Explicit Generalizations

Defenders of truth-telling as a literary virtue rarely rest their case on the presence of factual descriptions alone in literary works. Other propositions, thus other candidates for truth-assessment, of a more universal kind can seem more relevant to the debate. Larkin, for example, ends his poem "Dockery and Son", which we have looked at before, as follows:

> Life is first boredom, then fear.
> Whether or not we use it, it goes,
> And leaves what something hidden from us chose,
> And age, and then the only end of age.[25]

This is a general reflection arising at the end of a poem in which Larkin compares himself to a contemporary, Dockery, at his Oxford college; the Dean had informed Larkin that Dockery's son had recently joined the college and this prompted a process of thought – about having children, being set in one's ways – that culminated in these observations. The reflection is not a factual claim, part of the setting or subject, but a general thought arising from the setting. Novelists, too, frequently offer general comments in the course of a narrative: none more than Tolstoy, who, in *War and Peace*, makes numerous asides, for example on the nature of history: "Man lives consciously for himself but unconsciously he serves as an instrument for the accomplishment of historical and social ends."[26]

## Memorable sayings

From a theoretical point of view, what are we to make of such general reflections? Is their truth an issue in literary judgments? There is no doubt in the popular mind that general observations encapsulated in memorable sayings are part of what make authors "great." Shakespeare's contribution to the "quotation" industry is unrivalled. Anyone wanting a fine *mot* on, say, the seven ages of man could not do better than reach for the famous passage in *As You Like It* (Act II, scene vii) which starts

> All the world's a stage,
> And all the men and women merely players.
> They have their exits and their entrances,
> And one man in his time plays many parts,
> His acts being seven ages. At first, the infant,
> Mewling and puking in the nurse's arms.
> Then the whining schoolboy, with his satchel
> And shining morning face, creeping like snail
> Unwillingly to school.

and ends summarizing old age as

---

[25] Philip Larkin, "Dockery and Son," in *Collected Poems* (London: Faber and Faber, 1988), p. 153.

[26] Leo Tolstoy, *War and Peace*, trans. Rosemary Edmonds (Harmondsworth: Penguin, 1969), vol. 2, p. 718.

> ... second childishness and mere oblivion,
> Sans teeth, sans eyes, sans taste, sans everything.

Or a headmaster seeking stirring words at the end of term might want to share Polonius's advice to Laertes (in *Hamlet*, Act I, scene iii):

> This above all; to thine own self be true:
> And it must follow, as the night the day,
> Thou canst not then be false to any man.

Likewise, a politician might endorse these words from *Julius Caesar* (Act IV, scene iii):

> There is a tide in the affairs of men,
> Which, taken at the flood, leads on to fortune;
> Omitted, all the voyage of their life
> Is bound in shallows and in miseries.

It was Alexander Pope who saw the value of such "wit":

> True wit is nature to advantage dressed,
> What oft was thought, but ne'er so well expressed,
> Something, whose truth convinced at sight we find,
> That gives us back the notion of the mind.[27]

What great authors can offer are thoughts "ne'er so well expressed." It is not just the profundity that is admired but, probably more so, the precise and memorable expression. That is the "literary" achievement. But we should pause before accepting that literary value resides in "truths" of this kind. First of all, these well-known sayings from Shakespeare are all plucked out of context. The resonance the words have in the plays themselves, spoken by particular characters at particular dramatic moments for specific dramatic ends, is lost, and this drains them of the distinctive literary interest their contexts supply.

Another feature of the Shakespearean examples is that being spoken by characters they are, arguably, not directly asserted by the author. It might or might not be the case that Shakespeare intends them to be truths we should accept. After all, we are not invited to accept the cynical musings of Iago. Of course, whatever Shakespeare intended we might nevertheless take them as truths and appropriate them for our own purposes. We can accept the truth of propositions not asserted as such, but where we do so it does indeed look like appropriation. Even the Larkin and Tolstoy cases are not clear-cut as authorial assertions. A standard practice in reading poetry, as we have seen, is to postulate a dramatic speaker in place of the author. Larkin's proposition

---

[27] Alexander Pope, *An Essay on Criticism* (1711), part 2, ll. 297–300, in *Alexander Pope: The Major Works* (Oxford: Oxford University Press, 2006).

"Life is first boredom, then fear" cannot be assumed to be a sentiment that Larkin himself is endorsing. Even Tolstoy's pronouncement about history can be distanced from the author. After all, in an example we have used before, the opening sentence of *Pride and Prejudice* about "a single man in possession of a good fortune, [being] in want of a wife" would be wrongly taken as an assertion or as a proposition that Jane Austen accepts as true. But the defender of literary truth need not be too worried about whether the propositions are asserted. What seems to matter is whether they are candidates for truth.

### Generality and truth-assessment

A more serious problem, though, is that the generalizations are sometimes so general that their truth-value is hard to discern. Is it really true that "Life is first boredom, then fear"? At best that seems to hold only for some people, in some circumstances. Is it true that "All the world's a stage"? The latter is metaphorical, and perhaps the best we can say is that the metaphor is apt and telling. As for the seventh age of man, it is not *literally* true that all old people are "Sans teeth, sans eyes, sans taste, sans everything." Yet the image is vivid and memorable. Sometimes the fineness of the expression disguises the contentiousness of the content, as in Horace's stirring words: "Dulce et decorum est pro patria mori"[28] (It is sweet and honourable to die for one's country). So is truth really at issue? Or are these generalizations merely powerful prompters to get us to think along certain lines?

As with many proverbs ("Great minds think alike") it seems not just difficult but curiously irrelevant to try to *verify* certain literary reflections. Literary sayings are just as likely as proverbs to contradict each other: "Look before you leap"/"He who hesitates is lost." Yet with or without the possibility of verification the familiar quotations give pleasure because they offer precisely worded expressions of thoughts that people value. Peter Kivy has introduced the nice image of an "afterlife" to describe readers' reflections on works of fiction long after they have finished reading. Kivy maintains that thoughts about the verification of general thematic propositions – as he puts it, the "confirmation-disconfirmation" of live hypotheses – are central to literary appreciation even if there is little expectation of arriving at any final truth-valuation.[29]

A further worry about the emphasis on truth, aside from concerns about verifiability, is that these very general propositions are seldom *defended* or *argued for* in works of literature. This makes the literary context seem very different from the philosophic or scientific one, where reasoning and

[28]  Horace, *Odes*, Book III, 2, line 13, in *Horace: Odes and Epodes*, trans. C. E. Bennett, Loeb Classical Library (London: William Heinemann, 1927).

[29]  Peter Kivy, "The Laboratory of Fictional Truth," in *Philosophies of Arts: An Essay in Differences* (Cambridge: Cambridge University Press, 1997).

evidence are paramount. This criticism is often heard against defenders of literary truth. It is the basis for the rationalist suspicion felt by Plato against the seductive charms of poetry. If a thought is wittily and succinctly expressed we are likely to accept it, even if under colder analysis its truth is far from secure. The objection, though, is not decisive. It would be to beg the question against the special contribution of imaginative literature to insist that it employ the very methods of truth advancement found in science and philosophy. Literature, the truth-defender might reasonably insist, simply has different rhetorical strategies and different means of support from other truth-promoting modes of discourse; that's what's special about it.

A final consideration about these explicit generalizations is perhaps the most important of all. It concerns their function and status, in particular the role they play in their proper context. Consider an example again from Iris Murdoch who, as philosopher and novelist, is not averse to putting general reflections into her fiction. Here is one such, from her novel *The Black Prince* (1973):

> There is … an eternal discrepancy between the self-knowledge which we gain by observing ourselves objectively and the self-awareness which we have of ourselves subjectively: a discrepancy which probably makes it impossible for us ever to arrive at the truth. Our self-knowledge is too abstract, our self-awareness is too intimate and swoony and dazed.[30]

On the face of it, this is a philosophical observation about the limits of human self-knowledge. Readers can ponder its truth in that light. In context, though, its status is much more complicated and, arguably, more interesting. It is spoken by the narrator Bradley Pearson, whose quest, on his own admission, is "truth," but who reveals himself to be deeply self-deceived. Two central themes in the novel are the impossibility of a truly objective knowledge of any human being and the aspiration of art to tell the truth through its own "clarity" and honesty. The quoted statement is rich with irony because Bradley Pearson believes himself to be an artist and to have attained both truth and self-knowledge through his art (the narrative we are reading). The statement functions primarily as a thematic statement characterizing one of the themes just mentioned and offering a range of philosophical concepts to apply to the work as a whole. Events in the novel itself illustrate the very difficulty the statement alludes to (i.e., self-knowledge). The example thus shows a number of things about such generalizations: they can function as thematic statements as well as worldly truths, pointing inwards (to the work) rather than outwards (to the world); they can also acquire an ironic significance in context that is lost when they are crudely extracted. The example also shows the kind of support that a novel might give to its integral

---

[30]  Iris Murdoch, *The Black Prince* (London: Chatto and Windus, 1973), p. 155.

generalizations, short of philosophical argument or scientific evidence: a novel can *illustrate* through character and action what it might be for its thematic statements to be true about the world. Bradley Pearson's own narrative illustrates the "discrepancy" he speaks of between "self-knowledge" and "self-awareness." If we come to endorse the worldly truth of the thematic statement it might be because the fictional portrayal is so powerful or persuasive (it "rings true").[31]

## Implicit Theses

Literary truth is not always to be found spelt out explicitly in literary works. Often readers are called upon to construct their own generalizations. It is implicit in Franz Kafka's *The Trial* that human beings are victims of impersonal and indifferent forces outside their control or in Dickens's *Our Mutual Friend* that money has a remorselessly corrupting power. These propositions are not made explicit but are suggested by the works in question.

An issue sometimes raised about these implied truths is that there are no clear principles for deriving general propositions from works of literature.[32] Standard forms of inference familiar to philosophy, such as induction, logical deduction, or analytic entailment, do not seem relevant. However, there is no additional problem here beyond that of the validation of interpretive judgments in general for the propositions in question are precisely those associated with thematic interpretation, of the kind we examined in Chapter 4. There might be disagreements about the aims of interpretation and the nature of interpretive support but these do not challenge the fact that derived thematic content can take propositional and truth-assessable forms.

### Themes and truths

Now a deeper conflict arises, however, because the demands made on thematic interpretations and those on general truth-claims about human nature are very different. From the former we look for illumination about the literary work and underlying themes that help make sense of the work.

[31]    For a further discussion of Iris Murdoch's *The Black Prince* in the light of these issues, see Peter Lamarque, "Truth and Art," in *Fictional Points of View* (Ithaca, NY: Cornell University Press, 1996).

[32]    This preoccupies Mary Sirridge and is part of her anti-truth case: Mary J. Sirridge, "Truth from Fiction?," *Philosophy and Phenomenological Research*, vol. 35, no. 4 (1974–1975), pp. 453–471. It also concerns John Hospers in "Implied Truths in Literature," *Journal of Aesthetics and Art Criticism*, vol. 19, no. 1 (1960–1961), pp. 37–46.

From the latter we look for substantial insight into human lives. These do not necessarily go together. For example, Martha Nussbaum characterizes a theme of Euripides's *Hecuba* as "nothing human is ever worthy of trust: there are no guarantees at all, short of revenge or death."[33] As a thematic statement this captures well an implicit motif in this dark and troubling play. But as a generalization about human nature its truth is highly dubious. Only an utter pessimist would want to endorse it. Does this affect the value or interest of the play? No, we simply note that the play offers a dark and pessimistic vision, and even the optimists among us can value it for that reason. The example shows that a thematic statement might be true about a work but broadly false about the world at large. It also shows that worldly truth is not always relevant to literary value.

A related point is that quite different kinds of support are required for a thematic statement and a general truth. The former is supported by appeal to elements in the work. We note how Hecuba's faith in human trustworthiness is steadily eroded until she descends into the madness of revenge and murder. Her behavior through interactions with other characters reinforces the pessimistic theme. But, to change the example, no support for the proposition "Human beings are victims of impersonal and indifferent forces outside their control" is gained from the fact that this is a theme of Kafka's *The Trial*. That this proposition is implied by the novel is not a good reason to believe it. The novel does not *prove* the claim, at best it illustrates it, and if we were to try to prove it we would need arguments from philosophy or sociology.

It is striking also that critics themselves rarely move from identifying themes and locating them in the structure of a work to debating their truth as worldly generalizations. It is not part of the "practice" of reading, as characterized in Chapter 4, to engage in philosophical, psychological, or sociological debate about the great themes in literature: free will, desire, love, dejection, social responsibility, political action. Critics are content, as critics, to notice precisely how a point of view is developed and illustrated, relating it internally to features of the work and perhaps externally to works on similar themes. Confronted with works that present opposing points of view – free will vs. determinism, hope vs. despair, pessimism vs. optimism, political engagement vs. political quietism – they are not forced to defend one over the other. They might of course comment on the quality of the works in making a particular point of view plausible or interesting or attractive. But those are literary qualities, exhibiting consonance of means to ends. A novel that offers an unconvincing portrayal of a pessimistic or bleak outlook on life has failed not because what it portrays is literally false but

---

[33]   Martha Nussbaum, *The Fragility of Goodness: Luck and Ethics in Greek Tragedy and Philosophy* (Cambridge: Cambridge University Press, 1986), p. 419.

because, for example, its characters are wooden or stereotypical, its plot is contrived, its dialogue cliché-ridden, and its language use lackluster. These are literary, not philosophical or sociological, judgments.

## Triviality

The tension between interpretive validity and worldly truth emerges in another worry sometimes expressed about implied truths in literature, namely that the truths, when spelt out, are often trivial. The philosopher Jerome Stolnitz has fun trying to extract an "artistic truth" from the novel *Pride and Prejudice*. The best he claims he can come up with is: "Stubborn pride and ignorant prejudice keep attractive people apart," a truth he describes as "pitifully meagre."[34] Stolnitz points to a problem facing any attempt to derive worldly generalizations from literature, namely the need to abstract out all particularities of the work itself. Fine details about Elizabeth Bennet and Mr. Darcy, not to say "the feather-brained family members, the ne'er do well soldiers and priggish parsons," being all fictional, must be discounted when generalization is sought. But then it is no wonder that triviality results.[35]

When the literary critic, on the other hand, generalizes across the details of a work to formulate a thematic statement – a statement that illuminates the work rather than the outside world – triviality ceases to be an issue. The critic J. Hillis Miller has shown how the theme of the "power of money," how "people [are] turned into objects by money," is a strongly unifying thread in Dickens's *Our Mutual Friend*:

> The central intrigue of the Harmon murder shows the inheritance of a great fortune apparently corrupting its inheritors, Noddy Boffin, and his ward, Bella Wilfer, just as the desire to "become respectable in the scale of society" corrupts Lizzie Hexam's brother Charley. Money, one source of each character's station in life, separates Eugene Wrayburn and Lizzie Hexam. ... Class distinctions are shown in *Our Mutual Friend* to be closely intertwined with the power of money.[36]

It is illuminating to see just how the theme of the "power of money" develops and ramifies through the disparate details of the novel. But if we try

---

[34] Jerome Stolnitz, "On the Cognitive Triviality of Art," in Lamarque and Olsen, eds., *Aesthetics and the Philosophy of Art*, pp. 338–339.

[35] Further arguments to this effect can be found in Peter Kivy, "On the Banality of Literary Truths," *Philosophical Exchange*, vol. 28 (1997–1998). Noël Carroll introduces the expression "the banality argument" to capture the point: in "The Wheel of Virtue: Art, Literature, and Moral Knowledge," *Journal of Aesthetics and Art Criticism*, vol. 60, no. 1 (2002), pp. 3–26.

[36] J. Hillis Miller, "Afterword," in Charles Dickens, *Our Mutual Friend* (New York: Signet, 1964), p. 901.

to extract a worldly truth from all this, a truth independent of fictional particulars, such as "Money corrupts," we are back to banality. The corrupting power of money has been endlessly treated in literature, and it is implausible to suppose that the value of Dickens's novel lies in its presentation of this threadbare truth in itself. The novel's value resides in the working of the theme, not in the theme's bare propositional content.

## The Epistemology of Literature: Learning, Beliefs, Knowledge

What the preceding discussion has shown is that propositional truth, as favored by philosophers, does have a role to play in the characterization of the content of even the most overtly fictional works. Fictionality, in other words, is no bar to the advancement or illustration of worldly truth. However, the question of whether literal truth, either of a factual nature or of generalizations, is part of what gives literary works their distinctive value has not yet had a decisive answer. No one who gives primary focus to the discovery of propositional truths in literature, or who mines famous works for stirring quotations, would qualify as a subtle reader, even if it is admitted that there are pleasures to be had in reflecting on wise and well-expressed thoughts.

It might seem, though, that the narrow focus on propositional truth, factual or universal, does not do justice to the broadly "cognitive" benefits of literature, its power to "instruct." In particular, it does little to cast light on the admittedly vague thought that novels or poems can open our eyes to the world or present a vision which can change a reader's outlook on life.

### Vision

So how might we learn from literature beyond merely acquiring true beliefs? One notion commonly advanced is indeed that of "vision," which takes us back to Iris Murdoch, who has offered a telling defense of this idea. For Murdoch the "study of literature ... is an education in how to picture and understand human situations."[37] She expands this elsewhere:

> what we learn from contemplating the characters of Shakespeare or Tolstoy or the paintings of Velasquez or Titian ... is something about the real quality of human nature, when it is envisaged, in the artist's just and compassionate vision, with a clarity which does not belong to the self-centred rush of

---

[37]    Iris Murdoch, *The Sovereignty of Good* (London: Routledge, 1970), p. 34.

ordinary life. … [T]he greatest art … shows us the world … with a clarity which startles and delights us simply because we are not used to looking at the real world at all.[38]

The point is not that readers come to grasp propositional truths or acquire new beliefs but that their way of seeing the world has been affected. In a passage quoted earlier, she spoke of our being "led to a juster, clearer, more detailed, more refined understanding." The reader's vision comes to match that of the artist whose "compassionate" view of the world is manifested in the sympathy, generosity, and humanity of the portrayal of character and incident. This is far from the "truth" of the scientist, social scientist, or philosopher, and is not amenable to proof, verification, or argument. Instead it is deeply implicated in morality.

The connection of "vision" with morality is emphasized by philosophers of the Wittgensteinian school for whom the task of ethics is not to formulate general rules and principles but to explore "forms of life." The philosopher D. Z. Phillips remarks, in a discussion of Edith Wharton's novel *The Age of Innocence*:

Fundamental changes in moral perspectives need no longer be seen as the rejection and replacing of hypotheses or policies within a single framework within which moral beliefs must be determined. Old values do die, and new ones take their place. What separates Archer and his son is not a matter of different tentative beliefs within a common notion of reason but, rather, *different ways of looking at the world*, different conceptions of what is important in life.[39]

To come to a moral understanding of a complex real-life situation is not dissimilar to coming to grasp the vision presented in a work of art; in both cases a change of outlook might result. Both demand attention to fine-grained particularities, and neither is grounded on, or expected to issue in, a simple judgment. When we are guided by an artist to see things in new ways, to adopt a new perspective, we cannot formulate a lesson learned, for the particularities resist all effort of generalization. The philosopher R. W. Beardsmore expands the idea: "though we may speak of a novel or a poem's bringing a man to see what is possible for him, we can no longer

---

[38]   Ibid., p. 65.
[39]   D. Z. Phillips, "Allegiance and Change in Morality: A Study in Contrasts," in *Through a Darkening Glass: Philosophy, Literature, and Cultural Change* (Oxford: Blackwell, 1982), p. 25 (italics added).

conceive of these possibilities existing independently of the way in which he was brought to recognize them. ... For what it has to tell us is internally related to the work itself."[40] Writing of Celine's *Journey to the End of the Night*, Hilary Putnam remarks: "I do not learn that love does not exist, that all human beings are hateful and hating. ... What I learn is to see the world as it looks to someone who is sure that hypothesis is correct."[41]

How literally should we take the notion of "seeing" or "vision"? It cannot be literally true that one "sees" fictional characters, although "seeing" has an extended sense beyond the strictly visual in expressions like "seeing the point" or "seeing the best way forward." In this latter sense, seeing is a kind of grasping or recognition and no doubt has an application in responses to literature. It would be wrong, though, to rule out altogether the literal, visual, sense of seeing in this context, for it is an implication, certainly of Iris Murdoch's views, that great art has the capacity to change the way we literally look at the world. We *see* people and their actions differently when (in a non-literal sense) our *perspective* has been changed by great art.

## Imagination

A notion cognate to seeing is imagining, which is centrally involved in accounts of learning from literature. When Shelley offers his "defence of poetry," famously describing poets as "the unacknowledged legislators of the world," he makes the case for poetry's cognitive powers less in terms of truth than in terms of the imagination: "Poetry enlarges the circumference of the imagination by replenishing it with thoughts of ever new delight."[42] Later he continues: "The imagination is enlarged by a sympathy with pains and passions so mighty, that they distend in their conception the capacity of that by which they are conceived."[43] To enlarge the imagination is not to add new truths to it but in effect to "exercise" it through new applications. A fairly straightforward source of learning (or "insight") can result, and not only in poetry. A novelist's invented characters and incidents can stretch the imagination by causing readers to bring to mind imaginatively what otherwise might not have occurred to them. Further imaginative reflection

[40]    R. W. Beardsmore, "Learning from a Novel," *Philosophy and the Arts, Royal Institute of Philosophy Lectures*, vol. 6, 1971–1972 (London: Macmillan, 1973), p. 31.

[41]    Hilary Putnam, "Literature, Science, and Reflection," in *Meaning and the Moral Sciences* (London: Routledge, 1978), p. 89.

[42]    Percy Bysshe Shelley, "A Defence of Poetry" (1821), in *Percy Bysshe Shelley: The Major Works*, ed. Zachery Leader and Michael O'Neill (Oxford: Oxford University Press, 2003), p. 682.

[43]    Ibid., p. 684.

on this content, perhaps through supplementing detail, recognizing divergent points of view, judging the reliability of narrators, and so on, can extend this stretching process.

For the Romantic poets, however, imagination was sometimes thought to be more than that. It promised a new kind of apprehension, beyond bare reason or the senses, into a world otherwise inaccessible. Here is Wordsworth:

> That Poets, even as Prophets, each with each
> Connected in a mighty scheme of truth,
> Have each his own peculiar faculty,
> Heaven's gift, a sense that fits him to perceive
> Objects unseen before, thou wilt not blame
> The humblest of this band who dares to hope
> That unto him hath also been vouchsafed
> An insight that in some sort he possesses,
> A privilege whereby a work of his,
> Proceeding from a source of untaught things,
> Creative and enduring, may become
> A power like one of Nature's.
> (Wordsworth, *The Prelude*, Book 13, ll. 301–312)[44]

Although Wordsworth writes of "truth" it was a common thought of the Romantics that the imagination could offer something more "transcendent" than truth narrowly conceived. When Keats writes (in "Lamia," Pt. 2, ll. 229–237)[45] that

> Philosophy will clip an Angel's wings,
> Conquer all mysteries by rule and line,
> Empty the haunted air, and gnomed mine
> Unweave a rainbow

the implication seems to be that too much *cognition* can destroy what it touches. But it would be wrong to overemphasize the mystical strand in romantic thinking about the imagination. Under closer analysis, the imagination is revealed more as heightened awareness of the ordinary world than as special access to an extraordinary one: the "objects unseen before" are familiar things now apprehended through a quickening of those faculties of mind already acknowledged.[46] Hence Wordsworth, once again:

---

[44] William Wordsworth, *The Prelude: Four Texts (1798, 1799, 1805, 1850)* (Harmondsworth: Penguin, 1995).

[45] John Keats, *Complete Poems of John Keats* (New York: Random House, 1994).

[46] For a useful study, see T. J. Diffey, "The Roots of Imagination: The Philosophical Context," in Stephen Prickett, ed., *The Romantics: The Context of English Literature* (London: Methuen, 1981).

> Imagination, which, in truth,
> Is but another name for absolute strength
> And clearest insight, amplitude of mind,
> And Reason in her most exalted mood.
>
> (Wordsworth, *The Prelude*, ll. 167–170)

It is not obvious, however, that there is *intrinsic* value in having the imagination stretched in the sort of way Shelley envisages. It is easy to think of cases where the results are more harmful than beneficial (violence, pornography, despair, or hatred). Any value will depend on the material presented and the kind of involvement demanded. An important distinction here is between fantasy and imagination, described by Iris Murdoch as "two active faculties, one somewhat mechanically generating narrowly banal false pictures (the ego as all-powerful), and the other freely and creatively exploring the world, moving toward the expression and elucidation (and in art celebration) of what is true and deep."[47] She contrasts "trapped egoistic *fantasy*, and *imagination* as a faculty of transcendence."[48] On this account cognitive value will not be found in fantasy.

Another way of contrasting fantasy and imagination is to look at the kind of control authors have over the imaginative vision acquired by readers, or to put it more strictly, the interactions between authorial control and reader response. Sometimes readers simply *find themselves* in a certain state of mind, sometimes they shape their responses because they recognize they are being invited to do so. Fantasy belongs with the former, imaginative response with the latter. In the case of works of art readers will be (or should be) aware of how the structure of the work – its forms of expression, its use of literary convention – is controlling the perspective on offer. They have a reason for imagining as they do and they imagine for that reason. In contrast, the imaginings of fantasy are purely manipulative: attitudes and responses are the products of causes; readers fantasize, as we might say, *in spite of themselves*, with only minimal awareness of the representational

---

[47]   Iris Murdoch, *Metaphysics as a Guide to Morals* (Harmondsworth: Penguin, 1993), p. 321. Murdoch explicitly distances her distinction, and thus the one that concerns us here, from that drawn by Coleridge in *Biographia Literaria*, chapter XIII, between "fancy" and imagination. "Fancy," Coleridge writes, "has no other counters to play with but fixities and definites. The fancy is indeed no other than a mode of memory emancipated from the order of time and space, and blended with, and modified by that empirical phenomenon of the will which we express by the word CHOICE." One application of "fancy" in this sense occurs, as Murdoch points out, when "a story-teller creates a character by roughly tying together, in an unfused collection, separate characteristics from different people he knows" (*Metaphysics as a Guide to Morals*, p. 321).

[48]   Murdoch, *Metaphysics as a Guide to Morals*, p. 86.

modes in which the fantasy is embodied.[49] Two important points emerge: that a reader's imagination is to a large extent under the control of the author (and the work), and that merely free-floating imagination (i.e., fantasy) is remote from literary appreciation.

There has been much philosophical debate about the extent to which the imagination is involved in acquiring knowledge. In the epistemological theories of both Hume and Kant, imagination is given a fundamental role.[50] Recent philosophers have explored the relation between knowledge and imagination, often making the connection with literature. David Novitz has developed a thesis he calls "romantic realism" that emphasizes the indispensable role of the "fanciful imagination" in the acquisition of knowledge without abandoning objectivity and the basic tenets of science.[51] In a similar vein, Berys Gaut has stressed the potential of learning from our imaginings: "In ordinary life one can, through imagination, learn about what one really wants, what one ought to value, what it is like to undergo some experience one has not had, what it is like to be someone else by imaginatively projecting oneself into his place, and so on."[52]

*Learning what it is like …*

One of these uses of the imagination, imagining *what it is like* to be such-and-such, is often thought to be central to the learning function of fiction: e.g., learning *what it is like* to be a certain sort of character or in a certain sort of predicament.

> Readers of *Anna Karenina* do not only imagine or re-create the heroine's quandaries, but given sufficient interest, they actually ponder and explore them. They imagine what it is like to be assailed by such problems, they feel the fright and despair that accompany them, and, arguably as a result, they are able to discern their overwhelming complexity.[53]

In turn this "imaginative participation … furnishes us with empathetic beliefs, and … with a set of practical hypotheses for tackling similar quandaries in the

---

[49]  These ideas are further developed in Lamarque, *Fictional Points of View*, ch. 8.

[50]  For an account of this role, see Lamarque and Olsen, *Truth, Fiction, and Literature*, ch. 9.

[51]  David Novitz, *Knowledge, Fiction and Imagination* (Philadelphia, PA: Temple University Press, 1987).

[52]  Berys Gaut, "Art and Knowledge," in Jerrold Levinson, ed., *The Oxford Handbook of Aesthetics* (Oxford: Oxford University Press, 2003), p. 444; see also Berys Gaut, "Art and Cognition," in Matthew Kieran, ed., *Contemporary Debates in Aesthetics and the Philosophy of Art* (Oxford: Blackwell, 2006).

[53]  Novitz, *Knowledge, Fiction and Imagination*, p. 135.

actual world."[54] The ideas of "participation" and "empathy" are central in this theory. What is stressed is the experiential aspect of learning rather than the purely intellectual. Adding to Gilbert Ryle's distinction between "knowing how" and "knowing that," we now have "knowing what it is like." This "is not the acquisition of information, or the inferential knowledge about something, … it is knowing in the sense of realizing by living through."[55] "*Recognizing* that such and such is so with reference to some kind of human experience is not the same thing as *realizing* what this might be like as lived experience."[56]

Much has been written about the role of empathy in responding to fiction. That readers to different degrees can "identify" with fictional characters is not in dispute, although the precise mechanisms for this, and indeed the degrees to which it is possible, has been debated at length.[57] To empathize with a character is in some ways to share or "live through" the experiences of that character. Gregory Currie has presented a reading of Anne Brontë's novel *The Tenant of Wildfell Hall* (1846) to show that "empathy plays an important role in the reader's response to this novel, and that few readers would stay the course without its encouragement":[58]

> The book's success depends on establishing, with the reader, a number of conflicting emotions concerning Helen [Huntingdon], which Gilbert [Markham]'s perspective provides: we feel admiration for the spirited independence of her moral and aesthetic sensibility at the same time as we are irritated by her narrow attitudes. The second part [in the novel's three-part structure] enables us to explain all this by experiencing for ourselves something of the emotional journey that has shaped her. For this, it was essential that Helen's narrative should take the form it did: the much-criticized diary she places in Gilbert's hands. Those who would have preferred a direct telling fail to see that, being retrospective, this would have made it more difficult for us to empathize with Helen's younger self. The third part, while narrated by Gilbert, is somewhat complicated because the device of letters from Helen shifts the focus of empathy to her for some of the time. But the greater part of this, which is seen from Gilbert's perspective, sustains the narrative by reintroducing uncertainty about Helen's feelings.[59]

---

[54]   Ibid., p. 137.

[55]   Walsh, *Literature and Knowledge*, p. 101.

[56]   Ibid., p. 104.

[57]   E.g., Susan Feagin, *Reading with Feeling* (Ithaca, NY: Cornell University Press, 1996); Gregory Currie, "Imagination and Simulation: Aesthetics Meets Cognitive Science," in M. Davies and T. Stone, eds., *Mental Simulation* (Oxford: Blackwell, 1995); M. Kieran and D. Lopes, eds., *Imagination, Philosophy and the Arts* (London: Routledge, 2003).

[58]   Gregory Currie, "Anne Brontë and the Uses of Imagination," in Kieran, ed., *Contemporary Debates in Aesthetics and the Philosophy of Art*, p. 219.

[59]   Ibid.

Currie is not arguing that empathy is the only, even a predominant, experience of the work. His point is that it is a natural response and helps us, for example, to "sympathize with attitudes and behavior that would otherwise tend to alienate us from the characters." In fact, he believes that the intended empathy does not always work and leads to a (minor) weakness in the novel: "we are intended to empathize with Gilbert's anxiety, very late in the book, about whether Helen will accept him. But the intention fails; his reporting of her demeanor indicates clearly that she will."[60]

There are a number of questions about the nature and role of experiencing "what it is like" to be a character. The first is whether it is a common response among readers. In fact it is probably less common than its proponents suggest, and more genre-relative. Some popular genres – fantasy, romance, horror – seem to encourage empathy, but other kinds, say, modernist or postmodernist novels, do not. On the whole it seems more common for readers to act as observers rather than participants. This is evidenced by differences between a reader's and a character's emotions. A character feels grief, the reader feels pity; a character has a sense of hope and optimism, while the reader senses foreboding and disaster.[61] In general, readers are more likely to show sympathy than empathy toward characters. It has also been pointed out that at least in novels with omniscient narrators there is no need for readers to "simulate" a character's emotions – for example, with the aim of finding out more about them – because information about the character's feelings or thoughts is in ready supply.[62]

Is empathy integral to literary appreciation? Gregory Currie clearly thinks so, in his analysis of Anne Brontë's novel. Others do as well. For Susan Feagin "[h]aving emotional and other affective responses [including empathy] to a work of fictional literature is a very important part of appreciating it, and a capacity of a work to provide such responses is part of what is valuable about it."[63] She comments on a passage from Virginia Woolf's *To the Lighthouse*, where Mr. Ramsey is reacting to his wife's death. Feagin writes: "I *feel* his vulnerability, his emptiness and loss, as it is evoked by this passage and also how important Mrs. Ramsey was as his source of security. Though Mr. Ramsey is not an especially sympathetic character in the novel, this passage enables me, if briefly, to empathize with him."[64] Nor is this feeling merely an incidental response: it aids interpretation:

[60]   Ibid., p. 220.
[61]   See Noël Carroll, "Simulations, Emotions, and Morality," in *Beyond Aesthetics* (Cambridge: Cambridge University Press, 2001), p. 313.
[62]   Ibid., p. 313.
[63]   Feagin, *Reading with Feeling*, p. 1.
[64]   Ibid., p. 97.

With respect to Mr Ramsey, it does make interpretive sense of the novel to attribute the same sort of mental condition to him as I found in myself. Reflecting on my own psychological activity, I realised that it was important both for understanding Mr Ramsey and for understanding the novel that I identify what I was doing as empathizing with him.[65]

Jenefer Robinson too holds that "our emotional responses are a vital part of *understanding* a narrative text" and, in similar vein to Feagin, that "a critical interpretation of a work becomes *a reflection upon one's emotional experience of the work*."[66]

While it seems undeniable that empathetic and other emotional responses can heighten the pleasure a reader can get from a work (and thus its appreciation, broadly conceived), and even that this might aid understanding of the work and enlarge the imagination in Shelley's sense, it is far from clear that emotional responses can play a central role in literary criticism. Such responses tend to be too reader-relative or culture-specific, they tend to rely too much on first-time reading rather than careful and prolonged study, and they can do little to furnish a sense of the artistic unity of a work.[67]

In any case, while empathetic responses might, in certain cases, cast light on individual fictional characters, it remains a further question whether they contribute to a wider learning function. This returns us to the line of thought introduced earlier, where the claim was made that readers can learn *what it is like* to be or do such-and-such through their direct experiences of a work. Again, this is Jenefer Robinson's view: "To be told that *Anna Karenina* teaches us that betraying your husband can lead to misery is no substitute for reading the novel. One important reason why this is so is that it is only through an emotional experience of a novel that one can genuinely learn from it."[68] In general, according to Robinson, "the emotional process of engaging with characters and situations in a novel is part of a 'sentimental education', an education by the emotions."[69] For Feagin we can learn from literature what she calls "affective flexibility," which "expands our imaginative potential with respect to generating affects, so that it is possible to *imagine* a wider variety of possibilities, for instance, what it is like to *do* this or that, to be a certain sort of person, or to be in a certain sort of situation."[70]

---

[65]   Ibid., pp. 97–98.

[66]   Jenefer Robinson, *Deeper than Reason* (Oxford: Oxford University Press, 2005), pp. 122, 124 (italics in original).

[67]   For further comments on Susan Feagin's programme, see Peter Lamarque, Review of Susan L. Feagin, *Reading with Feeling*, *Mind*, vol. 109, no. 433 (2000), pp. 145–149.

[68]   Robinson, *Deeper than Reason*, p. 156.

[69]   Ibid.

[70]   Feagin, *Reading with Feeling*, p. 248.

Once again, though, we should distinguish the question whether such learning is possible, even desirable, from whether it is integral to *literary* value. The possibility and desirability can be readily conceded. Who could deny the value of being flexible in one's emotional responses? But the connection with literature can seem merely contingent. Reading stories in newspapers or watching documentaries on the television or even gossiping about one's neighbors can all engage and educate the emotions. In the context of these different kinds of narratives there doesn't seem any special contribution that *literary* narratives can make in "learning what it is like." In fact, if we think of literary works as being special in forging unity out of complexity, then a new difficulty arises for these narratives not found in others:

> Although individual aspects, characters, or incidents abstracted from a work might yield an empathetic response in a reader it is most unlikely that literary works taken as a whole — as *works* — will present situations that could provide a coherent and unified experience describable as "knowing what it is like." A Hamlet-situation, for example, is far too complex and specific to give rise to any single and sustained experience of this kind, certainly not one that will be relevant to a reader's daily life.[71]

## Conceptual knowledge

A variant on the "learning what it is like" view is the idea that literary works have a special way of enhancing our understanding of fundamental concepts. Wittgenstein suggested to Norman Malcolm that he read Tolstoy's *Hadshi Murat* to change his conception of war, in particular to grasp that war is not "boredom":

> Malcolm might have found a new idea of how it is possible to think and speak of war and of its relationship to a lot of other things, to love, to power, to fear, and to life and death. In this way, Malcolm's concept of war would have been enriched and extended, so that there would be new things which he would say about it, and things which he would no longer say – like perhaps that it was all boredom.[72]

Part of what is going on when this "enrichment" and "enhancement" happens is that a work offers a new and perhaps unfamiliar context of application for key concepts. Hilary Putnam elaborates: "Consider the experience of reading a novel like *Don Quixote*. One thing that happens to us is that our conceptual

---

[71]   Lamarque and Olsen, *Truth, Fiction, and Literature*, p. 378.

[72]   R. W. Beardsmore, *Art and Morality* (London: Macmillan, 1971), p. 74.

and perceptual repertoire becomes enlarged.... This enlargement of our stock of predicates and of metaphors is *cognitive*; we now possess descriptive resources we did not have before."[73] It is not just that we can enlarge our vocabulary through reading literature – although that is undoubtedly true – but we can extend the grasp of concepts we already possess by coming to imagine new instantiations.

Bernard Harrison, who calls the language of fiction "constitutive language," has argued that there is far more than semantic competence involved, namely a kind of self-knowledge and a shift in perspective that recalls the "vision" theories:

> The cognitive gains offered by constitutive language are of two kinds. On the first and simplest level they are gains in self-knowledge. As such they are of an essentially negative kind. They disturb the self in its natural but mistaken conviction that the terms in which it habitually construes the world are the only terms in which the world is capable of being construed, simply by displacing the language, the system of connections and differences between terms which articulates and constitutes that habitual way of looking at things. In the process of achieving this ... shift of perspective, constitutive language necessarily ... passes from reordering its own signs to reordering ... our perception of the limits and scope of natural possibility.[74]

The case for conceptual "enhancement" or the "reordering" of perceptions is only as substantial as the particular examples invoked to illustrate it. Eileen John has offered a careful analysis of a short story by Grace Paley, *Wants*, to support the thesis that

> works of fiction, rather than providing new ways of thinking, sometimes lead us to places of obscurity or untested areas in entrenched ways of thinking. In getting us there, the work provides a context in which we can think fruitfully about the conceptual issues raised, where the line of inquiry we pursue is integrated into our efforts to judge the characters and events.[75]

The story is about a woman who meets her ex-husband while returning books to a library, which evokes reflections in both on why their marriage

---

[73] Hilary Putnam, "Reflections on Goodman's *Ways of Worldmaking*," *Journal of Philosophy*, vol. 76, no. 11 (1979), pp. 603–618 at pp. 614–615.

[74] Bernard Harrison, *Inconvenient Fictions* (New Haven, CT: Yale University Press, 1991), p. 50.

[75] Eileen John, "Reading Fiction and Conceptual Knowledge: Philosophical Thought in Literary Context," *Journal of Aesthetics and Art Criticism*, vol. 56, no. 4 (1998), pp. 331–348 at p. 340.

of 27 years ended. John takes up the concept "wants" from the title and explores the ambiguity and resonance in the ex-husband's remark that his ex-wife "didn't want anything" and will "always want nothing":

> The sentence can be read both in terms of wanting as desiring and wanting as lacking. Although it is fairly clear that the ex-husband is thinking of her as desiring nothing, the reader is left to wonder which meaning is most appropriate and, I think, is likely to feel confused about how distinct the two meanings are. We think about *lack* shading into *need*, and *need* shading into *desire*, and perhaps we compare the negative, inert connotation of want-as-lack to the somehow forward-looking connotation of want-as-desire. The relation and tension between the two meanings becomes an underlying question of the story, though it takes on a more concrete focus as we try to understand the narrator [the ex-wife] and the claim that she *lacks desire*.[76]

The analysis is detailed and pertinent, yet it remains an open question whether it establishes the theoretical point in contention, namely whether it is part of the value of a literary work to impart this special kind of conceptual knowledge. As with so many of the cognitive claims already considered, the crucial move is from attention focused on the work to applications beyond the work to the extra-literary world. John's analysis looks to be a careful and insightful reading of the story identifying thematic concepts and making connections across the work. However, the further claim that a reader who follows and endorses this reading will have the additional benefit of conceptual clarification remains controversial. It might be true as a matter of fact that a reader emerges with a clearer and "enhanced" concept of *wants* or *desire*. But is this benefit any more attributable to an intrinsic literary quality than is the case when other readers of other stories emerge feeling more cheerful or resolved to spend more time with their families or determined to try to combat poverty? The outcome in all cases looks like a contingent by-product of reading. The issue of authority arises too, for it would seem just as possible for a story to distort or weaken a reader's grasp of a concept. Not all conceptual shifts are for the good.

### Cognitive strengthening

A final idea, which draws on several of the earlier ones, proposes that although literary works are unlikely to inform readers — at the level of broad human generalities — of things they did not already know, they do have the potential to "enhance" knowledge already possessed. This might be described as "cognitive strengthening." Mere knowledge is not enough, so the idea of

---

[76]   Ibid., p. 337.

"enhanced" or "enriched" knowledge is invoked. But these metaphors can mean different things. Gordon Graham frequently uses the epithets in respect of the arts: "enriching human understanding," "enhanced apprehension of human experience," etc.[77] Yet when he gives details it looks as if he is falling back on the idea of "learning what it is like":

> Novels and poems supply patterns of human relationship, its fulfilment, destruction, or corruption, and these can enter directly into the moral experience of those who are reflecting upon how best to live, because the devices of art reveal to us the internal 'how it feels' as well as the external 'how it is'.[78]

Another philosopher, John Gibson, has offered an explanation in terms of "acknowledgment," in the sense used by Stanley Cavell. Cavell draws the distinction between *knowledge* and *acknowledgment* as follows:

> It is not enough that I *know* (am certain) that you suffer, I must do or reveal something (whatever can be done). In a word, I must *acknowledge* it, otherwise I *do not know* what (yours, his) "being in pain" means … The claim of sympathy may go unanswered. We may feel lots of things — sympathy, *Schadenfreude*, nothing. If one says that this is a failure to acknowledge another's suffering, surely this would not mean that we fail, in such cases, to *know* that he is suffering?[79]

Gibson employs the idea of acknowledgment to explain the contribution that literature can make, using the example of *Othello*. No one can understand the play who lacks a fairly clear understanding of jealousy, so how could the play add to that understanding? The answer is that it can *strengthen* or *enhance* it, in a sense "bring it home" to us:

> *Othello* does not merely reflect our world back to us in the same form in which it presupposes that we are familiar with it. *Othello* returns to us this knowledge as embodied, as placed on the concrete stage of cultural practice and human comportment. That is to say, Othello acknowledges the knowledge he asks us to bring to the text. He calls upon it so that he can then go on to push it into that region of understanding left unmentioned in the skeptic's anti-cognitivist arguments.[80]

[77]   Gordon Graham, *Philosophy of the Arts: An Introduction to Aesthetics* (London and New York: Routledge, 1997), pp. 92, 128.

[78]   Ibid., p. 129.

[79]   Stanley Cavell, *Must We Mean What We Say?* (Cambridge: Cambridge University Press, 1976), p. 263 (italics in original).

[80]   John Gibson, "Between Truth and Triviality," *British Journal of Aesthetics*, vol. 43, no. 3 (2003), pp. 224–237 at p. 236.

A somewhat similar conception is labeled "clarificationism" by Noël
Carroll:

> Clarificationism does not claim that, in the standard case, we acquire interesting
> new propositional knowledge from artworks, but rather that the artworks in
> question can deepen our moral understanding by, among other things, encour-
> aging us to apply our moral knowledge and emotions to specific cases.[81]

When white audiences watch the play *A Raisin in the Sun* they probably
already endorse the general moral principle that people of different color
should be treated equally. So the play's theme at best amounts to "a discovery
about something [the audience] already knows." But "the characters and situations presented by the play afford an occasion to reorganize or reshuffle the
moral beliefs that the white audience already has at its disposal. Its system of
beliefs undergoes clarification. Its grasp and understanding of what it already
knows is deepened in a way that counts … as learning."[82]

The phenomenon of the eye-opening effect of reading some works of literature is familiar and can account for the impact of some works on political and
social change. Works that vividly bring home the horrors of slavery or war or
child poverty or capital punishment can, as clarificationism predicts, have an
effect even on people who would otherwise endorse general condemnation of
such things. This involves more than just adjusting concepts, and it may – but
need not – use the method of empathetic identification. However, clarificationism perhaps overreacts to the charge of triviality against propositional
views of literary content. The argument is motivated by the thought that summary thematic propositions will always be too trite on their own to advance
knowledge, leading to the suggestion that their message needs to be "clarified"
or "enhanced" to have a learning function. But the "triviality" of thematic
statements is only an issue when they are taken to be worldly truths. When
emphasis is given to their role in clarifying a work rather than clarifying the
world, and they are linked through interpretation to the particulars of the
work, then triviality is unimportant. Most of the perennial literary themes can
be given a trivial expression; what matters is how the themes are presented.

## Weighing up Pro-Truth and Anti-Truth Conceptions

We have come some way from discussions of truth per se. It is far from
clear that the theories about learning or empathy or clarifying or enhancing

[81] Noël Carroll, "Art, Narrative, and Moral Understanding," in *Beyond Aesthetics*, p. 283.
[82] Ibid., p. 284.

understanding are strictly "truth" theories, even granted the flexible range of concepts of "literary truth" we considered earlier. But all these theories, including the propositional theories, have in common the notion that literary works derive at least some of their value from a truth-like component or a component to do with human cognition. It was just such a component that Plato thought was fatally missing from poetry or fatally misused, enough to drive poetry from the Republic.

But for all the numerous efforts to capture this component the picture remains murky. There is no denying the fact of the matter that readers do learn all kinds of things from novels and poems; no doubt many of the additional benefits of "enriched" understanding and so on are in evidence as well. But some philosophers of literature are uneasy with the underlying thought that literary works can only be good if they have an educative function. That need not be the way to understand the "usefulness" of poetry. The mistake is to suppose that to be *serious* or *reflective* a work must in effect *teach* something. Yet there is no such implication. A work is serious if it treats of a serious subject matter. But it can do that without being true and without presenting a view that ought to be endorsed. The example of Euripides's *Hecuba*, with the theme that "nothing human is ever worthy of trust," shows that clearly.

Also it ought to be more surprising than it is to the pro-truth camp that critics have broadly negative attitudes to didactic works. Works are didactic that are overt in their teaching aim. A novel like Dickens's *Hard Times*, for example, is frequently criticized for its overbearing moral message and its extremes in characterization aimed at drumming home the point. If moral instruction is an important literary value then why should overt instruction be a fault? What the objection highlights is the difference between being a value per se and being a *literary* value. Learning seems to be a value, and truth preferable to falsehood, so anything that promotes learning and truth should, in that regard, be valued. Literary works can in their different ways do just that, so it seems a simple conclusion that literary works are good or better in virtue of their learning function. But the reservations over didacticism in literature show that while teaching might be a value, it is not for that reason a literary value.

Part of the anti-truth argument rests on a contrast between paradigmatic literary works (fiction and poetry) and what can be called *constitutively cognitive* discourses, such as philosophy. Philosophy *essentially* aims at advancing understanding and is valued accordingly. The core focus of interest in a philosophical work is on the theses it propounds and the arguments in support of them. Ill-supported, poorly argued, or unoriginal works are devalued for that reason. To read philosophy is to read for truth. In contrast, to read and value a work *from a literary point of view* seems quite different. As remarked, literary works that are too overtly didactic, that too obviously are trying to impart a message, are seldom valued highly. One of the pleasures of a literary reading is to notice different ways that the content can be imaginatively construed, not necessarily focused on a single "message" or "thesis" to be conveyed.

Also the expectations readers have in coming to a novel or poem for the first time are seldom "cognitive" expectations. Readers are not commonly motivated to read such works by the thought that they will learn something. Rather, they seek a distinctive kind of pleasure from their reading. The very process of reading a novel or poem is unlike that conventionally associated with philosophical or historical works. The differences have been spelt out in earlier chapters, notably in Chapter 4, where the *sui generis* practice of literary reading was explored. So the conclusion seems to be that, yes, learning is possible from works of literature, in all the ways outlined, and works can be valued for that reason. But the value is not indisputably a core literary value. Just what these core values are is the topic of the next chapter.

## Supplementary Readings

Useful secondary discussion of classical issues on the truth debate can be found in Iris Murdoch, *Fire and the Sun: Why Plato Banished the Artists* (Oxford: Oxford University Press, 1978); Amelie Oksenberg Rorty, ed., *Essays on Aristotle's "Poetics"* (Princeton, NJ: Princeton University Press, 1992); Christopher Janaway, *Images of Excellence: Plato's Critique of the Arts* (Oxford: Clarendon Press, 1998); and S. H. Butcher, *Aristotle's Theory of Poetry and Fine Art: With a Critical Text and Translation of the "Poetics"* (Mineola, NY: Dover Publications, 4th rev. ed., 2003).

The following philosophical works, broadly in the analytic tradition, pursue the debate about literature, knowledge, and truth: Richard Eldridge, *On Moral Personhood: Philosophy, Literature, Criticism, and Self-Understanding* (Chicago: Chicago University Press, 1989); Paisley Livingston, *Literary Knowledge: Humanistic Enquiry and the Philosophy of Science* (Ithaca, NY: Cornell University Press, 1990); Martha Nussbaum, *Love's Knowledge: Essays on Philosophy and Literature* (Oxford: Oxford University Press, 1990); Peter Lamarque and Stein Haugom Olsen, *Truth, Fiction, and Literature: A Philosophical Perspective* (Oxford: Clarendon Press, 1994); Stephen Davies, ed., *Art and Its Messages: Meaning, Morality, and Society* (University Park, PA: Penn State University Press, 1997); James O. Young, *Art and Knowledge* (London: Routledge, 2001); John Gibson, *Fiction and the Weave of Life* (Oxford: Oxford University Press, 2007); and John Gibson, Wolfgang Huemer, and Luca Pocci, eds., *A Sense of the World: Essays on Fiction, Narrative, and Knowledge* (London: Routledge, 2007).

# Chapter Seven
## Value

Questions of value permeate the philosophy of literature; nearly all the main topics we have examined have implications for value. The generic conception of literature as a species of "fine writing" already incorporates a value component, as does the notion of "appreciation" as a mode of attending to literary works of art. The discussion in the last chapter about literature and truth addressed the question whether truth is a literary value. What we found in that chapter has a bearing on the discussion to come. Truth is undoubtedly a value; it is what assertive discourse aspires to. Learning and knowledge are also values. Attaining knowledge, overcoming ignorance, and learning about ourselves and the world are among the highest aspirations of the human mind, enshrined in education and science. If literary works contribute to all this, then to that extent they are valuable. Our question was not whether learning is possible from reading novels and poems, which can be readily conceded, but rather whether that captures something essential to literature, whether it marks some special contribution and achievement, and explains literature's enduring value. We found reason to doubt this. The discussion suggested a distinction between a by-product of reading that is a contingent value of some works for some readers, and *sui generis* literary values associated with constitutive aims of literature shared by all works.

Are there such distinctive literary values? Is it possible to generalize across literary genres or are there only, at best, values of poetry, the novel, the short story, drama? And how are individual works to be valued? Are there objective values or only values relative to individual readers or "communities"? Is there a canon of great works? If so, how is it constructed? How do moral values relate to literary values? Can great works be immoral? These are questions for the philosopher of literature.

## The Varieties of Literary Value Judgments

It would be wrong to think that our only interest in literary value judgments resides in simple judgments to the effect that such-and-such is a good novel or a beautiful poem. Bald value claims of this kind have little intrinsic interest. Such interest as they have, and this is true of all value judgments, lies in the *reasons* offered in their support. A judgment that cannot be backed up is worthless. Those who are inclined to dismiss literary values as merely "subjective" or "personal opinion" are probably supposing that the only support for such judgments is of the form "because I like it." But although there is a place for personal preferences and likes and dislikes these cannot be the sole basis for considered critical judgments.

Literary criticism, as the term suggests, is inescapably connected to judgments of value, but these need not surface in a summative form (X is good, Y is bad); they might emerge, even implicitly, through detailed analysis. With well-established works – canonical works – a summative judgment is rarely needed. It is only when works in the canon are being challenged or non-canonical works being reassessed that explicit judgments seem pertinent. Sometimes, for example, global judgments are made about whole schools of writing, notably in a period of canon-revision:

> It is mainly due to him [T. S. Eliot] that no serious poet or critic today [i.e., 1932] can fail to realise that English poetry in the future must develop (if at all) along some other lines than that running from the Romantics through Tennyson, Swinburne, *A Shropshire Lad*, and Rupert Brooke. He has made a new start and established new bearings.[1]

The efforts of critics like T. S. Eliot and F. R. Leavis in the 1920s and 1930s, to demote Romantic poetry in favor of modernist poetry of the kind written by Eliot, Ezra Pound, and Gerard Manley Hopkins, was based on judgments of the comparative merits of the two schools of poetry, backed up by observations about the new social environment: "urban conditions, a sophisticated civilization, rapid change, and the mingling of cultures have destroyed the old rhythms and habits."[2]

Staying at a general level of value, some judgments refer to generic faults (or strengths) in works. Here is Virginia Woolf commenting on the novelist George Meredith identifying both a local flaw in his novels and a flaw in any novel:

> [Meredith's] teaching is too insistent. He cannot, even to hear the profoundest secret, suppress his own opinion. And there is nothing that characters in fiction resent more. If, they seem to argue, we have been called into existence merely to express Mr. Meredith's views upon the universe, we would rather

---

[1]  F. R. Leavis, *New Bearings in English Poetry* (Harmondsworth: Penguin, 1967), p. 28.

[2]  Ibid., p. 55.

not exist at all. Thereupon they die; and a novel that is full of dead characters, even though it is also full of profound wisdom and exalted teaching, is not achieving its aim as a novel.[3]

If academic critics are primarily concerned with established works, journalistic critics focus on new works and are paid to offer their assessments. Readers go to such critics to seek guidance on their reading. Here judgments do tend to be explicit, although again the judgments are worthless without support:

> Successful literary thrillers in the mold of Umberto Eco's "Name of the Rose" are the stuff of publishers' dreams, and in [Iain] Pears's novel [*An Instance of the Fingerpost*] they may have found a near-perfect example of the genre. It is literary — if that means intelligent and well written — and for the reader who likes to be teased, who likes his plots as baroque and ingenious as possible, "An Instance of the Fingerpost" will not disappoint.[4]

In a couple of sentences the critic has identified the genre of the novel, by comparing it to another highly acclaimed work, has valued it within that genre, and offered reasons why readers might enjoy it.

Sometimes critics are unsure of the overall quality of a work and find good and bad elements in it:

> [*Jane Eyre*] is a very remarkable book. We are painfully alive to the moral, religious, and literary deficiencies of the picture, and such passages of beauty and power as we have quoted cannot redeem it, but it is impossible not to be spell-bound with the freedom of the touch. It would be mere hackneyed courtesy to call it "fine writing". It bears no impress of being written at all, but is poured out rather in the heat and hurry of an instinct …[5]

Yet another kind of value judgment connects a summative assessment of a work with the success of localized detail in, or strategies of, the work:

> one of the triumphs of the novel [*Bleak House*] is the delicacy with which Dickens handles the knowledge, suspicions, guesses, and mistakes of the various characters. … Esther is never seen by the omniscient eye, nor does Tulkinghorn ever appear personally in Esther's narrative. This corresponds to

---

[3] Virginia Woolf, *The Common Reader*, Second Series (1932) (London: Hogarth Press, 1932), p. 234.

[4] *The New York Times*, March 22, 1998.

[5] Elizabeth Rigby, "Vanity Fair – and Jane Eyre," *Quarterly Review*, pp. 84–167, December 1848. Quoted in Charlotte Brontë, *Jane Eyre*, ed. Richard J. Dunn (New York: W. W. Norton, 1977), p. 452.

their limited knowledge; Tulkinghorn, for all his plotting, never knows of Esther's relation to Lady Dedlock while there is no substantial evidence that Esther knows anything of her father until after her mother's death.

Granted this, the opportunities for dramatic irony are clearly enormous and it is to Dickens's credit as an artist that with great tact he refuses many of the chances for irony offered by the interlocking narratives. How close — all unknowing — is Esther to meeting her father during her first visit to Krook's? Yet we scarcely perceive this, even on a re-reading of the novel. A lesser artist would have wrung dry the irony of such an incident, but Dickens is sound in his refusal to do so. For the novel, as it stands, is so taut, so potentially explosive, that to expatiate on, or to underline, its implications would make it quite intolerable.[6]

These are just some of the kinds of values that readers find in literary works. They show how natural and familiar such judgments are in the practice of reading, against an often heard complaint that talk of value in the arts is extraneous, elitist, or merely personal. Nevertheless the roots of these values need careful exploration.

## The Literary Institution and Appreciation

In many respects the fundamental bases for valuing literature as art have already been presented. The contextualist account of what kind of entities literary works are and the institutional account of conventional responses to them, laid out in Chapters 2 and 4, provide the framework within which literary value judgments must reside. If literary works are cultural artifacts grounded in determinate historical conditions of creation – contextualized texts governed by categorial intentions – inviting and rewarding a distinctive kind of appreciation as works of art, then their value within the norms of the institution will rest on how well they fulfill conventional expectations. In this sense literary value is internal to and defined by the institution.

We have looked at numerous examples of the various elements comprising a full appreciation of literature, as literature. These have revolved round expectations that readers bring to works viewed as works of art. As elaborated in Chapter 4, these expectations concern such matters as: the design, form, and structure of a verbal artifact; the presentation of a subject with a reasonable degree of coherence and connectedness; and the development of a thematic interest that allows for deeper, more far-reaching reflection on, and beyond, the particularities of the subject. To attend to a work with these expectations and to have them rewarded affords a species of

---

[6] W. J. Harvey, "The Double Narrative of *Bleak House*," in Charles Dickens, *Bleak House*, ed. George Ford and Sylvère Monod (New York: W. W. Norton, 1977), p. 969.

pleasure – aesthetic pleasure – that inclines readers to spend time exploring what the work can offer. Value resides in the quality of the experience a work yields, focused on two broad dimensions: imaginativeness or creativity evident in the design of the work, and the richness of its content at both subject and thematic levels.

The examples we have looked at have been drawn from poetry (e.g., *Epithalamion*), the novel (e.g., *Moll Flanders*), and drama (e.g., plays of Shakespeare). In each case we have pondered those factors in general that make the works worth attending to, from form to subject to theme, with a focus on the experience these extraordinary linguistic artifacts can sustain. It is a striking if obvious fact that those works that reward appreciation to the highest degree will be those that readers are inclined to return to and explore in depth. Valuable works of art are those that sustain this kind of interest. Consider an example that came up in Chapter 2, Gerard Manley Hopkins's sonnet "The Windhover." It was cited in that context because of the exceptional power and felicity of its language, seeming to epitomize the poetic, indeed the aesthetic:

> I caught this morning morning's minion, king-
>> dom of daylight's dauphin, dapple-dawn-drawn Falcon in his riding
>> Of the rolling level underneath him steady air, and striding
> High there, how he rung upon the rein of a wimpling wing
>> In his ecstasy!

But it is more than just its rippling mellifluous melodies that have struck readers. There is a remarkably large body of secondary critical writing about this single poem. Why should that be? Why should some poems such as this, and not others, draw so much attention? The answer is that readers derive pleasure from reflecting on the poem; different readers notice different aspects of it, further reasons for returning to it. Here is a not untypical example:

> The triumph of this poem is precisely that perception of the likeness in the unlikeness, and of the poet's own achievement — the association of bird, self, and Christ. The "buckling" in line 10, then is a sort of gravitational center, in the poem, where the conflation of figural levels "here," in the poem itself, takes place as analogy is lifted to the level of allegory and interpretation. The octave of "The Windhover" is to a large degree about perception, but the sestet, a formal revision of the octave, is about re-vision — seeing again. Mere perception has become a different kind of vision, and brings the poet access to what we call the visionary.[7]

---

[7]   Jennifer A. Wagner, "The Allegory of Form in Hopkins's Religious Sonnets," *Nineteenth-Century Literature*, vol. 47, no. 1, June (1992), pp. 32–48 at p. 37.

As is conventional, this critic notices factors about the poem's form, its immediate subject, and the wider context of what it is "about," of course interrelating all three. The poem elicits quite different interests from other readers:

> "The Windhover" most famously images Christ in highly equestrian terms, as an endearing "chevalier" (11). Yet, even there, amidst the aristocratic emblem of falconry, the kestrel is a symbol of "mastery" (8), iconizing "Brute beauty" (9), and the poem closes by falling heavily with the weight of the ploughman's "sheer plod" (12). Any reader of Hopkins's work, then, encounters a definitely masculine poetics.[8]

This reader pursues the partly biographical, partly literary critical theme in Hopkins of the "unswerving attention to the embodiment of divine power in differing types of working men," in the light of the idea that "the male body, especially the working-class male body, has such potency, vitality, and, it has to be said, no uncertain danger in Hopkins's aesthetics."[9]

It is a mark of the great works of literature that a tradition of "readings" builds up round them representing the fascination that readers have with the works and their desire to explore them further. Of course it is not just the quantity of readings that indicates literary value but the nature of what these readings reveal. Works that reward continued interest will be those that are amenable to different perspectives, that have the capacity to surprise, and that open up new imaginative possibilities. Lesser works will simply not reward renewed attention.

The framework of the literary institution also raises a further context for reflecting on value, and that concerns the value of the institution itself. The emphasis so far has been on the value attributed to individual works, but there are values attaching to participation in the institution. Perhaps only quite general comments are possible here, but there are clearly values associated with both the production of works and their appreciation. Artists derive, if nothing else, at least some personal satisfaction and sense of fulfillment in producing works that give pleasure to those that appreciate them. In turn, appreciators can find intrinsic as well as instrumental value (ideas we shall return to) in the experience of literature. A literary education is an education in how to acquire worthwhile experiences of this kind, and it takes the form of initiation into some such practice as described in Chapter 4.

---

[8]  Joseph Bristow, "'Churlsgrace': Gerard Manley Hopkins and the Working-Class Male Body," *ELH*, vol. 59, no. 3, Autumn (1992), pp. 693–711 at p. 697.

[9]  Ibid., p. 694.

It is possible to stand back even further and ask about the roots in human life and human society of an institution that reveres certain kinds of linguistic artifacts and which encourages the constitutive benefits to producers and appreciators alike. Perhaps an evolutionary explanation is at hand, identifying adaptive features of story-telling or poetry.[10] But given the essential features associated with literature – language, design, imagination, play, "imitation," broad themes of human interest – it is hardly surprising that the institution of literature is such a universal and inter-cultural phenomenon. The imaginative realization in narrative (story-telling) of fundamental human concerns, about life and death, love, and despair, seems to manifest itself in all cultures, and the roots of poetry are found in song, ritual, and oral traditions. It is hard to conceive of a society that could find no need for such activities. Whatever detailed explanation is forthcoming for the origins and durability of this phenomenon, its value within human life is there for all to see.

The philosopher of literature, though, needs to provide a more down to earth account of the nature of values in the literary sphere. There are many misconceptions to overcome.

## Key Distinctions about Value

### Valuing as x, as y

The value we are exploring is *literary* value or the value a work has *as literature* or *as art*. The innocent seeming "as" is important, because when we ask if something is good or valuable we usually need to know what kind of goodness or value is at stake. A paperweight might be good as a decorative object, poor as a paperweight, valuable as a family memento, valueless in financial terms, or good for propping a door open, bad for packing in a suitcase. When asked if it is valuable, it is reasonable to ask "valuable as what?" Note that to relativize values in this way is not to imply that values are relative in the sense that they are merely subjective or dependent on personal preference. Yes, values are relative to interests but once the interests have been identified there need be no further relativization. To judge something as a paperweight is to invoke clear, if basic, criteria: the object must be heavy enough to keep papers from blowing away, must be a manageable size (fit easily on a desk, for example), must not be so heavy that it takes two people to lift it, had better not be completely round as it would likely roll off, and so forth. Such criteria bear on the effective design of a paperweight and help determine good or bad examples.

---

[10]   See, for example, Steven Pinker, *How the Mind Works* (New York: W. W. Norton, 1997).

Similarly, in asking what value a work has *as literature* or *as art* is to relativize value to particular interests. The interests in question relate to relevant conceptions of literature. If the generic conception of literature as belles lettres is at issue then the question "Is it good as literature?" simply means "Is it fine writing?" Under the thicker conception of literature as art, the conception developed in Chapter 2, more than just fine writing is looked for. The question now concerns how well the work rewards a certain kind of attention ("appreciation"), how receptive it is to literary critical modes of reading, in general how well it conforms to the norms of the "institution." Exactly what that entails has been the subject of our inquiry.

Even works that are acknowledged to be literature (under the thicker conception) might reward attention other than a strictly literary one. Different interests can be involved. Social historians might have a legitimate interest in the nineteenth-century novel and judge some more highly than others for the purpose of shedding light on contemporary attitudes and conditions. Their judgments, arguably, are not literary judgments. Similarly philologists might rank novels and novelists according to the contributions they make to linguistic innovation. Freudian psychoanalysts admire certain works for "anticipating" Freud's theories of the unconscious; Freud himself singled out the relatively obscure novel *Gradiva* by Wilhelm Jensen and Schiller's play *Wallenstein* for just this reason. Again his interests, and thus his judgments, were not, and did not purport to be, strictly literary critical ones. The works were valued for illuminating his theories. Just as reading is directed, so too is evaluating.

More controversially, when readers choose novels for taking to the beach or going on holiday they are not characteristically concerned with literary merit. They want "light entertainment," "easy reading," something to help them relax and take their minds off work. Much genre fiction can be rated highly as fantasy or pure entertainment without having any literary aspiration. The distinction, though, is controversial because it is sometimes deemed to rest on elitism or snobbery rather than anything more intrinsic to the works. But the charge is unfair, at least partially, because the values concerned are incommensurate. It is not that there is a single scale of value on which "literary" works rate highly and genre fiction lowly, rather there are different scales. Judged as fantasy the Harry Potter novels rank high, *Middlemarch* ranks low. As tragedies, *Hamlet* is good, *What Ho, Jeeves* is a non-starter. Of course some genre fiction also aspires to literary status, and on that scale can perform well – Harry Potter might be an example, or the spy novels of John Le Carré. But the fact that many genre novels neither invite nor reward systematic literary analysis should not be taken as a negative feature of them. Their merits lie elsewhere.

The cheery but trite rhyming couplets in a birthday card might suit the purpose (of the card) very well but entirely lack literary interest.

Part of the reason why comparisons continue to be made between literary and genre fiction, often to the detriment of the latter, is that the generic conception of belles lettres is being assumed. Genre fiction, so the thought goes, is just not as well written. But then that judgment is subject to the charge of snobbism. Why should works that are sometimes difficult to read (e.g., Henry James's later novels) be more highly valued than straightforward story-telling? Only snobbism, it is said, could be the explanation. A number of confusions underlie this familiar spat. The first is that there is more to literary value, in the substantial sense of "literature," than fine writing. James's novels might fulfill the relevant criteria – beyond belles lettres – better than a standard murder mystery. The second is that the idea of fine writing is itself a relative value, as was noted earlier; it is a matter of means and ends. The convoluted prose of James's novels is only admired, if at all, because it serves the literary purpose of exhibiting the complexities, ambivalence, and fragility in human relations. If it were reproduced in a letter of condolence or a memo round the office or a popular whodunit the writing would not be praised but thought pretentiously inappropriate. In a genre novel where suspense, action, or fantasy is paramount the writing needs to conform to those ends.

Another overriding problem is that in principle any work can be read *as if* it were literature in the substantial sense. It is always possible to undertake a critical analysis of any work, looking for unifying themes, character development, formal complexity, internal connectedness, moral seriousness, etc., but most genre fiction would not reward such attention, and the inquiry would be seen to be pointless and irrelevant. But it should not be concluded that these works are of no value, only that their primary interest is not *as literature*.

The debate cannot quite be left there, although the points about incommensurable values are important. Even ardent fans of murder mysteries, or other genres, are likely to concede that there is a broader framework in which comparative value judgments across works can be made. Within this framework, literary works of art – those, as we have seen, that reward continued re-readings – seem to provide more lasting satisfaction, the chance for deeper and more reflective contemplation, than the self-confessedly ephemeral productions suitable for beach or birthday card. If there is a scale of lasting or rewarding pleasures then literary works are likely to score higher. The thought is familiar from John Stuart Mill's admittedly not uncontroversial discussion of "higher pleasures." As Mill puts it: "there is no known Epicurean theory of life which does not assign to the pleasures of the intellect, of the feelings and imagination, and of the moral sentiments, a much higher value as pleasures than to those of mere sensation."[11] In the literary context, it is important to draw the right inference from this: not that there is no value in the works of non-literary genre fiction or that they are intrinsically inferior or that canonical works of literature should always be promoted over these productions, only that the gains in quality of experience, lasting pleasure, and stimulation of the imagination, are likely to be more rewarding from the former over the latter. There is still no reason to run the categories together and to suppose that genre fiction is trying and failing to do something that literary fiction does better.

### Intrinsic and instrumental values

A distinction related to that between reading *as literature* and reading *as something else* is the distinction between intrinsic and instrumental values. It is common to speak of works of art as valued *for their own sake* rather than for some extrinsic end.[12] Clearly to value a work of art as something other than art is not to value it for its intrinsic merit. Instrumental values of literature are associated with values attached to the effects of reading where these effects seem remote from artistically relevant qualities: they might include reminding me of my childhood, giving me the ability to pass an exam, or providing examples of psychoanalytic theory. Reading the works is instrumental in bringing about these desired effects, but the effects do not indicate intrinsic values.

However, it cannot be quite right to draw the intrinsic/instrumental distinction exclusively in terms of the relevance or otherwise of effects. The intrinsic value of a work cannot be independent of all effects because works of art only have value for human beings. The very existence of works of art is dependent on the responses of humans to art. Artistic values and thus literary values are in that sense *response-dependent* values. So now the question is: which effects – or which responses – are directly related to a work's intrinsic value, and which are merely "contingent" or instrumental effects? The question points to a complexity in the idea of intrinsic value. Philosophers can mean different things by this.

---

[11]  John Stuart Mill, *Utilitarianism*, ed. Mary Warnock (London: Fontana Press, 1986), p. 258.

[12]  The concept of *extrinsic* is not identical to that of *instrumental*, even though both are commonly contrasted with *intrinsic*: an extrinsic property is a relational property, involving a relation to something beyond the object itself, while an instrumental value is a value arising from an object's use or consequences. Some relational properties – for example what a work represents, refers to, or is about – should not be excluded without further argument from the work's intrinsic value.

One idea is that a work's intrinsic value connects only to the properties of the work that are intrinsic to it, those properties that give it its unique character: these are primarily formal properties like structure or composition, but by extension would incorporate vocabulary, subject, and theme. Another idea locates intrinsic value with the value of an experience intimately bound up with the work: this is usually connected to the pleasure that the work gives. In fact the two ideas are related because the unique experience that a work yields is necessarily linked to the intrinsic properties of the work.

But once it is admitted that some effects of a work – like pleasurable experience – are linked to intrinsic value, where can the line be drawn between intrinsic and instrumental? Crucially, what becomes of properties like learning, moral knowledge, heightened awareness, increased sensitivity to human affairs, indeed any of the properties we have been considering under the heading of "cognitive"? Are these part of the intrinsic value of a work or are they instrumental values, i.e., merely beneficial consequences of reading? We seem to be pulled in two directions. Either we say that certain extrinsic-looking properties, like moral knowledge, are in fact intrinsic to a work and part of its intrinsic value, its value as a work of literature; or we say that certain genuinely extrinsic properties are a part of literary value, so literary value is not confined to intrinsic value. In both cases, though, we are caught with the problem of where to draw the line. After all, if we include all extrinsic properties – such as helping to win prizes, make money, impress friends – as part of the value of reading literature, then we are in danger of losing the notion of a genuinely literary value. But if we include some but not all effects of reading among intrinsic values, why should just those effects – associated with pleasurable experience – be counted?

One route out of the dilemma is not entirely satisfactory in the case of literature, namely to appeal to a narrowly defined kind of aesthetic pleasure or aesthetic experience, which is tied closely to the intrinsic, formal properties of a work. This idea is often linked to notions like "disinterested attention" or attention cut off from practical, utilitarian, political, or moral concern, involving contemplation of an object for its own sake. This might get round the problem of how pleasure could be both an effect wrought by a work and also in some way intrinsic to it; it does not do justice, however, to a genuine literary response which, as shown in Chapter 4, goes far beyond disinterested contemplation of a work's formal properties.[13]

A more subtle account keeps the notion of experience, even aesthetic experience, as integral to artistic value but broadens out this experience to

[13]   For objections to this account of aesthetic experience, see Noël Carroll, "Four Concepts of Aesthetic Experience," in *Beyond Aesthetics* (Cambridge: Cambridge University Press, 2001), pp. 41–62.

include more than bare formalism. Malcolm Budd has defended a view of the value of art in terms of the experience a work offers:

> The value of a work of art as a work of art is intrinsic to the work in the sense that it is (determined by) the intrinsic value of the experience the work offers. ... It should be remembered that the experience a work of art offers is an experience *of the work itself*, and the valuable qualities of a work are quali-ties *of the work*, not of the experience it offers. It is the nature of the work that endows the work with whatever artistic value it possesses; this nature is what is experienced in undergoing the experience the work offers; and the work's artistic value is the intrinsic value of this experience. So a work of art is valu-able as art if it is such that the experience it offers is intrinsically valuable.[14]

Budd is at pains to keep the connection, surely rightly, between what the work is like in itself and the valuable experiences it affords. But he rejects formalism and allows that the relevant experience might possess intrinsi-cally, not merely as consequences, all of the following: "the invigoration of one's consciousness, or a refined awareness of human psychology or politi-cal or social structures, or moral insight, or an imaginative identification with a sympathetic form of life or point of view that is not one's own."[15] So here cognitive – and other – values are reinstated among the intrinsic values of a work. While this might seem a desirable outcome, it does put pressure both on the idea of "experience" and on the intrinsic/instrumental distinction.

Budd builds a lot into the term "experience," requiring that an appropriate experience of a work be "imbued with an awareness of ... the aesthetically relevant properties of the work" and be "an experience of interacting with it in whatever way it demands if it is to be understood." The crucial point is that the experience on which the value of a work is based is not just *any* response that the work might elicit in individual readers but is subject to norms of appropriateness. If a reader misunderstands a work or is unaware of its important aesthetic properties, then any value judgment of that reader will be compromised.

It is a moot point whether Budd's conception of experience leaves room for a non-arbitrary distinction between intrinsic and instrumental values. It might, for example, be argued that acquiring a "refined awareness" or "moral insight" (two items on his list) must extend beyond an experience itself as both are dispositional properties, realizable in subsequent action long after

---

[14]   Malcolm Budd, *Values of Art: Pictures, Poetry and Music* (Harmondsworth: Penguin Press, 1995), pp. 4–5.
[15]   Ibid., p. 7.

any particular artistic experience has passed.[16] This would suggest they are distinct from experience and are consequences of experience, therefore not intrinsic values of the experience. On the other hand, employing a notion like that of "vision," as discussed in the previous chapter, might bring awareness and insight closer toward intrinsic experiential qualities.

A further example might help. It seems to be a clearly instrumental property of a work that it cheered me up when I read it – this is a beneficial effect, but an effect nonetheless. In contrast, being *cheerful* might be an intrinsic property of the work. Recognizing its cheerfulness might be integral to a proper appreciation of the work. It is a different move altogether, though, to say that feeling cheerful or being cheered up is an experience demanded by the work when properly understood. The work property and the experience property never quite come together as intimately as that. Being cheered up, we might say, is not an aesthetic experience.

However the issue of intrinsic/instrumental is resolved, it does seem that in seeking literary value we should seek it, as far as possible, in intrinsic rather than instrumental values, as that distinction is normally understood, although a good case can be made that intrinsic values include values associated with a fairly broadly conceived experience a work can offer. When focusing on literature, however, not merely art in general, a sharper conception of the relevant experiences is needed. That can be provided only by returning to core ideas of what literature is.

## Text / work

If we seek the intrinsic value of a literary work, the value it has as a work of literature, where do we look? It might seem a hopelessly indeterminate matter trying to discern the value of a stretch of writing even if the value is limited to intrinsic value. Why should we expect any single kind of experience shared by all readers? This is indeed a problem if the focus is on *texts*. A text, we recall, is just a string of sentences (or words) in a language endowed with the meanings assigned to the words by the language. It is hard to see how a *text* in itself can have any value. A text only acquires value when it fulfills a purpose: it is valuable just to the extent that it fulfills the purpose well. A sentence used in a conversation has value if it conveys information intended by a speaker and grasped by a hearer. A work of literature – a poem, a novel, a drama – is, as we have seen, not just a text in this sense but an "institutional object," a text located in a network of conventions and actions: i.e., a "work." If we are to identify literary value we must, as noted,

---

[16]    This point is made by Robert Stecker in *Aesthetics and the Philosophy of Art: An Introduction* (Lanham, MD: Rowman and Littlefield, 2005), p. 189.

do so with the resources uncovered in our investigation of the relevant conception of the literary work, and of the practice of reading associated with that conception.

A brief look at other institutional objects shows parallel cases of the locus of value. A chess piece, a playing card, or a banknote acquire their distinctive value only in the context of an "institution," in this case a game or a banking system. Taken as a physical object a chess piece has only the value, such as it is, of the object itself. If the piece is made of gold then it is indeed valuable, but that is not a "chess value." How do we account for its value *as a chess piece*? An explanation can only be given within the terms of the game. Within chess a queen has more value than a pawn. Why? Because a queen has greater maneuverability than a pawn. Maneuverability is a criterion of value in chess. Of course that is not to deny that in a particular game at a particular time a pawn might be more powerful than the queen: the queen might be trapped and rendered momentarily useless, while the pawn is threatening checkmate. But such circumstances do not undermine the general claim about the relative values of the pieces. Nor is there any inclination to think of these values as "merely subjective." Someone might have an eccentric personal preference for pawns over queens; if so, that is indeed "subjective." But it does nothing to impugn the objective fact that overall the queen has higher value than a pawn in the game of chess even though in some particular game, *this* pawn at *this* moment is more valuable than the queen in *this* position.

Similar points can be made about the values of a playing card and a banknote. A card's "face" value is its value determined by constitutive rules of card games: a 10 is higher than a 6, a King higher than a Jack, etc. Of course local rules in particular games might vary these values. Banknotes too have "face" values, invariably more than the intrinsic value of the paper on which they are printed. Their monetary value, like the value of a playing card, is not an arbitrary or subjective matter, rather it follows from agreed conventions. These simple examples show how uncontroversial it is in some cases to speak of an object's possessing value relative to a practice or system of rules.

The analogy between these cases and literature is only loose. The rules governing chess, for example, are stricter and more clearly defined than the conventions of literary practice. But that there are conventions governing responses to works "from a literary point of view" should not be denied. Not anything counts as a literary response; we saw in Chapter 4 broadly what kinds of attention literary works do invite. The key analogy is in the way that an object (a piece of wood, a piece of paper, a text) can acquire values it does not inherently possess in virtue of being assigned a status (a chess piece, a playing card, a work) when located in a "practice" or rule-governed framework.

To speak of the intrinsic value of a literary work is potentially confusing because works can be confused with texts. Those who express skepticism about literary values often succumb to that confusion, basing their skepticism on the thought that mere texts have little or no intrinsic value and acquire such value as they have by being assigned value, perhaps arbitrarily, by those using the text. But once we locate the text in a determinate practice and apply to it the conventions of literary critical analysis we have not just a text but a *work*. The intrinsic value of a work becomes like the intrinsic value of a chess piece and unlike the intrinsic value of the material of which the piece is made. Literary value then becomes subject to the conventions of literary practice just as chess value is dependent on the rules of chess. Exactly how the conventions of the practice determine value we will return to later although the idea is by no means obscure. In effect a work reveals its value by showing how well it rewards the kinds of reading procedures detailed in Chapter 4.

### Subjective / objective

Before considering the bases for particular literary value judgments, a few comments are needed about a distinction that frequently surfaces in this discussion, indeed which has done so already, between objective and subjective. These terms are notoriously ill defined yet they persist, and in doing so recall debates about "judgments of taste" going back to the eighteenth century. Objectivity is often associated with an ideal of science and as such is thought to be unobtainable in application to the arts. A truly objective judgment might be thought to be a judgment that characterizes an object *as it is in itself* quite apart from any attitude or viewpoint associated with a human observer.[17] Even if that is too stringent a requirement, then at least objectivity is associated with properties of an *object*, while subjectivity makes reference to qualities in a perceiving *subject*.

It became a fairly standard tenet in eighteenth-century aesthetics that beauty was not an inherent quality of an object but in some way or other referred to the impression the object made on a perceiving subject. But another equally standard tenet was to deny an out-and-out subjectivity to "judgments of taste," allowing at least for what subsequently became known as "intersubjectivity," a shared and non-arbitrary conformity of judgment. This was the line taken by both Hume and Kant, who felt that there was more to aesthetic judgment than just the expression of personal preferences. The idea of objectivity came to acquire connotations not so much of "belonging to the object" as of qualities in the judging subject, such as impartiality.

[17]   Something like this ideal of objectivity is described by Thomas Nagel, e.g., in *Mortal Questions* (Cambridge: Cambridge University Press, 1979), p. 208.

An objective judgment becomes one that is not tainted with prejudice, interest, personal desire, or ulterior motives. In this way it becomes possible to be "objective," or to take an objective stance, toward value or beauty, without denying that beauty, in the original sense, is inherently subjective.

## Lessons from Hume

There is no need to explore eighteenth-century theories in detail, not least because they were concerned with a more limited range of value judgments – about beauty – than are relevant in the philosophy of literature. However, of Hume and Kant, it was Hume who had the most to say about literary value; his contribution is important both for its insights and, arguably, for its mistakes. Hume notices that common sense moves in two directions on matters of aesthetic judgment: on the one hand, it affirms the maxim that "there is no disputing about taste" (extreme subjectivism, there being no dispute about an *object* as such), yet on the other it rejects certain judgments as wild and unacceptable (supporting a species of objectivity or at least intersubjectivity). Hume offers a notorious literary example for the latter:

> Whoever would assert an equality of genius and elegance between OGILBY and MILTON, or BUNYAN and ADDISON, would be thought to defend no less an extravagance, than if he had maintained a mole-hill to be as high as TENERIFFE, or a pond as extensive as the ocean. Though there may be found persons, who give the preference to the former authors; no one pays attention to such a taste; and we pronounce without scruple the sentiment of these pretended critics to be absurd and ridiculous.[18]

The reason this passage is notorious is that the comparative judgments, which seemed so certain to Hume, seem far less so to us, in the twenty-first century. Perhaps our contemporary common sense easily ranks John Milton, author of *Paradise Lost*, over the obscure seventeenth-century poet and translator John Ogilby, who few nowadays have heard of, but common sense is much less confident on the relative merits of John Bunyan, author of *Pilgrim's Progress*, and Joseph Addison, eighteenth-century essayist, poet, and editor of *The Spectator*. Bunyan seems to have passed the test of time (Hume's own criterion of value) as well as Addison. What the example shows, contrary to Hume's expectation, is that value judgments themselves do not always pass the test of time. Hume is reflecting a common opinion of his day that Addison was a wit and genius unsurpassed, but now Addison seems to be merely one clever author among others in a century of genius.

[18]  David Hume, "Of the Standard of Taste," in *The Philosophical Works of David Hume*, ed. T. H. Green and T. H. Grose (London: Longman, Green, 1874–1875), vol. 3, p. 269.

Nevertheless, Hume's purpose is not to rest value judgments on common sense in the "obvious" cases but on something more subtle and discriminating. What he hopes to show is that not anyone's judgment is as valid as anyone else's; to do that he needs to characterize the qualities of a "true judge" whose considered pronouncements acquire a higher authority. Value judgments, or judgments of "taste," are still subjective, in the sense of being founded on "sentiment," but they acquire an intersubjective validity through arising from the sentiments of experienced and discerning judges. What such a judge possesses is a "delicacy of taste" backed by practice and comparison, unprejudiced, and informed by "good sense." The lack of such qualities is nicely described by Hume:

> When the critic has no delicacy, he judges without any distinction, and is only affected by the grosser and more palpable qualities of the object: The finer touches pass unnoticed and disregarded. Where he is not aided by practice, his verdict is attended with confusion and hesitation. Where no comparison has been employed, the most frivolous beauties, such as rather merit the name of defects, are the object of his admiration. Where he lies under the influence of prejudice, all his natural sentiments are perverted. Where good sense is wanting, he is not qualified to discern the beauties of design and reasoning, which are the highest and most excellent.[19]

Such, Hume believes, is the state of most of us. True judges, who overcome these defects, are rare.

However, Hume allows for some variation even among the deliverances of the most qualified judges, resting on either personal taste or cultural and historical attitudes. Personal predispositions cannot be eliminated altogether. As Hume nicely puts it: "At twenty, OVID may be the favourite author; HORACE at forty; and perhaps TACITUS at fifty." He goes on:

> One person is more pleased with the sublime; another with the tender; a third with raillery. One has a strong sensibility to blemishes, and is extremely studious of correctness: Another has a more lively feeling of beauties, and pardons twenty absurdities and defects for one elevated or pathetic stroke. … Comedy, tragedy, satire, odes, have each its partisans, who prefer that particular species of writing to all others. It is plainly an error in a critic, to confine his approbation to one species or style of writing, and condemn all the rest. But it is almost impossible not to feel a predilection for that which suits our particular turn and disposition. Such preferences are innocent and unavoidable, and can never reasonably be the object of dispute.[20]

[19]   Ibid., p. 278.
[20]   Ibid., p. 281.

Hume is surely right that however hard we strive for a species of objectivity, or a "standard of taste," in our value judgments there can be no denying individual predispositions. He is on more controversial ground when trying to find a place for cultural variations. On the whole he thinks that a discerning critic should be able to make allowances for different manners and customs. But he offers a famous exception: "where the ideas of morality and decency alter from one age to another, and where vicious manners are described, without being marked with the proper characters of blame and disapprobation; this must be allowed to disfigure the poem, and to be a real deformity."[21] This species of "moralism," as it has been called, is not universally conceded. It is a point to which we shall return.

Hume's overall position on critical judgments has much to commend it, notably the ideas that criticism calls for skill and training, that a degree of objectivity is possible in value judgments, and that there remains an ineliminable residue of personal preference or cultural difference not open to reasoned dispute. But there are problems with Hume's account. One problem springs from what might be called his "naturalizing" of taste. He believes that by describing the dispositions, aptitudes, and attitudes of a true judge he has assured soundness of judgment. But he does so without reference to the peculiar nature of the objects being judged, in our case literary works. In a word, he does not acknowledge the "institutional" nature of literature and the conventions associated with literary reading. The "delicacy of taste" that Hume characterizes is of a generic kind applicable to different kinds of objects and different art forms. Admittedly, he requires that the true judges have "practice" over many examples and are able to affect "comparisons." He also emphasises that different arts have different ends or purposes, that of poetry being to "please by means of the passions and the imagination."[22] But our inquiry has shown that the conventions for reading literary works are more specific than that. So, given that the required discernment must be appropriately directed, a more detailed account of the object of the discernment, as well as of the discerning subject, is called for. This Hume does not provide.

Another problem for Hume's account, often remarked, is his assumption that human nature has sufficient uniformity across time and culture to yield reasonably similar "sentiments" in appropriately qualified observers responding to the same objects. Yet there is every reason to believe that at least aesthetic sentiments have the potential for deep cultural differences. This might suggest that there can be no universal true judges, only true judges within specific cultural traditions.

---

[21]   Ibid., p. 282.
[22]   Ibid., p. 277.

However, we must take care not to fall back on out-and-out relativism. As Hume himself observes – instancing the lasting appeal of Homer – there do seem to be works that are valued trans-culturally. Certain myths and certain literary motifs, love and conflict, honor and shame, self and other, generate human interest across times and places. Canonical works in all traditions will treat of such themes and as such can be open to non-relativistic appraisal. No doubt there are culture-specific literary modes or background assumptions, but Hume's true judges can either make allowances for these or acknowledge them in the residue of differences. Nevertheless, the point about "naturalizing" taste arises again, for what matters in the search for universal values are not just common sentiments among true judges but common expectations arising from the very conception of literature.

An important lesson from Hume is that literary appreciation is not based on merely arbitrary responses to literature but calls for powers of discernment that to a large extent can be cultivated through experience and training. The idea of "subjective" breaks down into at least two different senses: one refers to what Hume calls "sentiment," the other merely to personal preference. Value judgments are subjective in the first sense, in that they are ultimately response-dependent, there can be no literary values independent of the experience of readers of literature; but they need not be subjective in the second sense. Recall that "objective" can mean "belonging to the object," i.e., not subjective in the first sense, not dependent on human responses, or it can mean merely "impartial." It is not uncommon for one and the same person to make an objective (i.e., impartial) judgment that goes one way, and a subjective judgment (i.e., based on personal preference) that goes the other, over a single work. Such a person might acknowledge that a work is "great" or "important" or "significant" while offering a negative personal view: "a good work but it doesn't appeal to me." Or the other way round: "I like it but I agree it is not a great work." These familiar locutions imply that there are standards that transcend personal preferences.

## Being valued / being valuable

There is a species of relativism that holds that there is no more to literary value than the succession of local value judgments made at different times by different people. "'Value,'" writes one proponent of this view, "means whatever is valued by certain people in specific situations, according to particular criteria and in the light of given purposes."[23] On this view, literary value judgments will vary from era to era, from culture to culture, even from group to group: "literary value is radically relative and therefore 'constantly

[23]    Terry Eagleton, *Literary Theory: An Introduction* (Oxford: Blackwell, 1983), p. 11.

variable.' "[24] Any individual judgment that "X is good" means no more than "X is thought good by y." There might be reasons offered for these judgments but the reasons too will only be reasons *for y*.

But relativizing judgments in this way is problematic on several counts. First of all, there's Hume's point that not all judgments are of equal standing. We need to know the authority, as it were, of the judges. Then the question arises of how the group (the "certain people") is defined, whose values are being represented. Is it just any group of like-minded people? Or is it a larger cultural grouping, within which there might be dissenting voices? In the extreme it might reduce to a group of one individual, in which case the relativism collapses into radical subjectivism. Also, logic indicates that "is valued" is not equivalent to "is valuable." It is possible to state without contradiction that such and such *is valued* (e.g., by a group) but *is not valuable*. "X is valued" is a matter of fact, established by historical inquiry, while "X is valuable" is a matter of judgment. To be valuable is to be justifiably valued. It is often the case that authors are popular in their day but fall out of favor and are later judged to be "dated." The verdict of history, as it were, is that the work is not of lasting value, which is not to deny that it was once highly valued. Relativists might predict that this state of affairs is the norm, and that as social and cultural conditions change so too do values. What is difficult for relativists is to account for those works that do retain their value under changing conditions. Yet it is precisely such works that are deemed to be "canonical."

Before looking at canonicity, there is a further crucial point that counts against the radical relativizing of literary value: because the very concept of literature is already an evaluative term, there is no neutral starting point from which literary values can develop and diverge. To start simply with "texts" and to ask which of those are valued is not yet to determine a particular species of value. To start with "works" of the relevant kind is already to have incorporated a basic judgment which is not itself relativized: a judgment that this work is open to literary consideration, that it is the kind of work that merits attention of the appropriate kind. Of course relativists might insist that the identification of literature is indeed relative to parochial and changing contexts. What counts as literature, they insist, will differ at different times for different groups. But then it seems as if the concept of literature has been lost. If each group can decide what counts as a literary work then there is no common measure by which different value judgments *about literature* can be compared. To make the disagreements about the values of literature interesting there has to be a shared basis for identifying the objects of those values.

[24] Barbara Herrnstein Smith, *Contingencies of Value: Alternative Perspectives for Critical Theory* (Cambridge, MA: Harvard University Press, 1988), p. 11.

Yet one more problem for relativists is that they tend to run together the question of how something came to be valued and the question of the basis or justification for its value. Loosely speaking, the former is concerned with *causes*, i.e., the historical factors that led to some works over others being valued, while the latter is concerned with *reasons*, i.e., the grounds on which a work is deemed valuable. The history of reception is an intellectual or political history. There are interesting stories to tell about how particular movements or authors or works became prominent. F. R. Leavis's *New Bearings in English Poetry* (1932), mentioned earlier, was part of a concerted effort to change the taste of the poetry reading public from the Romantics and Georgians toward modernism. Efforts by other critics, for example in the 1950s, helped shift interest in drama toward writers like Samuel Beckett and John Osborne.

There can be no doubt that there are social and cultural factors influencing these shifts in taste. Arguably, neither could have taken place at an earlier point in history, even, say, 40 years earlier. But that is not to deny that there were aesthetic considerations as well as historical ones that underlay the change. Part of Leavis's case for preferring T. S. Eliot to Shelley is that Eliot skillfully deploys language to express the concerns of the modern age. Eliot, Leavis argued, was not just a good poet for the age but had found a new voice for traditional poetic themes: "*The Waste Land* remains a great positive achievement, and one of the first importance for English poetry. In it a mind fully alive in the age compels a poetic triumph out of the peculiar difficulties facing a poet in the age."[25] In our terms we might say that *The Waste Land* became *valued* partly because of the efforts of critics like Leavis (a matter of historical fact); it was shown to be *valuable* for many of the aesthetic reasons advanced by critics like Leavis (a matter of literary judgment).

## Canonicity

Few debates among literary critics are so heated as that over the nature and foundations of the so-called literary "canon." There are many vested interests in the debate, some of a quasi-political nature concerning the very basis on which literature is taught in schools and universities. The concern of the philosopher of literature is not with the underlying politics but with both the concept of canon itself and the validity of the arguments, for and against, as they bear on literary value.

---

[25]   Leavis, *New Bearings in English Poetry*, p. 95.

*The idea of a canon*

The idea of a canon was appropriated, relatively recently, by literary critics from theology:

> Over the last quarter of the twentieth century, the term *canon*, which previously had been restricted to the body of Sacred Scripture approved by ecclesiastical authority, attained general currency in academic circles as a designation for the corpus of secular literary works implicitly or explicitly endorsed by established cultural authority as worthy of preservation through reading and study.[26]

Prior to the introduction of this term, the idea of "tradition" held a more central place in critical vocabulary, as used by (for example) T. S. Eliot, in his essay "Tradition and the Individual Talent" and F. R. Leavis in *The Great Tradition*. Although some of the same questions arise about the constitution of the literary tradition, arguably the term "tradition" is less contentious as it does not so provocatively invoke the idea of authority. We looked at aspects of Eliot's idea of tradition in Chapter 3. Nevertheless, the notion that there are a number of key works across a long period of history, even across cultures, that help to shape and define literary value, is common to both "canon" and "tradition." The question is: on what basis do works acquire this status?

*Historical causes and aesthetic reasons*

Two prominent views show the polarization of the debate, each highlighting an aspect we have already encountered: the difference between cause and reason. On the one hand, first of all, there are those who explain the formation of the literary canon entirely in causal terms, specifically in terms of power:

> Since those with cultural power tend to be members of socially, economically, and politically established classes (or to serve them and identify their own interests with theirs), the texts that survive will tend to be those that appear to reflect and reinforce establishment ideologies.[27]

In answer to the obvious objection that many canonical works seem to challenge established norms, the suggestion is that they are not *really* or *deeply* doing so:

[26]  Robert Alter, *Canon and Creativity: Modern Writing and the Authority of Scripture* (New Haven, CT: Yale University Press, 2000), p. 1.

[27]  Herrnstein Smith, *Contingencies of Value*, p. 51.

However much canonical works may be seen to "question" secular vanities such as wealth, social position, and political power, "remind" their readers of more elevated values and virtues, and oblige them to "confront" such hard truths and harsh realities as their own mortality and the hidden griefs of obscure people, they would not be found to please long and well if they were seen *radically* to undercut establishment interests or *effectively* to subvert the ideologies that support them.[28]

As for the Humean thought that the test of time will weed out works of lesser value, such that only great works will survive from generation to generation, again appeal is made to the overwhelming power of the dominant classes:

Since the texts that are selected and preserved by "time" will always tend to be those which "fit" (and indeed have often been designed to fit) their [i.e., the dominant classes'] characteristic needs, interests, resources, and purposes, that testing mechanism has its own built-in partialities.[29]

The scriptural notion of a canon is useful for advancing an argument of this kind because it presupposes that canonical works are based on authority. Works are deemed to be canonical only because they serve the interests of those authorities that establish the canon:

The great author is great because he (occasionally even she) has managed to convey an authentic vision of life; and the role of the reader or critic is to listen respectfully to the voice of the author as it is expressed in the text. The literary canon of "great literature" ensures that it is this "representative experience" (one selected by male bourgeois critics) that is transmitted to future generations, rather than those deviant, unrepresentative experiences discoverable in much female, ethnic and working-class writing. Anglo-American feminist criticism has waged war on this self-sufficient canonization of middle-class male values.[30]

Arguments of this kind, citing the class and gender interests of critics, are used to promote "marginalized" works and authors. The danger with this style of argument, though, is that it can count against itself. If recognized literary virtues always reflect class and gender interests then there can be no *objective* grounds for literary evaluation. Any purported reasons for giving a high

---

[28]    Ibid.

[29]    Ibid.

[30]    Toril Moi, *Sexual/Textual Politics: Feminist Literary Theory* (London: Methuen, 1985), p. 78.

evaluation to some particular work will turn out simply to be self-serving or self-justifying rationalizations. But then what becomes of "marginalized" works exemplified by "female, ethnic and working-class writing"? What kind of value can they be ascribed? Presumably these works are no more subject to objective appraisal than the works promoted by "male bourgeois critics." So instead of having the desirable consequence of broadening the canon, reassessing neglected works, and promoting a debate about values, this kind of argument closes off debate and, at its extreme, simply asserts the non-rational and self-serving opinions of another interest group. It should be added, of course, that not all feminist critics or supporters of marginalized writing do reject objective standards or recognized literary virtues. They are more likely to see these virtues, or similar ones, exemplified in hitherto unacknowledged places. They can also mount a case for new virtues worthy to be considered.

Defenders of the canon seek reasons why works acquire canonical status, not merely causes. And the most obvious reasons invoke the intrinsic, or aesthetic, value of the works themselves. Harold Bloom has been one of the most vociferous literary critics both in defense of the aesthetic criterion of canonicity and in attacking those who propose ideological explanations:

> I myself would want to argue … that aesthetic choice has always guided every secular aspect of canon formation, but that is a difficult argument to maintain at this time when the defense of the literary canon, like the assault against it, has become so heavily politicized. Ideological defenses of the Western Canon are as pernicious in regard to aesthetic values as the onslaughts of attackers who seek to destroy the Canon or "open it up," as they proclaim. Nothing is so essential to the Western Canon as its principles of selectivity, which are elitist only to the extent that they are founded upon severely artistic criteria.[31]

Bloom puts up a spirited defense of what he calls "the autonomy of the aesthetic." Its "best defense," he writes, "is the experience of reading *King Lear* and then seeing the play well performed. *King Lear* does not derive from a crisis in philosophy, nor can its power be explained away as a mystification somehow promoted by bourgeois institutions. It is the mark of the degeneracy of literary study that one is considered an eccentric for holding that the literary is not dependent upon the philosophical, and that the aesthetic is irreducible to ideology or to metaphysics. Aesthetic criticism returns us to the autonomy of imaginative literature …."[32]

[31] Harold Bloom, *The Western Canon: The Books and School of the Ages* (New York: Riverhead Books, 1994), p. 21.
[32] Ibid., pp. 9–10.

Bloom's arguments in favor of the aesthetic criterion are perhaps not very strong and often rely more on passionate affirmation ("Shakespeare *is* the secular canon, or even the secular scripture; forerunners and legatees alike are defined by him alone for canonical purposes"[33]) or on name-calling (the "School of Resentment" characterizes his opponents). But the force of his case rests not on philosophical argument but on example. His careful readings of the canonical works *show* what reasons there are for evaluating them; he shows why the works reward attention. That is not to say his readings and his assessments couldn't be challenged, but at least he has offered reasons that invite critical debate.

As we saw in Chapter 1, the critic Frank Kermode also aims to relocate a notion of the aesthetic – specifically the idea of "aesthetic pleasure" – in the debate on canon formation as a counter to the view that the canon rests only on "collusion with the discourses of power."[34] However, we argued there that Kermode weakens his case by seeking to naturalize the pleasures of literature, via Freud and Roland Barthes, appealing to notions like sexuality (*jouissance*), transgression, and "dismay."

No doubt pleasure must play some role in the defense of intrinsic literary values, but it must be much more closely linked to the distinctive modes of reading and appreciating literature than implied by the debate between Kermode and his fellow symposiasts. Any substantial discussion of the values of canonical literature must both look at particular cases and show in detail the kinds of reasons that might be given in support of the evaluations. Case studies can be revealing.

The critic Willie van Peer, for example, has tested and sought to refute the hypothesis that canon formation arises exclusively from "collusion with the discourses of power," specifically the hypothesis that

> If ... two works of literature deal with the same subject matter (and are also similar in other respects), the one that reflects and reinforces prevailing ideologies of dominant groups most closely will have more chances of ending up in the canon than the one that expresses criticism of such ideologies.[35]

He compares two works, versions of the Romeo and Juliet story, which we looked at in Chapter 5: Shakespeare's and an earlier version by Arthur Brooke, *The Tragicall Historye of Romeus and Juliet* (1562). Van Peer shows how

---

[33]  Ibid., pp. 23–24.
[34]  Frank Kermode, *Pleasure and Change: The Aesthetics of Canon* (New York: Oxford University Press, 2004), p. 31.
[35]  Willie van Peer, "Canon Formation: Ideology or Aesthetic Quality?" *British Journal of Aesthetics*, vol. 36, no. 2, April (1996), pp. 97–108 at p. 98.

Brooke's work is didactic and moralistic, "anti-erotic and anti-utopian in style and spirit,""demanding absolute adaptation of the individual to the prevailing social conditions, however arbitrary these may be, without critique, without reflection," while Shakespeare's play "shows us a utopian outlook on sexual relations between men and women, without stifling constraints of a rigid social order."[36] In the light of this, and other evidence besides, if the "discourses of power" hypothesis were right then one might predict that of the two works it would be Brooke's that became canonical. Yet his novella is almost entirely forgotten. The analysis seeks to show, on the one hand, that Shakespeare's work is far more subversive of prevailing ideologies than is Brooke's, while, on the other, it is of a manifestly higher literary quality in its language, its structure, and expressiveness. It is Shakespeare's work, of course, that is canonical.

A single example will not settle a deeply contested issue. No doubt there are many factors influencing canon formation, and we should not have to choose between a causal story and a story based on value judgments underpinned by critical reasoning. Both factors no doubt play a part. Appeal to reductive notions of pleasure is not adequate to explain the constitution of canons any more than are reductive accounts in terms of ideologies. Nor are parallels with the canon of scripture particularly illuminating. In the sense of "canon" where it just means central and paradigmatic works of literature there is no coordinated authority issuing fiats as to what works do and do not belong. The literary canon is not a static body of works; there is constant "revaluation" round the edges. Critics endlessly return to established works, reflecting on them anew both positively and negatively, but they also seek out new ones.

The idea of a literary "tradition" weakens the notion of a controlling "authority" while introducing connotations of skills handed down. The skills of reading, reflecting on, and evaluating literature are defined not in terms of class or gender or race or nationality, or as the province of any social group, but in terms of a "practice." Those practitioners who engage in the practice are identified, not in social terms, but in terms of the conventions and concepts that constitute the practice. There is nothing self-serving about these practitioners – authors, readers, lovers of literature – so there are no externally defined interests they seek to promote.

## Description, Interpretation, and Evaluation

The practice of reading and appreciating literature as art, discussed in Chapter 4, shows the complex interplay of the descriptive and the evaluative in this process. It would be utterly simplistic to divide the process into

[36]   Ibid., p. 104.

statements of pure description on the one hand and value judgments on the other, especially with the additional assumption, sometimes made, that the former provide objectivity, rigor, and clarity, while the latter are subjective, open to bias, and extraneous. There are facts about literary works – about form, rhetoric, structure, genre, and textual and semantic properties – which it can be important to recognize. But the idea that anything beyond the identification of facts is mere opinion is not only a misapprehension but invites an over-simplified quest for inferential principles moving from fact to value.

## Thick and thin descriptions

One benefit of Sibley's aesthetics, outlined in Chapter 1, is his recognition of the subtly different ways in which descriptive and evaluative elements can interact in aesthetics concepts.[37] Sometimes aesthetic descriptions are "thin," in the sense that they do no more than offer a positive or negative evaluation: "beautiful," "ugly," "admirable." Aesthetic characterizations, though, are not merely ways of evaluating works; they can also reveal literally the *character* of the work, the kind of work it is. Arguably some aesthetic terms have a substantial descriptive content and function much like "thick" descriptions in ethics, such as *courageous*, *honest*, and *merciful*.[38] The correct application of these terms to characterize human conduct seems to rest as much on observable features as on moral judgment.[39] In paradigm cases it is not just a "matter of opinion" whether someone is courageous or honest. Similarly, there are fairly clear bounds on what can count as melancholic, tragic, or comic in verse or prose.

Hume, however, sounds a note of caution in the matter of "thick" descriptions in criticism:

> Every voice is united in applauding elegance, propriety, simplicity, spirit in writing; and in blaming fustian, affectation, coldness and a false brilliancy: But

---

[37]   See Frank Sibley, "Particularity, Art, and Evaluation," in Peter Lamarque and Stein Haugom Olsen, eds., *Aesthetics and the Philosophy of Art: The Analytic Tradition: An Anthology* (Oxford: Blackwell, 2003). Originally published in *Proceedings of the Aristotelian Society*, suppl. vol. 48 (1974), pp. 1–21.

[38]   The notion of "thick" and "thin" moral concepts comes from Bernard Williams, *Ethics and the Limits of Philosophy* (Cambridge, MA: Harvard University Press, 1985).

[39]   The point is made by Jerrold Levinson in "Aesthetic Properties, Evaluative Force, and Differences of Sensibility," in Emily Brady and Jerrold Levinson, eds., *Aesthetic Concepts: Essays After Sibley* (Oxford: Oxford University Press, 2001), p. 63.

when critics come to particulars, this seeming unanimity vanishes; and it is found, that they had affixed a very different meaning to their expressions.[40]

Hume is right that readers can agree that elegance is good and affectation bad in literature but disagree over cases. The readers might not mean the same or might apply different criteria. On the other hand not anything can count as elegant or affected, and someone might fail to recognize these qualities not because of disagreement over criteria but through a lack of perceptiveness, a failure to acquire the Sibleyan "gestalt."

## Interpretation and value

In just such a way can readers fail in literary appreciation of a broader kind that involves interpretation. They might fully understand a work at a linguistic level but not grasp its literary significance and thus not its literary value. Here is an example, referring to George Eliot's novel *Silas Marner*:

> The literary innocent will read *Silas Marner* ... merely as "a story of old-fashioned village life" (as George Eliot described it to her publishers). He will not see the features which he may notice in the novel as requiring any further construal. For him the association of Silas's gold and Eppie will be innocent of significance. He may notice, but he will attach no significance to, the fact that Eppie's golden hair, in Silas's first confusion after she walks through his open door, is seen by him as his gold; to the fact that Eppie is the daughter of the brother of the man who stole his gold; to the fact that Eppie takes the place in Silas's life that the gold has occupied; that while the gold turns Silas away from society and his fellow men, Eppie again brings him into contact with other people, etc. He may notice, but will not attach any significance to, Silas's short-sightedness, George Eliot's description of him as a weaving spider, the picture of Silas as linked to the loom and dominated by its rhythm, to the fact that he lives by the stone-pit, that the wasted land around the stone-pit is turned into a garden by Aaron, the gardener, under Eppie's guidance when she is to marry Aaron, that the theft of his gold makes Silas keep his door open, that Dunstan is found with the gold at the bottom of the stone-pit when this is drained, etc.[41]

The important terms here are "construal" and "significance." What the experienced reader of the novel offers the "literary innocent" is a way of construing

---

[40]   David Hume, "Of the Standard of Taste," p. 266.

[41]   Stein Haugom Olsen, "Value Judgments in Criticism," *Journal of Aesthetics and Art Criticism*, vol. 42, no. 2 (1983), pp. 125–136 at p. 134.

scenes that he or she otherwise might have passed over. The construal takes the form of assigning significance to passages that might seem merely incidental. This is partially the task of interpretation: to connect elements in a work by making them salient under a species of re-description. Eppie's golden hair is not just a minor narrative detail but symbolizes Eppie's substitution in Silas's life for the gold he has lost. To assign significance to a passage is to find a reason to attend to that passage.

Literary value enters the picture at several levels. To read a novel as literature – not merely as a diversion or escape – is to bring to the novel an expectation that it will yield rewards for this kind of attention. It invites construal, the quest for significance, and appreciation in the sense discussed. The pleasure the novel affords is a product of the successful realization of the expectation of value. Not all novels will reward such an expectation. Further value judgments arise in asking about the effectiveness of detail, either in a narrative or in poetic imagery. But it is not bare textual (i.e., linguistic) features that invite appraisal but features-assigned-significance-under-a-construal. We might ask of *Silas Marner*: how effective is the motif of gold in the overall vision of the novel? How well do the details hang together to make this interesting and powerful? This value question cannot be answered without first exploring, through interpretation, the ways the motif is developed. Thus is evaluation intimately tied to interpretation; it is not usefully contrasted with fact or description.

### *A hermeneutic circle*

An interesting version of the hermeneutic circle now presents itself with regard to evaluation. For when we come to assess the effectiveness of a feature-under-a-construal and we find that it seems strained or weak, we are often forced to ask whether the perceived weakness is in the feature itself (i.e., in the *work*) or in the way the feature is construed (i.e., in the *interpretation* of the work). A small example might be the death of Krook by "spontaneous combustion" in a notorious passage in *Bleak House*. Even early on in the novel's reception the passage was criticized for being fantastical and opposed to scientific fact. Dickens himself in his Preface to the novel is defensive, insisting that "before I wrote that description I took pains to investigate the subject" and gave putative examples of the real thing. If we construe Krook's death as simply the exaggerated dispatch of a despicable character we might criticize the scene for its lack of verisimilitude. But if we construe it symbolically it seems to have more power and interest. The critic Hillis Miller sees Krook's death as fitting into a pattern of physical corruption and decay which characterizes the whole world of the fiction: "Krook is transformed into the basic elements of the world of the novel, fog and mud. The heavy odor in the air … and the 'thick yellow liquor' which forms on the windowsill as Krook burns … are particularly horrible versions of these elements."[42]

Value assessments of whole works characteristically develop out of judgments at the level of detail; indeed, reasons given for global judgments will be drawn from judgments at the local level. The interactions can occur down to the level of diction:

> These are lapses of style, and they extend, also, into Eva and Ruth's interior voices. Boyd makes occasional resort to formulaic constructions: "There was something very odd happening here, I told myself," says Ruth when she first notices her mother's strange behaviour, and later: "Life is very strange, I told myself, you can never be sure of anything." This is laziness from a writer capable of local, as well as global, brilliance. Take Ruth's recollection, for example, of her dying father's mania for turning out lightbulbs, a detail which is Chekhovian in its strange, unsolvable truth.
>
> It's the interest, and insight, of Boyd's overarching story that overwhelms these small complaints.[43]

A close interplay between interpretation and evaluation occurs at the global level too. When we judge a work as literature, we judge it not simply as a text or a story or as lines of verse but always under some conception of what we think the work is seeking to achieve, or what underpins its claim to our attention as a work of art. We arrive at that conception through interpretation. If we see the work as "biting political satire" or an "exposure of the horrors of war" or a "comic romance" we judge its success in those terms. Another reader might conceive the work in different terms with different emphases. This might affect the value attributed to it.

## Ethical Criticism and Value

One kind of assessment of literature has caused considerable debate, arguably going back to the ancient Greeks, concerning literature's ethical content. That literary works often – though not always – have ethical content is not in dispute, nor even that they can be judged for the ethical stance they take. The disputed question concerns the precise relation between ethical value and literary value. This is sometimes formulated, by philosophers, more

---

[42] J. Hillis Miller, "The World of *Bleak House*," in Charles Dickens, *Bleak House*, ed. George Ford and Sylvère Monod (New York: W. W. Norton, 1977), p. 955.

[43] David Mattin, Review of William Boyd's *Restless*, in *The Independent on Sunday*, September 10, 2006.

narrowly as the question whether aesthetic value ever encompasses ethical value, such that "the moral defects and/or merits of a work may figure in the aesthetic evaluation of the work."[44] The issue is important, for it demands a more precise delimitation of what we have called intrinsic and instrumental values and what it is to value a work "as literature."

In fact two separate issues can be identified on the status of "ethical criticism": the first might be labeled the "edification" issue, the second the "ethical flaw" issue.

## The edification issue

The edification issue relates back to the more general debate about cognitive values in Chapter 6: is it a key literary value to educate or impart knowledge? A debate between, on the one hand, the philosopher Martha Nussbaum and the literary critic Wayne Booth, and, on the other, Richard A. Posner, a Circuit Judge at the United States Court of Appeals, has given focus to the edification issue, specifically in the context of ethics.[45] For Nussbaum and Booth, one central and important function of criticism is to elicit from literary works clarity and enlightenment on moral questions. Nussbaum's book *Poetic Justice* set out to "commend ... certain works of literature to citizens and public officials, as a valuable source of deliberative enrichment."[46] As she explains, "[f]ocusing on the analysis of compassion and on the role of the imagination in promoting compassion, I argue that certain specific literary works develop these imaginative abilities in a valuable way and are therefore helpful to citizens."[47]

There is no need to argue whether certain works *can* be valuable in this way; that is not in dispute. And there might be agreement over which works are better or worse for this purpose. What is at issue is whether this is a genuine *literary* value or just an instrumental value, even a kind of appropriation.

---

[44] Noël Carroll, "Moderate Moralism," *British Journal of Aesthetics*, vol. 36, no. 3 (1996), pp. 223–238 at p. 236.

[45] Richard A. Posner, *Law and Literature* (Boston, MA: Harvard University Press; rev. and updated ed., 1998); Posner, "Against Ethical Criticism," *Philosophy and Literature*, vol. 21, no. 1 (1997), pp. 1–27; Posner, "Against Ethical Criticism: Part Two," *Philosophy and Literature*, vol. 22, no. 2 (1998), pp. 394–412. Martha C. Nussbaum, *Poetic Justice: The Literary Imagination and Public Life* (Boston, MA: Beacon Books, 1997); Nussbaum, "Exactly and Responsibly: A Defense of Ethical Criticism," *Philosophy and Literature*, vol. 22, no. 2 (1998), pp. 343–365. Wayne C. Booth, *The Company We Keep: An Ethics of Fiction* (Berkeley: University of California Press, 1989); Booth, "Why Banning Ethical Criticism Is a Serious Mistake," *Philosophy and Literature*, vol. 22, no. 2 (1998), pp. 366–393.

[46] Nussbaum, "Exactly and Responsibly," p. 350.

[47] Ibid.

Many of the relevant considerations have already been canvassed in the previous chapter. But in the Nussbaum–Posner debate there is a sharp political and moral edge worth remarking. The value judgments at stake are not merely abstract but involve, as was the case with Plato, what books should appear on a syllabus.

First of all, Nussbaum is aware of the distinction between intrinsic and instrumental values:

> Our thesis about the effects of literature is only in part a causal thesis, a thesis about what reading literature does to the personality. It is also, clearly, a conceptual thesis. We claim that the activities of imagination and emotion that the involved reader performs during the time of reading are not just instrumental to moral conduct, they are also examples of moral conduct, in the sense that they are examples of the type of emotional and imaginative activity that good ethical conduct involves.[48]

Moral edification can appear *in* the process of reading, not just *as a result* of it. On the other hand, if edification is the desired end, perhaps the distinction is not that important. Posner responds by claiming not only that "there is nothing morally improving *in literature itself*,"[49] but that even in the favorable cases "[e]thical readings of works of literature tend to be reductive — and digressive."[50] And he regards as "repugnant" a view of literature that invites "ideological screening" of works that have a "bad influence."[51] Furthermore there is little evidence, he argues, that edification of any significant kind occurs: "[m]oral philosophers, their students, literary critics, and English majors are no more moral in attitude or behaviour than their peers in other fields."[52]

For Posner we only have to look at the acknowledged canon of works to see how unsuitable most are for moral edification and, indeed, how widespread, by our contemporary lights, are ethical blemishes:

> The classics are full of moral atrocities — as they appear to us today, and sometimes as they appeared to the more enlightened members of the author's own society — that the author apparently approved of. Rape, pillage, murder, human and animal sacrifice, concubinage, and slavery in the *Iliad*; misogyny in the *Oresteia* and countless other works; blood-curdling vengeance; antisemitism in more works of literature than one can count, including works by Shakespeare and Dickens; racism and sexism likewise; homophobia

---

[48]  Ibid., p. 355.

[49]  Posner, "Against Ethical Criticism," p. 16.

[50]  Ibid., p. 12.

[51]  Posner, "Against Ethical Criticism: Part Two," p. 398.

[52]  Posner, "Against Ethical Criticism," p. 12.

(think only of Shakespeare's *Troilus and Cressida* and Mann's "Death in Venice"); monarchism, aristocracy, caste systems and other illegitimate (as they seem to us) forms of hierarchy; colonialism, imperialism, religious obscurantism, militarism, gratuitous violence, torture (as of Iago in *Othello*), and criminality; alcoholism and drug-addiction; relentless stereotyping; sadism; pornography; machismo; cruelty to animals (bullfighting, for example); snobbism; praise for fascism and communism, and for idleness; contempt for the poor, the frail, the elderly, the deformed, and the unsophisticated, for people who work for a living, for the law-abiding, and for democratic processes. The world of literature is a moral anarchy.[53]

Such ethical failings, according to Posner, are no more than one might expect from works of earlier periods: "[m]ost readers accept the presence of obsolete ethics in literature with the same equanimity that they accept the presence of obsolete military technology or antiquated diction or customs."[54] He also makes the point that the rare books that do promote ethically sound views are not for that reason highly regarded. *Uncle Tom's Cabin*, for example, "has not survived as literature ... even though its author's opposition to slavery now commands universal assent."[55] And Dickens's *Hard Times*, one of Nussbaum's case studies for edification, "illustrates ... the ... banality of literary moralizing."[56]

The idea that literature is and should be valued as a source of moral edification has a long history appealing to Puritans and to Marxists, as well as cultural critics like Matthew Arnold or F. R. Leavis, and eccentrics like Leo Tolstoy. Few have been overly concerned with whether edification is an intrinsic literary value or merely a convenient instrumental one. Arguably, though, the weakness of the instrumental case reveals a weakness in the intrinsic value case. If the end result is hard to detect or uneven, and if most literary works are unsuitable for this purpose, then there seems no strong case for promoting moral edification as a *deep* achievement of literature. Furthermore, if ethical criticism, in its more polemical manifestations, entails attending to a literary work primarily to see how far it endorses the reader's own moral and political beliefs, valuing it just to the extent that it does so, and promoting it to others as part of a moral education with the aim of spreading those beliefs, then this does not fit any paradigmatic conception of reading literature *as literature*. It looks more like the appropriation of literature for some further end. And if the ethical reading is presented as

[53] Ibid., p. 5. For a similar list, making the same point, see Bloom, *Western Canon*, p. 28.

[54] Posner, "Against Ethical Criticism," p. 7.

[55] Ibid.

[56] Posner, "Against Ethical Criticism: Part Two," p. 412.

literary interpretation then the possibility remains of other ways of construing the work. Construed in a different way the work might reveal different values.

## The ethical flaw issue

It is interesting that those who address the "ethical flaw" issue, to which we now turn, take care from the outset to focus on the connection between the ethical and the *aesthetic*. The point of "moralism" of this kind is to argue that an ethical blemish in a work – perhaps akin to those in Posner's list above – can at least in some cases amount to an aesthetic blemish, therefore a flaw in the work *as art*. Two prominent arguments have been advanced in support of such moralism: an argument from "uptake" and an argument from "merited response."

## Moderate moralism and the failure of uptake

The uptake argument originates with Noël Carroll's defense of "moderate moralism," the view that "in some instances a moral defect in an artwork can be an aesthetic defect … and sometimes a moral virtue can count as an aesthetic virtue."[57] Carroll points out that narratives are "incomplete" and invite audiences to fill in details imaginatively and to respond in ways that the work invites. Classical tragedy invites audiences to respond with pity and fear at the downfall of the tragic hero, but, as Aristotle noted, if the hero is of the wrong kind – too perfect or too evil – then the response becomes impossible and the tragedy fails on its own terms. Carroll comments: "Failure to elicit pity and fear is a failure of tragedy *qua* tragedy, an aesthetic failure, a failure in the design of the work."[58]

Sometimes the failure to secure the invited uptake rests on moral factors. Carroll gives the example of Brett Easton Ellis's novel *American Psycho*:

> The author intended it as a satire of the rapacious eighties in the USA. He presented a serial killer as the symbol of the vaunted securities marketeer of Reagonomics. However, the serial killings depicted in the novel are so graphically brutal that readers are not able morally to get past the gore in order to savour the parody. Certainly Ellis made an aesthetic error. … He failed to appreciate that the readers would not be able to secure uptake of his themes in the face of the unprecedented violence. He invited the audience to view the murders as political satire and that was an invitation that they could not

[57] Noël Carroll, "Moderate Moralism versus Moderate Autonomism," *British Journal of Aesthetics*, vol. 38, no. 4 (1998), pp. 419–424 at p. 419.

[58] Ibid., p. 420.

morally abide. His moral understanding of the possible significance of murders, such as the ones he depicted, was flawed, and he was condemned for promoting it. But that defect was also an aesthetic defect, inasmuch as it compromised the novel on its own terms.[59]

The structure of Carroll's argument for moderate moralism can be captured like this:

1   The perspective of a work in question is immoral.
2   The immorality portrayed subverts the possibility of uptake by a morally sensitive audience. (In the parallel case of tragedy, the response of pity is precluded.)
3   Any work which subverts the possibility of uptake by a morally sensitive audience would subvert the work *qua* work of art and is aesthetically defective.
4   Therefore, the work in question is aesthetically defective.[60]

The argument is subtle and has generated much debate, but it is far from clear that it establishes the strong position that in some cases a moral defect actually *is* an aesthetic defect.[61] After all, the aesthetic defect arises from a mismatch of aim and response, the ethical defect arises from a flawed ethical stance, so the bases of the two defects are distinct. Also by introducing the idea of a "morally sensitive audience" Carroll makes the question of response normative. The suggestion seems to be that the right kind of audience *ought* not to pursue the uptake invited. Then the question is what the standard should be for appropriate uptake. Might not the "right" audience be less one that is morally sensitive, more one that is sensitive to *literature*? It would beg the question to presume that the ideal reader of literature, one best able to recognize literary value, must have a heightened moral sensibility. Perhaps the ideal reader (like Hume's "true judge") is someone able to set aside his or her own moral beliefs to enter the world of the work, someone who is not morally squeamish.

---

[59]   Noël Carroll, "Moderate Moralism," *British Journal of Aesthetics*, vol. 36, no. 3 (1996), pp. 223–238 at p. 232.

[60]   This version of the argument is derived from James Anderson and Jeffrey Dean, "Moderate Autonomism," *British Journal of Aesthetics*, vol. 38, no. 2 (1998), pp. 150–166 at pp. 156–157, and George Dickie, "The Triumph in *Triumph of the Will*," *British Journal of Aesthetics*, vol. 45, no. 2 (2005), pp. 151–156 at pp. 151–152.

[61]   This is the objection of Anderson and Dean in "Moderate Autonomism," and Dickie in "The Triumph in *Triumph of the Will*."

According to a position labeled "immoralism" "there can be, and indeed are, works whose value as art is enhanced in virtue of, rather than despite of, their morally defective character."[62] Arguably, too much moral sensitivity might blunt a critic to the appreciation of such works. It has even been suggested that Carroll's own example of a morally reprehensible and aesthetically flawed work, *American Psycho*, might be open to reappraisal. The critic Anthony Lane comments: "Now, at a distance, the book reads better than it did; it feels lit with a kind of cold hellfire, and Ellis has become our most assiduous tour guide ... to the netherworld of the nineteen-eighties." The hero of the novel "is a type taken to the limit, and, if his story did not offend us, then Ellis ... would not be doing [his] job."[63]

It should be noted that Carroll's moralism is similar to, but not identical with, Hume's. Hume, we recall from a passage quoted earlier, holds that: "where vicious manners are described, *without being marked with the proper characters of blame and disapprobation*; this must be allowed to disfigure the poem, and to be a real deformity" (emphasis added). It is not the "vicious manners" themselves that disfigure the poem but the fact that they are endorsed (or not disavowed) by the poet. But in Carroll's example, Brett Easton Ellis is not actively promoting serial murder, only using it as a satirical device. Admittedly he doesn't show obvious "disapprobation," but that is not the focus for Carroll's uptake argument, which highlights instead Ellis's failure to elicit the required response in his aim that readers should view gruesome killing as somehow humorous. In other respects, though, Carroll is close to Hume, who writes: "I cannot, nor is it proper I should, enter into such sentiments." The key to the uptake argument is that sometimes readers are unable or unwilling to engage imaginatively with an author's project, and on such occasions uptake fails and an aesthetic flaw results.

Set in this context, though, it seems as if morality is not the crucial issue so much as imaginability. Any work that is implausible or fantastical to a degree that readers cannot engage with it is an artistic failure. That "vicious manners" – rather than, say, a fantastical portrayal of a race of people or a weird kind of building – should prompt such a failure does not change the character of the artistic failure. Arguably, there is nothing special about immorality in explaining failure of this kind. In fact, underlying this kind of failure is a criterion centrally associated with literary value, namely coherence.

[62] Matthew Kieran, "Forbidden Knowledge: The Challenge of Immoralism," in J. Bermudez and S. Gardner, eds., *Art and Morality* (London: Routledge, 2003), p. 72. See also D. Jacobson, "In Praise of Immoral Art," *Philosophical Topics*, vol. 25, no. 1 (1997), pp. 155–199.

[63] Anthony Lane, "To the Limit," *The New Yorker*, April 17, 2000. Quoted in Daniel Jacobson, "Ethical Criticism and the Vice of Moderation," in M. Kieran, ed., *Contemporary Debates in Aesthetics and the Philosophy of Art* (Oxford: Blackwell, 2006), p. 353.

A work might be simply incoherent if it portrays states of affairs, immoral or otherwise, that are unimaginable or utterly implausible.[64]

However, there is a debate closely related to Carroll's that does seem to suggest there is something special about the immorality cases with respect to imaginability. This is the so-called "puzzle of imaginative resistance."[65] Philosophers have been puzzled by what looks like an asymmetry between kinds of imagining: imagining physical variations in the world and imagining moral variations. While there is little difficulty in, and little resistance to, imagining wildly bizarre and fantastical physical departures from reality (in sci fi, fantasy, etc.), it can sometimes seem more difficult, more open to resistance, to imagine extreme moral deviations from moral norms. Once again, Hume is thought to have noticed some such asymmetry:

> Whatever speculative errors may be found in the polite writings of any age or country, they detract but little from the value of those compositions. There needs but a certain turn of thought or imagination to make us enter into all the opinions, which then prevailed, and relish the sentiments or conclusions derived from them. But a very violent effort is requisite to change our judgment of manners, and excite sentiments of approbation or blame, love or hatred, different from those to which the mind from long custom has been familiarized. And where a man is confident of the rectitude of that moral standard, by which he judges, he is justly jealous of it, and will not pervert the sentiments of his heart for a moment, in complaisance to any writer whatsoever.[66]

This is an observation about what we are prepared to tolerate in literature from distant times and lands. For Hume it can be harder to stomach alien morals than alien science. But where exactly is the "puzzle"? If it rests just on the psychological fact that some people find some things more or less difficult to imagine then it does not seem of much philosophical interest.

---

[64] Matthew Kieran has proposed a criterion of "intelligibility": "The quality of the imaginative experience afforded by a narrative concerns its value as art and is, in part, a function of how intelligible that experience is. Intelligibility is thus internal to the evaluation of a work as art." See Matthew Kieran, "In Defence of the Ethical Evaluation of Narrative Art," *British Journal of Aesthetics*, vol. 41, no. 1 (2001), pp. 26–38 at p. 35.

[65] Tamar Szabó Gendler, "The Puzzle of Imaginative Resistance," *Journal of Philosophy*, vol. 97, no. 2 (2000); Kendall Walton, "Morals in Fiction and Fictional Morality," *Proceedings of the Aristotelian Society*, suppl. vol. LXVIII (1994); Richard Moran, "The Expression of Feeling in Imagination," *Philosophical Review*, vol. 103, no. 1 (1994); Derek Matravers, "Fictional Assent and the (so-called) 'Puzzle of Imaginative Resistance,'" in M. Kieran and D. Lopes, eds., *Imagination, Philosophy, and the Arts* (London: Routledge, 2003).

[66] Hume, "Of the Standard of Taste," p. 283.

It is sometimes taken to be an issue about the limits of imagination. Can we imagine what is logically impossible? It is often thought that the limits of imaginability are the limits of conceivability, although even that is disputed.[67] But does imagining a morally deviant world, a world in which our cherished norms are reversed or mocked, demand something inconceivable? For Hume such imagining is not impossible but requires a "very violent effort." Again, it is important to distinguish works that merely present morally repugnant characters – Posner reminds us how many there are in the literary tradition – and those that approve their actions or endorse their attitudes. For Hume only the latter are blameworthy. Yet from a reader's point of view, *imagining* endorsing disagreeable attitudes is not the same as actually doing so.

Is there, though, anything special about the immorality cases? There are plenty of things that readers resist imagining, for all kinds of reasons: too improbable, frightening, repulsive, absurd, boring, badly expressed. There is no compelling evidence that resistance is always stronger on moral matters, that "too immoral" will always stand out in such a list. A further question is whether resistance to morally deviant fictions rests on an *inability* to imagine or an *unwillingness* to do so. The latter is weaker. There might be many reasons, as listed, why readers are unwilling to imagine what a work prescribes. Likewise, an inability to imagine something might also have many sources, from incoherent content to a reader's imaginative impoverishment. That brings us back to value considerations and the uptake argument. Clearly a reader who refuses to go on reading – for whatever reason – is making an implicit (negative) value judgment. And readers who cannot imagine something because it exceeds the limits of their imagination also fail in uptake. We can, then, concede the presence of imaginative resistance, in some cases, and it can be connected to literary value, but its sources seem far more varied than suggested by any simple dichotomy between the physical and the moral.

## Ethicism and merited response

The "merited response" argument does rest crucially on the immoral viewpoint being endorsed or prescribed by the author. Berys Gaut uses the argument in defense of a view he calls "ethicism," defined as follows:

> the ethical assessment of attitudes manifested by works of art is a legitimate aspect of the aesthetic evaluation of those works, such that, if a work manifests

---

[67]  For a useful discussion, see Kathleen Stock, "The Tower of Goldbach and Other Impossible Tales," in M. Kieran and D. Lopes, eds., *Imagination, Philosophy, and the Arts* (London: Routledge, 2003).

ethically reprehensible attitudes, it is to that extent aesthetically defective, and if a work manifests ethically commendable attitudes, it is to that extent aesthetically meritorious …[68]

Here is a summarized version of Gaut's argument:

1  Prescribed responses to art works are subject to evaluation.
2  Some of the evaluative criteria for prescribed responses are ethical ones.
3  If a work prescribes a response that is unmerited, then the work has to that extent failed *qua* work of art.
4  Any defect in a work of art *qua* work of art is an aesthetic defect.
5  Therefore, ethical defects are aesthetic defects.[69]

Merited responses take different forms: "tragedies which do not merit fear and pity, horror films which do not merit horror, comedies which do not merit amusement, and so on, all fail aesthetically."[70] An issue parallel to that of immoral art concerns jokes, notably whether offensive or vicious jokes can succeed *as jokes*. The merited response line suggests not.[71] Yet some would argue that a joke succeeds, as a joke, simply if it is funny and people are amused by it; whether they *ought* to be amused, whether the joke "merits" the response, is beside the point.[72] On the specifically moral application of the merited response view a work fails aesthetically if it prescribes a response that is immoral, e.g., being amused by sadistic cruelty.[73]

The trouble is there are genres of fiction that deliberately, and arguably innocently, make light of sadistic cruelty and we laugh at it. An obvious case would be cartoons: when Tom beats Jerry into the ground with a mallet until he disappears we are intended to laugh, and do so. It would be absurd to think there was an aesthetic failure here because laughing at sadistic cruelty is unmerited. But it is not uncommon for fiction to suspend conventions of

---

[68]  Berys Gaut, "The Ethical Criticism of Art," in Jerrold Levinson, ed., *Aesthetics and Ethics* (Cambridge: Cambridge University Press, 1998), pp. 182–203 at p. 182.

[69]  Taken from Anderson and Dean, "Moderate Autonomism," p. 158.

[70]  Berys Gaut, "Art and Ethics," in B. Gaut and D. Lopes, eds., *The Routledge Companion to Aesthetics* (London: Routledge, 2001), p. 351.

[71]  Berys Gaut has explicitly applied ethicism to jokes, arguing that "ethically bad attitudes tend to diminish or undercut the funniness of a joke: the joke is flawed," in "Just Joking: The Ethics and Aesthetics of Humor," *Philosophy and Literature*, vol. 22, no. 1 (1998), pp. 51–68 at p. 64.

[72]  For a discussion of the morality of jokes, see Jacobson, "In Praise of Immoral Art"; and Ted Cohen, *Jokes: Philosophical Thoughts on Joking Matters* (Chicago: University of Chicago Press, 1999), ch. 6.

[73]  Gaut, "The Ethical Criticism of Art," p. 192.

propriety that hold in the real world. When Bertie Wooster steals a silver jug for his Aunt Dahlia to get out of a predicament we urge him on imaginatively, as the author encourages us to do. Does that mean we are endorsing stealing and dishonesty? Is our gleeful response immoral and thus unmerited? Worse still, is there a flaw in the work? With these consequences the argument itself seems flawed.

Another objection sometimes raised to Gaut's ethicism is that premise 4, "Any defect in a work of art *qua* work of art is an aesthetic defect," is unsubstantiated.[74] Aesthetic defects might seem better limited to formal or structural features of a work, among which prescribed unmerited responses would surely not be included. Gaut himself simply stipulates that he is using "aesthetic value" to encompass any value of an object *qua* work of art. Our interest is in the intrinsic values of literature *qua* literature, and even if we grant the broadening of the aesthetic to include the artistic more generally it is not proven that a literary work fails *as literature* when it prescribes a response that is immoral. A work might deliberately set out to flout conventional morality and might gain its impact as literature from its use of powerful imaginative resources to that end. The work might be "shocking" or "dangerous" but not obviously a literary failure in the way that, admittedly, a tragedy fails if it is not tragic, or a horror story if it is not horrific. These latter cases can be conceded as literary failures (on the assumption, of course, that the initial interpretive construal as "tragedy" and "horror" can be sustained). Ethicism is convincing only if moral propriety is already accepted as an overriding literary constraint; but of course that is hopelessly circular.

### *Moralism and formalism*: *rejecting the choice*

The debate over versions of moralism has been extensively pursued; the problems raised are far from decisive. Although the argument has been focused on positions with labels like "moderate moralism" and "moderate autonomism," there is always a tendency to abandon moderation in favor of sharper divides. The divide between formalism on the one hand and species of moralism on the other can seem unbreachable, with two clear visions of literary value:

> The first insists that the preservation of literary value rests on the containment of literature as an autonomous and non-cognitive discourse, made safe from the encroachments of political or moral or commercial interests and defended through a formalist criticism with its own rigorous methodologies. The second acknowledges that literary texts have ethical and cognitive values

---

[74]  E.g., Dickie, "The Triumph in *Triumph of the Will*."

and effects in the world, and that they must therefore be defended through containment within a minority culture serviced by an appropriately trained clerisy.[75]

Thus when Posner attacks ethical criticism, he seeks to replace it with "aestheticism" of a Wildean kind,[76] asserting that "the moral content of … a work of literature has little to do either with the value of the work … or with the pleasure to be derived from the work."[77]

But we are not forced to choose between formalism and moralism. Posner's claim that moral content has little to do with the value of literature is surely extraordinary if taken literally. The great works of literature are full of "moral content," but it doesn't follow that they are engaged in moral education or that they must be valued for the lessons they impart.

The great canonical works afford immense pleasure to those who know and love them. They are monuments to the enduring human effort at revealing and understanding our deepest concerns about what it is to be human. To value them in their own right, as literary not scientific or philosophic explorations of these concerns, is to recognize them first and foremost as works of art. Few cultures have not had their own literary traditions, oral or written, and those story-telling or poetic traditions have helped sustain the identity of the cultures in question, not to say the very possibility of their being cultures in the first place.

## Supplementary Readings

On the idea of artistic value, with some but not exclusive reference to literature, see R. W. Beardsmore, *Art and Morality* (London: Macmillan, 1971); Eva Schaper, ed., *Pleasure Preference and Value: Studies in Philosophical Aesthetics* (Cambridge: Cambridge University Press, 1983); George Dickie, *Evaluating Art* (Philadelphia, PA: Temple University Press, 1988); Malcolm Budd, *Values of Art: Pictures, Poetry and Music* (Harmondsworth: Penguin Press, 1995); Alan Goldman, *Aesthetic Value* (Boulder, CO: Westview Press, 1995); Stephen Davies, ed., *Art and Its Messages* (University Park, PA: Penn State University Press, 1997).

---

[75]   Patricia Waugh, "Value: Criticism, Canons, and Evaluation," in Patricia Waugh, ed., *Literary Theory and Criticism* (Oxford: Oxford University Press, 2006), p. 78.

[76]   He often quotes Oscar Wilde's well known dictum from the Preface of *Picture of Dorian Gray*, that "there is no such thing as a moral or immoral book. Books are well written, or badly written. That is all."

[77]   Posner, "Against Ethical Criticism: Part Two," p. 394.

For philosophical treatments of literary values in particular, see
D. Z. Phillips, *Through a Darkening Glass: Philosophy Literature and Cultural
Change* (Oxford: Blackwell, 1982); Peter Lamarque and Stein Haugom
Olsen, *Truth, Fiction, and Literature: A Philosophical Perspective* (Oxford:
Clarendon Press, 1994); Peter Lamarque, *Fictional Points of View* (Ithaca,
NY: Cornell University Press, 1996); Peter Kivy, *Performance of Reading: An
Essay in the Philosophy of Literature* (Oxford: Blackwell, 2006).

For discussions of the literary canon from a literary critical perspective,
see Harold Bloom, *The Western Canon: The Books and Schools of the Ages* (New
York: Riverhead Books, 1994); John Guillory, *Cultural Capital: The Problem of
Literary Canon Formation* (Chicago: Chicago University Press, 1995); Robert
Alter, *Canon and Creativity: Modern Writing and the Authority of Scripture* (New
Haven, CT: Yale University Press, 2000); Lynette Hunter, *Literary Value /
Cultural Power: Verbal Arts in the Twenty-First Century* (Manchester: Manchester
University Press, 2002); Frank Kermode, *Pleasure and Change: The Aesthetics of
Canon* (New York: Oxford University Press, 2004).

On literature and ethics or ethical criticism, see Wayne C. Booth, *The
Company We Keep: An Ethics of Fiction* (Berkeley: University of California Press,
1989); Martha Nussbaum, *Poetic Justice: The Literary Imagination and Public Life*
(Boston, MA: Beacon Press, 1995); Richard A. Posner, *Law and Literature*
(Cambridge, MA: Harvard University Press; rev. and updated ed., 1998);
Colin McGinn, *Ethics, Evil, and Fiction* (New York: Oxford University Press,
1999); Jerrold Levinson, ed., *Aesthetics and Ethics: Essays at the Intersection*
(Cambridge: Cambridge University Press, 2001); Berys Gaut, *Art, Emotion,
and Ethics* (Oxford: Clarendon Press, 2007).

# Bibliography

The items listed below are those cited in the notes. (Additional readings, in the form of books not articles, are given at the end of each chapter.)

M. H. Abrams, *The Mirror and the Lamp: Romantic Theory and the Critical Tradition* (Oxford: Oxford University Press, 1953)

M. H. Abrams, "Structure and Style in the Greater Romantic Lyric," in *Sensibility to Romanticism: Essays Presented to Frederick A. Pottle*, ed. Frederick W. Hilles and Harold Bloom (New Haven, CT: Yale University Press, 1965)

M. H. Abrams, E. T. Donaldson, et al., eds., *The Norton Anthology of English Literature*, 4th ed., Vols. 1 and 2 (New York: W. W. Norton, 1979)

Thomas Adajian, "On the Cluster Account of Art," *British Journal of Aesthetics*, vol. 43, no. 4 (2003), pp. 379–385

Robert Alter, *Canon and Creativity: Modern Writing and the Authority of Scripture* (New Haven, CT: Yale University Press, 2000)

James Anderson and Jeffrey Dean, "Moderate Autonomism," *British Journal of Aesthetics*, vol. 38, no. 2 (1998), pp. 150–166

G. E. M. Anscombe, *Intention* (Oxford: Blackwell, 1959)

Aristotle, *The Complete Works of Aristotle: The Revised Oxford Translation*, ed. Jonathan Barnes, 2 vols. (Princeton, NJ: Princeton University Press, 1984)

J. L. Austin, *How to Do Things with Words* (Oxford: Oxford University Press, 2nd rev. ed., 1976)

Annette Barnes, *On Interpretation* (Oxford: Blackwell, 1988)

Roland Barthes, *The Pleasure of the Text* (*Le Plaisir du texte* [Paris: Seuil, 1975]), trans. R. Miller (London: Cape, 1976)

Roland Barthes, "The Death of the Author," in *Image-Music-Text*, Essays Selected and Translated by Stephen Heath (London: Fontana/Collins, 1977)

Roland Barthes, "From Work to Text," in *Image-Music-Text*, Essays Selected and Translated by Stephen Heath (London: Fontana/Collins, 1977)

Roland Barthes, "The Reality Effect," in *The Rustle of Language*, trans. Richard Howard (Oxford: Blackwell, 1986)

Monroe C. Beardsley, *The Possibility of Criticism* (Detroit, MI: Wayne State University Press, 1970)

Monroe C. Beardsley, "Aesthetic Intentions and Fictive Illocutions," in Paul Hernadi, ed., *What Is Literature?* (Bloomington: Indiana University Press, 1978)

Monroe C. Beardsley, *Aesthetics: Problems in the Philosophy of Criticism*, 2nd ed. (Indianapolis, IN: Hackett, 1981)

Monroe C. Beardsley, "Fiction as Representation," *Synthese*, 46 (1981), pp. 291–314

Monroe C. Beardsley, "Intentions and Interpretations: A Fallacy Revived," in *The Aesthetic Point of View*, ed. Michael J. Wreen and Donald M. Callen (Ithaca, NY: Cornell University Press, 1982)

Monroe C. Beardsley, "The Concept of Literature," in Eileen John and Dominic McIver Lopes, eds., *Philosophy of Literature: Contemporary and Classic Readings: An Anthology* (Oxford: Blackwell, 2004)

R. W. Beardsmore, *Art and Morality* (London: Macmillan, 1971)

R. W. Beardsmore, "Learning from a Novel," *Philosophy and the Arts, Royal Institute of Philosophy Lectures,* Vol. 6, 1971–1972 (London: Macmillan, 1973)

Catherine Belsey, *Critical Practice* (London: Methuen, 1980)

Andrew Bennett, "Expressivity: The Romantic Theory of Authorship," in Patricia Waugh, ed., *An Oxford Guide to Literary Theory and Criticism* (Oxford: Oxford University Press, 2006)

Harold Bloom, *The Western Canon: The Books and School of the Ages* (New York: Riverhead Books, 1994)

Ronald Blythe, "Introduction," Jane Austen, *Emma* (Harmondsworth: Penguin, 1972)

Wayne C. Booth, *The Company We Keep: An Ethics of Fiction* (Berkeley: University of California Press, 1989)

Wayne C. Booth, "Why Banning Ethical Criticism Is a Serious Mistake," *Philosophy and Literature*, vol. 22, no. 2 (1998), pp. 366–393

Jorge Luis Borges, "Pierre Menard, Author of the *Quixote*," in *Labyrinths* (Harmondsworth: Penguin, 1971)

Bijoy Boruah, *Fiction and Emotion: A Study in Aesthetics and the Philosophy of Mind* (Oxford: Clarendon Press, 1988)

Pierre Bourdieu, *Distinction: A Social Critique of the Judgement of Taste* (London: Routledge, 1984)

A. C. Bradley, "Poetry for Poetry's Sake," in *Oxford Lectures on Poetry* (London: Macmillan, 1909)

Joseph Bristow, "'Churlsgrace': Gerard Manley Hopkins and the Working-Class Male Body," *English Literary History*, vol. 59, no. 3, Autumn (1992), pp. 693–711

Charlotte Brontë, *Jane Eyre*, ed. Richard J. Dunn (New York: W. W. Norton, 1971)

Cleanth Brooks, *The Well Wrought Urn: Studies in the Structure of Poetry* (London: Methuen, 1968)

Malcolm Budd, *Values of Art: Pictures, Poetry and Music* (Harmondsworth: Penguin, 1995)

Edward Bullough, "'Psychical Distance' as a Factor in Art and an Aesthetic Principle," *British Journal of Psychology*, vol. 5 (1912), pp. 87–117

Lord Byron, *The Poetical Works of Lord Byron* (London: Oxford University Press, 1928)

David Carrier, "Art Without Its Artists," *British Journal of Aesthetics*, vol. 22, vol. 3 (1982), pp. 233–244

Noël Carroll, *The Philosophy of Horror, or Paradoxes of the Heart* (New York: Routledge, Chapman, and Hall, 1990)

Noël Carroll, "Moderate Moralism," *British Journal of Aesthetics*, vol. 36, no. 3 (1996), pp. 223–238

Noël Carroll, "Moderate Moralism versus Moderate Autonomism," *British Journal of Aesthetics*, vol. 38, no. 4 (1998), pp. 419–424

Noël Carroll, "Art and Aesthetic Experience," ch. 4 of *Philosophy of Art* (London and New York: Routledge, 1999)

Noël Carroll, "Interpretation and Intention: The Debate between Hypothetical and Actual Intentionalism," in *Beyond Aesthetics: Philosophical Essays* (Cambridge: Cambridge University Press, 2001)

Noël Carroll, "Art, Intention, and Conversation," in *Beyond Aesthetics: Philosophical Essays* (Cambridge: Cambridge University Press, 2001)

Noël Carroll, "Four Concepts of Aesthetic Experience," in *Beyond Aesthetics: Philosophical Essays* (Cambridge: Cambridge University Press, 2001)

Noël Carroll, "Art, Narrative, and Moral Understanding," in *Beyond Aesthetics: Philosophical Essays* (Cambridge: Cambridge University Press, 2001)

Noël Carroll, "Simulations, Emotions, and Morality," in *Beyond Aesthetics: Philosophical Essays* (Cambridge: Cambridge University Press, 2001)

Noël Carroll, "The Wheel of Virtue: Art, Literature, and Moral Knowledge," *Journal of Aesthetics and Art Criticism*, vol. 60, no. 1 (2002), pp. 3–26

Stanley Cavell, *Must We Mean What We Say?* (Cambridge: Cambridge University Press, 1976)

William Charlton, "Feeling for the Fictitious," *British Journal of Aesthetics*, vol. 24, no. 3 (1984), pp. 206–216

Frank Cioffi, "Intention and Interpretation in Criticism," in David Newton-de Molina, ed., *On Literary Intention* (Edinburgh: Edinburgh University Press, 1976)

A. J. Close, "*Don Quixote* and the 'Intentionalist Fallacy,'" *British Journal of Aesthetics*, vol. 12, no. 1 (1972), pp. 19–39

P. S. Churchland, *Neurophilosophy: Toward a Unified Science of the Mind/Brain* (Cambridge, MA: MIT Press, 1986)

Ted Cohen, *Jokes: Philosophical Thoughts on Joking Matters* (Chicago: University of Chicago Press, 1999)

Samuel Taylor Coleridge, *Biographia Literaria* (1817) in *The Collected Works of Samuel Taylor Coleridge*, Vol. 7, ed. James Engell and W. Jackson Bate (Princeton, NJ: Princeton University Press, 1985)

R. G. Collingwood, *The Principles of Art* (Oxford: Clarendon Press, 1938)

W. A. Craik, "Emma," in Jane Austen, *Emma*, ed. Stephen M. Parrish (New York: W. W. Norton, 1972)

Charles Crittenden, *Unreality: The Metaphysics of Fictional Objects* (Ithaca, NY: Cornell University Press, 1991)

Jonathan Culler, *Structuralist Poetics: Structuralism, Linguistics and the Study of Literature* (London: Routledge, 1975)

Valentine Cunningham, "Theory, What Theory?" in D. Patai and W. Corral, eds., *Theory's Empire* (New York: Columbia University Press, 2005)

Gregory Currie, *An Ontology of Art* (Basingstoke: Macmillan, 1989)

Gregory Currie, "What Is Fiction?" *Journal of Aesthetics and Art Criticism*, vol. 43, no. 4 (1985), pp. 385–392

Gregory Currie, *The Nature of Fiction* (Cambridge: Cambridge University Press, 1990)

Gregory Currie, "Work and Text," *Mind*, vol. 100, no. 3 (1991), pp. 325–340

Gregory Currie, "Imagination and Simulation: Aesthetics Meets Cognitive Science," in M. Davies and T. Stone, eds., *Mental Simulation* (Oxford: Blackwell, 1995)

Gregory Currie, "Anne Brontë and the Uses of Imagination," in Matthew Kieran, ed., *Contemporary Debates in Aesthetics and the Philosophy of Art* (Oxford: Blackwell, 2005)

E. M. Dadlez, *What's Hecuba to Him? Fictional Events and Actual Emotions* (Philadelphia, PA: Penn State University Press, 1997)

Arthur C. Danto, *The Transfiguration of the Commonplace* (Cambridge, MA: Harvard University Press, 1981)

Arthur C. Danto, "The Artworld," in Peter Lamarque and Stein Haugom Olsen, eds., *Aesthetics and the Philosophy of Art* (Oxford: Blackwell, 2004). Originally published in *Journal of Philosophy*, 61 (1964), pp. 571–584

Arthur C. Danto, *The Philosophical Disenfranchisement of Art* (New York: Columbia University Press, 1986)

Donald Davidson, "What Metaphors Mean," in Sheldon Sacks, ed., *On Metaphor* (Chicago: University of Chicago Press, 1978)

David Davies, *Art as Performance* (Oxford: Blackwell, 2004)

Stephen Davies, *Definitions of Art* (Ithaca, NY: Cornell University Press, 1991)

Stephen Davies, "Relativism in Interpretation," *Journal of Aesthetics and Art Criticism*, vol. 53, no. 1, Winter (1995), pp. 8–13

Stephen Davies, "The Cluster Theory of Art," *British Journal of Aesthetics*, vol. 44, no. 3 (2004), pp. 297–300

Stephen Davies, "Authors' Intentions, Literary Interpretation, and Literary Value," *British Journal of Aesthetics*, vol. 46, no. 3 (2006), pp. 223–247

Charles Dickens, *Our Mutual Friend* (1865) (New York: Signet, 1964)

Charles Dickens, *Bleak House* (1853), ed. George Ford and Sylvère Monod (New York: W. W. Norton, 1977)

George Dickie, *Art and the Aesthetic: An Institutional Analysis* (Ithaca, NY: Cornell University Press, 1974)

George Dickie, *The Art Circle* (New York: Haven, 1984)

George Dickie, *Introduction to Aesthetics: An Analytic Approach* (Oxford: Oxford University Press, 1997)

George Dickie, "The Triumph in *Triumph of the Will*," *British Journal of Aesthetics*, vol. 45, no. 2 (2005), pp. 151–156

T. J. Diffey, "The Roots of Imagination: The Philosophical Context," in Stephen Prickett, ed., *The Romantics: The Context of English Literature* (London: Methuen, 1981)

Julian Dodd, "Musical Works as Eternal Types," *British Journal of Aesthetics*, vol. 40, no. 4 (October 2000), pp. 424–440

Julian Dodd, "Defending Musical Platonism," *British Journal of Aesthetics*, vol. 42, no. 4 (October 2002), pp. 380–402

Jonathan Dollimore, "*King Lear* and Essentialist Humanism," in John Drakakis, ed., *Shakespearean Tragedy* (London: Longman, 1992)

Robert Alan Donovan, "The Two Heroines of *Moll Flanders*," in *Moll Flanders*, Norton Critical Edition, ed. Edward Kelly (New York: W. W. Norton, 1973), p. 403. Originally published in *The Shaping Vision: Imagination in the English Novel from Defoe to Dickens* (Ithaca: NY: Cornell University Press, 1966)

Denis Dutton, "'But They Don't Have Our Concept of Art,'" in Noël Carroll, ed., *Theories of Art Today* (Madison: University of Wisconsin Press, 2000), pp. 217–238

Ronald Dworkin, *Law's Empire* (London: Fontana Press, 1986)

Terry Eagleton, *Myths of Power: A Marxist Study of the Brontës* (London: Macmillan, 1975)

Terry Eagleton, *Literary Theory: An Introduction* (Oxford: Blackwell, 1983)

Terry Eagleton, *The Ideology of the Aesthetic* (Oxford: Basil Blackwell, 1990)

Terry Eagleton, *After Theory* (London: Allen Lane, 2003)

Marcia Muelder Eaton, "Art and the Aesthetic," in Peter Kivy, ed., *Blackwell Guide to Aesthetics* (Oxford: Blackwell, 2003)

Umberto Eco et al., *Interpretation and Overinterpretation*, ed. Stefan Collini (Cambridge: Cambridge University Press, 1992)

T. S. Eliot, "Tradition and the Individual Talent," in David Lodge, ed., *20th Century Literary Criticism* (London: Longman, 1972)

John M. Ellis, *The Theory of Literary Criticism: A Logical Analysis* (Berkeley: University of California Press, 1974)

William Empson, *Seven Types of Ambiguity* (London: Chatto and Windus, 2nd ed., 1947)

Jeanette Emt, "On the Nature of Fictional Entities," in J. Emt and G. Hermerén, eds., *Understanding the Arts: Contemporary Scandinavian Aesthetics* (Lund: Lund University Press, 1992)

Victor Erlich, *Russian Formalism: History-Doctrine* (The Hague: Mouton, rev. ed., 1965)

Susan Feagin, *Reading with Feeling: The Aesthetics of Appreciation* (Ithaca, NY: Cornell University Press, 1996)

Leslie Fielder, "'Come Back to the Raft Ag'in, Huck, Honey,'" in *An Age of Innocence* (Boston, MA: Beacon Press, 1966)

Stanley Fish, *Is There a Text in This Class? The Authority of Interpretive Communities* (Cambridge, MA: Harvard University Press, 1980)

Stanley Fish, *There's No Such Thing as Free Speech, and It's a Good Thing Too* (New York: Oxford University Press, 1994)

Michel Foucault, "What Is an Author?" in *The Foucault Reader*, ed. Paul Rabinow (Harmondsworth: Peregrine Books, 1986)

Marilyn French, "The Late Tragedies," in John Drakakis, ed., *Shakespearean Tragedy* (London: Longman, 1992). Originally published in *Shakespeare's Division of Experience* (London: Abacus, 1982), pp. 219–251

Paul L. Garvin, ed. and trans., *A Prague School Reader on Aesthetics, Literary Structure and Style* (Washington, DC: Georgetown University Press, 1964)

Berys Gaut, "The Ethical Criticism of Art," in Jerrold Levinson, ed., *Aesthetics and Ethics* (Cambridge: Cambridge University Press, 1998), pp. 182–203

Berys Gaut, "Just Joking: The Ethics and Aesthetics of Humor," *Philosophy and Literature* 22.1 (1998), pp. 51–68

Berys Gaut, "'Art' as a Cluster Concept," in N. Carroll, ed., *Theories of Art Today* (Madison: University of Wisconsin Press, 2000), pp. 25–44

Berys Gaut, "Art and Ethics," in B. Gaut and D. Lopes, eds., *The Routledge Companion to Aesthetics* (London: Routledge, 2001)

Berys Gaut, "Art and Knowledge," in Jerrold Levinson, ed., *The Oxford Handbook of Aesthetics* (Oxford: Oxford University Press, 2003)

Berys Gaut, "The Cluster Account of Art Defended," *British Journal of Aesthetics*, vol. 45, no. 3 (2005), pp. 273–288

Berys Gaut, "Art and Cognition," in Matthew Kieran, ed., *Contemporary Debates in Aesthetics and the Philosophy of Art* (Oxford: Blackwell, 2006)

Tamar Szabó Gendler, "The Puzzle of Imaginative Resistance," *Journal of Philosophy*, vol. 97, no. 2 (2000), pp. 55–81

John Gibson, "Between Truth and Triviality," *British Journal of Aesthetics*, vol. 43, no. 3 (2003), pp. 224–237

Nelson Goodman, "About," *Mind*, 70 (1961), pp. 1–24

Nelson Goodman, *The Languages of Art* (New York: Bobbs-Merrill, 1968)

Nelson Goodman, "Fiction for Five Fingers," *Philosophy and Literature*, vol. 6, nos. 1/2 (1982), pp. 162–164

Nelson Goodman, *Of Mind and Other Matters* (Cambridge, MA: Harvard University Press, 1984)

Nelson Goodman and Catherine Elgin, "Interpretation and Identity: Can the Work Survive the World?" in Eileen John and Dominic McIver Lopes, eds., *Philosophy of Literature: Contemporary and Classic Readings: An Anthology* (Oxford: Blackwell, 2004). Originally published in *Critical Inquiry*, 12 (1986), pp. 567–574

Gordon Graham, *Philosophy of the Arts: An Introduction to Aesthetics* (London and New York: Routledge, 1997)

André Green, "*Othello*: A Tragedy of Conversion: Black Magic and White Magic," in John Drakakis, ed., *Shakespearean Tragedy* (London: Longman, 1992)

Stephen Greenblatt, *Will in the World: How Shakespeare Became Shakespeare* (New York: W. W. Norton, 2004)

Thomas M. Greene, "Spenser and the Epithalamic Convention," in *Edmund Spenser's Poetry*, sel. and ed. Hugh Maclean (New York: W. W. Norton, 1968)

H. P. Grice, "Meaning," *Philosophical Review*, vol. 66, no. 3 (1957), pp. 377–388; reprinted in *Studies in the Way of Words* (Cambridge, MA: Harvard University Press, 1989)

H. P. Grice, "Utterer's Meaning and Intentions," *Philosophical Review*, 78 (1969), pp. 147–177; reprinted in *Studies in the Way of Words* (Cambridge, MA: Harvard University Press, 1989)

H. P. Grice, *Studies in the Way of Words* (Cambridge, MA: Harvard University Press, 1989)

E. Gron, "Defending Thought Theory from a Make-Believe Threat," *British Journal of Aesthetics*, vol 36, no. 3 (1996), pp. 311–312

Bernard Harrison, *Inconvenient Fictions* (New Haven, CT: Yale University Press, 1991)

W. J. Harvey, "The Double Narrative of *Bleak House*," in Charles Dickens, *Bleak House*, ed. George Ford and Sylvère Monod (New York: W. W. Norton, 1977)

Terence Hawkes, *Structuralism and Semiotics* (London: Methuen, 1977)

G. W. F. Hegel, *Introductory Lectures on Aesthetics*, trans. Bernard Bosanquet, ed. with an introduction and commentary by Michael Inwood (Harmondsworth: Penguin Books, 1993)

Barbara Herrnstein Smith, *Contingencies of Value: Alternative Perspectives for Critical Theory* (Cambridge, MA: Harvard University Press, 1988)

E. D. Hirsch, Jr., *Validity in Interpretation* (New Haven, CT: Yale University Press, 1967)

Gerard Manley Hopkins, *The Poetical Works of Gerard Manley Hopkins*, ed. Norman H. Mackenzie (Oxford: Clarendon Press, 1990)

Horace, *Odes and Epodes*, trans. C. E. Bennett, Loeb Classical Library (London: William Heinemann, 1927)

John Hospers, "Literature and Human Nature," *Journal of Aesthetics and Art Criticism*, vol. 17, no. 1 (1958), pp. 45–57

John Hospers, "Implied Truths in Literature," *Journal of Aesthetics and Art Criticism*, vol. 19, no. 1 (1960–1961), pp. 37–46

A. E. Housman, *The Name and Nature of Poetry* (Cambridge: Cambridge University Press, 1933)

William G. Howard, ed., *Laokoon and Other Prose Writings: Lessing, Herder, Goethe* (New York: Henry Holt, 1910)

Irving Howe, "The Center of Hardy's Achievement," in Thomas Hardy, *Tess of the d'Urbervilles*, ed. Scott Elledge (New York: W. W. Norton, 1979)

Robert Howell, "Fictional Objects: How They Are and How They Aren't," *Poetics*, 8 (1979), pp. 129–177

David Hume, *The Philosophical Works of David Hume*, ed. T. H. Green and T. H. Grose (London: Longman, Green, 1874–1875), vol. 3

William Irwin, *Intentionalist Interpretation: A Philosophical Explanation and Defense* (Westport, CT: Greenwood, 1999)

Gary Iseminger, ed., *Intention and Interpretation* (Philadelphia, PA: Temple University Press, 1992)

Daniel Jacobson, "Ethical Criticism and the Vice of Moderation," in M. Kieran, ed., *Contemporary Debates in Aesthetics and the Philosophy of Art* (Oxford: Blackwell, 2006)

Daniel Jacobson, "In Praise of Immoral Art," *Philosophical Topics*, vol. 25, no. 1 (1997), pp. 155–199

Henry James, "The Art of Fiction," in *Longman's Magazine* 4 (September 1884), reprinted in *Partial Portraits* (London: Macmillan, 1888)

Christopher Janaway, "Borges and Danto: A Reply to Michael Wreen," *British Journal of Aesthetics*, vol. 32, no. 1 (1992), pp. 72–76

Alice A. Jardine, *Gynesis: Configurations of Woman and Modernity* (Ithaca, NY: Cornell University Press, 1985)

Eileen John, "Reading Fiction and Conceptual Knowledge: Philosophical Thought in Literary Context," *Journal of Aesthetics and Art Criticism*, vol. 56, no. 4 (1998), pp. 331–348

Eileen John and Dominic McIver Lopes, eds., *Philosophy of Literature: Contemporary and Classic Readings: An Anthology* (Oxford: Blackwell, 2004)

Samuel Johnson, *Preface to Shakespeare* (1755) in *Johnson on Shakespeare*, ed. Arthur Sherbo, Vol. VII, The Yale Edition of the Works of Samuel Johnson (New Haven, CT and London: Yale University Press, 1968)

Samuel Johnson, "The Life of Gray," in *Samuel Johnson: A Critical Edition of the Major Works*, ed. Donald Greene (Oxford: Oxford University Press, 1984)

Samuel Johnson, *Rasselas* (1759) in *Rasselas and Other Tales*, ed. Gwin J. Kolb, vol. XVI, The Yale Edition of the Works of Samuel Johnson (New Haven, CT: Yale University Press, 1990)

Samuel Johnson, "Prefaces to Shakespeare's Plays," in *Shakespeare: The Critical Heritage*, vol. 5, 1765–1774, ed. Brian Vickers (London: Routledge, 1974)

Richard Joyce, "Rational Fear of Monsters," *British Journal of Aesthetics*, vol. 40, no. 2 (2000), pp. 209–224

P. D. Juhl, *Interpretation: An Essay in the Philosophy of Literary Criticism* (Princeton, NJ: Princeton University Press, 1980)

Immanuel Kant, *Critique of Judgment*, trans. James Creed Meredith (Oxford: Clarendon Press, 1952)

John Keats, *Complete Poems of John Keats* (New York: Random House, 1994)

William Kenrick, comments on Dr. Johnson, in *Shakespeare: The Critical Heritage*, vol. 5, 1765–1774, ed. Brian Vickers (London: Routledge, 1974)

Arnold Kettle, "In Defence of *Moll Flanders*," in *Moll Flanders*, Norton Critical Edition, ed. Edward Kelly (New York: W. W. Norton, 1973), p. 395. Originally published in *Of Books and Humankind*, ed. John Butt (London: Routledge, 1964), pp. 55–67

Matthew Kieran, "In Defence of the Ethical Evaluation of Narrative Art," *British Journal of Aesthetics*, vol. 41, no. 1 (2001), pp. 26–38

Matthew Kieran, "Forbidden Knowledge: The Challenge of Immoralism," in J. Bermudez and S. Gardner, eds., *Art and Morality* (London: Routledge, 2003)

Matthew Kieran and Dominic McIver Lopes, eds., *Imagination, Philosophy and the Arts* (London: Routledge, 2003)

Frank Kermode, *Pleasure and Change: The Aesthetics of Canon* (New York: Oxford University Press, 2004)

Peter Kivy, *Speaking of Art* (The Hague: Martinus Nijhoff, 1973)

Peter Kivy, "Platonism in Music: A Kind of Defense," *Grazer philosophische Studien*, vol. 19 (1983), pp. 109–129, reprinted in Peter Kivy, *The Fine Art of Repetition: Essays in the Philosophy of Music* (Cambridge: Cambridge University Press, 1993), pp. 35–58

Peter Kivy, "Platonism in Music: Another Kind of Defense," *American Philosophical Quarterly*, vol. 24, no. 3 (July 1987), pp. 245–252 (reprinted in Kivy, *The Fine Art of Repetition*, pp. 59–74)

Peter Kivy, "The Laboratory of Fictional Truth," in *Philosophies of Arts: An Essay in Differences* (Cambridge: Cambridge University Press, 1997)

Peter Kivy, "On the Banality of Literary Truths," *Philosophical Exchange*, 28 (1997–1998)

Steven Knapp and Walter Benn Michaels, "Against Theory," in W. J. T. Mitchell, ed., *Against Theory: Literary Studies and the New Pragmatism* (Chicago: University of Chicago Press, 1985)

Steven Knapp and Walter Benn Michaels, "The Impossibility of Intentionless Meaning," in Gary Iseminger, ed., *Intention and Interpretation* (Philadelphia, PA: Temple University Press, 1992)

L. C. Knights, "How Many Children Had Lady Macbeth?" in *Explorations* (Harmondsworth: Penguin, 1964)

Michael Krausz, *Rightness and Reasons: Interpretation in Cultural Practices* (Ithaca, NY: Cornell University Press, 1993)

Michael Krausz, *Limits of Rightness* (Lanham, MD: Rowman and Littlefield, 2000)

Fred Kroon, "Make-Believe and Fictional Reference," *Journal of Aesthetics and Art Criticism*, vol. 52, no. 2 (1994), pp. 207–214

Peter Lamarque, "How Can We Fear and Pity Fictions?" *British Journal of Aesthetics*, vol. 21, no. 4 (1981), pp. 291–304, reprinted in *Fictional Points of View* (Ithaca, NY: Cornell University Press, 1996)

Peter Lamarque, "On the Irrelevance of Psychoanalysis to Literary Criticism," in Peter Clark and Crispin Wright, eds., *Mind, Psychoanalysis and Science* (Oxford: Basil Blackwell, 1988)

Peter Lamarque, Essay Review of Kendall Walton *Mimesis as Make-Believe*, *Journal of Aesthetics and Art Criticism*, vol. 49, no. 2 (1991), pp. 161–166

Peter Lamarque, *Fictional Points of View* (Ithaca, NY: Cornell University Press, 1996)

Peter Lamarque, "Truth and Art," in *Fictional Points of View* (Ithaca, NY: Cornell University Press, 1996)

Peter Lamarque, Review of Susan L. Feagin, *Reading with Feeling*, *Mind*, vol. 109, no. 433 (2000), pp. 145–149

Peter Lamarque, "Work and Object," *Proceedings of the Aristotelian Society*, vol. CII, pt. 2 (2002), pp. 141–162

Peter Lamarque, "How to Create a Fictional Character," in Berys Gaut and Paisley Livingston, eds., *The Creation of Art* (Cambridge: Cambridge University Press, 2003)

Peter Lamarque, "On Perceiving Conceptual Art," in Peter Goldie and Elisabeth Schellekens, eds., *Philosophy and Conceptual Art* (Oxford: Oxford University Press, 2007)

Peter Lamarque and Stein Haugom Olsen, *Truth, Fiction, and Literature: A Philosophical Perspective* (Oxford: Clarendon Press, 1994)

Peter Lamarque and Stein Haugom Olsen, eds., *Aesthetics and the Philosophy of Art: The Analytic Tradition: An Anthology* (Oxford: Blackwell, 2003)

Anthony Lane, "To the Limit," *The New Yorker*, April 17, 2000, p. 124

C. H. Langford in "The Notion of Analysis in Moore's Philosophy", in Paul A. Schilpp, ed., *The Philosophy of G. E. Moore* (La Salle, IL: Open Court, 1942)

Philip Larkin, "Dockery and Son," in *Collected Poems* (London: Faber and Faber, 1988)

Philip Larkin, "Absences," in *Collected Poems* (London: Faber and Faber, 1988)

Philip Larkin, *Selected Letters of Philip Larkin*, ed. Anthony Thwaite (London: Faber and Faber, 1992)

F. R. Leavis, *The Great Tradition* (Harmondsworth: Penguin, 1962)

F. R. Leavis, *New Bearings in English Poetry* (Harmondsworth: Penguin, 1967)

Jerrold Levinson, Review of Terence Parsons, *Nonexistent Objects*, *Journal of Aesthetics and Art Criticism*, vol. 40 (1981), pp. 96–99

Jerrold Levinson, *Music, Art, & Metaphysics* (Ithaca, NY: Cornell University Press, 1990)

Jerrold Levinson, "What a Musical Work Is," in *Music, Art, & Metaphysics* (Ithaca, NY: Cornell University Press, 1990)

Jerrold Levinson, "What a Musical Work Is, Again," in *Music, Art, & Metaphysics* (Ithaca, NY: Cornell University Press, 1990)

Jerrold Levinson, *The Pleasures of Aesthetics* (Ithaca, NY: Cornell University Press, 1996)

Jerrold Levinson, "Intention and Interpretation in Literature," in *The Pleasures of Aesthetics: Philosophical Essays* (Ithaca, NY: Cornell University Press, 1996)

Jerrold Levinson, "Emotion in Response to Art: A Survey of the Terrain," in M. Hjort and S. Laver, eds., *Emotion and the Arts* (Oxford: Oxford University Press, 1997)

Jerrold Levinson, "Aesthetic Properties, Evaluative Force, and Differences of Sensibility," in Emily Brady and Jerrold Levinson, eds., *Aesthetic Concepts: Essays after Sibley* (Oxford: Oxford University Press, 2001)

George Henry Lewes, Review of Charlotte Brontë, *Jane Eyre*, *Fraser's Magazine*, December 1847

David Lewis, "Truth in Fiction," *American Philosophical Quarterly*, vol. 15, no. 1 (1978), pp. 37–46

Paisley Livingston, "Literary Aesthetics and the Aims of Criticism," in D. Patai and W. Corral, eds., *Theory's Empire* (New York: Columbia University Press, 2005)

David Lodge, ed., *20th Century Literary Criticism* (London: Longman, 1972)

David Lodge, *The Modes of Modern Writing: Metaphor, Metonymy, and the Typology of Modern Literature* (London: Edward Arnold, 1977)

David Lodge, *Therapy* (Harmondsworth: Penguin, 1995)

David Lodge, "Fact and Fiction in the Novel," in *The Practice of Writing* (Harmondsworth: Penguin, 1997)

Elizabeth Longford, *Byron* (London: Arrow Books, 1976)

György Lukács, "Realism in the Balance" (1938), in Vincent B. Leitch, ed., *The Norton Anthology of Theory and Criticism* (New York: Norton, 2001)

Colin Lyas, "The Semantic Definition of Literature," *Journal of Philosophy*, vol. 66, no. 3 (1969), pp. 81–95

Colin Lyas, "The Relevance of an Author's Sincerity," in Peter Lamarque, ed., *Philosophy and Fiction: Essays in Literary Aesthetics* (Aberdeen: Aberdeen University Press, 1983)

Colin Lyas, "Wittgensteinian Intentions," in Gary Iseminger, ed., *Intention and Interpretation* (Philadelphia, PA: Temple University Press, 1992)

J. W. Mackail, "communication" (1906) on "poetry," in Oxford English Dictionary (*The Compact Edition of the Oxford English Dictionary*, volume II, Oxford: Oxford University Press, 1971, p. 2,220)

Louis MacNeice, *Modern Poetry: A Personal Essay* (London: Oxford University Press, 1938)

Joseph Margolis, *Art and Philosophy: Conceptual Issues in Aesthetics* (Atlantic Highlands, NJ: Humanities Press, 1980)

Joseph Margolis, "Reinterpreting Interpretation," in John W. Bender and H. Gene Blocker, eds., *Contemporary Philosophy of Art: Readings in Analytic Aesthetics* (Englewood Cliffs, NJ: Prentice Hall, 1993). Originally published in *Journal of Aesthetics and Art Criticism*, vol. 47, no. 3 (1989), pp. 237–251

Joseph Margolis, *What, After All, Is a Work of Art?* (University Park, PA: Penn State Press, 1999)

Robert Bernard Martin, "Religious Discovery in *Jane Eyre*," in Charlotte Brontë, *Jane Eyre*, ed. Richard J. Dunn (New York: W. W. Norton, 1971). Originally published in *The Accents of Persuasion: Charlotte Brontë's Novels* (New York: W. W. Norton, 1966)

Terence Martin, "The Unity of *Moll Flanders*," in *Moll Flanders*, Norton Critical Edition, ed. Edward Kelly (New York: W. W. Norton, 1973), p. 363. Originally published in *Modern Language Quarterly*, XXII (1961), pp. 115–124

David Mattin, Review of William Boyd's *Restless*, in *The Independent on Sunday*, September 10, 2006

Derek Matravers, "Fictional Assent and the (So-called) 'Puzzle of Imaginative Resistance,'" in M. Kieran and D. Lopes, eds., *Imagination, Philosophy, and the Arts* (London: Routledge, 2003)

Alexius Meinong, "Theory of Objects," in R. M. Chisholm, ed., *Realism and the Background of Phenomenology* (Glencoe, IL: Free Press, 1960)

John Stuart Mill, *Utilitarianism*, ed. Mary Warnock (London: Fontana Press, 1986)

Arthur Miller, *Timebends: A Life* (New York: Grove Press, 1987)

J. Hillis Miller, "Afterword," in Charles Dickens, *Our Mutual Friend* (New York: Signet, 1964)

J. Hillis Miller, "The World of *Bleak House*," in Charles Dickens, *Bleak House*, ed. George Ford and Sylvère Monod (New York: W. W. Norton, 1977)

J. Hillis Miller, *On Literature* (London and New York: Routledge, 2002)

Toril Moi, *Sexual/Textual Politics: Feminist Literary Theory* (London: Methuen, 1985)

Richard Moran, "The Expression of Feeling in Imagination," *Philosophical Review*, vol. 103, no. 1 (1994), pp. 75–106

John Morreall, "Fear without Belief," *Journal of Philosophy*, vol. 90, no. 7 (1993), pp. 359–366

Andrew Motion, *Philip Larkin: A Writer's Life* (London: Faber, 1993)

Iris Murdoch, *The Sovereignty of Good* (London: Routledge, 1970)

Iris Murdoch, *The Black Prince* (London: Chatto and Windus, 1973)

Iris Murdoch, *Metaphysics as a Guide to Morals* (Harmondsworth: Penguin, 1992)

Thomas Nagel, *Mortal Questions* (Cambridge: Cambridge University Press, 1979)

Alexander Nehamas, "Writer, Text, Work, Author," in Anthony J. Cascardi, ed., *Literature and the Question of Philosophy* (Baltimore, MD: Johns Hopkins University Press, 1987)

Alex Neill, "Fear, Fiction and Make-Believe," *Journal of Aesthetics and Art Criticism*, vol. 49, no. 1 (1991), pp. 47–56

Alex Neill, "Fiction and the Emotions," *American Philosophical Quarterly*, vol. 30, no. 1 (1993), pp. 1–13

Alex Neill, "Fear and Belief," *Philosophy and Literature*, vol. 19, no. 1 (1995), pp. 94–101

David Newton-de Molina, ed., *On Literary Intention* (Edinburgh: Edinburgh University Press, 1976)

David Novitz, *Knowledge, Fiction and Imagination* (Philadelphia, PA: Temple University Press, 1987)

Winifred M. T. Nowottny, "Formal Elements in Shakespeare's Sonnets: Sonnets I–IV," in William Shakespeare, *The Sonnets* (New York: Signet Classics, 1964), pp. 227–228. Originally published in *Essays in Criticism*, II (January, 1952), pp. 76–84

Winifred Nowottny, *The Language Poets Use* (London: Athlone Press, 1968)

Martha Nussbaum, *The Fragility of Goodness: Luck and Ethics in Greek Tragedy and Philosophy* (Cambridge: Cambridge University Press, 1986)

Martha C. Nussbaum, "Flawed Crystals: James's *The Golden Bowl* and Literature as Moral Philosophy," in *Love's Knowledge*: *Essays on Philosophy and Literature* (Oxford: Oxford University Press, 1990)

Martha C. Nussbaum, *Poetic Justice: The Literary Imagination and Public Life* (Boston, MA: Beacon Books, 1997)

Martha C. Nussbaum, "Exactly and Responsibly: A Defense of Ethical Criticism," *Philosophy and Literature*, vol. 22, no. 2 (1998), pp. 343–365

Richard Ohmann, "Speech Acts and the Definition of Literature," *Philosophy and Rhetoric*, vol. 4 (1971), pp. 1–19

Stein Haugom Olsen, "Do You Like Emma Woodhouse?," *Critical Quarterly*, vol. 19, no. 4 (1977), pp. 3–19

Stein Haugom Olsen, *The Structure of Literary Understanding* (Cambridge: Cambridge University Press, 1978)

Stein Haugom Olsen, "Value Judgments in Criticism," *Journal of Aesthetics and Art Criticism*, vol. 42, no. 2 (1983), pp. 125–136

Stein Haugom Olsen, *The End of Literary Theory* (Cambridge: Cambridge University Press, 1987)

Stein Haugom Olsen, "Literary Aesthetics and Literary Practice," in *The End of Literary Theory* (Cambridge: Cambridge University Press, 1987)

Stein Haugom Olsen, "Literary Theory and Literary Aesthetics," in *The End of Literary Theory* (Cambridge: Cambridge University Press, 1987)

Stein Haugom Olsen, "The 'Meaning' of a Literary Work," in *The End of Literary Theory* (Cambridge: Cambridge University Press, 1987)

Stein Haugom Olsen, "On Unilluminating Criticism," in *The End of Literary Theory* (Cambridge: Cambridge University Press, 1987)

Stein Haugom Olsen, "Text and Meaning," in *The End of Literary Theory* (Cambridge: Cambridge University Press, 1987)

Stein Haugom Olsen, "The Concept of Literature: An Institutional Account," in Stein Haugom Olsen and Anders Pettersson, eds., *From Text to Literature: New Analytic and Pragmatic Approaches* (Basingstoke: Palgrave Macmillan, 2005)

Judith Owens, "The Poetics of Accommodation in Spenser's *Epithalamion*," *Studies in English Literature, 1500–1900*, vol. 40 (2000), pp. 41–62

Terence Parsons, *Nonexistent Objects* (New Haven, CT: Yale University Press, 1980)

Barrie Paskins, "On Being Moved by Anna Karenina and *Anna Karenina*," *Philosophy*, vol. 52, no. 201 (1977), pp. 344–347

Torsten Pettersson, "The Literary Work as a Pliable Entity: Combining Realism and Pluralism," in Michael Krausz, ed., *Is There a Single Right Interpretation?* (University Park, PA: Penn State University Press, 2002)

D. Z. Phillips, "Allegiance and Change in Morality: A Study in Contrasts," in *Through a Darkening Glass: Philosophy, Literature, and Cultural Change* (Oxford: Blackwell, 1982)

Steven Pinker, *How the Mind Works* (New York: W. W. Norton, 1997)

Plato, *Ion*, in *The Works of Plato*, trans. with analysis and introductions by Benjamin Jowett, Four Volumes Complete in One (New York: Tudor Publishing, 1937)

Plato, *The Republic*, trans. Robin Waterfield (Oxford: Oxford University Press, 1994)

Plato, *The Laws*, trans. Trevor J. Saunders (Harmondsworth: Penguin, 1976)

Alexander Pope, *An Essay On Criticism* (1711), in *Alexander Pope: The Major Works* (Oxford: Oxford University Press, 2006)

Richard A. Posner, "Against Ethical Criticism," *Philosophy and Literature*, vol. 21, no. 1 (1997), pp. 1–27

Richard A. Posner, "Against Ethical Criticism: Part Two," *Philosophy and Literature*, vol. 22, no. 2 (1998), pp. 394–412

Richard A. Posner, *Law and Literature* (Boston, MA: Harvard University Press; rev. and updated ed., 1998)

C. G. Prado, *Making Believe: Philosophical Reflections on Fiction* (Westport, CT: Greenwood, 1984)

John Press, *The Chequer'd Shade: Reflections on Obscurity in Poetry* (Oxford: Oxford University Press, 1963)

Hilary Putnam, "Literature, Science, and Reflection," in *Meaning and the Moral Sciences* (London: Routledge, 1978)

Hilary Putnam, "Reflections on Goodman's *Ways of Worldmaking*," *Journal of Philosophy*, vol. 76, no. 11 (1979), pp. 603–618

W. V. O. Quine, "On What There Is," in *From a Logical Point of View* (Cambridge, MA: Harvard University Press, 1953)

Colin Radford, "How Can We Be Moved by the Fate of Anna Karenina?" *Proceedings of the Aristotelian Society*, suppl. vol. 49 (1975), pp. 67–80

I. A. Richards, *Principles of Literary Criticism*, 2nd ed. (London: Routledge and Kegan Paul, 1926)

I. A. Richards, *The Philosophy of Rhetoric* (New York: Galaxy Books, 1965)

Christopher Ricks, "Literature and the Matter of Fact," in *Essays in Appreciation* (Oxford: Clarendon Press, 1996)

Jenefer Robinson, "Style and Personality in the Literary Work," *Philosophical Review*, vol. 94 (1985), pp. 227–247; reprinted in Peter Lamarque and Stein Haugom Olsen, eds., *Aesthetics and the Philosophy of Art: The Analytic Tradition: An Anthology* (Oxford: Blackwell, 2003)

Jenefer Robinson, *Deeper than Reason* (Oxford: Oxford University Press, 2005)

Richard Rorty, "Is There a Problem about Fictional Discourse?" in *Consequences of Pragmatism* (Brighton: Harvester Press, 1982)

Richard Rorty, *Contingency, Irony, and Solidarity* (Cambridge: Cambridge University Press, 1989)

M. W. Rowe, "Lamarque and Olsen on Literature and Truth," *Philosophical Quarterly*, vol. 47, no. 188 (1997), pp. 322–341

M. W. Rowe, "Poetry and Abstraction," in *Philosophy and Literature: A Book of Essays* (Aldershot: Ashgate, 2004)

Bertrand Russell, *Logic and Knowledge*, ed. R. C. Marsh (London: George Allen and Unwin, 1956)

Bertrand Russell, *Introduction to Mathematical Philosophy* (London: Routledge, 1993)

Gilbert Ryle, "Imaginary Objects," *Proceedings of the Aristotelian Society*, suppl. vol. 12 (1933), pp. 18–43

Gilbert Ryle, *Collected Papers, Vol. II: Collected Essays 1929–1968* (London: Hutchinson, 1971)

Nathan Salmon, "Nonexistence," *Nous*, vol. 32 (1998), pp. 277–319

Anthony Savile, *The Test of Time: An Essay in Philosophical Aesthetics* (Oxford: Clarendon Press, 1982)

Roger Scruton, "Photography and Representation," in Peter Lamarque and Stein Haugom Olsen, eds., *Aesthetics and the Philosophy of Art: The Analytic Tradition: An Anthology* (Oxford: Blackwell, 2003)

John R. Searle, *Speech Acts: An Essay in the Philosophy of Language* (Cambridge: Cambridge University Press, 1969)

John R. Searle, "Reiterating the Differences: A Reply to Derrida," *Glyph*, vol. 1 (1977), pp. 198–208

John R. Searle, *Expression and Meaning: Studies in the Theory of Speech Acts* (Cambridge: Cambridge University Press, 1979)

John R. Searle, "The Logical Status of Fictional Discourse," in *Expression and Meaning: Studies in the Theory of Speech Acts* (Cambridge: Cambridge University Press, 1979)

John R. Searle, *The Construction of Social Reality* (London: Allen Lane, 1995)

Percy Bysshe Shelley, "A Defence of Poetry," in *Percy Bysshe Shelley: The Major Works*, ed. Zachery Leader and Michael O'Neill (Oxford: Oxford University Press, 2003).

Viktor Shklovsky, "Sterne's *Tristram Shandy*," in Lee T. Lemon and Marion J. Reis, eds., *Russian Formalist Criticism: Four Essays* (Lincoln: University of Nebraska Press, 1965)

Elaine Showalter, "Representing Ophelia: Women, Madness, and the Responsibilities of Feminist Criticism," in Patricia Parker and Geoffrey Hartman, eds., *Shakespeare and the Question of Theory* (London: Methuen, 1985)

Frank Sibley, "Aesthetic Concepts," in Peter Lamarque and Stein Haugom Olsen, eds., *Aesthetics and the Philosophy of Art: The Analytic Tradition: An Anthology* (Oxford: Blackwell, 2003). Originally published in *Philosophical Review*, vol. 68, no. 4 (1959), pp. 421–450

Frank Sibley, "Particularity, Art, and Evaluation," in Peter Lamarque and Stein Haugom Olsen, eds., *Aesthetics and the Philosophy of Art: The Analytic Tradition: An Anthology* (Oxford: Blackwell, 2003). Originally published in *Proceedings of the Aristotelian Society*, suppl. vol. 48 (1974), pp. 1–21

Philip Sidney, *Defence of Poesie*, from the Scolar Press facsimile of the British Museum's copy (Shelf-mark: C.57.b.38) of the Ponsonby edition (1595)

Mary J. Sirridge, "Truth from Fiction?" *Philosophy and Phenomenological Research*, vol. 35, no. 4 (1974–1975), pp. 453–471

Quentin Skinner, "Motives, Intentions and the Interpretation of Texts," *New Literary History*, 3 (1972), pp. 393–408

Susan Sontag, "Against Interpretation," in *Against Interpretation* (New York: Farrar, Straus, and Giroux, 1961)

Edmund Spenser, *Edmund Spenser's Poetry*, sel. and ed. Hugh Maclean (New York: W. W. Norton, 1968)

Robert Stecker, "What Is Literature?" in Eileen John and Dominic McIver Lopes, eds., *Philosophy of Literature: Contemporary and Classic Readings: An Anthology* (Oxford: Blackwell, 2004). Originally published in *Revue Internationale de Philosophie*, 50 (1996), pp. 681–694

Robert Stecker, "The Constructivist's Dilemma," *Journal of Aesthetics and Art Criticism*, vol. 55, no. 1 (1999), pp. 43–51

Robert Stecker, *Artworks: Definition, Meaning, Value* (University Park, PA: Penn State University Press, 1997)

Robert Stecker, "Is It Reasonable to Attempt to Define Art?" in Noël Carroll, ed., *Theories of Art Today* (Madison: University of Wisconsin Press, 2000)

Robert Stecker, *Interpretation and Construction: Art, Speech, and the Law* (Oxford: Blackwell, 2003)

Robert Stecker, *Aesthetics and the Philosophy of Art: An Introduction* (Lanham, MD: Rowman and Littlefield, 2005)

Kathleen Stock, "The Tower of Goldbach and Other Impossible Tales," in M. Kieran and D. Lopes, eds., *Imagination, Philosophy, and the Arts* (London: Routledge, 2003)

Jerome Stolnitz, "On the Cognitive Triviality of Art," in Peter Lamarque and Stein Haugom Olsen, eds., *Aesthetics and the Philosophy of Art: The Analytic Tradition: An Anthology* (Oxford: Blackwell, 2003). Originally published in *British Journal of Aesthetics*, vol. 32, no. 3 (1992), pp. 191–200

P. F. Strawson, "Aesthetic Appraisal and Works of Art," in Peter Lamarque and Stein Haugom Olsen, eds., *Aesthetics and the Philosophy of Art: The Analytic Tradition: An Anthology* (Oxford: Blackwell, 2003). Originally published in *Oxford Review*, vol. 1, no. 3 (1966), pp. 5–13, and reprinted in P. F. Strawson, *Freedom and Resentment* (London: Methuen, 1974), pp. 178–188

Raymond Tallis, *In Defence of Realism* (London: Hodder Arnold, 1988)

Amie L. Thomasson, *Fiction and Metaphysics* (Cambridge: Cambridge University Press, 1999)

E. M. W. Tillyard and C. S. Lewis, *The Personal Heresy: A Controversy* (London: Oxford University Press, 1939)

Tzvetan Todorov, *Littérature et signification* (Paris: Larousse, 1967)

William Tolhurst, "On What a Text Is and How It Means," *British Journal of Aesthetics*, vol. 19, no. 1 (1979), pp. 3–14

L. N. Tolstoy, *War and Peace*, trans. and with an introduction by Rosemary Edmonds (Harmondsworth: Penguin, 1969)

J. O. Urmson, "Fiction," *American Philosophical Quarterly*, 13 (1976), pp. 153–157

Dorothy Van Ghent, "On *Tess of the d'Urbervilles*," in Thomas Hardy, *Tess of the d'Urbervilles*, ed. Scott Elledge (New York: W. W. Norton, 1979)

Peter van Inwagen, "Creatures of Fiction," *American Philosophical Quarterly*, vol. 14, no. 4 (1977), pp. 299–308

Willie van Peer, "Canon Formation: Ideology or Aesthetic Quality?" *British Journal of Aesthetics* vol. 36, no. 2 (1996), pp. 97–108

Jennifer A. Wagner, "The Allegory of Form in Hopkins's Religious Sonnets," *Nineteenth-Century Literature*, vol. 47, no. 1, June (1992), pp. 32–48

Dorothy Walsh, "The Cognitive Content of Art," *Philosophical Review*, vol. 52, no. 5. (1943), pp. 433–451

Dorothy Walsh, *Literature and Knowledge* (Middletown, CT: Wesleyan University Press, 1969)

Kendall L. Walton, "Fiction, Fiction-Making, and Styles of Fictionality," *Philosophy and Literature*, vol. 7, no. 1 (1983), pp. 78–88

Kendall L. Walton, "Do We Need Fictional Entities? Notes towards a Theory," in *Aesthetics: Proceedings of the Eighth International Wittgenstein Symposium* (Vienna, 1984)

Kendall L. Walton, *Mimesis as Make-Believe* (Cambridge, MA: Harvard University Press, 1990)

Kendall Walton, "Morals in Fiction and Fictional Morality," *Proceedings of the Aristotelian Society*, suppl. vol. LXVIII (1994), pp. 27–50

Kendall L. Walton, "Spelunking, Simulation, and Slime: On Being Moved by Fiction," in Mette Hjort and Sue Laver, eds., *Emotion and the Arts* (Oxford: Oxford University Press, 1997)

Ian Watt, *The Rise of the Novel* (Harmondsworth: Penguin, 1966)

Patricia Waugh, ed., *Oxford Guide to Literary Theory and Criticism* (Oxford: Oxford University Press, 2006)

Patricia Waugh, "Value: Criticism, Canons, and Evaluation," in Patricia Waugh, ed., *Literary Theory and Criticism* (Oxford: Oxford University Press, 2006)

Morris Weitz, "Truth in Literature," *Revue Internationale de Philosophie*, IX (1955), pp. 1–14

Morris Weitz, "The Role of Theory in Aesthetics," in Peter Lamarque and Stein Haugom Olsen, eds., *Aesthetics and the Philosophy of Art: The Analytic Tradition: An Anthology* (Oxford: Blackwell, 2003). Originally published in *Journal of Aesthetics and Art Criticism*, vol. 15 (1956), pp. 27–35

René Wellek and Austin Warren, *Theory of Literature* (Harmondsworth: Penguin, 1973)

Oscar Wilde, "The Decay of Lying," [1891], in *Complete Works of Oscar Wilde* (London and Glasgow: Collins, 1966)

Bernard Williams, *Ethics and the Limits of Philosophy* (Cambridge, MA: Harvard University Press, 1985)

G. Wilson Knight, "*Macbeth* and the Metaphysic of Evil," in *The Wheel of Fire: Interpretations of Shakespearean Tragedy* (London: Methuen, 1949)

W. K. Wimsatt, *The Verbal Icon: Studies in the Meaning of Poetry* (Lexington: University Press of Kentucky, 1954)

W. K. Wimsatt, "Genesis: A Fallacy Revisited," in David Newton-de Molina, ed., *On Literary Intention* (Edinburgh: Edinburgh University Press, 1976)

W. K. Wimsatt and M. C. Beardsley, "The Intentional Fallacy," in David Lodge, ed., *20th Century Literary Criticism* (London: Longman, 1972)

Ludwig Wittgenstein, *Philosophical Investigations*, trans. G. E. M. Anscombe (Oxford: Blackwell, 1968)

Richard Wollheim, *Art and Its Objects*, 2nd ed. (Cambridge: Cambridge University Press, 1980)

Richard Wollheim, "Criticism as Retrieval," Essay IV, in *Art and Its Objects*, 2nd ed. (Cambridge: Cambridge University Press, 1980)

Nicholas Wolterstorff, *Works and Worlds of Art* (Oxford: Clarendon Press, 1980)

Virginia Woolf, *The Common Reader*, First Series (1925) (London: The Hogarth Press, 1957)

Virginia Woolf, *The Common Reader*, Second Series (1932) (London: The Hogarth Press, 1932)

William Wordsworth, "1802 Preface to the Lyrical Ballads," in *Romanticism*, ed. Duncan Wu (Oxford: Blackwell, 1994)

William Wordsworth, *The Prelude: Four Texts (1798, 1799, 1805, 1850)* (Harmondsworth: Penguin, 1995)

Michael Wreen, "Once Is Not Enough?" *British Journal of Aesthetics*, vol. 30, no. 2 (1990), pp. 149–158

Robert J. Yanal, *Paradoxes of Emotion and Fiction* (University Park, PA: Penn State University Press, 1999)

Edward Zalta, *Abstract Objects* (Dordrecht: Reidel, 1983)

Eddy Zemach, "Tom Sawyer and the Beige Unicorn," *British Journal of Aesthetics*, vol. 38, no. 2 (1998), pp. 167–179

# Index